The Punitive Turn in American Life

The Punitive Turn in American Life
How the United States Learned to Fight Crime Like a War

Michael S. Sherry

THE

UNIVERSITY OF

NORTH CAROLINA

PRESS

Chapel Hill

*This book was published with the assistance of
the William R. Kenan Jr. Fund of the University of
North Carolina Press.*

© 2020 The University of North Carolina Press

Designed by Richard Hendel
Set in Miller and Geogrotesque
by codeMantra, Inc.
Manufactured in the United States of America

The University of North Carolina Press has been
a member of the Green Press Initiative since 2003.

Jacket illustration: special ops police officer by
Getmilitaryphotos, shutterstock.com.

Library of Congress Cataloging-in-Publication Data
Names: Sherry, Michael S., 1945– author.
Title: The punitive turn in American life : how the United States
learned to fight crime like a war / Michael S. Sherry.
Description: Chapel Hill : University of North Carolina Press, 2020. |
Includes bibliographical references and index.
Identifiers: LCCN 2020026484 | ISBN 9781469660707
(cloth : alk. paper) | ISBN 9781469660714 (ebook)
Subjects: LCSH: Criminal justice, Administration of—Political aspects—
United States—History—20th century. | Criminal justice, Administration of—
Political aspects—United States—History—21st century. | Punishment. |
Militarization. | Intelligence service—United States.
Classification: LCC HV9950 .S547 2020 | DDC 364.973—dc23
LC record available at https://lccn.loc.gov/2020026484

Contents

A gallery of illustrations begins on page 127.

The Punitive Turn in American Life

Introduction

Advertisements urging civilians to buy guns suggest how the punitive turn had played out by the 2010s. "As Close as You Can Get without Enlisting"—that is, get to war—stated one rifle ad, while another ad promoted a semiautomatic shotgun with the slogan "Iraq Afghanistan, Your Livingroom," and a handgun ad pictured an infantryman above the words "BUILT FOR THEM . . . BUILT FOR YOU."[1] The message: Americans at home could carry the same weapons of war that soldiers carried in battle. Many Americans believed, or at least were asked to imagine, that the line between war-fighting and crime-fighting had almost disappeared. This book is about how that happened.

The title of this work, *The Punitive Turn in American Life: How the United States Learned to Fight Crime Like a War*, captures the sweeping process, starting in the 1960s, that moved punishment and surveillance to the center of American life and imbued them with militarized language and practices. Its obvious forms were mass incarceration, as the United States became the world's foremost jailer, and "the militarization of policing," as critics called it. But the punitive turn also encompassed other practices—public schools entered through metal detectors and patrolled by police, gated communities shooing away the unwanted, cameras peering to catch red-light offenders, armies of private police, familiar rituals of airport screening, and fads like the child-spanking movement. Scholars often refer to "the carceral state." The "punitive turn in American life," a phrase I first used in 2005,[2] signals a broader process that included what the state did but went beyond it.

The punitive turn faced countercurrents—it did not move forward inexorably and uniformly. As a result of authorities' indifference, court rulings, or legislative action, some acts once deemed criminal no longer were: most abortions after *Roe v. Wade* in 1973, and sodomy between adults later on. Military conscription, certainly a coercive system and to some draftees a punitive one, ended in 1973, and the death penalty faced persistent and partially successful opposition. These countercurrents churned the waters but did not halt the onrushing tide, at least until the 2010s. The punitive turn made America a meaner, punishment-obsessed nation, with vengeance at home and abroad its ruling impulse. And it made the United States a more distinctive nation, as it departed from norms in comparable countries.

What caused the punitive turn in American life? Scholars, pundits, and, on occasion, politicians have offered many explanations, most centered on race, class, economics, and the state. This book seeks not to supplant those explanations but to add to them, locating another engine driving the punitive turn—the nation's messy entanglement of war-fighting with crime-fighting. No great historical shift has a single cause, but a major cause of the punitive turn was the Vietnam-era crisis in the militarized order that had dominated the nation and disciplined its youth since the late 1930s. Under that order, the United States had harnessed industry, science, people, and propaganda to amass world-destroying weapons in its efforts to defeat Axis enemies in World War II, contain communism during the Cold War, justify an expansive state, and sustain its global hegemony. As the U.S. war in Vietnam faltered, that order frayed, and the state's legitimacy came into question.

In response, political leaders embarked on a war on crime in order to reassert that legitimacy, to preserve their power, and to quell the era's disorder, starting a process whereby resources devoted to war and national security were partly redeployed to wage "war on crime," to use the term that became commonplace. Redeployment was often halting, improvised, half intended. But when President Lyndon Johnson proclaimed on September 22, 1965, that "the policeman is the frontline soldier in our war against crime," the process was starting.[3] By then, an already substantial apparatus of law enforcement and a powerful apparatus of national security allowed the state to act vigorously in criminal justice and to do so on militarized terms. Soon, the waning of America's war in Vietnam created a surplus of war-making capacity—people, institutions, machines, words—that was recycled into crime-fighting. As the Vietnam War raged, responses to crime got encased in the language and institutions of war making. Political leaders worked to rebuild a state under siege on the basis of a new punitive order, one that borrowed from an older militarized way of life.

That process was hardly alone in causing the punitive turn. But it was consequential, it overlapped other sources of the punitive turn, and it was a causal force that Americans long overlooked. Over several decades, Johnson and others reconstructed the old militarized order and rebuilt the state on a new foundation of crime-fighting. No one political faction, ideology, institution, leader, or vested interest made that project happen. Most Americans were complicit in it or oblivious to it, and those keen to resist were often powerless to do so. But all were not equally culpable. Political leaders and institutions—presidents, Congress, state legislatures, and so forth—bore the most culpability. Americans did not en masse demand the punitive turn. Leaders and institutions led them into it.

Many Americans considered crime-fighting to be like war-fighting because of long-standing political habits and the immediate circumstances of the 1960s. Their nation had gone to war often, by some measures almost continuously. Americans had often regarded national problems as warranting a warlike response because war seemed like the mechanism that had most purposefully organized the nation and the state. President Franklin Roosevelt, for example, had cast the nation's response to the Great Depression as a warlike effort, saying at his first inaugural that he might need to respond as "if we were in fact invaded by a foreign foe," and the New Deal modeled some of its efforts on World War I's institutional apparatus. The bigger the wars, the stronger that habit in their wake. After World War I, and even more so after World War II, countless proposed national programs were analogized to wartime efforts like the atom bomb–building Manhattan Project or built on their apparatus.[4] Less successful wars after 1945 complicated exercise of that habit without stopping it.

But customs are not automatic; they intersect with circumstances. In the 1960s, they intersected with still-powerful memories of World War II, with the war in Vietnam, and with rising racial conflict and crime at home. For President Johnson and many others, war, World War II in particular, provided the template for national action on many fronts. The language of war arose easily, almost reflexively, as these Americans confronted poverty, disease, social conflict—and crime. But the conditions of the 1960s, above all a floundering U.S. war in Southeast Asia, made that intersection especially fraught. The state slowly steered the institutions and modes of war toward crime-fighting. But the era's analogies of crime-fighting to war-fighting were so numerous, conflicting, and explosive that the nation's punitive turn was at its start both energetic and uncertain.

This book tells a story hardly unknown in its particulars but hidden in plain sight overall. Many people know that war talk enveloped late twentieth-century campaigns against crime, especially in the war on drugs. But few scholars do more than note the presence of such talk, failing to map its emergence and tenacity, its twists and turns.[5] As the punitive turn accelerated, apparent lines between spheres of

action—war-fighting and crime-fighting, the military and the civilian—
faded in political rhetoric and institutional practice. A robust and
persistent language of war on crime enmeshed the two spheres. The
blurring of lines encountered little opposition, even though shrill presidential rhetoric often revealed it, because war and crime tapped similar fears and ambitions, overlapped institutionally, and served similar
purposes. To move from a war on foreign foes to a war on domestic ones
did not seem like a big shift. Likewise, the phrase "war on crime"—often
waged on those deemed criminals—seemed natural enough to Lyndon
Johnson and the scores of others who came to use such phrasing.

The narrative spine of this book is the public rhetoric and record of
presidents and other high officials, but much branches out from that
spine, since those officials hardly did it all. Unlike the most analogous
realms, defense and foreign policy, for which authority was centralized,
crime policy was scattered among many local, state, and national authorities. Even at the federal level, jurisdiction splintered among many
agencies, and Congress and the courts played powerful roles. And initiatives often arose at the local level and in the marketplace with little
or no presidential awareness.

Yet presidents were hardly impotent. Indeed, one trajectory in the
punitive turn was the ascending role of the presidency and the federal government in crime-fighting. With the punitive turn, presidents
from Lyndon Johnson on (Jimmy Carter was the exception) often set
the tone and got their way. Dividing the story by presidencies is an
old-fashioned way to write history, and many developments in the punitive turn spilled beyond the confines of any one administration, as
readers will see. But that organization highlights what much scholarship neglects—the revealing role of presidents. Even when they were
not prime movers, their words provided a major lens through which
Americans understood criminal justice and punitive practice. And for
presidents, crime was not just a national story but a supercharged local
one of crime and violence in Washington, D.C., right under their noses.
Given that the federal government had jurisdiction over that city that
it lacked elsewhere, these leaders could not ignore how the local intersected the national.

Presidents' roles differed. Johnson's initiation of the punitive turn,
chapter 1 suggests, was caught up in the convulsive politics of war and
race in the 1960s. His efforts featured the first sustained exposition of
war-on-crime rhetoric, with policies roughly to match. Richard Nixon,
chapter 2 shows, echoed LBJ's rhetoric in a mean-spirited but less sustained fashion, and to less consequence than is often credited to him.

Gerald Ford, chapter 3 indicates, provided a robust ideological framework for a state rebuilt on crime-fighting. However, he had little chance to implement that framework, and even less given resistance to the punitive turn by his successor, Jimmy Carter

Ronald Reagan and George H. W. Bush, detailed in chapter 4, offered a concerted, ugly, and consequential punitive conservatism saturated with the words and mentalities of war-fighting. Setting aside those words, Bill Clinton, chapter 5 argues, offered a softer language of prevention that obscured the militarization of American criminal justice. Responding to the 9/11 attacks, George W. Bush, as chapter 6 lays out, further exposed the currents of vengeance long coursing through the punitive turn.

Pushed by many activist and legal forces, Barack Obama, chapter 7 suggests, resisted the punitive turn but did so cautiously and with limited success. Donald J. Trump, sketched in the epilogue, embraced the currents of vengeance viciously even as he faced the strongest resistance to the punitive turn yet seen. These presidents and other leaders effected no conspiracy to enact a punitive turn, which is a story of unplanned and contingent shifts in political culture. Nonetheless, step by step (with a few steps backward), they helped to advance it.

Most people believe that changes in punitive systems are driven by public attitudes—by the waxing and waning of fears of crime and tough-on-crime sentiments. Many crimes inflicted real horror and pain: the assassinations of John F. Kennedy in 1963 and of Robert Kennedy and Martin Luther King Jr. in 1968, the murder of seventeen people in 1966 by ex-marine Charles Whitman shooting from atop a tower at the University of Texas, and the Manson murders in 1969, as well as unparalleled urban violence, right-wing and left-wing terrorism, and much else. But the atrocity of crimes and the overall crime rate did not alone drive the punitive turn. Horrible lawlessness occurs in many eras without producing a large-scale punitive response. (Who remembers the Bath, Michigan, school bombing in 1927, which took forty-four lives and may still be the deadliest school massacre in American history?) Changes in criminal justice correlated loosely with public fears, and sometimes not at all, and public figures provoked fear of crime as much as they responded to it. What drove the punitive turn was not just the horror of lawbreaking, but the responses to it of state authorities, politicians, the media, and others in a position to interpret the horror. Crime and fear of it were hardly the only forces at work.

Critics and scholars have argued that the punitive turn was a project of racial control that replaced a system of overt racism with a nominally color-blind one of law and order. As Michelle Alexander explains, "In the era of colorblindness, it is no longer socially permissible to use race explicitly, as a justification for discrimination, exclusion, and social contempt. So we don't. . . . We have not ended racial caste in America; we have merely redesigned it."[6] This book connects that dimension of the punitive turn to other currents flowing through it. In America, criminal justice is always about race, and never only about that.

And law and order was not the only color-blind language. Apparently, the loud, sustained language of war was also color-blind, even as it carried thinly coded racial meanings, especially in the war on drugs. "War" is never just an abstract, neutral term for the clash of armies or nations. In the United States in the late twentieth century, the word had cultural and racial valences. The nation's deadliest war, the Civil War, had been about race, and had been waged in part by African Americans. Much of the nation's war making had been against nonwhite enemies. And the term "war on crime" rose to prominence in the mid-1960s amid racial upheaval and at the peak of America's war against another nonwhite foe. Not everyone who bandied about such terms intended them to carry a racial charge. But the ostensibly race-neutral language of war also cloaked the racial assumptions and animus often undergirding the project of those supporting a war on crime. The language of war, like that of law and order, had a powerful undertow of racial meanings.

This book is more about connections, associations, and feedback loops than causation, which is harder for historians to prove than many admit. The connections between war-fighting and crime-fighting were numerous, dense, charged, and ever evolving. They helped drive the punitive turn and give it its character. These connections' persistence and ubiquity were as striking as their content. I trace the language of war that presidents, officials, police, arms peddlers, and others used. That language took many forms. Sometimes it involved a simple metaphor like "war on drugs." Often it involved analogies and comparisons—for example, cops on the beat were like soldiers in war. And sometimes it was meant literally. In turn, that language propelled the use of warlike institutions and practices in crime-fighting. Thus, language lay at the top of a slippery slope down to practice.

Insofar as Americans saw fighting war as a model for fighting crime, not just as a breezy metaphor, their adoption of the war-fighting model implied a shrugging acceptance of the risks that combat entails: collateral damage to bystanders, danger to warriors as well as their targets, erosion of civil liberties and constitutional procedures, secrecy and deception, wasteful expenditures, abuse of enemies, distrust of those who resist the cause. Americans entered their war on crime having experienced such risks in World War II, Korea, and Vietnam, and in the threat of nuclear war. They were accustomed to such dangers, in part because they fell heaviest on others beyond their shores. Risks like these were so woven into the fabric of Americans' historical experience that few questioned their reappearance in a war on crime. This was especially the case since the dangers of a war on crime were less obvious than those of a real war, creeping into consciousness and practice without the terrifying suddenness of Pearl Harbor or the 9/11 attacks. It was easy to analogize crime-fighting to war-fighting.

Measured against the full run of American history, the punitive turn may seem less distinctive, only a new version of old patterns. After all, what was slavery if not a disciplinary system? And there was much else that fell into this category: the killing of Native Americans and their forced removal to reservations; the violent repression of workers by state and private authorities; the cruelties of Jim Crow and lynching for African Americans, with similar systems for Hispanic and Asian Americans; the mass repression during World War I of those deemed insufficiently loyal to the American cause; the incarceration of Japanese Americans during World War II; the confinement of hundreds of thousands in mental health facilities. And that is only a short list. Was the United States a more punitive nation in 1990 than it had been in 1890 or 1790? Perhaps not. Yet even new versions of old patterns deserve explanation. In American history, punishment is ever present but hardly unvarying, and there was nothing in that earlier history quite like the rhetoric and practice of the war on crime late in the twentieth century. Moreover, people usually understand their times in reference to a recent past, not a distant one. By that standard, the United States of 1990 was a much more punitive nation than it had been in 1950.

This book is not a comprehensive history of the punitive turn, which was too vast and long-lasting for one study to encompass. Instead, this book offers a selective, sometimes idiosyncratic take on the words and practices that illustrate how war-fighting and crime-fighting intersected, crossed paths, collided, or more often blended together. Readers will know other words and practices, especially regarding the high-tech dimensions of criminal justice, that I have neglected. By the same token, this book engages others' scholarship selectively.[7] For primary sources, it relies on published materials, some obvious and some obscure. At a few points, it digs into archival sources. Sections on cultural representations of criminals, victims, cops, and lawyers suggest how the punitive turn slowly spread into many facets of American life beyond the formal workings of criminal justice.

This work is an exercise in the history of political culture, thus differing in methods, aims, and style from much scholarship in the social sciences and political history on mass incarceration, the carceral state, and other aspects of the punitive turn. By and large, this study does not refute that scholarship. It instead offers a complementary way to explain the punitive turn, one focused on the language, institutions, and politics of war. As such, the book is a provocation designed to open a fresh way to think about the punitive turn rather than to offer the final say on it.

The emotive dimension of the punitive turn—ugly demands for vengeance ("kill the bitch" in reference to Hillary Clinton during and after the 2016 presidential campaign), visceral hatreds, racist furies, indignant cries of injustice—is one I only partially account for. I do, however, show how presidents and others voiced that dimension or gave others license to do so, and how that aspect of the punitive turn was often linked to the emotive thinking and language that war usually entails. Long living "in the shadow of war," as I phrased it in an earlier book,[8] Americans learned how to make substance of that shadow among themselves.

As I write this and you read this, the punitive turn continues to spill forward and splatter its harm widely. It does not seem destined to end soon.

Readers will find it useful to understand how I use key words and phrases. I place the word "war" and phrases like "war on crime" and "war on drugs" in quotation marks when quoting the words of historical actors or when referring to the aforesaid phrases as metaphors and dominant terms. Otherwise I use those words and phrases without quotation marks. Doing so risks appearing to normalize the phenomena involved, as if there were an actual war on crime, not a metaphorical one. But readers will see that is not my intent.

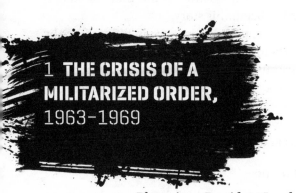

1 THE CRISIS OF A MILITARIZED ORDER, 1963-1969

Blame it on President Lyndon Johnson, among others.[1] In 1965 LBJ declared "war on crime," and in his usual way of making extravagant promises that often backfired, he pledged "not only to reduce crime but to banish it."[2] He did much to start the punitive turn and to shape its nature. Because his crime-fighting efforts carried an aura of liberal social uplift and got lost in the sea of his many other initiatives and failures, they gained him little credit at the time from law-and-order types, little attention for a long time from scholars, and little blame from critics of American criminal justice.[3] But his administration did help start the punitive turn in response to the Vietnam-era disruption of a militarized order, thereby enmeshing it in the attitudes and institutions of war.

Johnson hardly intended to create the massive punitive system that soon emerged, a development so incremental that almost no one foresaw it, much less advocated it, in the 1960s. But he was as instrumental in that development as law-and-order luminaries like Barry Goldwater, George Wallace, and Richard Nixon. True, LBJ sometimes disavowed responsibility—he had "no choice" but to sign the Omnibus Crime Control and Safe Streets Act of 1968, he told Doris Kearns, explaining, "Nixon has forced me into it by all the election bullshit blaming the Democrats for crime in the streets."[4] But his reluctance to sign that bill can be misleading. Johnson was a vigorous proponent of new crime-fighting efforts, and he saw crime as warranting "war" against it. In tying crime-fighting and war-fighting so closely, LBJ helped set the punitive turn in motion, redirecting the state from war abroad to war at home. Liberalism, at least some strands of it, was as responsible for the punitive turn as conservatism. Liberals had a deep association with war, not because they loved it but because the midcentury peak of liberalism coincided with the midcentury peak of American war-making, which often underwrote the liberal state. They shared responsibility for the river of words, images, weapons, and personnel of war that flowed into crime-fighting. It is the place to begin this story.

This chapter locates the start of the punitive turn in the embrace by Johnson and others of war's rhetoric and institutions, and in their ability to draw on the midcentury buildup of those institutions, which provided state capacity that could be turned to crime-fighting. As such, this chapter differs from other explanations of Johnson-era crime politics that seldom mention either that embrace or the Vietnam War context of crime politics in the 1960s and 1970s.

LBJ and the Punitive Turn

The pressures within and beyond the Johnson administration to tackle crime were numerous, big, and volatile. Rising crime rates— as always, more malleable and subjective than almost anyone admitted, and partly the product of more systematic reporting—were the most obvious concern. According to the Federal Bureau of Investigation (FBI), violent crime rose 11 percent from 1965 to 1966, and 165 percent between 1965 and 1975. In addition, "the national homicide rate doubled between the mid-1960s and early 1970s" and soared even more in some big cities.[5] Crime rates would have registered even higher had they reflected the illegal acts of racist southern sheriffs and police, scared National Guardsmen patrolling campuses and cities, angry cops unloading sticks and guns, and urban red squads and federal agents snooping on and provoking violence by alleged radicals. But such people were rarely arrested, much less convicted, barely leaving a trace in crime statistics. At least as unsettling to people in power like LBJ, more and more prison inmates, especially black ones organized by the Nation of Islam, were rebelling or taking legal action against their treatment.[6]

In 1966, the young expert James Q. Wilson, later to champion a crackdown on crime and to influence presidents and crime policy for decades, assayed the statistics skeptically. Stating that he had found "as yet no good evidence to justify the assertion that American society is becoming more criminal or less moral," he also suggested, "We are . . . *less* likely to commit a truly serious crime today than twenty or thirty years ago." Far from "going to hell in a handbasket," he added, "we are a long way from hell, and in fact may not even be in that particular handbasket." Wilson did speculate that the "middle classes" might be "now *consuming* more crime, even though our society, as a whole, may be said to be *producing* less." And he warned that crime "can become the major domestic issue of the far right, replacing 'communist subversion' and even 'socialism.'" Unless "liberalism" addresses crime, he declared, "it will become a notable victim of crime in the streets." But like many experts, Wilson attributed rising crime to the huge baby-boom cohort of the 1960s, given that younger people are more prone to crime: *"What appears to be a crime explosion may in fact be a population explosion."*[7]

Moreover, in some categories like murder and robbery, crime rates only rose above their historically low levels in the 1950s, reflecting the periodic fluctuations such rates always experience rather than a march into unknown territory. Indeed, the rising crime rates of the 1960s might have attracted little attention by themselves — absent, that is, the political disorder, urban uprisings, racial conflict, and antiwar protest of the period (which, to be sure, contributed to the crime statistics).

But crime rates never exist "by themselves," and the public voices of politicians and law enforcement leaders rarely acknowledged demography or the other complexities Wilson examined. A spike in public fears of crime seemed obvious at the time. Increasing anxiety was measurable in an "explosion of fear of crime stories . . . easily traced to around 1965," and more tentatively in public opinion polls. But pollsters' leading questions (do you agree that "Law and Order has broken down in this country"?) did as much to provoke fear as to measure it, and crime did not ascend to a major place in polling until 1968. Even then, "recorded concerns over the Vietnam War" far outpaced concerns about crime.[8]

Indeed, over the long haul politicians and other elites nurtured public fear of crime more than they responded to it, much like they led rather than followed public opinion preceding America's entry into many of its wars. One LBJ biographer postulated a "national desire for substantive and symbolic responses to the country's growing lawlessness." However, that desire was more conjured than palpable — in the early stages of its construction, as scholars like to put it.[9]

Americans' desire for crime control was hardly uniform or stable across class, racial, and other lines, and it was certainly less pronounced late in the LBJ years than a national desire to end (one way or another) America's war in Vietnam. As Marie Gottschalk stresses, "It is misleading to portray the public as overwhelmingly punitive," and "the widespread impression that public concern about crime skyrocketed in the 1960s . . . is not solidly supported." Indeed, it was only "in the mid-1990s" that "the public began to identify crime as a leading problem." Americans did not focus on crime as a goad to leaders' initiatives; rather, they pinpointed the issue in reaction to how leaders had harped on it for decades. Political scientist Peter K. Enns has challenged those formulations, arguing that "politically motivated elites have been marching in step with the mass public."[10] But it is more accurate to say that in the

1960s politicians tried to make hay out of crime, and they did so with only mixed success (it did Goldwater little good in the 1964 election).

Still, the social production of fear—the claim that fear was rampant—surged at mid-decade, even if the grassroots reality of fear was less evident. And beyond crime of a familiar sort, urban riots, campus conflicts, antiwar agitation, black militancy, youthful rebelliousness, pornography, and godlessness added to a generalized sense of social disorder for numerous Americans. In response, many whites sought to throttle African Americans for their violence or simply for their assertion of equality. This distinction was rarely clear to many white Americans, for whom policing had a deep antiblack history. ("The first real organized policing systems in America arguably began in the South with *slave patrols*," argues Radley Balko.)[11] Much crime was committed by whites intimidating or terrorizing blacks—by "Bull" Connor's Birmingham, Alabama police, for example—although most public debate framed the aggressors' actions as an issue of civil rights rather than criminality.

Most worrisome to Johnson and those around him, their political enemies seemed to gain traction by lambasting crime and blaming it on the liberalism of the ruling Democrats and key judges (especially Chief Justice Earl Warren, though he was a Republican nominated by President Dwight Eisenhower). As president, Eisenhower had made little public mention of crime. President John Kennedy had not discussed the matter much more, except for organized crime and race relations. But law and order moved to center stage in Goldwater's 1964 campaign, assisted by former president Eisenhower's denunciation that year of "maudlin sympathy for the criminal" who was "roaming the streets with switchblade knife and illegal firearms seeking a prey."[12] Lawbreaking was also emphasized in state and local races, including Ronald Reagan's successful campaign to become California's governor in 1966, and independent Wallace's and Republican Nixon's presidential campaigns in 1968. The crime issue plausibly accounted for Nixon's tiny margin of victory over Wallace and Vice President Hubert Humphrey.

Often enough, politicians presented crime in gendered and racialized terms. "Our wives, all women, feel unsafe on our streets," Goldwater declared in 1964. Given that the candidate connected the civil rights movement to "mobs in the street," critics interpreted Goldwater as saying that white women felt vulnerable at the hands of black men.[13] Nixon announced in 1968, "50 per cent of American women are frightened to walk within a mile of their homes at night."[14] Women's fear of crime, especially sexual violence, was powerful, but male politicians also exploited it, posing as protectors of defenseless women even though many crime victims were men. Not infrequently, critics in turn presented law-and-order crusaders as protofascists driven by an out-of-whack masculinity—charging, for example, that Goldwater was a "counterfeit figure of a masculine man, namely, Adolf Hitler."[15] Lawlessness was enmeshed with race, gender, and class, issuing a gusher of volatile politics that rained down on the White House.

But Johnson was not simply a beleaguered respondent to these pressures who sought "to co-opt some of his critics' momentum by adopting the crime issue himself."[16] He was also an active agent in expressing and channeling those burdens. He came into office because of a great crime, Kennedy's assassination in 1963, and he agonized over the alleged criminality of people close to him. In the heat of the 1964 campaign, Walter Jenkins, Johnson's chief of staff and longtime confidante, was arrested for sexual activity in a D.C. YMCA men's room. In 1967, Bobby Baker, the party wheeler-dealer close to LBJ, was indicted and convicted on tax evasion, theft, and fraud charges after years of sex and corruption allegations.

For sure, LBJ did not engage crime as intensely as he did the Vietnam War and race relations, matters that presented him with almost daily crises. But crime worried LBJ in itself and as a threat to his efforts to build the Great Society, which he in turn saw as a means to combat crime. Like many liberals, he understood his "war on poverty," publicly launched on March 16, 1964, as one way to get at the root causes of criminality. In the same way, he regarded civil rights laws as a means to quell black discontent that might erupt into lawlessness. As the President's Commission on Law Enforcement put it in 1967, "Warring on poverty . . . is warring on crime. A civil rights law is a law against crime."[17] Humphrey's 1968 campaign retort to Nixon's law-and-order stance captured that liberal view: "For every jail Mr. Nixon wants to build I'd like to build a house for a family. And for every policeman he wants to hire I'd like to hire another good teacher."[18]

But it was not that neat: LBJ, too, wanted more police. He repeatedly, if sometimes waveringly, backed new measures to deal with crime, among them the Law Enforcement Assistance Administration, begun in 1965 and expanded in 1968, which funneled federal money and resources to local agencies (New Orleans police got an armed personnel carrier).[19] Johnson also supported a major, impressively staffed national crime commission. Capping off the legislative record was the Omnibus Crime Control and Safe Streets Act, so sprawling that "Omnibus" was indeed a fitting title. That law was the federal government's biggest intervention to date into the highly localized business of crime control, and it was so stripped of liberal provisions Johnson originally proposed (he wanted stronger gun control and better protection of privacy rights) that it took much squirming for him to sign it. Also, insofar as warring on poverty was equated with warring on crime, the instruments and resources of the former process were often redeployed to the latter one in the twilight of Johnson's presidency and under his successor.[20]

Just as important, Johnson employed the language of a "war on crime" repeatedly. That metaphor was hardly new, and it was easily lost in the blizzard of war metaphors LBJ issued—there was hardly a problem he did not declare war on. But Johnson used war-on-crime language abundantly and elaborately. He first publicly mouthed a similar phrase on the campaign trail, proclaiming on October 16, 1964, that "the war on poverty . . . is a war against crime and a war against disorder." In the months after, he mentioned "war against crime" occasionally, and on September 22, 1965, he insisted that "the policeman is the frontline soldier in our war against crime."

Johnson escalated his rhetorical war on crime on roughly the same schedule that he expanded America's war in Vietnam (major U.S. ground forces arrived there in 1965, and their number rapidly grew thereafter). In his special message to Congress on crime and law enforcement on March 9, 1966, LBJ proposed a long list of punitive, preventive, and rehabilitative measures, elaborating the war metaphor at length. The country would witness a "unified attack" and an "immediate attack" and a "three-stage national strategy," with the local policeman again "the frontline soldier in the war on crime." On October 15, Johnson told a crime-fighting group, "We are today fighting a war within our own boundaries. . . . This war is a war against crime in America." Entangling combat in Vietnam with combat against crime, he added, "This Nation can mount a major military effort on the other side of the globe, and we can transfer hundreds of thousands of men 10,000 miles away from home without too much difficulty. Yet this Nation tolerates criminal activity, right here at home, that costs the taxpayers far more in both lives and dollars than the Vietnam conflict has ever cost them." He used war-on-crime phrasing frequently for the rest of his presidency.

Others employed similar language. Nebraska Republican senator Roman Hruska, for example, claimed, "The task of law enforcement agencies is really not much different from military forces: namely, to deter crime before it occurs, just as our military objective is deterrence of aggression."[21] But other public figures often used the war metaphor in a generic or offhand way—as rhetorical chest thumping or in formulaic calls for stiffer laws, tougher judges, harsher penalties. Johnson gave the image specific, extended warlike content. For him, combating crime sometimes meant using the institutions of war to deal with it, including having troops patrol the streets in the face of big-city riots.

Johnson's equation of the cop and the "frontline soldier" broke from earlier images of police. In 1953, a sociologist noted that police had been widely "regarded as corrupt and inefficient by" a hostile "public" during the 1940s and 1950s.[22] Movies, film noir in particular, often presented cops, prosecutors, prison wardens, and other law enforcers as dangerous or crooked; only a thin line, or none at all, distinguished them from lawbreakers. More benign images appeared, but many were at best condescending. Cops in films were often laughably bumbling, slow witted, overweight, or old, characteristics of the stock Irish cop in films. Consider Officer Krupke struggling to match wits with teenagers in *West Side Story* (1957; film, 1961).

Some law enforcers in cinema were heroic, but these were often detectives, other nonuniformed officials, or members of elite forces like the FBI, which, under director J. Edgar Hoover, had clawed its way out of the bad press FBI agents had once gotten. Others, like the plainclothes juvenile officer who takes charge of James Dean in *Rebel Without a Cause* (1955), warranted viewers' admiration as protective, patriarchal social workers rather than as gun-toting cops. But however presented, the cop was not figured as a "frontline soldier." Nor was the policeman much noticed by Johnson's predecessors, in part because World War II had produced an abundance of real soldiers, whose heroism had helped to win that titanic war.

Johnson's comparison of cops to soldiers was as significant for who said it as for its content. Governors, mayors, and others sometimes praised law enforcement officers for their soldierly qualities, but when the president did so, he raised the comparison to the national stage. Since he was also commander in chief of the armed forces, he virtually enlisted cops into a national crime-fighting force—they, too, would be the president's soldiers. The president had no legal authority over local police, and that would have been the last responsibility LBJ would have wanted given the tumult in America's cities. Moreover, as the Vietnam War ground on, the cops-as-soldiers line became fraught. If, as many Americans came to believe, U.S. soldiers were exploited victims of America's war makers, perpetrators of war crimes, or drug-addled malcontents, what cop would want to be compared to them? But Johnson's words marked the start of a process whereby crime-fighting was recast as war-fighting and police as soldiers in a war. Police were "the men who wage the war on crime day after day in the streets and roads and alleys in America," as Johnson put it in signing the 1968 Omnibus Crime Control and Safe Streets Act.[23] Likewise, law enforcement officers were by then emerging "as a special victim class of its own needing special federal attention," and as a symbolic stand-in for all those victimized by crime.[24]

Why did Johnson and others cast their campaign against crime as a war? Among their reasons was that doing so framed crime as a national issue. Only the nation, after all, can wage war. States or localities cannot, however much their actions may have warlike dimensions. A "war" on crime helped Johnson's administration to mobilize the energies that war presumably summons, just as World War II had done for a generation of leaders like Johnson who regarded that war as the template for national action.

Before LBJ

In associating war-fighting with crime-fighting and soldiers with cops, Johnson was hardly operating from scratch. Those associations threaded through the history of the United States and other nations, with the lines between a state's military and policing functions blurry and shifting. In the 1920s, with World War I as a template, declarations sounded of a "war on crime." The *New York Times* used the phrase in summarizing a 1922 pronouncement by Chicago mayor "Big Bill" Thompson, not squeaky clean himself, though objections to that language also arose.[25] Drugs occasionally provoked similar language. "Leads War on Morphine," proclaimed a headline in the *Washington Post*, while the *Los Angeles Times* touted a "war on narcotics."[26] Indeed, "In California, unsavory cultures of drug-law enforcement that are still trappings of the drug wars date from the turn of the 20th century."[27]

In addition, what one historian dubs "the War on Alcohol" raged during Prohibition. While the term "war" was not widely used at the time with regard to banning alcohol, Prohibition sometimes took on warlike dimensions, drew on institutional machinery developed during World War I, and expanded the crime-fighting machinery of the state, including federal prisons.[28] At the same time, gang violence and defiance of Prohibition were imagined as a war against the social order. The ease with which Americans saw their armed forces as engaged in "police actions" in Latin America was another example of the political and linguistic traffic between war-fighting and crime-fighting. Above all, in a nation that saw its wars as its most triumphant endeavors, combat was a compelling model for understanding America's efforts in other realms like crime-fighting.[29]

The traffic between war and crime operated in practice as well as in language. The armed forces and state militias had recurrently policed the nation through breaking strikes and responding to riots, subduing Native Americans and enforcing Reconstruction in the South, and responding to natural disasters. The military also had policing functions abroad—occupying defeated enemies, patrolling strife-torn Caribbean nations, and quelling political opposition in these same locales. America pioneered policing and surveillance practices abroad that sometimes came back home (and vice versa).[30] And the armed forces had to police themselves, with their own large criminal justice systems. By the same token, criminal justice forces—the FBI and other federal, state, and local agencies—had war-related functions. They helped to police the armed forces, enforce conscription, track down alleged subversives, and spy on luminaries.

As the state's capacity to catch and hold criminals increased during the 1930s and 1940s, the connections between war-fighting and crime-fighting got rewired. Something of a New Deal for convicts emerged, championed by James Bennett, the reformist director of the Federal Bureau of Prisons from 1937 to 1964, and pushed by a lively prison journalism he endorsed. Bennett insisted that rehabilitation was the primary purpose of imprisonment, that facilitating reentry was vital, that inmates should have maximum contact with families and others on the outside, and much else. Except by example and advocacy, Bennett could have little impact on state and local prisons. Even so, the New Deal's reformist zeal hung over his efforts, aided by the professionalization of federal prison administration.[31]

That zeal carried over into World War II, when the nation's mammoth needs and proclaimed ideals sometimes made inmates assets to be valued, even patriots to be celebrated, rather than burdens to be borne. Prisoners touted their contributions to a war for freedom, the benefits of releasing prisoners for military duty or war industry jobs—in contrast to the slave labor practices of Axis enemies—and the restored citizenship for the incarcerated that might ensue. At one federal prison, the *Washington Post* reported in May 1941, months before the United States' formal entry into the war, "Atlanta Prisoners Jeer at Hitler, Double Output to Aid Defense." Soon, the Atlanta prison's inmate newspaper demanded that a fifth freedom, "the right to fight for one's country," be added to the four FDR proclaimed in 1941.[32] Yet there was push as well as pull. Indignant citizens wondered why their sons faced death overseas while other men sat out the conflict behind bars with a kind of get-out-of-war card.

The military, desperate for manpower for its ground forces, could hardly turn a blind eye to the opportunity. The result was the entry into the armed forces of ex-convicts and of convicts paroled or given early release—to this end, army recruiters even visited prisons. The practice was poorly tracked at the time because it varied among states, which held most prisoners, and among local Selective Service boards. Ex-felons also entered military service if they managed to hide their criminal records or if Selective Service boards exercised their discretion to admit them under some conditions. All in all, at least 100,000 former convicts served in the armed forces, a striking number given a total incarcerated population of only a quarter million at any one point during the war. For many, that service was the ticket to full restoration of their citizenship. Experts judged prisoners' military service favorably and touted it as proving the potential for rehabilitation of many such individuals. These servicemen's record was another reason the rehabilitative ideal held wide sway at midcentury.[33]

Thousands more convicts deployed to war production duties outside prison walls or churned out war goods in prison factories. There was, after all, a shortage of bodies not only for the armed forces but also for factories and farms. Convicts' production and patriotism were widely touted. "The inmates of San Quentin are doing our part by purchasing United States defense bonds and stamps and working in prison industries to furnish vital materials for the defense programs," boasted the 1942 crime-drama film *The Men of San Quentin*.[34] No less a figure than Attorney General Francis Biddle visited the Atlanta prison in 1942 to shower thanks on its inmates for their contribution to the war effort, leading one inmate to comment, "[What] a remarkable thing that a cabinet member and a convict can meet like this . . . shake hands and wish each other well."[35] Prison administrators now "found on their hands a prison population filled with enthusiasm, rather than paralyzed by a sense of gloom and futility."[36]

The war also had effects beyond its current batch of prisoners. It diverted millions of men of a crime-prone age into the armed forces before they could commit serious offenses (though some broke laws in service). Millions more men and women attained economic security, one bulwark against crime, in the gigantic apparatus of war production. The civilian imprisoned population accordingly shrank by a fourth between 1940 and 1945 (a lesser dip came during the Vietnam War).[37]

The World War II experience had varied repercussions. The flow of personnel between military and police work swelled. Aided by veterans' preference, many ex-servicemen from World War II and the Korean War flocked into police work; as of 1968, 70 percent of FBI Special Agents were veterans.[38] "By 1968," recalled one Chicago cop who also joined the National Guard, "I would say a great percentage of the police department, probably as high as eighty-five percent, was World War II and Korean War veterans." As he added, "When you joined up they called it a semimilitary organization. It was actually more than semimilitary."[39] Consequently, many Americans wore two hats—cops in their day jobs and military police in the National Guard.

With 16 million men serving during World War II and millions more after it, many veterans also made their way to prisons as guards, supervisors, wardens, counselors, doctors, chaplains, and the like—or as inmates, often after checkered records in military service and dishonorable discharges from it. Therapeutic methods and practitioners also made the move from the wartime armed forces, whose psychiatric experts devised new methods to treat men under duress or damaged by their service, and into the criminal justice arena. This was especially common in states like California that were inclined to try new practices. Institutional cooperation between the armed forces and criminal justice institutions was sometimes close, especially among prison psychologists and social workers who had done a stint in the military and had trained in Veterans Administration (VA) facilities, which were arguably the nation's biggest and best sites for medical and psychiatric research. For the VA, cooperation with prison staff and criminological experts made equal sense. "In many ways," notes one scholar, "the rehabilitative practices in postwar corrections fit squarely within the structure of the military welfare state."[40] That the armed forces used some inmates for radiation and other medical experimentation was another, perverse, link between the two realms.[41]

But at least before World War II, the imaginative and practical associations between war-fighting and crime-fighting had usually been episodic, improvised, and seldom articulated in the public square, unlike the sustained, high-profile, institutionally robust, and consequential connections that emerged during and after LBJ's presidency. The institutional apparatus to buttress those associations also had been limited.[42] The aftermath of World War II differed so much from the turmoil and aftermath of the Vietnam War. It occurred amid postwar prosperity so that veterans lacked the desperation that drove many of them to take on police and prison jobs later. Applied to both veterans and convicts, the rehabilitative ethos of the period curtailed the punitive thrust of military-civilian interchange. The national security state was gobbling up resources, not shedding them, as it did to a degree after 1970.

In the early postwar years, the men who switched from soldier's uniform to cop's outfit were a small slice of a vast veterans population, and they moved into a comparatively stable, small-scale policing and prison system. By the 1970s, those making that move were a larger slice of a smaller veterans cohort who moved into a fast-expanding criminal justice system amid more intense fears of crime. Older institutional links persisted, but to new purposes. In California, new "technologies" designed to predict crime and control criminals "came, once again, from military research," but they emerged after the 1960s with the goal of identifying "those most deserving of punishment and incapacitation."[43] And the wars themselves differed so much. Whereas World War II was fought mostly against an external enemy and ended with a powerful sense of U.S. triumph, the Vietnam War abroad featured "war at home" without the healing balm of victory.

"From Uniform to Uniform"

It was into this thicket of historical patterns and associations that Johnson stepped, not only with words but with policies. The Pentagon's Project 100,000, implemented in 1966 but sketched as early as 1964, pointed the way. That venture sought to pull into military service disadvantaged, especially black, young men who failed to meet the army's standards for draftees, and prepare them for service through extensive education and training. Its primary purpose was to provide more manpower for the expanding army as the Vietnam War heated up, with nearly 400,000 men cycling through Project 100,000 before its discontinuation in 1971. But the project was also underpinned by rationales about crime prevention.

Those underpinnings showed in *The Negro Family: The Case for National Action*, Assistant Labor Secretary Daniel Patrick Moynihan's famous March 1965 report that influenced Defense Secretary Robert McNamara and others who devised Project 100,000. Moynihan saw military service, especially for black youth, as an antidote to crime and other urban ills. Lamenting "matriarchy" and disorganization in poor black families, Moynihan, in line with many black and white experts, concluded bluntly, "Negro children [referring to sons, not daughters] without fathers flounder—and fail." One marker of failure was "a disastrous delinquency and crime rate," with fellow blacks the primary victims. Another was the high rate of rejection for military service when black youth were drafted or sought to enlist, denying them the advantages that service might bring. At least for those who survived it, "service in the Armed Forces over the past quarter-century has worked greatly to the advantage of those involved," Moynihan noted. "The training and experience of military duty itself is unique; the advantages that have generally followed in the form of the GI Bill, mortgage guarantees, Federal life insurance, Civil Service preference, veterans hospitals, and veterans pensions are singular, to say the least."[44]

As Moynihan saw it, military service could redeem vulnerable black boys, steering them away from joblessness, crime, and family dysfunction.

> There is another special quality about military service for
> Negro men: it is an utterly masculine world. Given the strains
> of the disorganized and matrifocal family life in which so many
> Negro youth come of age, the Armed Forces are a dramatic and
> desperately needed change: a world away from women, a world
> run by strong men of unquestioned authority, where discipline, if
> harsh, is nonetheless orderly and predictable, and where rewards,
> if limited, are granted on the basis of performance.

"The theme of a current Army recruiting message," the assistant labor secretary pointed out, "states it as clearly as can be: 'In the U.S. Army you get to know what it means to feel like a man.'"[45] "For Moynihan," one historian notes, "the military seemed like a vast, untapped agent of social uplift," just as Project 100,000 was "a significant component of the administration's 'war on poverty.'"[46]

But it was also a major component of an emerging war on crime, a component based on the assumption that flawed men commit crime and "strong men," made strong by military service, do not. Even before Project 100,000 got started, Johnson had pressed McNamara about salvaging "poor children," declaring, "I know that you can do better by them than the NYA [the New Deal–era National Youth Administration] or the Job Corps can." The Department of Defense "can do the job best," LBJ insisted. "We can teach them work discipline," McNamara promised. No wonder McNamara soon spoke of Project 100,000 as a way to salvage those he grimly labeled the "subterranean poor."[47]

As its planners saw it, Project 100,000 would take black youth out of a matriarchy that emasculated them, and all poor youth out of a culture of poverty that disadvantaged them. The shiftlessness, low expectations, and cultural deprivation that potentially made them criminals—and poor soldiers—would be disrupted. Military training and stern supervision would make men who could take responsibility for themselves in war or peace. Meanwhile, and not incidentally, it would take off the streets many of the young black men prone to crime and urban violence. Project 100,000 was widely judged a failure at the time, even as a mechanism for enlarging the army. Its soldiers' training was often poor, their service often unreliable. Many officials and commanders complained bitterly, and unfairly, that Project 100,000 was "just flooding [them] with morons and imbeciles."[48] And insofar as it aggravated among some men the very anger and discontent it sought to quiet and redirect, the scheme was arguably worse than a failure. But it did suggest how policymakers linked military service and military institutions to crime prevention and crime-fighting.

Johnson and almost everyone in politics, nearly all of whom were men, professed familiarity with the virtues of military service. Like Johnson and Moynihan, most had been members of the armed forces, especially during World War II, or worked as civilians in America's defense apparatus. They understood military service to civilize, discipline, and provide opportunities for those who survived it. For a generation, it had been the path to adult male responsibility, enriched citizenship, generous GI benefits, and political success. In that spirit, Johnson promised in 1967 that Project 100,000 would "help" its recruits "become good soldiers—and later, productive citizens."[49]

LBJ's men also knew the lore about errant youth straightened out by military service. That service might come through a draft call or a decision to enlist in the face of trouble at home, dead-end jobs, or personal criminal activity. Judges and social workers could give young men a choice between jail and military service, or they could simply order enlistment. To be sure, much of this lore was just that, not social science—a large stock of stories, gossip, and newspaper accounts that overlooked the kids who washed out of the military. And veterans benefits had been spread unevenly—denied to men and women discharged for homosexuality and more difficult for African Americans and other minorities to access. Still, the widespread post–World War II assumption, supported by some data, was that military service turned boys into men. This notion prevailed not just among white men but in African American families and among men who enlisted or were drafted. The marines were a "shortcut to manhood," as one 1966 enlistee later put it.[50] Indeed, one attraction of linking crime-fighting to military service was how this assumption crossed class, racial, gender, and partisan lines, at least as of the mid-1960s.

The beneficial links national leaders saw among military service, citizenship, and crime prevention also played out at the state level. For example, California politicians and corrections officials turned many convicts into conservation workers and disaster responders through a system of rural camps. Championed by Edmund G. Brown, California's Democratic governor from 1959 to 1967, the camps drew on the model, and sometimes the facilities, of the New Deal's Civilian Conservation Corps. Further inspiration came from the example of World War II service by California convicts, who were "transformed by the war from public enemies to public assets in seasonal harvest and forest camps and in manufacturing industries in the San Quentin and Folsom prisons." Camps drew local support from businessmen, civic leaders, and residents eager for protection from natural disasters and for assistance in developing local economies. The camps were often remarkably permissive concerning inmates' mobility and public roles. By removing inmates from the dead-end or barbaric effects of prison, "forest camps could turn prisoners into citizen soldiers," it was hoped. Lauding inmates' role in fighting a June 1966 fire near Santa Barbara, California's Department of Corrections "praised these 'specially trained and conditioned' prisoners for attacking the fire 'like soldiers [in] battle.'" Just as some World War II–era convicts had been paroled for military service or harnessed as war workers, postwar inmate "citizen soldiers" might restore their manhood and citizenship. "Turning public enemies into martyrs," it seemed, "was the apogee of rehabilitation." While national leaders hoped that service in the armed forces would turn at-risk youth away from crime, California leaders hoped that quasi-military service in their "forest army" would rescue many who had already succumbed to it.[51]

As Project 100,000 unfolded, officials pursued the linkage between war and crime in other ways. Project 100,000 had a limited shelf life since the Vietnam War would eventually end, the huge Vietnam-era force would shrink, and the draft, so provocative of political turmoil, might be abandoned, as some politicians and planners were already advocating late in the Johnson presidency. The notion that military service was an antidote to crime rested on a time-bound and romanticized sense of how it had functioned during and after World War II. By the late 1960s, it seemed that military service might instead provoke crime, in turn threatening the armed forces. Those inclined to lawbreaking might be rejected for service, or if they got in, they might undermine discipline and morale. As a tool for disciplining crime-prone youth, military service would have declining utility insofar as it had any at all, for the signs were abundant that service might attract or nourish the very misbehavior it was supposed to curtail. Resistance to conscription, dissent against the war, desertions (roughly 70,000 in the army and marines in 1969), AWOL rates, discharges, courts-martial, and drug use all climbed in the late 1960s, and military stockades filled up (and mutinies inside them multiplied).[52]

As a result, official attention shifted away from the young civilians pulled into the military and toward the young vets getting out. The numbers of discharged servicemen swelled in the late 1960s because of legal limits on the length of draftees' service, the rapid rotation of troops in and out of Vietnam (one-year tours of duty were standard for enlistees), the sheer size of the Vietnam War force (over a half million by 1968), and low rates of reenlistment. Only about a third of the 1964–75 cohort of nearly ten million men and women defined by the Defense Department as Vietnam-era veterans actually served in the Vietnam War.[53] But their return to civilian status elicited a simmering, protracted anxiety in and out of official circles about how they would fit back into American life.

Such anxiety had accompanied every major U.S. war—the damaged, deranged, or dangerous World War II vet appeared frequently in reporting, fiction, and film during the 1940s and 1950s. But the fear assumed a different form and length with each war. Insofar as World War II and the Korean War were benchmarks, the Vietnam War was distinctive, with its duration longer (veterans were returning for nearly ten years), its outcome less certain, and its politics of antiwar protest, racial upheaval, youthful rebellion, and urban unrest more volatile and resistant to elite control.

Americans worried that veterans of duty in Vietnam would be crime-prone for a variety of reasons: because they had been crime-prone even before their service, because they learned the ways of crime while in service, because their time in the military had damaged or angered them, because postservice joblessness would alienate them, because racial turmoil would radicalize them. Officials, pundits, and veterans also speculated on a host of other motives for veterans' potential lawlessness. LBJ did not publicly articulate his anxiety. Yet it was implicit in the strenuousness of his initiatives to support and appease veterans, and others made it explicit. According to one newsmagazine, Johnson's policies were designed "to make sure that Negroes returning to civilian life [were] headed for good jobs—and not for troublemaking in the big cities."[54] All the virtues once assumed to inhere in military service now appeared up for grabs.

The Pentagon and the Johnson White House scrambled to respond to these concerns by directing veterans into police jobs. A new scheme,

Project Transition, an ideological and programmatic follow-up to Project 100,000 announced by LBJ in 1967, supported that effort. Operating in tandem with other veterans programs, Project Transition aimed especially at the "disadvantaged" (as LBJ called them) men taken in by Project 100,000 who were unlikely or unable to find good jobs or to tap GI benefits for college attendance, homeownership, and the like.[55] Channeling black vets into civilian jobs, including police work, was among the program's goals. Johnson championed the use of veterans to police strife-torn cities, especially Washington, D.C.—the nation's "goldfish bowl," he dubbed it—as he begged big-city mayors to accept federal crime-fighting largess.[56] Beyond Project Transition, Defense Secretary McNamara directed in November 1967 that active-duty personnel offered civilian police jobs be given early discharges, and that urban police forces be encouraged to recruit on military bases. As the title of a *Washington Post* article put it, such measures helped vets move "From Uniform to Uniform."[57]

After all, as Johnson commented on November 3, "The time has come . . . when the American people are going to rise up and revolt against the lawbreaker in this country," as he offered, in his patriarchal style, to make the nation's capital "a model child" instead of a "stepchild." Proposing a new veterans act, LBJ argued that "we should continue to enlist him [the veteran]—in service to his community, when military duty is over." Among other things, ex-servicemen could "help man understrength police forces and fire departments."[58] If military service turned youth away from crime, then postservice duty could make them crime-fighters, a redeployment that veterans programs were designed to facilitate. War-fighting and crime-fighting were similar, argued LBJ, who again analogized policemen to soldiers. "If America were to send its Armed Forces into combat ill-equipped, underpaid, under-trained and unappreciated, it would be a national scandal," he stated, adding that, at the same time, such conditions were often "a way of life for America's 420,000 policemen."[59]

Johnson's veterans programs served multiple purposes. He had earlier resisted special benefits for Vietnam veterans, fearing they would undercut his Great Society programs and constitute an embarrassing acknowledgment that the United States really was at war in Vietnam. Only under pressure, illustrated by a thumping 381–0 vote for the "Cold War GI Bill" in the House, did he reluctantly sign the new law in 1966.[60] Johnson's programs and proposals in 1967 and 1968 marked a capitulation to that pressure and to the war's mounting toll on American forces in Vietnam. His plans were aided by repackaging vets' benefits as instruments of, rather than obstacles to, his liberal vision, since he also wanted ex-servicemen to "teach the children of the poor" and join VISTA (Volunteers in Service to America).[61] LBJ's proposed ventures addressed public restlessness about a new generation of veterans set adrift. And they deflected charges that his administration had exploited young men sent to Vietnam, only to discard them. They positioned him as a friend of the veteran, a position all modern presidents have claimed. Johnson's programs attempted to pull veterans into the traditions and programs established for the World War II generation, and they also served his war on crime, building on associations between war-fighting and crime-fighting.

LBJ's late-term efforts on this front were modest in scale and impact. And in seeking to turn vets into cops and analogizing the soldier to the policeman, he avoided another step in the underlying logic. If policemen were like soldiers, then were their foes akin to the enemies faced abroad, ones who threatened the nation's safety and lacked rights to its protection? For LBJ, criminality remained a complicated and rather abstract social problem. He viewed criminals as victims as well as agents of the nation's disorders, and he said little to demonize them. Still, he saw war against crime, if not against criminals themselves, as warranted, even urgent.

Militarization from Below

As the LBJ administration sought to bolster and militarize law enforcement from above, state and local law enforcement and corporate interests did so from below in a process that extended far beyond the Johnson years. Like the federal government, these entities had access to an infusion of crime-fighting capacity—institutions, companies, technologies, tactics, personnel, words—built up during decades of militarization and during escalation of America's war in Vietnam. Then, as that war faltered, they had its leftover capacity to cope with, to discard in some ways, but also to exploit and redeploy.

Law enforcers had linked their task to the waging of war before the Vietnam era. In 1960, for example, the police chief of Kansas City, Missouri, drew "an analogy between a state of war existing with an external enemy and a state of war existing with an internal enemy—in this instance the criminal element in our land." Lawmen, he claimed, were "engulfed in war" and in "a battle against surging, violent internal evilness." Just as in war abroad, that conflict might require "a suspension of our broad democratic principles."[62]

During the Vietnam era, federal officials, local law enforcers, and companies peddling new wares went about translating that rhetorical link into operational reality. From the mid-1960s on, publications for law enforcers bristled with calls for heavier armaments, advertisements for new equipment, and images of the policeman as a better-armored and sterner professional than his predecessor. In the 1950s, advertisements had often depicted police as Good Samaritans. A 1956 ad by uniform maker Metcalf Brothers featured a smiling policeman ringing a doorbell while holding a lost boy. An older girl appeared at the cop's side and no weapon but a nightstick was in view. A 1960 ad depicted the cop as a school crossing guard.[63] By the late 1960s, advertisements often showed cops as tough, sometimes hypermasculine figures saluting like soldiers or sternly facing the advertiser's camera—hardly the smiling officers whom a lost boy might approach, although those images did not disappear altogether.[64] "Command Respect!," the explicit message of Badger Uniforms in 1967, was the implied message of many advertisers by the late 1960s. These companies went some distance to ridicule "the Keystone Cops" of the past.[65]

New weapons and equipment on offer backed up that message. Fearsome armaments were hardly new to police forces, but the sixties saw a surge in police chiefs' pleas and corporations' pitches for heavier weaponry and protection to provide "the instant, superior firepower" police wanted "to combat violent crime and riots in . . . urban areas."[66] Better weapons, armored vans, flak vests, tougher headgear, riot-control tools—these filled the pages of law enforcement journals and the equipment rooms of police forces, who often faced more civilian hostility and violence now than in the recent past. Against an urban "mob," for example, officers could wield "the Curdler," a sonic weapon tried out by U.S. forces in the Vietnam War. It could unleash an "ear-splitting sound . . . comparable to standing behind a jet fighter during take-off," an advertisement promised, and "break up the slogan-shouting, chanting, handclapping that unifies and hypnotizes a mob incited to riot."[67]

Words of war, combat, and battle often accompanied the new products. *Law and Order* (a trade journal, not the later TV show) introduced armed vehicles that were "military types and alien to the average municipal policeman," at the same time noting, "The situation that requires their use is also regrettably alien," necessitating "an armed assault platform."[68] Aerojet General's design for a new "Peacekeeper" police car (see figure 1) came with body armor and a gun turret on top.[69] B&H Enterprises' "new MPPV (Multi-Purpose Police Vehicle)" could protect fifteen men against "armor piercing ammunition," deploy "a veritable arsenal of supporting weapons," and "easily [ram] through masonry walls"—it looked almost ready for duty in Vietnam.[70] Smith and Wesson's Model 15 .38 revolver was advertised as a "Combat Masterpiece."[71] And as newspapers and television circulated images of the new equipment in operation, it came to seem a normal part of urban policing, however unwelcome for many on the receiving end.

Where did the push for a more militarized look, equipment, and operation by police come from? Politicians and officials cited the obvious—urban riots, campus violence, rising crime, and better-armed or more crazed criminals (a favorite example was Charles Whitman, the ex-marine whose shooting rampage at the University of Texas Tower in 1966 killed seventeen people). Race and racial tensions were cited less often as reasons for police militarization, but they were implied in much of the material that law enforcement officers disseminated or received. (In thousands of illustrations for articles and advertisements in law enforcement journals of the 1960s, a black face almost never appeared as an official or a cop.) Even less often did police officials and trade journals mention antiwar agitation and other political protests. These phenomena were surely on cops' minds, but they were troublesome to single out lest it appear officers were trying to throttle political expression. Law enforcement officials also pointed to the growing hazards of police work: police, their bosses, their unions, and their allies wanted better protection. Annual total deaths for law enforcement officers—many from traffic accidents and causes other than engagement with offenders—rose from just over 100 in the late 1950s to 280 in 1974 (after which came a sharp falloff). However, the steepest increase came in the early 1970s, well after the militarization of policing was under way, and the number of officer deaths still did not reach the 1930 level of 312, occurring when the size of the population and policing forces was much smaller.[72]

But the militarization of policing far outlasted the disorder of the sixties, suggesting that other forces were at work. Militarization also went forward because law enforcement officials pursued professionalization, one standard for which was more militarized equipment and operations.[73] Even before the rising crime and disorder of the 1960s, police officials sought to overcome the image of cops as hapless buffoons, overaged crossing guards, or corruptible hacks, much as the FBI (itself a major influence on police forces) had done in the 1930s and 1940s. *Police Chief*, a magazine started in 1953 by the International Association of Chiefs of Police as "the professional voice of law enforcement," was one marker of the effort to professionalize. Police leaders likewise sought something like the respect and authority that the armed forces had achieved at midcentury. That hostility toward police was often loud and ugly (officers were called "pigs," "fascists," etc.) added to their wish to gain respect. No few hints of envy of the military crept into the speeches, editorials, and articles of trade magazines in the 1950s and 1960s. As the *FBI Law Enforcement Bulletin* informed readers in 1967, "Criminals are at war with society. Our armed forces are heroes, but policeman is a dirty word," even though often "the police and military forces simultaneously fight the same enemy."[74]

By the late 1960s, the language of war was widespread, both as a generic descriptor of conflict at home and as a specific association with fighting men abroad. "Not all the heroes are in Vietnam," Federal Laboratories reminded *Police Chief* readers, touting a "Silver Badge of Courage" for police chiefs fighting "the subversive effort by a tiny minority to discredit and malign public safety officials." After all, *Police Chief* editorialized, "the killing or maiming of dedicated men . . . is as tragic when it occurs in the jungles of our cities as when it occurs in the jungles of Vietnam."[75] The death rates in those two "jungles" were vastly different, but the metaphor of "jungles," with its implication that racially savage peoples inhabited both, was a common way to conflate the two. A more professional police force engaged in something like war would be better armed like the soldiers who went into the "jungles of Vietnam."

Professionalization took a further step when police officials tried to take lessons from American efforts at counterinsurgency and counter-revolution in the Dominican Republic, Vietnam, and elsewhere. For *Police Chief* readers, an air force colonel presented counterinsurgency at home as indistinguishable from its pursuit abroad, insisting on "the potent possibilities the police can contribute to counterinsurgency" and equating the soldier and policeman in the fight against "totalitarian" rule.[76] Professionalization, that is, was conflated with militarization. There were other ways to define professionalization—for example, learning how forces in Western Europe took nonmilitarized approaches to policing. But in the 1960s, most politicians and officials did not see or grasp those alternatives.

Just as the urge to militarize swelled within American policing, the Johnson administration provided resources and guidance to help police forces do so. Some police chiefs waging "the nation's war against crime" resented the loss of local autonomy that federal bounty might entail, warning of "a powerful clique of central planners" who might bring to policing something akin to "the Federal Government's use of naked coercive authority over local educational affairs."[77] Nonetheless, the largess continued. The federal Law Enforcement Assistance Administration, which "allowed state and local law enforcement agencies to go on huge shopping sprees," especially for military-grade equipment, saw its budget soar "from $63 million in 1968 to nearly $1 billion-a-year in its heyday in the 1970s."[78] The funds involved operations as well as financing. For example, "some 600 police officers" gathered in 1967 at Fort Belvoir, Virginia, under the auspices of the U.S. Army and the FBI "to view the latest techniques in riot and mob control."[79] In another Cold War blurring of the lines, the federal Office of Public Safety, operating from 1962 to 1974, sent "hundreds of municipal and state police officers . . . abroad to instruct foreign police in modern, professional methods and develop their counterinsurgency capacities."[80]

Hawking new wares at trade shows and in police journals, companies not only tapped a new market for better weapons and sharper uniforms, they helped create that market. As always, advertising both instills and satisfies needs. In the 1960s, many companies were old-line suppliers of police equipment (Badger Uniforms, Smith & Wesson), but defense contractors also spotted the market. "Chrysler is building its special purpose police patrol vehicles around the existing components used in its . . . military versions resulting in cost savings," *Law and Order* reported in 1967. Meanwhile, Hughes Aircraft was selling its Hughes 300 Helicopter to local forces ("Shouldn't your town be next?" one advertisement asked), and Aerojet General was creating its "Peacekeeper" police car in response to a federally sponsored design competition.[81]

With withdrawal from Vietnam and foreseeable retrenchment in the armed forces, defense contractors turned more vigorously to the law enforcement market. The shift was hardly effortless; the thousands of law enforcement agencies had far more varied and less monumental needs than the armed forces, and they had no centralized purchasing system as the Pentagon had. For a company like Aerojet, then building the giant Saturn rocket, this was a new game to enter. But the militarization of policing and the spread of federal law enforcement standards helped to bridge the gap. And there was soon more than the American military experience to draw on. By 1977, a notice informed police chiefs that they could order the "Latest Issue Israeli Army Helmet."[82]

The most dramatic example of police militarization was the rise of SWAT (Special Weapons and Tactics) teams. The origins of these elite paramilitary units have been little studied but commonly attributed to an initiative in 1968 by Los Angeles police inspector Daryl Gates. His actions hardly stood out amid all the other efforts to toughen policing until the city's SWAT team undertook highly publicized raids against the Black Panthers in 1969 and the Symbionese Liberation Army (SLA) in 1974. Urban riots, mass murders, political assassinations, and other high-risk challenges were the alleged prompts for developing SWAT units, but like most developments of the 1960s, this one outgrew its presumed origins.[83]

SWAT teams were notable for their paramilitary equipment, ethos, and tactics. SWAT units—"heavy weapons units," as cops often called them—soon bristled with "lace-up combat boots, full body armor, Kevlar helmets," helicopters, and other military paraphernalia, just as they adopted some of the trappings and secrecy of military systems.[84] With these modifications, police aspired to be more like the military's elite units. Comparing beat cops to army grunts—low-status individuals, indeed—conferred little prestige, but comparing SWAT teams to U.S. Navy SEALs and other special military units, themselves bulking up and gaining status, did.

Even as Gates told his SWAT origins story, distinguishing the military from the police ("To no avail," he later complained), his account was saturated with military language and systems. He and his colleagues "began reading everything . . . concerning guerrilla warfare," studied "Vietnam," "looked at military training," and learned about "counter-insurgency and guerrilla warfare." "Regularly," he recalled, "we sent squads to train at Camp Pendleton, trading expertise with the marines." SWAT "operates like a quasi-militaristic operation," Gates acknowledged. He recalled that the SWAT team's bloody encounter with the SLA in Los Angeles "was a war zone, something out of a World War II movie, where you're taking the city from the enemy, house by house." Gates offered no extended explanation for why SWAT tactics were necessary. He only referred briefly to criminals who were better armed and organized, and to the notion that America's streets "had become a foreign territory"—thus placed in the realm of war abroad. As a New Jersey state police spokesman put it in 1969, "We're following through on the military concept in tackling" the "problem" of crime. War metaphors also captured the resistance to SWAT-type policing, as when a Chicano Los Angeles paper complained that police were "waging a 'cold war in East L.A.'"[85]

The full flowering of SWAT units came in the 1980s and 1990s, leading some scholars to identify them as a "post–Cold War" phenomenon.[86] But the first seeds were scattered in the late 1960s and 1970s, marked by the brief TV appearance in 1975–76 of the cop show *S.W.A.T* and a flurry of kids' SWAT games, lunch boxes, puzzles, and the like. LBJ's "war on crime" was also Chicago's, New York's, and LA's.

Prison practices also migrated from the arena of defense. "In the 1960s," experiments in the isolation and brainwashing of prisoners "were imported directly from military experiments into U.S. prisons," in part through efforts by those conducting the experiments to sell their work to prison officials.[87] Their endeavors helped lead to the revival of solitary confinement in the 1970s and after, even though the practice had been widely deemed inhumane in the nineteenth century by people as diverse as Charles Dickens and members of the U.S. Supreme Court. Isolation and brainwashing also led to the subsequent rise of "supermax" prisons. What seemed justified in war also seemed justified in waging war on crime.

When empire retreats, it brings many of its toys home. Soldiers, hardware, tactics, and corporations migrated into criminal justice in a process hardly commanded from the top, but instead driven by the shifting fortunes and ambitions of the institutions involved. In a nifty later instance of "imperial recycling," as Victoria Hattam calls it, steel mats used for U.S. airfields in Vietnam later became components of barriers along the U.S. border with Mexico.[88]

Other institutions also redeployed. Campus-based institutes and think tanks that provided strategic and social science expertise for defense agencies scurried off campus at the end of the 1960s, when their attachment to ivory towers came under fire from antiwar protestors. But they hardly disappeared. In the slithering way that institutions, especially ones at the far reaches of congressional and executive oversight, can adapt, they reconstituted, often lock, stock, and barrel, as independent entities. Sometimes they further spun off into for-profit organizations. These organizations still supplied expertise to defense and security agencies, but as they were now free of university oversight, campus visibility, and a single defense patron, they also moved into work concerning civil order and criminal justice.

The Special Operations Research Office (SORO), for example, a federal contract research center set up by the army in 1956 and once operated by American University, simply "checked in with a new parent organization" in 1969. SORO was now a subsidiary of the "large, private, nonprofit contract research agency American Institutes for Research (AIR)." In its new guise, SORO's expert on communist insurgency now "used the same techniques he had applied in previous studies" of revolution and protest abroad to his Justice Department–funded studies of "American student movements." In 1971, AIR drew on earlier army-funded research into "enmity between American soldiers and Korean nationals" to examine, under contract with the city of San

Francisco, "the relationship between the city's police department and minority communities."[89]

Social scientists contracted with federal and local agencies to study (generally in secret) campus turmoil, radical movements, urban unrest, and black militancy, applying the models they had earlier developed for the Cold War abroad. As one expert explained the shift in the 1970s, "I have the feeling that, when you get a group of bright guys together you have a responsibility to cope with the problems not only of Saigon and Prague, but places like Washington as well." One historian concludes that, instead of demilitarizing in the face of criticism and reduced budgets, "the military's experts extended their purview to domestic contexts" and "imposed the logic of population control, underdevelopment, and containment on American cities, university campuses, and minority populations." And so in still another way, the developing war on crime tapped the institutions, logic, and rhetoric of military institutions.[90]

New tools for electronic surveillance, detection, and control also emerged, propelled by advances in computer technology tied to defense and space initiatives. Some were pioneered in the war in Vietnam: "virtual fence" technology from Vietnam started migrating to the United States–Mexico border in the 1970s. Many such developments arose for commercial reasons, sold as advantages for the consumer, not as systems of control. New credit-card technologies, for example, allowed for storing and tracking vast records created by shoppers and travelers, records gradually tapped by law enforcement agencies. Satellite technology could not yet zero in on the color of someone's eyes, but its advances were remarkable, just as they were with ground-based systems. The first police use of closed-circuit television "to monitor public streets" came in Olean, New York, in 1968. Banks, other businesses, and other cities (with grants from the federal Law Enforcement Assistance Administration) subsequently used the televisions for surveillance.

Many new systems had little immediate payoff for law enforcement, but their potential for constructing what Christian Parenti calls "the soft cage" of surveillance and control was quickly glimpsed and promoted. Abundant precedents encouraged this promotion. Precomputer forms of private and state surveillance dated to slavery, advanced with the development of passport and fingerprinting technology, took another form with use of filmed surveillance of public events, and spurted forward in 1939 when FBI director J. Edgar Hoover gained FDR's authorization to access Social Security records, already semicomputerized by the 1940s. As with SWAT policing and social science research, electronic surveillance and snooping did not start the punitive turn, but they did accelerate it. All owed a debt to American war making.[91]

These developments also indicated how talk of a war on crime was not just a rhetorical device to underline the urgency of crime-fighting. Such talk also drew on quite specific connections that many Americans, from LBJ on down, drew between war abroad and war at home. Whether as experience, hardware, model, or object lesson, the Vietnam War, alongside a broader discourse about counterinsurgency, saturated rhetoric and thought about crime and policing. "Our readiness to jump into wars when they are outside the three-mile limit seems much greater than our willingness to jump into wars inside our national boundaries," Detroit mayor Jerome Cavanagh complained to the National League of Cities in 1966. For good measure, he compared "guerilla war in the Mekong Delta" to "guerilla war on our streets."[92] In the Johnson years, and for LBJ in particular, it became difficult to think about the one without thinking about the other, and in turn to think of fighting lawlessness as something other than waging war. The dizzying connections between them gave the idea of a war on crime its traction, its immediacy, its weight.

2 WAR ON CRIME IN VIETNAM'S WAKE, 1969-1973

Crime politics were supercharged during the last years of America's war in Southeast Asia. Richard Nixon, through his shrill words, harsh actions, and backstage scheming, advanced the punitive turn, and he was soon regarded as a founding father of the modern war on crime and drugs. Yet he was neither a singular nor a steadfast figure in that regard. His impulses were punitive, but he was hardly alone in having them, and he met major challenges to them. He played the law-and-order card for political advantage, but that advantage faded when the Watergate crisis engulfed his second term. Nixon had little interest in substantive issues of crime, certainly less interest than in crushing his political enemies. His crime politics were angry but scattershot—more a Nixon project than the state project they had been under Johnson. The Vietnam War's convulsive politics both promoted and ensnared Nixon's law-and-order agenda. He was the agitated bellwether of crosscutting national impulses inflamed by war and racial conflict, not their creator. Changes often beyond his control—a faltering faith in rehabilitating convicts, a rising share of inmates who were black, a sped-up militarization of policing—did as much as Nixon to advance the punitive turn.

Nixon's Crime Politics

Nixon came to office amid mounting crime, violence, and political agitation about lawbreaking. He assumed the presidency just after the assassinations of Martin Luther King Jr. and Robert Kennedy in 1968, and the protest and brutality that engulfed the Democratic National Convention in Chicago in August. Urban turmoil was also ongoing. Over the next few years, radical offshoots of the New Left and the antiwar movement carried out campus bombings and raids on Selective Service offices, with some leaders calling for overthrow of the government.

Nixon's politics and most media coverage presented crime as the product of liberals, left-wingers, and blacks, but criminal action by others also surged. The result was vigilante attacks on real or imagined radicals ("an epidemic of hippie lynchings in New Mexico," for example), police violence (as at the Democratic Convention), illegal acts perpetrated by angry mayors and the White House, and deeds that defied political classification. "If anyone was keeping score, right-wing vigilantes were far worse," Rick Perlstein notes, although "people weren't keeping score." "The berserk was breaking out on every side. Sometimes it was hard to *tell* the sides," though Nixon's team "harbored no such doubts. The left were the aggressors. Everyone else was just playing defense." Nixon's "dirty trickster" Tom Huston "embodied a certain paradox of the right: to those who believed civilization unraveling at the hands of barbarians, it was principled to be unprincipled." In contrast to that view, a prestigious New Jersey commission investigating the July 1967 riots in Newark spotted "a pattern of police action for which there is no possible justification" and claimed that "the single continuously lawless element operating in the community is the police force itself."[1]

But outside of besieged minorities, leftist students, and radical critics—in the aggregate, no token number—many Americans judged the forces of "law and order" as "just playing defense." Convulsing matters further was illegality in America's war in Vietnam, especially the My Lai massacre of March 17, 1968, a story that emerged in newspapers late in 1969. Hanging over it all was a broader apprehension—or for some, wish—that the war in Vietnam had bequeathed a war at home. Even those who hardly wanted to conflate the two wars stumbled into doing so. "It would be ironic," the liberal Democrat George McGovern had told the Senate in 1967, "if we devoted so heavy a proportion of our resources to the pacification of Vietnam that we are unable to pacify Los Angeles, Chicago, and Harlem."[2]

All of Nixon's instincts went toward exploiting crime, violence, and antiwar agitation (he conflated the three) for political purposes, as he had in his 1968 campaign. He sought to use these issues to divide Democrats and peel some of them off, and to stir the very passions he said he wanted to calm. Nixon wanted to throttle black militancy and antiwar activism. Perhaps more important to him, he wanted to inform the "silent majority" of Americans that he was doing so, solidifying the GOP's emerging hold on the white South and on many white Democrats elsewhere. As a biographer characterized Nixon's 1970 campaign in behalf of Republicans running for office, "He ran against pot, permissiveness, protest, pornography, and dwindling patriotism," though doing so did Republicans no good in that year's congressional elections.[3]

Of course, some show of actual action against presumed lawbreakers was necessary to back up the message, lest it seem empty, and to satisfy Nixon's vindictive impulses. His crackdown on radical activism, often through illegal means, was real. So was the skeletal start of a war on drugs and a "new Jim Crow," as Michelle Alexander has labeled it—the use of mass incarceration to control black Americans now that legal Jim Crow had collapsed.[4] Yet Nixon hardly foresaw or cared much about long-term consequences. Gestures at solutions to problems of crime and violence served his political purposes, but Nixon's heart was in the politics, not the results.

In pursuing those purposes, he offered an uncertain follow-up to the political and rhetorical precedents Johnson set for a war on crime. Nixon did not tap the symbolic and substantive connections between war and crime to the extent that LBJ had. His was more a standard law-and-order approach, sometimes offered with nods to the complexities involved. In Nixon's first years in the White House, he made crime-fighting a signature policy and a vote-getting device. His three big priorities, he told Republican women in 1969, were to bring peace, halt the rise in taxes and prices, and "stop the rise in crime and reestablish respect for law and order." As his phrasing on that and many other occasions suggested, Nixon linked crime to the upheavals of the 1960s and to resistance to his policies. He blamed crime and the fear it elicited on "permissiveness in high places," "a failure to back up our law enforcement officials," "pornography and filth and obscenity," and "narcotics and drugs."[5] He thunderously denounced the conclusions of a commission set up by LBJ that pornography "did not contribute to crime, delinquency, or sexual deviation." Smut, Nixon insisted, "should be outlawed in every State in the Union." With campus protest in mind, he warned publicly, "This is the way civilizations begin to die."[6] Nixon gave those themes, plus organized crime and crime in the nation's capital, high-profile attention at the start of his presidency.

And his administration was consequential on this front. It ramped up law enforcement, funneled more federal aid and military hardware to local agencies, denounced "soft-headed judges and probation officers," waged "war" on drugs, urged the death penalty for some federal crimes, pressured states to follow its tough-on-crime line, loosened restrictions on warrants, pondered preventive detention, got a Democratic Congress to approve much of what it wanted in 1970, and cultivated fear of crime.[7] Nixon's presidency helped account for a tenfold increase in the federal narcotics-control budget, for spectacular (sometimes violent) displays of antidrug vigilance at home, and for an antidrug campaign in Southeast Asia that pioneered practices like aerial surveillance and urinalysis that were soon brought home.[8] His politics fit the model Jonathan Simon offers: "The attraction of crime control as a basis for executive power begins with its immunity from the political collapse of support for both the liberal welfare state and the conservative message of global military dominance."[9] Even when Nixon's initiatives had little immediate consequence, they enlarged the political and institutional platform for crime-fighting, one that others could build on.

The Decline of the Rehabilitative Ideal

Buttressing Nixon's campaign against crime was the decline of the rehabilitative ideal for imprisoned criminals. That ideal had been honored as much in rhetoric as in practice, but it was also widely embraced at midcentury in academic, political, criminal justice, and judicial circles. Justice Hugo Black robustly stated it for the Supreme Court in a 1949 decision: "Retribution is no longer the dominant objective of the criminal law. Reformation and rehabilitation of offenders have become important goals of criminal jurisprudence."[10]

The rehabilitative ideal had rested in part on the notion that criminality was as much a social as an individual responsibility. "It is vain to write about the particular motivation of an individual who succumbs and commits a crime," *Commonweal* argued in 1946, for "the general public maladies that lead or tempt [people] to crime are everybody's fault."[11] The armed forces emphasized social responsibility for different reasons—their need to retain personnel for their vast forces. In 1947 one official expressed pride that half or more of general court-martial offenders had been "restored to duty," identifying the military's "unusually heavy responsibility for men who had been drafted from all walks of life" and could not adjust to service. These soldiers "need your help and mine," the official stated, so that they would be "social assets to our country in the days of peace ahead."[12] That notion of "social assets" to be salvaged rather than squandered or locked away still guided the Johnson administration.

Its eclipse in the late 1960s and 1970s was rapid, signaled by Nixon's attack on his opponent Hubert Humphrey in the 1968 campaign: "Doubling the conviction rate in this country would do far more to cure crime in America than quadrupling the funds for Mr. Humphrey's war on poverty." The Democrats' platform that year expressed a milder form of this notion, asserting that "anyone who breaks the law must be held accountable."[13] Soon the rehabilitative ideal was under assault from opposing forces. A wave of prisoner strikes and riots and legal and political activism critiqued prisons as cruel and brutalizing rather than restorative. As the American Friends Service Committee judged the prison in 1971, "This two-hundred-year-old experiment has failed," at least as an instrument for rehabilitating criminals. Prominent writers like Jessica Mitford echoed this opinion. Law-and-order types embraced that judgment but drew an opposite conclusion from it: prisons should not be abolished, but instead repackaged as places to incapacitate and punish criminals, a function they had often served. "Prison critics had sought less incarceration, but ended up with more," as a scholar puts it. The assertion attributed to Robert Martinson that "nothing works" in rehabilitation—as his 1974 *Public Interest* article was glibly glossed— seemed to triumph. Lost was the obvious point that rehabilitation, in prison or elsewhere, worked in some instances but not others and depended on many factors.[14]

Contrary to most accounts, the assertion that "nothing works" was hardly the revelatory bolt from the blue that suddenly demolished the rehabilitative ideal. Martinson was a jaded radical who had done serious time in the Trotskyite circles of the Berkeley Left in the 1950s (running for that city's mayoral post in 1959) and in the civil rights movement of the 1960s (for which he did time at Mississippi's dreaded Parchman State Farm). By the 1970s, he was a criminologist helping New York State examine rehabilitation and recidivism. He saw his work as a blow against the whole prison system—it "cannot be reformed and must gradually be torn down," he wrote in the *New Republic* in 1972— not against rehabilitation alone, whose practice he believed was often a form of liberal authoritarianism. Martinson had his day in the sun (an appearance on CBS's *60 Minutes* in 1975), but he soon backpedaled on his claims and railed against the punitive purposes to which they were put, but to little avail. He committed suicide in 1979 for poorly understood reasons. The phrase "nothing works" caught on because it was hijacked to justify a punitive impulse already swelling before Martinson's writing appeared.[15]

As Martinson recognized, no comforting equation can be made between the rehabilitative and the benign. A rehabilitative regime may also be cruel if undertaken in brutal ways (there is a long history of seeing punishment of the body and solitary confinement as restorative of the soul). It can be coercive if it is mandated for inmates or made the condition of early release or other benefits. Often enough, "the latent function of the rehabilitative theory is to camouflage punitive measures that might otherwise produce protest in the community," a scholar observed in 1981.[16] The theory can be racist given how white officials often regarded African American and other minority inmates as less capable or deserving of rehabilitation. By the same token, a custodial regime may be benign. If its purpose is simply to house inmates until release, there is great leeway about whether to do so gently or brutally, and good reason not to antagonize inmates. Even a punitive regime need not be brutal, for if imprisonment alone is punishment, no further punishment is needed. And even punitive practices may be welcomed by some inmates (there may be a worse fate than tending a vegetable garden or picking up highway trash in the fresh air). In practice, much depends on the attitudes and behavior of prison administration and staff, on the cues they get from politicians and the public, on the funding they receive, and on the nature of the prison population, not on abstractions about the purpose of prisons.

American prisons had always been an unstable mix of the rehabilitative, the custodial, and the punitive. They remained so after the mid-1970s, since the prison system was too lumbering and decentralized for any one abstraction to govern it. The mantra that "nothing works" did not make for an abrupt turn in practice, as many administrators and prisoners continued to pursue rehabilitation.[17] But it rebalanced that mix of recuperation, guardianship, and punishment, moving beyond prison walls, filtering out into criminal justice, and reinforcing a general punitive impulse.

Combined with swelling prison populations and militarized modes of operation, that idea that "nothing works" helped shift the prison system to a more punitive, or at best custodial, mode. In prisons where beds, staffing, food, and toilet paper were in short supply, rehabilitation withered even if prison administrators did not want it to. California's legislature put its punctuation mark on this shift in 1976 when it revoked earlier sentencing provisions based on rehabilitation and bluntly declared "that the purpose of imprisonment for crime is punishment."[18] Judicial blessing of that shift came years later. In 2011, the U.S. Supreme Court unanimously embraced the wording of a 1984 federal statute declaring that "imprisonment is not an appropriate means of promoting correction and rehabilitation," leaving only punishment and public safety as "appropriate" rationales for incarceration.[19]

Girding the "nothing works" outlook were reactions to the Attica prison uprising of 1971 and other prisoner rebellions of the era. As spun by New York State officials in their protracted campaign of deception and dishonesty, that insurrection demonstrated the rebellious, murderous, bestial mentality of the inmates who took corrections guards hostage. Officials tried their best to hide the killing by state police and others of some twenty-nine prisoners and nine hostages during their guns-blazing retaking of the prison (these deaths were followed by torture of inmate survivors). As a result, this story was only revealed after years of leaks, investigations, court proceedings, and resistance from surviving inmates. Attica was less a prisoners' riot than a police riot, whose carnage one "member of law enforcement" compared to "wartime conditions in the Guadalcanal."[20]

To be sure, like much else in the muddled 1970s, reactions to Attica cut several ways. For a while at least, they invigorated efforts to reform and humanize prison life, resulting in "vital victories for prisoners across the country in general and at Attica in particular." But for President Nixon, Governor Nelson Rockefeller, and many others, Attica revealed the emergence of a "New Type of Prisoner," one more dangerous and rebellious—not least because he was so often black. This development paved the way for the "maxi-maxi facility" in New York and elsewhere, and for increased use of solitary confinement. Here, seemingly, was a class of inmates beyond rehabilitation or redemption, even beyond normal means of confinement. Yet many Attica prisoners had been jailed only for minor or petty offenses, and many found their way to rehabilitation after the uprising.[21] Buttressing those reactions to Attica was the rising share of African Americans in the nation's increasing prison population; they constituted 22 percent of state and federal prison admissions in 1930, 32 percent in 1960, and 41 percent in 1980.[22] Many white Americans viewed black prisoners as incapable or undeserving of rehabilitation. Then too, many Americans at mid-decade doubted that the state, and the experts who served it in places like prisons, could do anything right.

Did "nothing works" reflect the war mentality now emerging in criminal justice? There was no direct tie-in. Yet it is intriguing to ponder how "nothing works" echoed a widespread sense that "nothing" had also worked in Vietnam—not pacification, not money, not herbicides, not attrition, not negotiations, not bombing, not torture. "Nothing works" gained traction at precisely the moment when the final evidence emerged that nothing had been successful in Vietnam. The state had failed in its two major arenas of coercion. Yet few people connected those failures. Instead, most politicians doubled down on the one arena, crime-fighting, where they could still take action.

That shift was underlined by Ernest Van den Haag's high-toned 1975 book, *Punishing Criminals: Concerning a Very Old and Painful*

Question. Offering a quasi-philosophical analysis of long-standing theories and recent empirical evidence about crime, the Dutch-born sociologist and critic eschewed the language of immediate crisis—he was above all that. He had few words about a war on crime, or the war in Vietnam, or race, or class. But he treated "street crime as if it were the only kind," according to two critics who asserted, "The candor of his viciousness is unusual. No sheep's clothing for him." As one of the "new 'realists'" on crime, Van den Haag ended up where Martinson seemed headed, dismissive of rehabilitation, determined to crack down. "Order," as he approvingly glossed Adam Smith, "necessitates a punishment far above what justice would countenance." Because nothing else worked, prolonged incapacitation, even postrelease detention or exile for dangerous criminals, seemed wise. At a moment when, as one reviewer claimed, "Liberals and radicals are either recanting in the face of the crime statistics or fighting rearguard actions against the punishment school," Van den Haag's analysis met little resistance. Few reviewers noted his longtime belief in white superiority, opposition to school integration, and support for South Africa's apartheid system, much less pondered whether that record had a connection to his views on crime. Groaning under the weight of racial issues, discourse about crime was sometimes remarkably detached from them.[23]

Nixon's (Not-So) "Winning War against Crime"

Nixon's voice in these matters was loud but indistinct. He did echo LBJ's war rhetoric, declaring his intent to "win the war against the criminal elements" and "wage a winning war against crime in this country."[24] But unlike Johnson, he neither fleshed out the metaphor nor connected it to the institutions and challenges of war making. Nixon used such words in a formulaic way, when he used them at all. His public statements about crime mostly avoided the war metaphor, and his references to "law enforcement officials" as "frontline soldiers" were perfunctory.[25] But he spoke publicly about Peace Officers Memorial Day, which was another way to cast policemen as soldiers; not until Bill Clinton did that day routinely receive presidential attention. The first president to speak often of terrorism, Nixon presented cities as "terrorized by crime" and saw "a rising rate of terrorism and crime across this country," implying, amid rising fears of international terrorism, that criminals themselves were terrorists.[26] Denouncing "appeasement" of "thugs and hoodlums" during the 1970 campaign, he made criminals akin to foreign foes—"appeasement" of communists was the great bugaboo of American Cold Warriors.[27] He also fulminated often about drugs. As he once put it in a White House conversation, while also identifying another favorite enemy, "You see, homosexuality, dope, uh, immorality in general: These are the enemies of strong societies. That's why the Communists and the left-wingers are pushing it."[28] Nixon's rants aimed to discredit the antiwar movement by linking it to drugs, tarnishing all things associated with liberal and radical currents, and mobilizing a "silent majority" behind him.

Yet for all the importance later attributed to him, the thirty-seventh president took a stance on drugs that showed the limits of his war-on-crime politics. It was not the case that "the term 'War on Drugs' was first used by President Richard Nixon on June 17, 1971," as one source claims, or that, as a leading scholar asserts, he was on that day "officially declaring a 'War on Drugs.'"[29] He did not use the term then, though he came close ("war against heroin addiction") in a message laced with war talk ("wage a new, all-out offensive" against "America's public enemy number one"). Nixon came close again in March 1973 when announcing the establishment of the Drug Enforcement Administration, insisting that he had "declared all-out global war on the drug menace." And he occasionally used phrases like "our total war on drug abuse." But his only public use of the term "war on drugs" came as a throwaway line in a brief 1972 statement released in his name.[30]

Nixon's drug war only went so far. During his presidency, the term "war on drugs" lacked the status of official nomenclature that it gained under Reagan, and it was only used occasionally by others (some of them critics of Nixon). Nor did Nixon ever publicly refer to a "drug czar," though that term is linked to him. Moreover, his lengthiest statements on crime (two on June 17, 1971) rightly cited "bipartisan" congressional support for new initiatives. And while Nixon emphasized the "offensive" and touted "minimum mandatory penalties for all violators," he also stressed "rehabilitation." Rehabilitation was expanded under Nixon-era legislation and initiatives supported by both parties in Congress. At the same time, Nixon's "support for the rehabilitation model went only so far as it benefitted him politically," after the White House failed to scuttle a provision in the 1970 Controlled Substances Act for federal support of rehabilitation. Meanwhile, reflecting "the forthright view that white middle-class Americans should not have their futures ruined by policies to protect them from international trafficking and urban drug markets," some "eleven states decriminalized simple marijuana possession during the 1970s and most of the rest adopted the federal misdemeanor model."[31]

Nixon's private and public rants about drugs were numerous, angry, apocalyptic, and factually inaccurate. But they lacked the volume, rhetorical consistency, and singularly punitive stance of President Ronald Reagan's declarations about drugs. And given all that he and the nation were angry about, Nixon's diatribes did not dominate the political landscape—stand out from the other chatter—as much as Reagan's did. His White House antidrug office was "strictly for show," notes Radley Balko. "No one [in the administration] had any idea if these [anticrime] policies would work, but in a way it didn't matter. The strategy was as much about symbolism and making the right enemies as it was about effectiveness." Or as White House counsel John Dean colorfully recalled later, "I was cranking out that bullshit on Nixon's crime policy before he was elected." Dean added, "It was bullshit, too. We knew it. The Nixon campaign didn't call for anything . . . that [Attorney General] Ramsey Clark wasn't already doing under LBJ. We just made more noise."[32]

Whether the Nixon White House even perceived a serious crime problem, or cared about it if it did, was doubtful. As White House aide Egil Krogh told John Ehrlichman, Nixon's domestic affairs advisor, in 1971, "The crime problem is more apparent than real."[33] Nixon's anticrime initiatives were designed to serve his political needs, not to make a substantive difference, and crime rates rose rapidly on his watch. Those initiatives did make a difference, of course, but not one Nixon much intended or cared about.

Moreover, the perception of a drug crisis was hardly confined to conservatives spotting rot among America's youth. Calling attention to a drug-addled U.S. Army served the purposes of many antiwar activists in their effort to underline the damage the Vietnam War was doing to the country and its soldiers. Though often denounced as the voice of hippies and druggies, George McGovern, Nixon's 1972 Democratic opponent, also championed a campaign against drugs. "You're never going to get on top of crime," McGovern urged in a 1972 campaign ad, "until you get on top of drugs, because half of all the crime in this country is caused by the drug addict. They'll kill, they'll steal, they'll do anything to get that money to sustain that drug habit." For editors of the leftist magazine *Ramparts*, "the war has come home" through drugs that were "like an intercontinental missile" arriving in America. Arising out of a war, the apparent flow of drugs and drugged vets from Southeast Asia in turn elicited a surge of war (and disease) metaphors. It was like "an invasion of our shores producing casualties as surely and as horribly as any bullet or bomb," stated Democratic congressman Lester L. Wolff in 1976. Democrats "and the antiwar left," one historian concludes, "helped to promote the myth of the addicted army and bolstered public demand for antidrug legislation—lest the country be subsumed by drug-addicted and crime-prone veterans." Numerous journalistic, television, and movie treatments sustained that image of veterans through and beyond the 1970s.[34]

Furthermore, much of the impetus for a war on drugs arose at the state or local level, not the federal one. This was especially true of the hard-driving efforts of New York governor Nelson Rockefeller, the "liberal" Republican who was no ally of Nixon, and who pushed through the 1973 Rockefeller drug laws, as they came to be called. With this legislation, New York greatly expanded the writ of drug statutes and the severity of their penalties. Rockefeller had the backing of a "black silent majority" that was hardly silent and perhaps not a majority, but was incensed by black drug users and criminals "committing genocide," as one pastor put it. The governor insisted, "Drug addiction represents a threat akin to war in its capacity to kill, enslave and imperil the nation's future." In black-majority Washington, D.C., radical activists, religious leaders, and police officials defeated a white-led effort in 1975 to decriminalize marijuana use. Some opponents saw drugs as a white plot to destroy black communities "devastated by historically unprecedented levels of crime and violence," as James Forman puts it. On the "offensive" against drugs, Nixon was no reluctant warrior. But he was also no singular one, least of all in using war metaphors. As Heather Ann Thompson puts it, "Postwar liberals had been high-ranking generals in the nation's new war on crime, not its unhappy conscripts."[35]

Regarding drugs and their links to the Vietnam War, Nixon's scattershot impulses helped to enmesh drug crime, and crime generally, in the context and language of war. That enmeshment far outlasted Nixon's presidency and the Vietnam War, only deepening in the Reagan and Bush presidencies. Nixon could only help set the stage for a later "war on drugs" from which the quotation marks can be omitted. But already it was difficult to think "drugs" without thinking "war"—the war in Vietnam that presumably stoked drug taking, the drug use that so many foes of the war seemed to indulge, the war that might be needed to stop drug use.

Beyond the specifics of his anticrime initiatives, Nixon's role was limited for a broader reason: he saw so many enemies that criminals were lost in the crowd. The political enemies he identified usually had names and faces that triggered his fury, whereas "thugs and hoodlums" were mostly anonymous to him. Battling privately or publicly with blacks, Jews, homosexuals, reporters, bureaucrats, liberals, and others, Nixon put his war on crime on autopilot, letting it serve its political purposes but devoting little passion or imagination to it. He occasionally raged about criminals with staff. In the deadly aftermath of the Attica prison revolt, he worried that "radicals" would exploit the incident, and he condemned "the homosexual rape of young boys" in prisons.[36] But Nixon could fulminate about many subjects without consistently engaging them.

Hence it is not surprising that, as one scholar stresses, "rates of imprisonment fell during his first term." Nor is it surprising that in 1973 Nixon's advisory commission "was recommending a ten-year moratorium on penal construction and closing existing facilities for juveniles." In Congress, too, the impulse to crack down on crime still bumped up against the lingering rehabilitative ideal. Thus "illegal drugs were not integral to the early calls for law and order," Marie Gottschalk notes, and in 1970 "leaders of both parties applauded when Congress eliminated almost all federal mandatory minimum sentences for drug offenders." That Democrats (albeit many of them conservatives) controlled Congress throughout his presidency constrained Nixon further. Amid the national crosscurrents about drugs and crime, he could only go so far, insofar as he even tried to.[37]

Of course, Nixon's most profound engagement with the law was the criminal actions he and others took and the Watergate crisis that ensued. These events led to the House Judiciary Committee's vote in favor of articles of impeachment in July 1974, Nixon's resignation, and President Gerald Ford's pardon of Nixon. (Facing criminal charges, Nixon's vice president, Spiro Agnew, had resigned in October 1973 and been replaced by Ford.) The Watergate crisis holds an uncertain and little-studied relationship to the punitive turn. Insofar as many Americans celebrated the work of Watergate special prosecutors Archibald Cox and Leon Jaworski, the crisis justified prosecutorial zeal—the prosecutor as public hero, a key dimension of the punitive turn.[38] The crisis also unleashed currents of anger and recrimination, for and against Nixon and in other ways, that might have found their way into other dimensions of criminal justice. But those currents are hard to trace. So, too, is the possibility that Watergate, by reaffirming that the law reached people in high places, salved consciences about turning it harshly against others. The punitive turn was already in motion before Watergate, and its primary targets were not people like Nixon. Indeed, the Watergate crisis halted Nixon's tough-on-crime campaign. Once scandal embroiled his presidency, flagging others' wrong-doing became self-defeating for Nixon. In that way, Watergate marked a pause in the punitive turn, which was restarted under Ford.

Nixon did engage the crisis of America's militarized order, both aggravating and calming it in the ways that served his sense of his political talents and interests. He hoped that détente with the Soviet Union and China, victory (or the pretense of it) in Vietnam, and elimination of conscription would stabilize the world, disarm dissent at home, and tamp down the size and costs of America's defense establishment. Confronting a tenacious enemy in Southeast Asia, disintegrating U.S. ground forces, and antiwar protest at home and abroad, Nixon reduced U.S. troop levels from their peak of 536,000 (with thousands more at bases near Vietnam) in 1968 to near zero by January 1973. Until the Paris Peace Accords in January presumably ended the war, brutal and sometimes secret bombing campaigns in Southeast Asia compensated for the forces' withdrawal. Nixon's theatrical embrace of U.S. prisoners of war (POWs) returning from Vietnam in 1973 served some of the same purposes, and he cultivated prowar veterans and veterans groups.

But most vet-related issues either failed to engage him or put him in an awkward position. Asked "about the tens of thousands of American soldiers . . . coming back from Vietnam with an addiction to heroin," Nixon did not challenge the shakiness of the claim, but instead slid away from it. "It is not simply a problem of Vietnam veterans; it is a national problem," he stated, offering his standard antidrug stance.[39] The flood of young men leaving military service, the millions who would no longer enter it, and their changed relationship to American society never galvanized him. While he felt the impulse to attack the likes of veteran and antiwar activist (and future senator, secretary of state, and presidential nominee) John Kerry, whom he feared and scorned, or to clasp the likes of POW aviator (and future senator and presidential aspirant) John McCain, Nixon considered the masses of young men a trifle.

Soldiers to Cops

But these young men were not a trifle to others in politics, government, journalism, and elsewhere. Thus the initiatives that had started under Johnson continued, albeit with little push from Nixon. Programs to move black and white vets into law enforcement, often in concert with private groups like the Urban League and agencies like the Veterans Administration, continued in the Nixon years, as did the use of military equipment and training programs to help police. These actions were in keeping with J. Edgar Hoover's 1968 declaration in the magazine *Army Digest*: "There is another battlefield encompassing an entire Nation" besides the one in Vietnam, a battlefield at home that "increasingly involves guerrilla-type tactics" against "a criminal element which is bold, arrogant, and constantly increasing in numbers."[40]

Like Hoover, military and civilian commanders of the armed forces and ordinary personnel connected military service to police work. Publications for military personnel boasted about the Defense Department's Civilian Police Recruiting Program, which gave those in uniform early release for switching "from a green to blue uniform." Meanwhile, police forces, urged by the Defense Department to recruit on base as well as among veterans, sought out current and discharged servicemen. After all, police were a "semi-military police profession," one "as honored as military service."[41] By 1971, efforts to turn vets into cops were so familiar that the military press could make gentle fun of them (see figure 2).

Civilian publications echoed the military press. Many of the men in Project Transition were "enrolled in classes in law enforcement," according to *Nation's Business*. In addition, "dozens of municipal police departments lined up to offer jobs," which in turn would gain soldiers an early discharge. "The No. 1 market for police recruits," the *New York Times* reported in 1970 about the Los Angeles Police Department, "is among men just separated from the military service."[42] Located in a strife-torn city, the *Washington Post* reported often on campaigns to recruit veterans as police and editorialized approvingly: "[It] may seem to be a far-out effort, but the police in Washington and many other cities are in such desperate need of manpower that any hopeful device is worth a try." Washington's police recruiters had "scoured East Coast military bases," the *Post* soon reported, as it also tracked the growing percentage of recruits who were blacks rather than Appalachian whites. With a fresh infusion of funds for Washington's police from the Nixon administration in 1970, the city, the *Post* reported, was renewing its effort to recruit from the armed forces.[43]

As police forces opened their doors to young vets, factories did the opposite, especially once the peak of Vietnam War mobilization had passed and a crisis in heavy industry emerged. Here was the biggest difference between the job market that Vietnam-era vets faced and the one that World War II and Korean War veterans entered: In the late 1940s and the 1950s, vets enjoyed the advantages of a booming market for their labor and veterans preference for many jobs. By the early 1970s, however, the auto industry faced the first of many crises, high interest rates and gas shortages curbed home construction, and "old" industries like steel and railroads were in disarray. Policymakers rarely cited these obstacles to vets' employment and rarely offered them as a reason to channel former soldiers into fields like police work, but the economic situation was obvious.

For political and military leaders, putting black veterans into blue uniforms had special appeal. It tamped down their reenlistment in the armed forces, which offended some white personnel and made officials fear that blacks were doing too much of the combat in Vietnam. Recruiting African Americans into the police force also addressed anxieties that untethered veterans would foment urban alienation and violence. And the increasing number of black law enforcement officers reflected concern that confronting urban blacks with white cops aggravated big-city tensions, or just looked bad. As one official argued in the last days of LBJ's presidency, having more African Americans in the reserves would "reduce [the] lily-white character of units assigned to urban disorder duty." Thus mayors, city councils, and civic leaders rushed to recruit blacks for criminal justice jobs, often seeking service members and veterans. Even "the Navy's in-house newspaper ran ads featuring Bunker Bunny," who teased black sailors by asking, "Bet you didn't know that gals like me are big on the fuzz, did you?" By the mid-1970s many cities had high-ranking black "police executives" as a result, with thousands more African American officers in the ranks. Not all of them were veterans, to be sure, and many of them held attitudes toward policing similar to those of their white colleagues.[44] But since African Americans enlisted at higher rates than whites after 1973—by 1983 they comprised 33 percent of the army and 22 percent of the marines—they provided a pool of veterans for criminal justice work disproportionate to their share of total population.

But there were powerful countercurrents, mounting during the Nixon years, to any makeover of veterans into cops. Some vets were too disabled to enter police work.[45] Others, like many young people, were too disaffected from authority to countenance such careers. Budget crises kept many states and cities from hiring even with new federal aid. And there was also a mismatch between the armed forces' practices regarding crime and those emerging in civilian criminal justice. Just when civilian institutions were moving to a punish-and-contain model, the military model for criminal punishment remained rehabilitative (including "even yoga or transcendental meditation") because the end of conscription increased the armed forces' need to reclaim troubled or convicted soldiers and sailors.[46]

Soldiers' and veterans' criminality, real but sensationalized at the time, also cut against programs to turn vets into cops. The military's crime problem was "bad," the provost marshal general bluntly told

Soldiers, the official U.S. Army magazine, in 1973—not surprisingly, since, he also said, "18-through-29-year old males statistically [are] the most crime-prone group in the country."[47] That statistic hardly made vets promising prospects for police work. Nor did incidents, some well publicized, of soldiers in Vietnam turning mutinous or murderous, with enlisted men "fragging" officers.[48] Accounts of atrocities by American soldiers—above all, the My Lai massacre in 1968—added to the image of servicemen's criminality. The behavior of discharged vets often seemed scarcely better. Well into the 1970s, stories and images of shiftless, unemployed, distraught, crazed, or damaged soldiers circulated in journalism, film, congressional hearings, and elsewhere. An ex-soldier was an "unemployed killer," as one vet's 1976 verse put it.[49] Many Americans believed that antiwar veterans practiced another form of criminality through their actions opposing the war, or simply because any such opposition seemed treasonous, as it did to Nixon. Were these the men to patrol the streets and keep the lid on explosive prisons?

To be sure, Vietnam vets were also portrayed as victims, not villains. They were the prey of national leaders who sent them into a hopeless or evil war, as the antiwar Left usually saw it, or who sent them into a noble war while denying them the tools of victory, as hawks usually saw it. Many parties agreed that these soldiers had been further damaged by the VA. That sense of ill-treatment attached especially to army soldiers, and less so to officers and navy and air force personnel because of their class background, military duty, or race. But POWs held by the enemy—most of them white officers on warplanes—also emerged as victims, either of a Hanoi regime that brutalized them and exploited them as bargaining chips, or of a Nixon administration that long refused the peace terms to gain their release.[50] The sense of victimization was so acute that people of quite varied politics regarded Lieutenant William Calley Jr., the key figure in the My Lai massacre, as a victim as much as a villain. As one scholar puts it, "A slow, thirty-year process" of creating imagery about military personnel "had transformed soldiers who seemed *better* for their time in the military into ones who seemed *devastated*."[51] That process sped up as the war ended, when the hopeful beliefs about service expressed in the Moynihan report seemed to belong to a long-ago past. Even the sympathetic view of veterans as victims still tagged them as damaged or dangerous.

Nothing tied Vietnam veterans to criminality more than rampant reports of their use of drugs overseas and back home after service. As the story was usually told, combatants got addicted in Vietnam, where drugs were cheap and prized for helping personnel get through their hellish or dispiriting duty. As damaged men, the soldiers continued to use drugs back home, especially if they had gotten hooked on heroin. As the military's contemporary studies asserted and subsequent scholarship maintained, servicemen's drug use was rare in combat operations. It had little impact on military effectiveness, helped many men survive their duty emotionally, and constituted less of a problem than the use of alcohol, a substance ubiquitous in Vietnam, on leave, and after discharge. None of these facts diminished the spread of a powerful "myth of the 'addicted army,'" as one scholar puts it, perpetuated in both serious hand-wringing and popular humor. While visiting troops in 1970, comedian Bob Hope got his "biggest cheers" when he joked, "Instead of taking away marijuana from the soldiers, 'we ought to give it to the negotiators in Paris.'"[52]

The crime panic of the early 1970s stoked by politicians and the media focused heavily on veterans' drug use—on the criminal behavior they engaged in to get drugs or as a result of taking them. As *Time* maintained in June 1971, drug-addled vets were tied to a rise in crime. "Each planeload of returned GIs adds to the drug malaise at home," the magazine stated, adding that the problem was spreading from the "black urban ghettos" to "the heartland of white, middle-class America." *Time* was echoing Nixon, who, for all his efforts to embrace POWs and veterans, had days earlier warned publicly of drug-crazed servicemen returning from Vietnam to "slip into the twilight world of crime, bad drugs and all too often premature death." Leading Democrats said much the same thing while accusing the president of doing too little about the threat. How could vets be a solution to crime if they were a major source of it?[53]

Of all the crosscurrents, none was more charged than race, which elicited a bundle of concerns that overlapped those about veterans' drug use and criminality. The specter of the violent, crazed, or drugged black veteran was widespread, even if the image of white vets was scarcely better. For example, in 1972 *Newsweek* characterized De Mau Mau, a black urban group, as "gun-happy . . . black Vietnam veterans bent on random slaughter of whites." Moreover, a vet-led black war against white America was widely feared among mainstream black and white figures, and sometimes threatened by vets, from the Johnson administration through the Nixon years.[54]

Pundits did praise how black soldiers deepened their masculinity in Vietnam, "perhaps as a corrective to the matriarchal dominance of the Negro ghetto back home," as *Time* put it in 1967 in reference to the Moynihan report. But pundits offered this commentary while nervous that this new black masculinity might get out of hand. The long tradition whereby African Americans entered military service for its opportunities or its refuge from discrimination seemed in danger.[55] It survived — black men and women flowed into the all-volunteer armed forces established in 1973 — but in the Vietnam years, many black soldiers, especially draftees, expressed bitterness about racial maltreatment. Stories emerged of black servicemen "fed up with the racist bullshit not only in our detachment but all through the Army," as one soldier put it in 1973, and of combatants perhaps willing to shoot whites to express their resentment.[56] It seemed these veterans needed to be policed, rather than to do the policing.

The challenge of race went beyond matters of African American veterans' image and attitudes. Turning black vets into police also met resistance from white cops who saw their jobs as their racial privilege, from white citizens hardly eager to see blacks patrol their neighborhoods, and from those African Americans who regarded black cops as no improvement on white ones, or even as betrayers of their race. Leaders of the armed forces were under pressure to show racial progress and retain personnel with the end of conscription. Therefore, they tried to keep the best black officers and enlistees — precisely those most qualified for civilian criminal justice work — in uniform. Whether black or white, those in "the discarded army," as one notable 1973 study called it, were less promising.[57]

As the Vietnam War upended assumptions about military service making good citizens of young men, the links between service and citizenship at the state level also weakened, though for reasons less related to the war itself. When urban blacks and Latinos came to dominate California's swelling prison population in the late 1960s, its "forest camps" housed inmates less attuned to rural ways. These prisoners were taken farther from their home communities, and they were more inclined to escape. Like the friends and family members who came to visit them or settled nearby, these inmates were also less acceptable to local white populations. For many whites, African Americans were linked to the urban violence that wracked California cities — to the urban "jungle," as Ronald Reagan called it while running for governor in 1966. Despite heroic service by some black camp inmates, rural communities that once embraced convicts as disaster workers secured the camps' shrinkage in the 1970s. But they did so without relinquishing the state's resources, often demanding prisons in the camps' place. As a result, "prisons would channel urban men into the country on an unprecedented scale for rigid exclusion — not liminal camp experiences." More directly than at the national level, race drove the shift to mass incarceration at the state level, not least because the alternatives — service to the nation as real soldiers or to states as forest soldiers — were in disarray.[58]

Yet these crosscurrents loomed as reasons for action as well as obstacles to it, stoking the urgency with which politicians, mayors, pundits and others sought to turn veterans into soldiers of law and order. Without articulating their position this way, advocates of soldiers as law enforcement officers sought to bifurcate the emerging tide of veterans, steering the good ones into police work and the bad ones toward jail. This was a new form of social engineering, but unlike the older one under conscription, it dealt with exodus from the armed forces, not entry into them. While vets flooded into criminal justice jobs, they also crowded into prisons, totaling 20 percent of state and federal inmates by 1986, serving longer sentences and for more violent crimes than other convicts (as veterans aged, this percentage diminished, as did their overall numbers).[59] The war on crime was to be waged in part by veterans against veterans.

This conflict emerged as the old order fell apart. For nearly four decades, war had been a primary mechanism for sustaining internal order, particularly through conscription of the youthful male population most likely to commit crime. The draft helped draw sixteen million people into military service during World War II and over three million during most years of the Cold War. Military service had often been seen as a tool for disciplining and civilizing male youth, not just as a means of national defense. Although the draft had snagged only a small slice of each age cohort after World War II — it was called Selective Service for good reason — it reached far beyond those conscripted. Many young men considered college, jobs, or marriage to secure deferments, or the officer corps or reserves rather than the enlisted ranks that draftees entered.

The draft's registration and screening system shaped the lives even of those not drafted, including young women, since conscription helped promote early marriage and shaped the job and education choices boyfriends and brothers made. But the Vietnam War disrupted that order, producing strife and chaos at home and within the armed forces, rather than discipline and stability. And conscription ended in 1973, freeing millions of men from draft calls. The Vietnam War era thus ushered in the punitive turn, which was a product of the era — especially of its lively traffic between military and police service — not simply a backlash against it.

Above all, given the United States' failure in Vietnam and all that came with it, the utility of war itself—as an instrument of American power, a source of national identity, a justification for powerful government, a forger of internal cohesion, and a site of social engineering—was in doubt. The 1970s reverberated with claims or laments about the declining utility of combat for the United States. Nixon's "Vietnamization" of the Vietnam War implicitly validated those claims. No major political figures proposed disarmament; a formidable American deterrent to Soviet or other enemies still seemed necessary. But deterrence was about preventing war, not waging it. An acute hostility to actual war spread across the political spectrum in the 1970s, and the downsizing of America's armed forces met little resistance. With the dwindling of a mass army went the long-standing conviction that military service would turn American boys into manly and law-abiding citizens.

By the early 1970s, what had been a major path to economic security and upward mobility for less advantaged Americans since the 1940s was a shrinking outlet. At the same time, criminal justice was a growth industry that vets, at least high-functioning ones, were well placed to enter. The number of ex-soldiers who took such work was large, in the hundreds of thousands. However, it was difficult to count given the many federal programs in play, the delayed decisions to enter police work that many vets made, and the plethora of agencies that employed them. According to a 1990 study, 4.6 percent of male Vietnam-era veterans (5.2 percent of those who had served in the Vietnam theater) had work in "protective services" as of 1987, a rate double that for nonveterans of the era. That was a small percentage, but it was taken from a large cohort of 7,902,000 Vietnam-era veterans. Thus, some 370,000 were in "protective services" in 1987, and many more were employed in this manner over the 1964–87 period as veterans cycled in and out of such work, with many older former servicemen retired by 1987.[60]

But even more important than the numbers was the embedding in politics, institutions, and rhetoric of close associations between war work and crime work. Given a costly war abroad and political tumult at home, Johnson and Nixon had only limited opportunity to promote the turn from war-fighting to crime-fighting. But their efforts also met little resistance. Liberals and conservatives alike applauded both the specific programs and the broader effort to beef up metropolitan police forces with veterans. With the end of the Vietnam War and the swearing in of a new president after Nixon's resignation on August 9, 1974, political leaders' opportunity to act remained, with the words and institutions of war still framing their efforts.

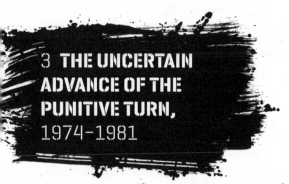

3 THE UNCERTAIN ADVANCE OF THE PUNITIVE TURN, 1974-1981

The post-Nixon years, the ones least examined by scholars of the punitive turn, offered a fascinating muddle of impulses from the president and others regarding crime. Gerald Ford's willingness to act on crime was large, but his ability to do so was limited, while Jimmy Carter's willingness was scant. And politics and culture pulled in conflicting directions. But the punitive turn advanced, especially its underpinnings in the language and systems of war, as Ford offered a new war on crime to replace the lost one in Vietnam. After all, in his odd analogy, "one man or woman or child becomes just as dead from a switchblade slash as from a nuclear missile blast."[1] Also advancing the punitive turn was the shrinkage of the armed forces, long a mechanism for controlling presumably crime-prone young men. As crime and incarceration rates rose, a supercharged discourse on crime, sex, and youth, one that blindsided Carter, pointed toward the full-fledged war on crime his successor would wage.

Gerald Ford, Forgotten Promoter

On April 25, 1975, with Saigon's fall days away and America's failure in Vietnam seizing headlines, Gerald Ford, the unelected president who had replaced Spiro Agnew as vice president in October 1973, delivered his first major address on crime. He spoke at his alma mater, Yale Law School, on a campus that had seen radical activism and occasional violence and where, he reminded his audience, he once had been "an assistant football coach." Ford highlighted the "problem of crime," remarking, "[It] obsesses America day and night. " He referred to crime "in high places" (his oblique reference to Watergate) but even more to crime "that invades our neighborhoods and homes—murders, robberies, rapes, muggings, holdups, break-ins—the kind of brutal violence that makes us fearful of strangers and afraid to go out at night." A conservative imbued with "the Spirit of Moderation" (as aides told

White House chief of staff Donald Rumsfeld), Ford warned against making the nation "one huge prison" and declined to speak of criminals as evil. But he championed beefed-up policing, prosecution, and courts; long sentences for repeat violent offenders; and action to make "more sentences mandatory." As he asserted in his memoirs, "The primary purpose of imprisonment was *not* to rehabilitate the convicted criminal ... but to punish him and keep him off the streets."[2]

The date was striking. Ford might have addressed the collapse of America's South Vietnamese ally, a momentous development. Instead, he changed the subject. To be sure, it was a coincidence that Ford ramped up on crime just when Saigon was falling: his administration had been preparing an initiative on crime since the fall of 1974, and his Yale address had long been scheduled. And Yale Law School would have provided a hostile audience for a defense of America's Vietnam War or a last-ditch plea to assist South Vietnam. Yet Ford had choices. His address coincided with the school's conference on international law and with the thirtieth anniversary of the United Nations' founding, subjects he might have addressed. Instead he announced a new war at home just as a war abroad ended.

There was no direct connection between the two conflicts in the White House's overt calculations. Ford's anticrime campaign reflected the White House's desperation to find a new issue for the unelected president, as well as its eagerness to get ahead of the crime issue before it trapped him, and its desire to trap Democrats instead (Ford's June "Special Message on Crime" should show, Donald Rumsfeld advised, that "Congress won't pass it").[3] Vetted by the relevant bureaucracies, Ford's anticrime campaign also bore the imprint of prominent conservative advisors like Irving Kristol and Harvard professor James Q. Wilson (the Nixon-Ford White House sneered at Ivy League professors, except those it agreed with). Wilson briefed White House staff in the fall of 1974, joined a "dinner seminar" with the president on December 9, added his unsolicited views on a range of topics, and offered sycophantic flattery of the administration. Armed with data and skilled at parsing it, Wilson provided complex considerations on crime and dismissed some conservative shibboleths. But his basic views were blunt, eagerly embraced in the White House, and widely publicized when his book *Thinking about Crime* appeared in 1975. "During the 1960s," he wrote, "we were becoming two societies—one affluent and worried, the other pathological and predatory," indeed, downright "wicked." As White House staff summarized his views, "Our correctional institutions do not correct." How could they, after all, when criminals were intrinsically "wicked," not merely desperate, disadvantaged, or deranged? As the *New York Times Magazine* titled a March 1975 piece by Wilson, well timed for Ford's initiative, "Lock 'Em Up."[4]

In the months after his Yale address, Ford returned to crime perhaps more than any other subject, even though doing so provoked reporters' frequent questions, which he blandly shrugged off, about his pardon of Richard Nixon. Ford repeatedly compared war-fighting to crime-fighting and suggested a shift from the first to the second. "Peace in our neighborhoods," he insisted on September 5, "is almost as important as peace in the world," and police "who work the night shift" are as "heroic and essential" as "military personnel and civilian technicians standing watch around the world."[5] With such words, he was moving from an older militarized order to a new punitive order built on a reconstructed state.

Not that later scholars noticed. Standard accounts of crime policy make little or no mention of Ford (or Jimmy Carter), while standard accounts of Ford (or Carter) make little or no mention of crime.[6] Scholars have dwelled on Vietnam, the subject Ford was trying to leave behind, not the one he was latching onto. In these analyses, it is as if the punitive turn came from below—in the multitudes angry about crime, in the lower reaches of government—rather than from on high. If Nixon kick-started the move toward punishment, these academics claim, Ford was incidental to it. "During the 1970s, law and order faded from the national limelight," one scholar writes. Another argues that Ford's administration, like Carter's to follow, seemed to mark "a time-out in the escalation of the war on crime."[7] Far from it, in Ford's case.

By emphasizing the pursuit of "domestic tranquility," a phrase from the Constitution's preamble, Ford's Yale address indicated that he had more than crime per se in mind. For him, the opposite of more crime was not just less crime. Nor was it personal security or other down-to-earth things. Rather, it was an elusive "tranquility"—that is, social harmony and order. Ford highlighted that phrase for instrumental reasons. It attached his effort to the wishes of the Founding Fathers, distinguished his language from Nixon's law-and-order rhetoric, and offered constitutional legitimacy for federal initiatives in crime control, still primarily a state and local responsibility. But "domestic tranquility" also evoked the urban and campus convulsions of the Vietnam era and Yale's recent history. Ford also emphasized victims' rights, flagging an emerging concept of a citizenship defined by victimhood and denied to criminals, who, after all, were "strangers," Ford suggested, even though in many crimes—especially ones of domestic violence, feminists stressed—perpetrators were family members or acquaintances of victims. Binary categories of citizenship were hardly new (slave and free, American and un-American, for example). But the notion of victimhood as citizenship was newer, and perhaps resonant with a sense among Americans that they were victims of the Vietnam War.

Ford's Yale address appeared amid a new round of public alarms about crime and violence, ones that often made war their reference point. Americans' concern about lawbreaking gained traction from an FBI report citing what one columnist called a "whopping" 17 percent increase in "serious crime" over the past year. Indiana Democratic senator Birch Bayh called Senate subcommittee findings on public schools "a ledger of violence ... that reads like a casualty list from a war zone." In its conclusions, the committee described "hallways and playgrounds of fear and terror" and gangs taking on a "martial or quasimilitary" character. Conservative columnist William F. Buckley, assailing the idea that inadequate South Vietnamese "will to resist" contributed to Saigon's impending collapse, analogized Saigon's plight to New York City's: "I assume, for instance, that the metropolitan population of New York City deeply desires to resist the city's murderers, rapists, robberies, and muggers." That April the director of the Federal Bureau of Prisons, Norman Carlson, announced the organization's partial retreat from the rehabilitative ideal. "The old theory that you could take an inmate, diagnose his problem and cure it in an institution didn't work," at least not for many inmates, he declared. Balance would therefore shift to deterrence and retribution, a change now endorsed by many crime experts, politicians, and the White House. Even pushback against that shift drew on the Vietnam experience. Arguing for gradual, rehabilitative release of long-term inmates, an Oregon official maintained, "We recognized this with our Vietnam prisoners of war. . . . You can't just let a man walk out of prison at the end of his sentence." The new alarms, loudly sounded in the media, also reached U.S. military personnel abroad who could read condemnations of "demagogic politicians of the superliberal stripe" whose "do-gooder theory" had presumably stoked crime and "anarchy."[8]

Associations between war-fighting and crime-fighting were hardly the Ford administration's only theme. Attorney General Edward Levi voiced his resentment toward big-city "communities" that distrusted law enforcement and showed a "strange tolerance of crime." Regarding the suspicion among inner-city residents "that criminal-law enforcement is very unfair because it's so kind to the rich and so tough to the poor," Levi implausibly argued that "in some sense the opposite is true."

He deplored those who thought it "unfair to stop" street crime "because Watergate occurred or some banker only went to the penitentiary for two years and they think he should have gone for five."[9] Levi's remarks were a clumsy entry into both the ugly class and racial politics of crime and Ford's pardon of Nixon, but they were also red meat to attract conservatives leaning toward Ronald Reagan, Ford's strongest rival for the 1976 GOP presidential nomination.

Ford's words linking war and crime might have been a rhetorical gloss on an anticrime initiative he pursued for other reasons. He often put such formulations into his speeches at the last moment and over staff objections. Yet the language stayed. Comparisons between war and crime came readily to leaders like Ford and Nixon and LBJ, World War II veterans who saw war as a model for national action but no longer had an overseas war they dared or needed to wage. Because such comparisons came so readily, no labored policy process was needed to produce them. Rhetoric mattered—it might not have driven the policy process, but it illuminated the political imagination at work. The state once deployed against enemies abroad was redeploying against enemies at home. As they seemed to have been doing in the 1960s, Americans would battle each other.

The timing and rhetoric of Ford's anticrime initiative suggest its connection to the Vietnam War and that conflict's end. "The judiciary is the Nation's standing army in defense of individual freedom," he declared on July 13. On September 5, he told the California Legislature that fighting crime required "the abandonment of partisanship on a scale comparable to closing the ranks in wartime against an external enemy," just as the Constitution "puts the obligation to ensure domestic tranquility in the same category as providing for the common defense against foreign foes." It was on that occasion that Ford compared police on "the night shift" to soldiers "standing watch around the world." Looking back on 1975 in his 1976 State of the Union address, the president offered a reminder to listeners: "The longest, most divisive war in our history was winding toward an unhappy conclusion. Many feared that the end of that foreign war of men and machines meant the beginning of a domestic war of recrimination and reprisal." His language connected the end of the Vietnam War to fears of "domestic war" and his campaign against crime.[10]

Even as Ford connected crime to the Vietnam era, he cordoned off the war itself as a source of the troubles the United States now faced. To be sure, crime was on a long list of ills he attributed to the Vietnam era. On November 1, 1974, Ford stated, "Confidence in America's institutions has been deteriorating since the early 1960's. There were, unfortunately, assassinations, upheavals in great cities and in school systems throughout our country, riots and terrorism, crime, drug abuse, pollution, the Vietnam war, the Watergate affair with the first Presidential resignation in America's history," and the energy crisis—events delivering "almost unbelievable blows to America's self-image."[11] But Nixon's Republican successor could hardly blame these ills on the corrosive effects of the war or on the leaders who waged it. In Ford's rendering, all that swirled around the war stoked crime, but the war was exempt. He instead located crime in an urban underclass—his references to street crime and terrorized residents evoked a dark urban setting, not rural or white-collar America. Movies like *Chinatown* (1974) and *All the President's Men* (1976) placed crime in high places, but Ford did not. Neither did James Q. Wilson, whose *Thinking about Crime* barely mentioned the Vietnam War.

Few observers at the time noted the conjunction of the Vietnam War's end and the crime war's start in Ford's rhetoric. Most media ignored Ford's Yale Law address (the *New York Times* gave it front-page coverage, then fell silent). Attention instead ran to South Vietnam's demise, the state of Ford's presidency, his pardon of Nixon, and the economy. Media outlets paid more attention to Ford's "Special Message on Crime" in June and to his later comments, but these remarks were treated largely as a political move to bolster his chances in 1976, not as a shift in the nation's priorities. Thus even as Ford loudly announced it, the punitive turn sneaked in through the back door of American political life.

Of course, correlation—in this case between one war's end and another's start—does not prove causation. After all, campaigns against crime were as old as the republic. LBJ had declared "war on crime," and Nixon had exploited the law-and-order issue. But Ford paid attention to crime more persistently than LBJ and Nixon had. In his special message on the subject in June and in his speeches thereafter to state legislatures, lawyers, police groups, GOP gatherings, and other audiences, he pounded away at the themes of his Yale address. Ford's surrogates did the same.

Moreover, his efforts coincided with other changes in the arena of criminal justice. The rehabilitative ideal for imprisonment gave way to a punish-and-contain model, and the 1973 Rockefeller laws on mandatory minimum sentences in New York gained traction there and influence elsewhere. Meanwhile, some states resumed the death penalty, and the Law Enforcement Assistance Administration moved into a pivotal role in shaping state, local, and private organizations. Above all, the imprisoned population grew rapidly: the number of sentenced inmates in prison (only one subset of the total jailed population) jumped from 196,429 in 1970 to 315,974 in 1980, with all the increase coming after 1972 and per capita sentencing rates also rising.[12]

A weak president holding office only briefly and facing a Democrat-controlled Congress, Ford alone did not cause those changes. Reflecting his cautious temperament, the volatile politics of 1975, and his effort to run for the White House as an unelected president, he zigzagged between urgency about the crime problem, efforts to downplay it, and skepticism about solutions for it. "Crime is a threat so dangerous" as to imperil "domestic tranquility," Ford said. Yet he noted that lawlessness was caused primarily by a "tiny minority of habitual lawbreakers," and it would not be solved by either "throwing every convicted felon in jail and throwing the key away" or adopting some "updated vigilante mentality." Furthermore, Washington had only limited responsibility and resources to combat crime, he often pointed out. All Ford could offer California lawmakers was his plea "that we must take one sure step at a time."[13]

But the president's words marked a major shift, as he kept restating connections between peace abroad and at home, and between making war and fighting crime, on which he offered his most vivid rhetoric. "Peace on 10th Street in Sacramento," ran the closing words of his California Legislature address, "is as important to the people who walk and work there as peace in the Sinai Desert," over which Israel and Egypt had just fought a war. "One man or woman or child becomes just as dead from a switchblade slash as from a nuclear missile blast. We must prevent both," Ford declared. These odd comparisons — "a switchblade slash" to "a nuclear missile blast"? — struck one staffer as "too negative," perhaps especially as the last words of a big speech. Yet no one in the White House seemed to find them silly or baffling.[14] Of course "peace" was an appealing goal, especially for the many Americans fearful of crime and weary of war. But analogizing its achievement to the task of preventing or waging war suggested a warlike approach to attaining that peace. That Ford's words made sense underlines how, in the political imagination of the mid-1970s, the war state was evolving into the punitive state. Ford sought internal stability not through the discipline of war abroad, which had failed, but through a war-inflected discipline of law and order.

Demographic changes that predated and outlasted his administration abetted that shift. With conscription ended and America's war in Southeast Asia over, the armed forces shrank from over 3 million members in 1970 to 2.05 million in 1980 despite a growing youth population. The share of men in service receded as women entered the military in larger numbers. That decline corresponded roughly in scale and chronology with increases in the numbers of people imprisoned by or working for the criminal justice system. The population of sentenced prisoners grew by over 100,000 during that period, and arrests for violent crimes leapt 65 percent after 1970, reaching 475,160 in 1980. At the same time, employment in criminal justice rose sharply, by more than one third, between 1971 and 1979, reaching 1,275,031 that year.[15]

Men, especially young ones, dominated all those population categories. Again, correlation does not prove causation. The transfer of people from one regime to the other—veterans into criminal justice jobs or into jails—was large. But prisons also received discards of another system, as mental health hospitals shuttered in reaction to their apparent dehumanizing and coercive practices, leaving many discharged patients to fend for themselves.[16] Still, there was a substantial post-Vietnam transfer of young men from the coercive machinery of military service to the coercive machinery of criminal justice.

Notably, the two mechanisms had similar social and political bases. The young men attracted to criminal justice jobs might once have sought or submitted to military service, and criminal justice was a common postservice occupation for veterans. By the same token, the young men in prison as inmates often had the same background as those who had been drafted. Criminal justice and military forces also shared an autonomous place in the state: courts and legislatures usually deferred to their authority, budgets for both were treated by many Americans as necessities exempt from their customary antistatism, and the secret parts of both were invisible to the public. In theory, the realms of criminal justice and the military each addressed the same need. They both provided security, from external threats in one case and internal ones in the other. While he was urging Ford to support federal aid for prison building now that judges were getting tough, James Wilson noted this connection between war-fighting and crime-fighting: "Just as he [Ford] has advocated that we increase our spending to meet our critical defense needs, so he now advocates, for the same reason, that we increase our spending on domestic defense against the criminals who prey on us."[17]

In 1975, Americans faced, and Ford faced, the prospect that millions of young men once tucked away in the armed forces or facing conscription were now free to roam the streets. (Whether their freedom in fact increased crime rates is an empirical claim I do not make—the point is that their freedom underwrote fear of such an increase.) The role of military service in taming youth had long been claimed. As Michigan's governor put it in 1863 regarding the Civil War, "The sound of the fife and drum on the Southern border has called to the camp most of those restless and reckless spirits who are easiest tempted to the commission of crime."[18]

Now, the fife and drum called fewer men. Ford worried publicly in 1975 that the decline in the size of the armed forces was aggravating unemployment among young men.[19] Moreover, the new volunteer military was not likely to draw in those youth deemed most susceptible to criminal behavior. The army believed its "best" recruiting prospects to be in "rural or small-town America" and generally in "a broadly defined middle class." It did not court "the 'good' but less desirable prospects who had dropped out of high school or who saw few other options in their futures." Of course, the army did not always get what it wanted, but the volunteer system was less likely to pull in "at-risk" youth than the draft had been. And with the armed forces encouraging long-term service, military personnel slowly aged, making service even less of a destination for males of crime-prone age, especially since women were slowly occupying more slots in the armed forces.[20]

Those shifts in military demographics promoted the turn to criminal justice as a means of social control, all the more so because other mechanisms—mental hospitals, social welfare systems, jobs in industry—were under siege. That change also helps explain why much of the punitive turn soon entailed a "war on drugs" targeting young men with fewer advantages. It was not just a generalized sense of order that inspired the punitive turn. Rather, the punitive turn was spurred by particular forms of order for particular Americans—those who were adrift as the armed forces shrank and the cities decayed.

The armed forces' downsizing also helped sustain the punitive turn after the 1970s, for the number of servicemen continued decreasing into the 1980s and 1990s. Active-duty strength slid from over 3 million in 1970 to just over 2 million in 1980, and after an uptick in the Reagan years, to under 1.5 million by the end of the 1990s.[21] Measured against a growing population, the military's shrinkage was even sharper, and it unfolded amid a young population more mired in poverty and more alien to many white Americans as Hispanic, Asian, and African immigration soared. Insofar as the Vietnam War upended an older militarized order, the effects were hardly passing ones of the 1970s: there was no return to that order afterward. The high-tech weapons kept piling up, the reach of American power kept growing, but the use of uniformed personnel kept shrinking.

That contraction, like deindustrialization, was not the only impetus to the punitive turn. Regional and local differences suggested that nationwide forces only went so far to drive that turn. The "prison boom" incipient in the 1970s emerged "in the most dynamic, expansive, and future-oriented sections of the country rather than in its abandoned urban-industrial core," and above all in the Sun Belt states of Florida, California, and Texas.[22] But just as the older militarized order had unfolded unevenly across the nation—Florida, California, and Texas were key nodes in it as well—so, too, did the new punitive order.

Toward a Punitive State

Thought of this way, the punitive turn was also a project in state rebuilding. According to many historians, the state was in crisis during the 1970s as the Vietnam War, Watergate, and federally mandated desegregation stirred distrust of national government. At the same time, POW/MIA groups charged that the state betrayed Americans left behind in Southeast Asia, deregulation of the economy began, welfare for the poor met growing resistance, antitax conservatives gained power, and neoliberalism took hold. As one account claims, the "slow march of privatization had pervaded the entire Seventies," after which "Reagan delegitimized government." In turn, some scholars note, the weakness of the American state made it more vulnerable to demands for "law and order" than Western European criminal justice systems that were freer from political control. Such frailty contributed to the United States' "harsh justice." That notion of a weak state has made it hard to see the state as shifting ground rather than giving it up, taking on new tasks even as it diminished others.[23]

In the punitive turn, that shifting of ground both responded to and outflanked the distrust of central authority characteristic of the 1970s. The punitive turn addressed a major source of that distrust—the assertion that government was failing to protect Americans from crime or, for that matter, failing to act effectively in any arena.[24] Yet in echoing Nixon's "new federalism," the Ford administration also outflanked suspicion of national government by offering an agenda in which state and local governments played a leading role while gaining new resources from the federal government. At the same time, the president and his administration maintained continuity through the elaborate analogizing of crime-fighting to war-fighting that they offered. Americans would redeploy their rhetoric, their soldiers, and their institutions, not abandon them. Here was a way to relegitimize the state that was conservative in one sense—restoration of order was the apparent goal. But it was not overtly partisan, since many moderates and liberals endorsed it, and for the following three decades, few of the most prominent ones vigorously opposed it. Indeed, the punitive turn endured in part because no one label—"conservative," "liberal," "neoliberal," and the like—easily attached to it.

As a state rebuilding project, crime-fighting had other advantages as well. The failure of America's war in Vietnam invalidated major combat as a rationale for the state. At mid-decade, the problems of energy, inflation, and economic stagnation were perhaps greater than those of crime. But those issues resisted state intervention, at least any that could produce quick results, survive conservative opposition, and yield vivid rhetoric and favorable headlines (witness Ford's much ridiculed "Whip Inflation Now" campaign). Efforts to address racial and economic inequalities had met growing resistance, and national leaders no longer enjoyed the Cold War pressures and trust in the state that had undergirded major initiatives by President Dwight Eisenhower with the Interstate Highway System, and by Democratic presidents in the 1960s with the space program.

Really, what else was left? Politicians were learning that *Governing through Crime*, as Jonathan Simon calls his account, rather than through war or social policy, was their only, or at least their best, option as they "began to turn to crime as a vehicle for constructing a new political order." At the same time, since crime-fighting seemed so much like war-fighting, the older rationales for the state could meld easily into the new one. As Simon captures the connections between them, the Department of Justice, emerging as "a planetary giant within the executive solar system," was becoming "what the Department of Defense was in many respects during the Cold War: The agency . . . that most naturally provided a dominant rationale of government through which other efforts must be articulated and coordinated."[25]

Crime-fighting also had other political advantages that Ford implicitly underlined. The White House could take the initiative and grandstand while passing much responsibility off to state and local government, whereas for national security and economic policy, the buck clearly stopped in D.C. And something of a consensus about the urgency of combating crime had emerged among leading politicians. It was evident in Governor Nelson Rockefeller's success in passing draconian antidrug measures in New York. It was also evident in the "hard line" on lawlessness taken in June 1975 by Edmund (Jerry) Brown Jr., California's young liberal governor and presidential aspirant. Apparently influenced by James Wilson, Brown bluntly rejected rehabilitation: "I think you rehabilitate jails, not people," he declared. He further asserted that the purpose of prisons is simply "to lock people up." As a 1976 California law promoted by Brown put it, "The purpose of imprisonment for crime is punishment."[26] Moreover, the crude hostility to judges alleged to be soft on crime indicated widespread agreement on the importance of harsh justice: Alabama governor George Wallace stated in 1976, "Vote for George Wallace and give a barbed wire enema to a federal judge."[27]

Americans remained bitterly divided about the wisdom of their war in Vietnam and the threat of the Soviet Union, but not about the urgency of curbing crime. To be sure, the political advantages of crime-fighting were neither instant nor decisive—Ford was defeated in 1976. But other issues were at play in that election, Ford's crime-fighting met the undertow of his pardon of Nixon, and he was moving awkwardly on this front rather than commanding it with confidence. Still, he advanced a politics of crime that later figures, especially Republicans, exploited.

Crime-fighting also tapped into familiar ideological patterns. American leaders had often branded foreign enemies as criminals. Roosevelt dubbed fascists "gangsters," and after Pearl Harbor he condemned "the sudden criminal attacks perpetrated by the Japanese" and called the Axis powers "powerful and resourceful gangsters" who "banded together to make war upon the human race."[28] Japanese and German officials were prosecuted in war crimes trials; the very term "war crimes" linked the categories together. Fascists and communist sympathizers had faced U.S. criminal prosecution, politicians and ideologues portrayed fascism and communism as criminal enterprises, and some blamed civil rights agitation on communist agents. Just as foreign enemies had been likened to criminals, criminals were sometimes likened to foreign threats in the 1970s, as the slippage from the domestic to the foreign began to reverse. As crime-fighting supplanted war-fighting, criminals supplanted communists, especially among conservatives, as James Q. Wilson had anticipated in 1966 when he warned that crime might end up "replacing 'communist subversion' and even 'socialism.'"[29]

Of course, many conservatives remained more vexed by communism than by crime, alarmed by the Nixon-Ford efforts at détente with the Soviet Union and China. But they rarely needed to make a hard-and-fast choice between the two, while anticommunism lost some of its political traction after a failed war and détente. Crime-fighting served many of the same ideological and political purposes, as analogies of war-fighting to crime-fighting suggested.

The state changed rather than shrank: it was reinvented, not reduced. Distrust of the state was real but hardly monolithic. No inconsistency was felt by antitax conservatives who championed prison building, nor by feminists suspicious of the male-run state who championed tough action against the rape and abuse of women. Nor was the state helpless before the suspicion it faced, for politicians sensed and manipulated the pressures on the state to do more as well as less. Indeed, scholars should abandon their notion of a "weak" American state. The U.S. state may be disorderly and porous, vulnerable to capture by various interests and enthusiasms. But a state that had the world's strongest armed forces, waged expensive wars, tried to impose its will on much of the world, presided over its most powerful economy, and soon imprisoned extraordinary numbers of people was not "weak." The trick is to understand how the state could be at once decisive, diffuse, disorderly, and distrusted. Because the U.S. state was weak in areas where liberal scholars prize action—social welfare, health care, economic regulation, progressive taxation—they have regarded it as weak. The punitive turn suggests otherwise.[30]

It also suggests state-building's gendered dynamics. Ford's campaign against crime advanced a masculinist agenda at a time of ascendant feminism. Congress passed the Equal Rights Amendment in 1972, the Supreme Court issued its *Roe v. Wade* decision on abortion in 1973, the United Nations proclaimed 1975 "the international year of the woman," and women entered military academies at mid-decade. But nearly all national voices on crime were men, as were nearly all those urged to become cops and hand out stiffer sentences, as well as those seen as criminals (striking increases in women's imprisonment came later). No hostility toward women or feminism animated Ford, who supported the Equal Rights Amendment. But in making crime his signature issue, he prized male leadership and action. And the particular thrust of his crime agenda mattered. He confronted the problem not with a social welfare model that many feminists and Western Europeans embraced, involving aid for crime's victims and rehabilitation for its perpetrators, but with a crack-down-on-crime approach. The call from Washington was for soldiers, not social workers, to become cops. It signaled a "conservative project of state reconstruction" designed "to replace social welfare with social control."[31] As Ford and others saw it, crime-fighting was men's business.

The punitive turn also helped to open a divide between the United States and Western Europe evident in many arenas of social policy. The two areas had shared roughly equal incarceration rates in the 1950s and 1960s until the great divergence began in the 1970s.[32] Whatever the fundamental differences in values and politics between the United States and Western Europe, specific circumstances also drove their discrepancy on crime at this point. In the 1970s, only the United States sharply shrank its armed forces and ended conscription. Only America (along with Portugal in its futile effort to retain its colonies) coped with the aftermath of a large failed war, and only America discounted rehabilitation for treatment of the convicted. The fact that rehabilitation had wide sway in U.S. legal and political circles before the 1970s further suggests that specific circumstances, rather than fundamental values, shaped the new transatlantic divide on crime. Another circumstance might also have operated: for Europeans struggling with the record of their continent's totalitarian regimes of mass incarceration and genocide, the large-scale imprisonment to which the United States was moving had, to put it mildly, little appeal.

The punitive turn began in response to the turmoil of the Vietnam era and to a crisis in the militarized order. Mass imprisonment and other punitive regimes complemented, colonized, and to a degree replaced various older coercive regimes—those of Jim Crow and mental asylums, but also those of mass conscription and militarized values. Of course, no one flipped a switch and said, "Let's replace armies with prisons," but the switch was hardly invisible to its makers. Nixon understood the advantages of calling out drug users while his war in Vietnam floundered, and Ford knew he was changing the subject from that war to crime. The punitive turn derived from the logic of politics and institutions in the 1970s. That hypothesis hardly discounts the role of race, class, sex, and power in the punitive turn, but it helps place them in a national framework.

Ford might also have been up to something else less witting—groping for scapegoats for the failure of America's war in Vietnam. In explaining the punitive turn, no scholar has explored that possibility, which lies beyond the standard proofs that historians offer. Yet the United States hardly escaped the search for scapegoats that most nations endure in the wake of failed wars. Indeed, that quest had started when the U.S. war was still at its peak, and by 1975 it had splattered across the political spectrum, placing blame on a bewildering array of actors and forces—Johnson and the Democrats for ramping up the war, Nixon and Henry Kissinger for cynically masking defeat as victory, antiwar activists and the media for emboldening the enemy, Congress for failing to aid a tottering Saigon regime, successive administrations for scheming to "abandon" Americans presumably left behind in Southeast Asia, and so on. Yet none of those targets of blame served the Ford administration well. Dead by 1973, Johnson faded fast as a target. Nixon's alleged misdeeds in war were swallowed up in the Watergate drama, and Ford was hardly inclined to blame his Republican predecessor, just as his pardon of Nixon signaled his absolution of the thirty-seventh president. And scapegoating works best when its targets are powerless to fight back, which was hardly the case with past presidents, the "liberal" media, or even antiwar activists. Criminals rarely can fight back.

The fact that Ford inaugurated his law-and-order campaign almost on the same day of final U.S. defeat in Vietnam suggested that he was trying not only to change the subject, but also to find an outlet for Americans' frustration about the failed war. Ford's repeated analogizing of crime-fighting and war-fighting suggested that the new enemies—from criminals to the weak-willed politicians and judges who failed to crack down on them—had a connection to the war just ended. The scapegoating also involved the swirl of disorder, contention, and violence that characterized the Vietnam era, now implicitly blamed on a criminal class rather than on powerful villains. That many white Americans understood criminals racially gave that scapegoating an implicit racial tilt. It was impossible to make an empirical case that criminals caused America's defeat in Vietnam, but scapegoating does not rely on empirical evidence.

Sold as a response to rising crime, the punitive order was never just that, as its growth even in periods of falling crime suggested. Rather, it was one way that leaders chose, or stumbled into choosing, to maintain their legitimacy and to restore what Ford had called "domestic tranquility" as an older order crumbled.

Jimmy Carter, Outlier

Jimmy Carter provided a pause in the punitive turn, at least in presidential politics. No other post-1963 president until Barack Obama said so little publicly about the danger of crime, did as little to crack down on crime, or spoke so little of crime-fighting as a war. As in many dimensions of politics, Carter stood off by himself regarding crime, proving hard to place in the standard categories. Precisely because he said little on this score, it is hard to know what he was thinking beyond the obvious point that he did not make crime a priority.

But clues emerged before he took office. Allaying fears about his Baptist faith and his southern politics, candidate Carter maintained that his version of Christianity required caution about judging others and made it "ridiculous" to imagine that he would "run around breaking down people's doors to see if they were fornicating." Interviewer Robert Scheer summed up Carter as follows: "a guy who believes in his personal God and will let the rest of us believe whatever the hell we want." During a 1976 presidential debate, Carter needled Ford about his pardon of Nixon and his awkward policy of "no amnesty, no revenge" for Vietnam War draft evaders and resisters. The Democratic candidate pointed to "a sharp distinction drawn between white collar crime [and other crime]," observing, "The big shots who are rich, who are influential, very seldom go to jail. Those who are poor and who have no influence quite often are the ones who are punished."[33]

Emphasizing from the start of his presidency that energy and inflation were the big issues confronting him, Carter relegated crime to the sidelines less by explicitly demoting it than by simply failing to mention it except when pressed to do so. And notably, reporters at his numerous press conferences and the people who phoned in to his televised question-and-answer sessions rarely forced the issue. Perhaps other problems shoved crime offstage. Yet presidents do much to signal what they wish to be queried about. Carter rarely put crime on the agenda.

And when he did discuss lawlessness, or when he found the subject inescapable, he broke sharply from his predecessors. In one of his first and most controversial decisions, Carter pardoned men who had resisted the Vietnam-era draft by refusing to register or by fleeing to resistance-friendly nations like Canada (he was careful to call the act a "pardon," not an "amnesty," and to exclude those who had deserted once in uniform). That decision was likely shaped in part by his strain of Christian tolerance and forgiveness, though he did not say so publicly. Carter came closest to explaining his stance on crime when he spoke to a group of lawyers in March 1978. He condemned "excessive litigation and legal featherbedding" and complained of a nation "over-lawyered and under-represented." He talked about his upbringing in Georgia, which "often did not provide simple justice for a majority of our citizens" because wealth, political power, and race predetermined the outcomes. Stressing that "nearly all inmates are drawn from the ranks of the powerless and the poor," he insisted that "making criminal justice fairer," not harsher, was his goal, with decriminalization of "such crimes as drunkenness and vagrancy" and "alternatives to incarceration" major steps toward that fairness.[34] As the White House made clear, "both the President and the Attorney General endorse[d] the principle of concentrating Federal law enforcement efforts on attacking large, organized crime operations" and "large-scale narcotics traffickers" instead of "minor offenders."[35]

Carter portrayed crime, except perhaps as committed by "large" operations and white-collar offenders, as the product not of individual evil but of societal failure. "The major cause of crime in those downtown areas is unemployment," he insisted in 1977, bragging that he was putting people into public service jobs at "a greater rate than Franklin Roosevelt put people in the CCC camps." Carter likewise condemned the creeping militarization of crime control, including the "waste" involved in using Law Enforcement Assistance Administration funds for "buying very expensive and fancy machines." "Carter's moralistic rhetoric," one scholar claims, "suggests little awareness of the ways in which established social structures and historical legacies may imprison even good people in tragic circumstances."[36] But regarding the thirty-ninth president's positions on crime, that claim is unfounded: he was quite aware of those "structures" and "legacies." Carter could sound tough on some matters, as he urged action against undocumented immigrants and particularly their employers. But even on that issue, he conveyed a sense of the complexities involved.

Carter could hardly escape the issue of drug abuse, and he probably did not want to escape it. Drug abuse and the criminality associated with it offended him. He championed efforts against drug traffickers, prosecuting a quasi-military campaign against them in Asia and the Americas that included aerial spraying of drug crops with toxic substances. But he never demonized drug users (or undocumented immigrants), and he never declared "war" on them. Indeed, Carter urged decriminalization (already done by some states) at the federal level for possession of small amounts of marijuana. (As he argued, "Penalties against possession of a drug should not be more damaging to an individual than the use of the drug itself.") And he insisted, sometimes in detailed ways, that abuse involved both legal and illegal substances, alerting Congress to his "strong concern about the crime and sickness and death caused by the abuse of drugs, including barbiturates and alcohol." For Carter, the misuse of any substance, not the illegality of some, was the problem. Reflecting his stance, the Democratic Party platform of 1980 said little about crime and declared no war on it. Instead, the platform promised to "enhance rehabilitation of offenders," and it urged the nation to "treat addiction as a health problem," bracketing "substance abuse" with health rather than with a later section on law enforcement. For a president often derided as waffling and indecisive, Carter was consistent and forceful in his stance about crime and justice through the 1980 campaign.[37]

Sex, Children, Evil

But Carter's stance hardly meant that the punitive turn paused. Instead, the engines set in motion before he came to office continued to operate, and new ones kicked into gear. They did so less in reaction to Carter's presidency than coincidental with it, but their speed and force put him at odds with them. In wide areas of life, "many Americans adopted a more pessimistic, more threatening interpretation of human behavior," Philip Jenkins argues. Jenkins further asserts that "the post-1975 public was less willing to see social dangers in terms of historical forces, instead preferring a strict moralistic division: problems were a matter of evil, not dysfunction," yielding "an absolutist moral vision" regarding foreign policy, crime, and other challenges. Official rates of murder and overall crime (perhaps amped up by better reporting) reached historic highs in the 1970s, triggering alarm, as did a new round of sensational crimes. But these factors alone did not account for the particular character of that anxiety, with its emphasis on evil. As James Q. Wilson explained in 1975 while advising the Ford administration, "Wicked people exist. Nothing avails except to set them apart from innocent people," while others "neither wicked nor innocent . . . ponder our reaction to wickedness as a cue to what they might profitably do."[38] Some young people are given to "sheer evil," as *Time* put it. The magazine summarized recent horrific crimes (one of a fifteen-year-old boy who castrated and beheaded an eleven-year-old), claiming that "more than half of all serious crimes in the United States [were] committed by youths aged ten to 17" and that it was "all too literally true" that youngsters were "getting away with murder."[39]

Of course in practice, then and later, no "absolutist moral vision" could be readily applied. People disagreed about what constituted evil, who embodied it, and how to punish it, and some rejected the notion of evil altogether. Acting on that vision required the use of power, which was most easily applied against those lacking power by virtue of race, class, or other markers—above all, African American boys and men. To some, Nixon was evil. But Ford's pardon of Nixon meant that his criminal acts got a legal pass. Yet however compromised in application, an "absolutist moral vision" was widely shared, or at least trumpeted, by the late 1970s in America. It was one reason that Carter's proposal to decriminalize possession of small amounts of marijuana under federal law failed. The plan was also dealt a blow in 1978 when a new parents movement claimed to expose Dr. Peter Bourne, a former antiwar activist serving as Carter's drug "czar," for writing an illegal prescription and using cocaine and marijuana (Bourne resigned).

Panic about the sexual abuse of children illustrated that moral vision, serving as the point of condensation for the complex politics and emotions that vision involved. Though it had precedents, the panic emerged abruptly in 1977, when "sexual abuse and molestation appeared quite suddenly on the political agenda," according to Jenkins. No crime wave, sensational incident, or new research sparked the alarm. The closest to something new was a wave of exposés about child prostitution and child pornography in New York and other cities, and "a vogue for outrageous figures about child exploitation that were scarcely even challenged until the mid-1980s," unleashing "hysterical campaigns against imagined networks of sexual criminals." Hence "the sudden shift . . . demands explanation," though even Jenkins struggles to offer one.[40]

That shift owed in part to the real ways in which children's vulnerability increased in the 1970s, as divorce rates climbed, economic flux and stagnation eroded incomes for families and mothers, and school systems floundered. Unease about such realities got displaced and acted out, as such unease often is, in the symbolic and supercharged arena of sex. Then too, changes in American cities provoked indignant reactions. An eruption of erotica, prostitution, public sex, and gay visibility led many Americans to view New York City "as a latter-day Sodom teetering on the verge of ruin." Like many cities, it seemed "a lawless metropolis on the brink of destruction amid ballooning crime rates, impending fiscal collapse, serial killers, racial strife, and rampant public indecency." Sensational movies and television news broadcast that image to the nation. The new erotic landscape in cities was hardly the major cause of "ballooning crime rates" and hardly the only target of onlookers' indignation. But it was an easy proxy for everything else that troubled cities, as well as a shock to many Americans who were hardly willing to see "the heroic overtones of this mass experiment in pleasure seeking." Even more than crime—but also conflated with crime—sex elicited bewilderment and outrage, and the perceived threat of urban sexuality was easily understood as a threat to children in particular.[41]

As in much crime politics of the 1970s, conservative and liberal forces converged, largely unwittingly and for very different reasons, on the same point of panic about sex crimes against children. For many feminists concerned about male violence, children's endangerment at the hands of male predators seemed akin to women's vulnerability to brutal men. "The contemporary women's movement in the United States helped facilitate the carceral state," Marie Gottschalk points out, through its "demands . . . to address the issues of rape and domestic violence."[42] The movement's facilitation was often unintended—its efforts were sometimes captured by law-and-order hard-liners—but nonetheless important. For many conservatives, children's vulnerability was the linchpin of their arguments against the Equal Rights Amendment, Carter's cautious liberalism, and gay rights. Singer Anita Bryant's 1977 campaign to overturn a new law in Dade County, Florida, barring discrimination on the basis of "sexual preferences" captured the conservative—and dominant—tone of the panic. Her crusade was titled Save Our Children, and its leaflets screamed, "There is no human right to corrupt our children."[43]

The notion that gay people sexually exploit children was hardly new, but its sudden and sensational reappearance was part of a calculated effort to reverse the tide of gay liberation that had been surging since the 1960s. "Homosexuals cannot reproduce themselves, so they must recruit" was Reverend Jerry Falwell's version in 1980 of what was already a formulaic claim. Falwell added, "It is shocking how many feminists are lesbians."[44] Race also lurked beneath the sex panic of the late 1970s, whose proponents often had roots in earlier anti-integration campaigns. Thus "a movement born in the struggle to preserve segregation had largely 'de-raced' its rhetoric" but left intact "the figure of the white child . . . first imperiled by federal desegregation orders" and now "by gay rights and women's reproductive freedom."[45]

The New Right's campaign against homosexuality met resistance, but resistance largely disappeared regarding child pornography and endangerment. Feminists were sometimes enthusiastic about the cause, and liberals were at best disarmed. Who wanted to go on record as supporting child pornography? Amid this atmosphere in 1977 the House passed a new law against child porn by a smashing 401-0 vote, and Carter signed the bill early in 1978, making no public note of doing so except a terse announcement to a group of prominent feminists.[46] Both heartfelt and cynically exploited, alarm about endangered children propelled the punitive turn to a considerable degree.

For that subject, Carter was utterly unprepared. His primary framework for understanding crime, which he deemed the product of systemic injustices, was irrelevant to the subject of sex crimes, for which few proposed a socioeconomic explanation. Instead, evil was the operative rationale. Like Carter, most presidents were ill prepared by precedent and temperament to address sex crimes. To be sure, they had commented on the upheavals of the 1960s (Nixon had weighed in loudly against pornography), and they could not avoid entanglement in the related arenas of abortion and gender (both Ford and Carter endorsed the Equal Rights Amendment). But before the 1970s, the regulation and prosecution of presumed sexual misbehavior had been mostly a state and local matter. It did sometimes involve federal authority, as in post office bans on mailing pornography, gay magazines and newsletters, and birth control information, as well as in the purge of queer federal employees and the federal government's construction of "the straight state," as Margot Canaday has called it.[47] But that authority had usually operated at arm's length from the White House.

Scandal did drag presidents into the public arena of sex, as it did LBJ in 1964 with the Walter Jenkins affair, but presidents scurried away from that subject as fast as they could. As a candidate in 1976, Carter famously admitted in an interview for *Playboy* magazine the "lust in his heart" he had felt for women besides his wife. But that was a confession of his sinfulness, not a statement of his attitudes about sex. As head of state he had no taste for this topic. Insofar as initiatives about sex propelled the punitive turn, enlarging or shrinking what was legal, presidents played little role before the 1980s. The late 1970s sex panic was a dimension of the punitive turn not only beyond chief executives' control but even beyond their full awareness.

To be sure, the prosecution of sex crimes hardly filled America's jails in the years ahead. And even as some sex-related offenses were created or more vigilantly enforced, others fell off the books or met declining enforcement: abortion was decriminalized, and sodomy laws were slowly removed by courts or state legislatures. In the punitive turn, everything did not move in the same direction, as if pulled by some single magnetic force. But sodomy and abortion statutes had rarely crowded prisons before the 1970s; gay men were more vulnerable to laws on public indecency and the like that remained in effect than to sodomy statutes. The significance of the sex crime panic of the 1970s (and after) was less the number of inmates it produced than the way it legitimated prosecutorial zeal, pioneered extralegal practices soon exported to other arenas,[48] put evil at the center of understandings of crime, and unleashed a politics of criminality beyond presidential control.

Crime Cultures

In addition to a new crime politics, Carter faced an evolving media culture of crime, although one that followed political change more than drove it. Scholars have stressed how depictions of criminals as evil flooded into American culture during the 1970s, underwriting the punitive turn.[49] But they have exaggerated the scale and causative power of those portrayals, just as others, like college students in classrooms, now routinely blame "culture" or "the media" for the punitive turn and other ills of modern America. Hence the value of carefully examining culture's role in the punitive turn. Evil criminals were hardly new to American culture, and they had waxed (and waned) in the past without prompting a broad crackdown on crime. Just as no mass popular outcry set off the punitive turn, no sharp cultural shift propelled it. Politics—the ambitions and concerns of political elites, which Carter did not share—drove that turn.

Cultural change and its slowness appear in a comparison of popular 1950s presentations of crime to later depictions. Take the "The Big Producer," a 1954 episode of *Dragnet* (its first run aired from 1951 to 1959), the most famous of the decade's many cop, crime, law, and detective television programs (not to mention Westerns, usually crime shows themselves). At first the episode's perp, the "big producer," looks ominous. He distributes pornography through boys at Los Angeles schools, and he is marked by a weird Salvador Dalí mustache and dark sunglasses, like a dirty old man. Yet as often on *Dragnet*, the appearance of malice is deceiving. The man turns out to be a victim of cultural and economic change, an old Hollywood hand fallen on hard times. Shown amid the ruins of a stage set from Hollywood's glory days, and lost in memories of his time as a star producer, he turned to porn in desperation. Sergeant Joe Friday (Jack Webb, also the program's creator and producer) and his partner coax the truth out of the perp patiently and gently, almost as priests would behave toward a confessing sinner. With his sunglasses removed and tears streaming down a face full of shame, the man comes across as more pathetic than dangerous, if still deserving of the slammer. And the boys seem remarkably unstained by (and unapologetic about) their encounter with smut. They are victims more of family circumstance (one lives only with "his sister and brother-in-law," not his parents) than of a smut peddler. So it often was on *Dragnet*. In a famous episode ("The Big Crime," 1954), a swarthy man molests girls, a sensational subject for 1950s television. But after Friday's grilling, the guilty party seems more hapless and tortured than malicious—as much a discard of society as a threat to it, even as he confesses he had planned to murder the girls.[50]

Dragnet nailed how mass culture often depicted crime and punishment in the 1950s. Of course, culture was hardly uniform. Because network television sought a huge audience, advertisers' blessings, and regulators' approval, it operated on a tight leash at the time. Period movies, on the other hand, offered more criminal malice, often youthful: the violent motorcyclists of *The Wild One* (1953), the destructive high school kids of *Blackboard Jungle* (1955). Lingering into the 1950s, film noir often showed crime as horrific and smudged the line between lawbreaker and law enforcer.

But *Dragnet* showed few of the characteristics of late-century shows like *Law and Order* (airing from 1990 to 2010, with spin-offs continuing into 2020). It rarely trafficked in the language of evil. Criminals on the program have a problem that must be solved, but the problem does not define the criminals as people. Later shows homed in on the evil of perpetrators—the evil of their motivations as well as their actions. Only occasionally did *Dragnet*'s plots deal with murder, the sole focus of *Homicide: Life on the Streets* (1993–99), or with sex crimes. *Dragnet*'s rather generic approach to crime, including its minor and petty dimensions, contrasted with more recent shows' emphasis on its horrific forms. The detectives on *Dragnet* are methodically doing a job, not waging a moral crusade. They are unmuscled, lightly armed, and indifferently dressed—virtually unmarked as police—and they experience little danger to themselves. Moreover, the detectives are unhurried. *Dragnet* notes the time of each step of a story, doing so in the spirit of the dutiful record keeping of the police procedural, not the ticking clock of impending doom that *24* (2001–10) offers. Joe Friday's "way of doing his job is sometimes so passive as to seem alarming compared with more recent police dramas," Anne-Marie Cusac notes.[51]

Nor did *Dragnet* linger on crime's damage to victims. Porn is "obscene" and "rotten," Friday observes scornfully, but rather in passing. By the same token, *Dragnet* showed little interest in punishment. Catching the perp, not destroying him for his crime, was its focus. The programs featured no courtroom finale—no prosecutor flaring nostrils, victim testifying to damage, or cop recounting grisly details. In a coda to each episode, *Dragnet* simply noted that the criminal had been sentenced. In "The Big Producer," the titular criminal is "now serving his term in the county jail," the length of his sentence unspecified. Visual style also made a difference. Unlike the claustrophobic interiors of later crime shows, much of *Dragnet* was shot outside in sunny California because early TV technology made outdoor shooting easier.

Dragnet captured its matter-of-factness in Joe Friday's line "Just the facts, ma'am" (or the often-used "All we want are the facts").[52] It offered confidence that the state would catch bad guys in reasonable time, by reasonable means, with reasonable punishment after, and reasonable chances for rehabilitation. In contrast, later "television cops [gave] up trying to stop television criminals," having "morphed into the arbiters of good and evil" as "they tell their audiences who among the assortment of suspects deserves punishment."[53]

Popular TV shows of the 1970s marked halting steps toward that later era, ones foreshadowed in the reprise of *Dragnet* that ran from 1967 to 1970. Shown in color and executed in a more sensational style, the new *Dragnet* echoed its times and Jack Webb's ardent opposition to the counterculture, especially drugs. In its pilot episode, "The LSD Story," the drug wreaks havoc on Los Angeles, and in the second season a pot-smoking couple allow their baby to drown in a bathtub. Yet *Dragnet*'s understanding of criminality did not change much. Crime remained the product more of unfortunate circumstance, social rot, or (for youthful offenders) parental neglect than of individual depravity, and the show's criminals were still calculated to elicit more pity than rage from viewers. When it came to hardened criminals, *Dragnet* still gave their psychology and motivation little attention. These characters were plot devices, not the focus of the show, which remained Joe Friday and his partner.

So it often was with television shows and movies well into the 1970s. It took time for the politics of crime practiced by Johnson, Nixon, Ford, and others to percolate through popular culture, while the antiestablishment ethos commonly ascribed to the "sixties" only made it fully to big and little screens in the 1970s. Thus in the tame private eye series *The Rockford Files* (1974–80), Jim Rockford is a wrongfully imprisoned ex-con who remains close to the actual criminal and encounters his share of corrupt or vicious cops, while the perps whom Rockford lazily tracks down hardly "have inner lives worth investigating."[54] The murder mystery series *Columbo* (1968–78) also paid little attention to the psyches of its murderers, present largely to set the stage for Lieutenant Columbo's detective work. Those programs also spun another antiestablishment thread of 1970s culture, evident in films like *Network* (1976) and *The China Syndrome* (1979): The bad guys were often the high and mighty, spiritual cousins to Nixon and his Watergate gang, and mostly white. These programs' villains were not the racialized gang leaders, drug dealers, and street criminals evoked in much contemporary political rhetoric ("strangers," as Ford had called them). In their pallid way, 1970s television crime shows presented rot in American life as trickling down from above more than rising up from below. Even programs with an obvious law-and-order line echoed earlier themes. *Kojak*'s (1973–78) eponymous New York police detective rarely demonizes criminals; again, the show focused on the search for the villain, not the villain himself. While more inclined to depict danger to law enforcement personnel, 1970s shows were still optimistic about curbing crime and fostering rehabilitation. And though victims' rights was a rising cause, most 1970s TV shows gave victims and their distress little attention.

Criminal evil surfaced more often on the big screen, as with Scorpio, the serial killer in *Dirty Harry* (1971) whom Harry Callahan (Clint Eastwood) finally guns down. Yet that movie hardly inspired confidence that the state could impose order. Callahan is contemptuous of his own police department, and his is essentially vigilante justice. At film's end he tosses his inspector's badge into the river, just as Charles Bronson's vigilantism triumphs in *Death Wish* (1974). Both films were widely regarded as endorsing a new law-and-order politics and public attitude. But in their confused blend of law-and-order alarmism and suspicion of the state, they were at best uneasy allies of punitive politics. "Crime in these films is the result of an evil human nature, not of social conditions," two scholars noted later, but they added, "*Dirty Harry* was not a significantly popular film, at least in regard to box office receipts." An "audience survey" suggested "that it wasn't successful in winning large segments of the population over to its viewpoint."[55] That so many 1970s movies, especially the "slasher" genre, featured grotesque violence against women complicated things further. Insofar as they reveled in that violence, did these films call on the state to protect women or to ignore them?

In any event, it is silly to think that a few films alone captured some popular mood, especially when other movies offered different messages. In *Dog Day Afternoon* (1975), based on a 1972 *Life* magazine story of a real event, Al Pacino's addled and histrionic Sonny, a Vietnam vet, robs a bank in order to pay for his partner's sex-change operation—hardly a conventional crime of malice—only to get trapped in the bank, taking the people in it hostage. Sonny strikes back by taunting the horde of police types who lay siege to him and getting an angry crowd to join him in shouting, "Attica! Attica!"—referring to the New York prison where the state trained its guns on rebelling inmates in 1971. In much 1970s culture (*Chinatown* is another example), the institutional evil of the state or the corporation loomed larger than the individual evil of the criminal. The state that bungled Vietnam and much else was hardly to be trusted to impose law and order. Such depictions were hardly a clear goad to the punitive turn.

In other cultural sectors such as popular music, resistance to that turn was sometimes overt and loud. Eric Clapton's cover version of Bob Marley's "I Shot the Sheriff," its title signaling its antipolice politics, was a number one single in 1974. Punk often offered a defiant stance. Released in 1977, the Clash's version of Junior Murvin's "Police & Thieves" repeated the antipolice message, and "by the early 1980s, nearly every hardcore punk band worth its salt performed at least one anti-police song."[56] Nor was such music confined to big-city settings. The Ohio band Necros's "Police Brutality," released in 1981, depicts Maumee, Ohio, where "cops are all off the farm." "Police brutality—get it in Maumee," the song states. These lyrics spoke to tensions over policing in small towns that scholars, fixated on big-city problems, have yet to track. Rap and hip-hop gave the antipolice impulse new vitality in the 1980s and 1990s, as with N.W.A.'s 1988 single "Fuck tha Police" and Ice-T's lyrics for the 1992 release of "Cop Killer," the latter condemned by President George H. W. Bush, Vice President Dan Quayle, and Senator Al Gore's wife, Tipper. None of these songs defined all popular music any more than *Dirty Harry* defined all movies. But even country music, far whiter in authorship and audience and ascendant in the 1970s, offered the antipolice theme, especially in songs written and/or sung by the oft-arrested Johnny Cash. In the 1970s and beyond, popular culture had too much diversity to provide a sharp impetus to the punitive turn.

That impetus arose more at the margins of culture and in new forms of it less burdened by entertainment traditions. In the movies *Rosemary's Baby* (1968) and *The Exorcist* (1973), the offspring of mothers who succumbed to 1960s turmoil and temptation turn out to be evil, or at least possessed by evil, in plots with religion rather than criminal justice as the defining framework. "Social upheaval has birthed a Devil— a member of Generation X," Anne-Marie Cusac says of these films.[57] Alongside their vomit-spewing pyrotechnics, these movies' significance lay not just in discovering evil but locating it especially in children.

That emphasis on the evil in children got expressed in conservative Christian publishing and moviemaking far from mainstream culture. In *A Thief in the Night* (1972), a low-budget movie ("filmed on location in Iowa"), a ragtag group of teenagers (slightly slutty girls and randy boys, uncertain skeptics and pious believers) confronts the prospect of a divine judgment that sweeps up believers in the Rapture and condemns doubters to the rule of the Antichrist, who appears masked in the benign appearance of a United Nations–like official.

Shown widely in the church basements of Pentecostal and other denominations, *A Thief in the Night* roughly paralleled what Cusac calls "the Birth of the Christian Spanking Manual" in the 1970s. Such tracts offered scriptural justification and practical tips for parents in forestalling or driving out the evil in children. While "before the 1970s, how-to books on godly spanking were all but non-existent," treatises like *Spanking: A Loving Discipline* (1975), *Withhold Not Correction* (1978), *The Strong-Willed Child* (1978), and *What the Bible Says about Child Training* (1980) instructed parents that an "exceptionally willful" child would "require more frequent and more intense whippings" that might entail "stripes or even welts." As Cusac summarizes this literature, it was no longer "heretics and loud women who suffer God's violent concern. It's children." For its believers, "crime prevention," Cusac puts it, "begins with a swat on a toddler's rear." And what at first seemed a backwater of culture later was not. *A Thief in the Night* was the template for Tim LaHaye's popular *Left Behind* book series inaugurated in 1995, and for the widely distributed, richly budgeted *Left Behind* movie series (2000, 2002, 2005), which closely tracked the plot and theology of the original. Meanwhile, Christian spanking manuals and instruments emerged as a robust business.[58]

Cultural developments were also political. Conservative Christian literature offered a critique of the "sixties" as the moment when America, especially its children, succumbed to sin. Redemption required action on many fronts: committing to sexual purity, renewing anticommunism, strengthening defenses, defeating liberal politicians, and embracing Israel. But in particular redemption required harsh punishment for the sinner, and harsh punishment to throttle the sinful ways of children exposed to so many ploys of the wily devil. Major figures in conservative Christian culture forged its links to politics, as with Anita Bryant and her Save Our Children crusade, and Jerry Falwell, whose Moral Majority organization began in 1979. James Dobson, perhaps the most widely read and heard authority on parental discipline, made clear the link of family and discipline to criminality and the state. By yielding to his parents' "loving authority," Dobson stated, the "child learns to submit to other forms of authority which will confront him later in his life—his teachers, school principals, police, neighbors and employers." As a sign read that advertised a "God and Decency Rally" with Falwell as the headliner, "Are you tired . . . of paying traffic tickets when dope peddlers, armed robbers, murderers and the like get off scot free?"[59] For most Christian conservatives, criminal evil was an individual trait to be purged or punished. It was not the product of social evil, or so they claimed, although they too identified social evils, just different ones—secular values, permissiveness, and the welfare state, rather than poverty and inequality.

Their efforts also revealed divisions over class, race, and gender. Conservative Christians' public face was mostly white, and they appealed substantially to lower- and middle-income whites outside big urban areas. However, as usual in American life, social divisions were not absolute. Black conservatives also condemned moral rot. Women like Phyllis Schlafly assailed feminism. Conservative white Protestants feared a rising "underclass"—a bugaboo of many worried secular authorities as well—but also assailed a privileged liberal elite. Still, the middle-class, white, male character of the conservative Christian leadership and most of its products was unmistakable, and so was its patriarchal cast. All major conservative evangelical leaders were men who often asserted the husband's supremacy in the family system, just like the man's supremacy in churches and governance. The period's best-known female evangelist—Ruth Carter Stapleton, the president's sister—was known for her healing ministry, not for the cultural and political conservatism of people like Falwell.

Of course critiques of the "sixties" were a commonplace of the 1970s that spilled far beyond conservative Christian circles. From the high intellectual camp came Christopher Lasch's *The Culture of Narcissism* (1979), which briefly caught the attention of the Carter White House. "Retributive justice" had yielded to "therapeutic justice," Lasch complained, "destroying the very sense of moral responsibility" as it did. What bothered Lasch was the loss of a sense of self as narcissistic Americans in "a dying culture" found it hard "to lay to rest the terrors of infancy or enjoy the consolations of adulthood." "Evil" was not in his vocabulary as a secular intellectual, and crime was not his focus—he seemed to miss how much "retributive justice" was already back in vogue. Yet whatever Lasch's intent, it was not hard to read his lament as an argument for the reassertion of stern patriarchal authority in the state and in the family. That is, it dovetailed with arguments in conservative Christian culture even as it derived from different concerns. "Modern capitalist society," rarely the object of conservative Christian scorn, was for Lasch the ultimate source of a "culture of narcissism." Lasch's critique of homosexuality and promiscuity—regrettable products of narcissistic personalities, in his view—marked another point of congruence.[60]

Spectacular public dramas also served as vehicles for emphasizing individual culpability and sin, rather than social and environmental forces, as the prime source of criminality. For all that the Watergate crisis fed into a mounting critique of institutional rot and aggrandizement, most Americans still understood it as a story of Nixon's willful criminality. This understanding was reinforced by Ford's pardon of Nixon. For all the commentary produced by the case of heiress Patty

Hearst, kidnapped in 1974 by the Symbionese Liberation Army and then emerging as its gun-toting accomplice, she, too, was often viewed as a willful, or at least willing, criminal. "For many Americans, and especially those on the right, she came to represent . . . the permissive sixties; feminism run amok . . . , the pathology of left-wing politics," and "the coddling of criminals."[61] After assassinating San Francisco mayor George Moscone and gay supervisor Harvey Milk in 1978, Dan White offered an infamous "twinkie defense" scorned in and beyond the gay community—his homophobic murderousness, not the sugar overdose he pleaded, seemed the source of his crimes. Yet if these dramas tilted toward the willful criminality of individuals, the tilt was only partial. Each was understood in many ways, and each yielded a clutter of opposing views rather than a consensus.

In the culture of the 1970s, conservative religionists wielded the hard knife of demands to police the nation and its children, but secular and often liberal figures, from intellectuals like Lasch to Hollywood filmmakers, added their own soft power to the cause. Mainstream media added their imprimatur, offering secular versions of criminal evil, especially as a threat that children posed. As *Newsweek* put it in 1978, assaying new research in an article entitled "The Criminal Mind," "Some kids are just bad. They lie and cheat and skip school; they try to bully their parents, rejecting love if it is offered. When these children grow up, they rob, embezzle, rape and kill," not because they are mentally ill, according to a new "theory" that *Newsweek* summarized, but because "they are simply wicked." A similar stance emerged about Gary Gilmore, the murderer who in 1976 was the first person executed when capital punishment was reinstituted in some states, and the subject of Norman Mailer's Pulitzer Prize–winning book *The Executioner's Song* (1979). As Cusac notes, a diverse array of people, including Gilmore's mother, "understood Gilmore as evil" even as a young child, and "rehabilitation as having failed." In 1970s culture, Cusac argues, "no longer is the criminal redeemable. Rather, criminality is intrinsic, evidence of the Devil inside." "In the 1960s and early 1970s," explains William Graebner, "criminal theory emphasized social and psychological causes—the criminal as victim," but in mid-decade, "perpetrators were now understood to be evil or depraved, perhaps beyond help and rescue."[62] Previous outbursts of "moralism and punitiveness" often had had little impact on state policies and incarceration rates.[63] What was distinctive about the 1970s outburst was its scale and its congruence with state efforts to crack down on crime.

But much of that surge of moralism on the cultural front came in a rush near the end of the decade, and it reached full influence only in the following two decades. That is, a punitive culture emerged not before but in the wake of politicians' demands to crack down on crime, turn vets into cops, and build a crime-centered state. Immense and variegated as it is, the cultural record of this era can be cherry-picked to support almost any argument about the relationship between culture and politics in the punitive turn, for it offers a muddle of contending views about how criminality was to be understood and dealt with. But a rough trajectory is apparent: cultural validation of the punitive turn was partial, erratic, and often challenged earlier in the 1970s, and it was more decisive and sure of itself by decade's end. It was no coincidence that the ultimate crime-fighter returned to the screen in 1978 in *Superman*. He and similar figures had flourished at midcentury on radio, in movies, on television, and in comics, as they battled foes foreign and domestic, but they had receded, especially in screen culture, from the late 1950s through the early 1970s. In a new era of anxiety about crime, crime-fighting required the return of supernatural heroes, as if nothing else could defeat criminal evil.

Moreover, both imagined criminals and imagined cops were rendered more as combatants at war by the late 1970s. Films like *Assault on Precinct 13* (1976) and *The Warriors* (1979) "depicted gang members as inconceivably numerous, soldiers in vast armies capable of virtual human-wave assaults." *The Warriors*' "publicity blared, 'These are the Armies of the Night. They are 100,000 strong. They outnumber the cops five to one. They could run New York City.'"[64] *Dirty Harry* suggested a harsher view of the criminal and harsher means of pursuing him. Featuring a police chopper hovering and Harry well armed and sporting a bulletproof vest, the film pointed toward the militarization of policing. Harry was a long way from the doughy physiques and pedestrian garb of 1950s law enforcers on-screen. The logic, mostly unspoken, was that if criminals are more like foreign enemies, cops must be more like soldiers in war. Filmmakers, advertisers, and other cultural producers conveyed this message, contributing to a militarization of crime control that political authorities supported through cash, policy, and weapons.

Local television news abetted such trends with a surge in crime reporting in the spirit of the well-known adage "If it bleeds it leads."[65] Insofar as sensational crime reporting had long been a staple of print news, this development represented as much a shift of venue as of content, but television's visual imagery amped up the sensationalism, as the 1976 film *Network* savagely satirized. Federal controls, commercial pressures, and corporate caution largely kept local stations from overt editorializing about the causes and politics of crime. But more important was the sheer volume and vivid nature of attention to lawbreaking, with its implicit and sometimes explicit message that crime was ever more threatening and ever nearer the viewer's home. It was a daily dose of violence and death to replace the dose long administered by TV news during the Vietnam War.

Buffeted by so much, including much about crime, Carter proposed a different war in his televised "malaise" speech (in which he never used that word) on July 15, 1979. Explicitly, he offered a war to curb energy waste and develop new fuel sources in light of 1979's global crisis in oil supplies. Implicitly, Carter also proposed a war on Americans' funk and discontent—their "crisis of confidence," distrust of authority, materialist "emptiness of lives," and "paralysis and stagnation and drift"—that he and various experts (including Lasch) had identified. "War" was no passing notion in that speech. Carter spoke of the "energy crisis" as "a clear and present danger to our Nation." He aspired "to win the energy war," and he wanted "an energy mobilization board" that would be "like the War Production Board in World War II." A successful "energy battle" would both solve the energy crisis and mobilize Americans behind a common purpose. "On the battlefield of energy we can win for our Nation a new confidence," Carter declared.

As usual, a war on abstractions was problematic. A war on crime had obvious enemies—drug traffickers, murderers, and other criminals. For his proposed war, Carter named no human enemies, and the ones he implicitly identified were numerous and diffuse: all those Americans surrendering to "stagnation and drift"; all those Americans failing to conserve resources; all those companies abetting dependence on Arab oil and resisting new kinds of energy. The wagging finger Carter pointed at so many people left the real enemy in this war unclear—perhaps it was ordinary gas-guzzling Americans. That was one reason his speech, though initially applauded, gained no traction for his presidency or his programs. He had revived the tradition of finding a "moral equivalent of war," as William James had called it—of thinking of war as the mode in which the nation acts most forcefully. Others, especially Carter's successor, would find more success by applying that tradition to a war on crime with identifiable enemies.

In the mid-1970s, Philip Jenkins claims, "a public terrified of violent offenders demanded that its elected officials respond with sharp punishments." But it is not clear that "the public" ever "demands" anything, even if audiences for the film *Death Wish* "literally cheered the frustrated white vigilante who executes street criminals."[66] Public demands are inchoate and multiple. The public also seemed to be demanding cheap gasoline and clean government but did not get them, raising the question of why the state acted on some "demands" and not others. In some matters, those about crime, state leaders judged it useful and feasible to take action. Johnson, Nixon, and Ford waged "war on crime," as LBJ dubbed it. Carter was the outlier. Although some dimensions were not yet in play,[67] the punitive turn, measured by growing incarceration, continued despite him, and in many ways it simply bypassed him. For many Americans, notes Jenkins, defeating "evil predators . . . was a matter of war."[68]

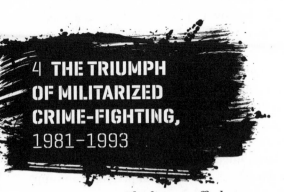

4 | THE TRIUMPH OF MILITARIZED CRIME-FIGHTING, 1981–1993

The busy traffic between war and crime intensified in the 1980s, taking on new rhetorical, political, and institutional forms. And though it met little resistance and often active support from liberals, the punitive turn took on a more conservative cast, leaving behind its origins in 1960s politics and being expressed more than ever in the language and institutions of war. Ronald Reagan and George H. W. Bush, his one-term successor, did much of the work in that regard, though much else went on beyond their administrations. Regarding crime, Ronald Reagan departed even more sharply from Carter than Carter had from Nixon and Ford, ushering in the most abrupt shift in presidential crime politics of the late twentieth century. The shift was most publicized in Reagan's declaration of a "war on drugs" and in a new gusher of war talk that he, Bush, and others offered. Scholars and critics have flagged Reagan's and Bush's role in that "war on drugs." But perhaps because of their public images (Reagan as genial, Bush as moderate and reasonable), their analyses have paid less attention to how harsh, sometimes ugly, and war-saturated their rhetoric and policies on crime were. Later critics of mass incarceration pounced on Bill and Hillary Clinton, Joe Biden, and others. They might also have pounced on Clinton's predecessors, who did much to usher in an age of militarized crime-fighting.

Reagan's New War

No public outcry drove Reagan toward a war on crime and a war on drugs. Criminality had hardly been a defining issue of the 1980 election, and opinion polls offered "no evidence of an upsurge in concern about drugs prior to Reagan's declaration of war," according to Katherine Beckett. Beckett finds "no evidence that the political elites' initial involvement in the wars on crime and drugs was a response to popular sentiments."[1] At most, public opinion was permissive rather than directive—fluid and opaque enough to leave the path open for Reagan, who drew less on polls than on his political success as a tough-on-crime California governor (1967–75), and on the politics of his two Republican predecessors.

Indeed, much of Reagan's public talk was standard-issue rhetoric about cracking down on crime, and little changed from what conservatives had been offering Americans since the 1960s. Likewise, much of the legislation he pushed and the initiatives his administration took came off that conservative shelf. The Reagan White House wanted to appoint tough-on-crime federal judges and justices; make sentences fixed and longer; fund new federal, state, and local prisons; ramp up prosecution of drug-related crimes; curb rights of the accused; expand rights of victims; and stamp out pornography and obscenity.

But Reagan often sounded harsher than his Republican predecessors. Not for him were the nods to rehabilitation for drug offenders that Nixon had offered and Congress had funded. Asked if "drug dealers" should be "executed, as Malaysia did," Reagan responded, "If you're talking about the death penalty, I know they deserve it." He then added that he would not pursue capital punishment for those offenders, explaining, "[It] would divide our ranks, because there are so many people who don't believe in the death penalty for anything." Reagan judged drug dealers "very prone to evil," thereby giving presidential imprimatur to a language of evil that gained force in the 1970s.[2]

Reagan echoed Nixon and Ford, minus their gestures to the role of poverty and social disorder in causing crime—explanations that Reagan scorned. For Reagan, crime was caused by individuals' moral and personal failure, by "an arrogance of the criminal mind, a belief in its own superiority over the rest of humanity," as he put it in 1981. His "portrait" of the criminal was "that of a stark, staring face, a face that belongs to a frightening reality of our time—the face of a human predator." Together, he claimed, "repeat offenders and career criminals" form "a new privileged class in America." Reagan once acknowledged that "sustained unemployment" for young people might "tempt some to channel their energies and ambitions into antisocial or criminal activities," but that was a rare departure from script. True, he offered his own social explanation—that permissive courts, indulgent welfare, and slack social mores gave license to criminality. But Reagan never addressed the tension between embracing one such explanation and judging others worthless. He scoffed in 1983 at the claim that declining "crime statistics in America" owed to fewer "people in the crime-prone age." The decline could only be for one reason, he said: "We are putting career criminals in jail in greater numbers and for longer periods."[3]

Likewise, Reagan rarely addressed the tension between asserting that the federal government was too big and intrusive and demanding that it expand to go after crime. "Government is not the solution to our problem; government is the problem," he declared in his January 20, 1981, inaugural. Yet he moved effortlessly between insisting that "Government's first duty is to protect the people, not run their lives" and proposing new initiatives to "run" some lives. Reagan's 1981 speech to police chiefs was a classic in that regard. "We've learned the price of too much government," he stated, adding, "The massive expansion of government is related to the crime problem" because it discourages individual responsibility.[4] Even so, he defended a "massive expansion of government" regarding lawlessness. Implicitly, the fortieth president resolved the tension by invoking a "war on crime," since war was exempt from strictures like his about big government. Just as Reagan's defense budgets rose sharply, so too did his crime-fighting budgets. Measured in dollars (rapidly depreciating in the 1980s), defense spending increased 60 percent between 1981 and 1989, while federal "administration of justice" spending more than doubled and soared further under George Bush and Bill Clinton.[5] Federal justice spending was far smaller than defense spending, in part because so much justice spending went through state and local budgets. However, justice expenditures were also rising more rapidly. As under Nixon and Ford, the state would retreat but also advance.

On crime, Reagan rarely allowed for complexity or strayed off message, except when the wrongdoing involved his own administration. He made it clear that by "crime" he meant "street crime" and "violent crime" and drug trafficking done by denizens of cities, often implicitly racializing all these behaviors. One advisor repudiated what he called Carter's "preoccupation with white-collar crime," and the Justice Department sharply cut back resources for its prosecution.[6] For Reagan, "violent" crime subsumed all crime—he skillfully conflated the two. And while he claimed that a "small number of criminals" were "responsible for an enormous amount of the crime," his war on drugs rhetoric cast the net wider, implicating millions in activity that presumably imperiled the nation.[7]

And even more than Nixon and Ford, Reagan harped on crime relentlessly. If Americans were not already afraid of lawlessness, Reagan tried to teach them to be. He also pushed citizens to embrace the tough-on-crime measures he advocated, ones designed to end "the liberal era of coddling criminals." As Reagan began a 1984 radio address, "Shouldn't we have the right as citizens of this great country to walk our streets without being afraid and to go to bed without worrying the next sound might be a burglar or rapist?"[8] His public stance on criminality had distinctive declarative and performative qualities. He proclaimed new crime-related events—Victims of Crime Week, National Correctional Officers Week, National Neighborhood Crime Watch Day, and so forth. And he included members of crime-fighting groups in his public appearances, doing so on a gendered basis: victims of crime were usually women (among them, actress Theresa Saldana, who later played the wife of Police Commissioner Tony Scali in the 1990s television series *The Commish*), and punishers of crime were usually men. Reagan not only said more about crime than his predecessors, he also did more to perform the crime issue, sometimes literally on the public stage. That he was a victim of crime—John Hinckley Jr. attempted to assassinate him on March 30, 1981—was the president's ultimate, though of course unintended, performance.

In the process, Reagan was often cavalier about facts and loose about history, as he was with many issues. He summarized complex criminal cases, some from his California governorship, in a sentence or two. The past he pushed against was vaguely located in time, as when he spoke of "the sad, often tragic story of years of judicial solicitation for every conceivable right of criminals and neglect for the victims of crime, of playing fast and loose with the first amendment rights in a way that gave too many pornographers free rein, of fanciful constitutional arguments used to throw out long and hard police work, and the price our nation has paid for all of this."[9] These remarks date from December 1987, before some officials caught in the Iran-Contra scandal (they had illegally funneled weapons to "contras" in Nicaragua) used arguably "fanciful constitutional arguments" to escape legal jeopardy (Oliver North, John Poindexter) or received pardons from Reagan's successor, Bush. Were the "years" of this "tragic story" those of Reagan's law-and-order GOP predecessors, Nixon and Ford, and were the "fanciful constitutional arguments" those often formulated by Supreme Court justices nominated by previous GOP presidents? This was a mythical past that listeners were free to imagine as the "'60s" and "'70s," set against an even more fanciful era—the 1950s, sort of—before a "tragic story" ensued.

Reagan also broadened the actions he deemed criminal. Some of that broadening was explicitly legal, as in new or enhanced federal penalties for various crimes in laws Congress enacted and Reagan signed. In other instances, widening the definition of unlawful acts was rhetorical and political. Reagan could not criminalize abortion, but by calling it a "great moral evil" and doing so alongside his discussion of crime, he suggested it was a criminal act, *Roe v. Wade* notwithstanding. For parents, he opined that "music and the media floods their children's world with glorifications of drugs and violence and perversity" and doubted that "the first amendment" should be "twisted into a pretext for license." Reagan wanted such "glorifications" to be regarded as criminal, even if he could do little to make that happen.[10]

Just as criminality was an expanding category, so was victimhood. Reagan established a President's Task Force on Victims of Crime in 1982, which in turn helped shape years of federal and state legislation that, despite the political diversity of the initial victims' rights movement, did little to compensate victims financially (a common practice in Western Europe). Instead, compensation was to be punitive—the satisfaction injured parties gained from advocating punishment for offenders and often from gaining the public limelight (sometimes a few feet from Reagan). With considerable success, Reagan and others worked to give victims a voice in criminals' sentencing. Future attorney general William Barr captured the thrust of Reagan-era victim politics when he commented in 1992, "We should not forget that justice is done when people"—meaning offenders—"get what they deserve."[11]

Reagan made it clear his administration was waging "war on crime."[12] He used war language routinely, as if everyone already understood that such a war was going on, and as if his phrasing was natural and settled, hence requiring no justification. Addressing Reagan, reporters also used such verbiage unquestioningly. In fact, this language was not settled at the start of his presidency, but Reagan's antidrug rhetoric hardly came out of nowhere. It was already entrenched in some right-wing circles, with roots in California during Reagan's governorship and in Nixon's presidency. On the fringes of those circles, Lyndon LaRouche's National Anti-Drug Coalition used its short-lived magazine *War on Drugs* to champion LaRouche for president in the 1980 elections. The periodical also alleged a vast conspiracy extending from Chinese Communists to Iran's Ayatollah Khomeini to Washington liberals who peddled drugs (and sex education and homosexuality) and posted on one cover a photo of a casually dressed Jimmy Carter surrounded by a hirsute rock band with the caption, "Who's Pushing Drugs on America?"[13] LaRouche's quirky politics probably had little influence on Reagan, but others were also weighing in on the issue of drugs. Agitation against drug dealing, drug use, and the resulting damage to communities swirled through many cities, especially Washington, D.C., Reagan's new home turf. African American politicians and activists often spearheaded that protest, and as African Americans entered police forces and mayors' offices in swelling numbers, they often championed mandatory minimum sentencing and tough militarized action against drugs.[14]

But Reagan was the one to give full-throated cry to those politics on the national stage and to cast antidrug policing as a war, even more than Nixon did. He did much to turn phrases like "war on crime" and "war on drugs" into a settled, even official, language, doing so through sheer repetition and by treating those phrases as givens (it was not his style to explain his language). Reagan first publicly declared "war on drugs" in an October 2, 1982, radio address, and he soon joined First Lady Nancy Reagan in a much-touted "Just Say No" campaign against drug use.

The Reagan years heralded a few other wars. Though there was no war on white-collar crime, there was a "war against the crime syndicates," also called "a war of abolition against the mob." A "war on terrorism," as Reagan called it in a September 22, 1986, United Nations address, also broke out, as did other wars that merited more passing mention. On occasion Reagan likened his tough-on-crime stance to his tough-on-communism foreign policy: "This administration seeks no negotiated settlement, no detente with the mob," with whom it was "war to the end," as he put it on another occasion. Sometimes Reagan's war analogies became odd or farfetched. He said of drugs, "The situation is not hopeless," any more than it was "at the Battle of Verdun in World War I," which had been a horrendous stalemate. In another instance, Reagan compared his situation to the one Abraham Lincoln had faced in the Civil War.[15]

And occasionally he tripped over words in revealing ways, as when he referred, regarding drugs, to "the other half of the law—or the war, I should say," inadvertently acknowledging the blurry line between crime-fighting and war-fighting, which his administration did much to blur further. To designate crime-fighting as a war was tricky insofar as it triggered suspicion about the questionable use of military "assets." Even as Reagan insisted on drawing "the line at not saying that we're suddenly going to make our military have a police capability," he was soon claiming, "Military forces have dramatically reduced drug use by 67 percent."[16] That assertion presumably referred to military efforts to interdict the flow of drugs across America's borders and to disrupt its sources abroad; if war invited using the armed forces, the obvious place to do so legally was beyond United States borders. But by then, National Guard units, U-2 spy planes, helicopters (some "blaring Wagner's 'Ride of the Valkyries'"), and weapons were also swooping down on alleged California pot growers. Reagan's rhetoric, like his policies, confused reporters, and probably many others, about just where he "drew the line." But his first attorney general successfully resisted budget cuts in 1981 by arguing that "the Justice Department is not a domestic agency" but instead "the internal arm of the nation's defense," or what budget director David Stockman derisively labeled the "Internal Defense Department."[17]

Even for Reagan and his subordinates, the war analogy had limits. Thus they rarely deployed it for their campaign against pornography and obscenity. The war analogy did not define the language of the Meese Commission—the Attorney General's Commission on Pornography run by Edwin Meese. Commissioner James Dobson, the right-wing religious and media figure, did declare, "We are engaged in a winnable war!" He also said the battle against "hard-core pornography" could be concluded "in 18 months."[18] *Newsweek* splashed "The War Against Pornography" in bold letters on the cover of its March 18, 1985, issue, on the eve of the Meese Commission's work, and other media outlets occasionally trumpeted "war" in their headlines about Meese's efforts. But these occasional uses rarely went beyond the headlines and found little place in official rhetoric. The war analogy also appeared in feminist antipornography campaigns, as in Andrea Dworkin's *Letters from a War Zone* (1989). However, for Dworkin, the "war zone" designated the clash between men and women, and pornography's way of creating a "concentration camp for women, the house of sexual slaughter," not a government crackdown on criminal activity.[19] In any event, Reagan had no truck with feminists, even though some sided with him on this issue. While a federal campaign against pornography went forward, it lacked the traction of Reagan's other crime wars.

War did frame activists' mounting campaign against abortion in the 1980s. Pro-lifers' countless comparisons of fetal deaths to the Holocaust analogized their campaign to World War II, and their demands to wage war against abortion surged, just as pro-choice activists often denounced the war against abortion. Yet because abortion remained (for the most part) legal, "war" could not frame state action against it. War imagery served as rhetorical summons for citizens to fight against (or for) abortion rights, but the Reagan administration could not plausibly declare war on abortion. The war against abortion was another example of the decade's promiscuous use of "war" to designate all sorts of campaigns—against AIDS, trade imbalances, and much else.[20]

Sometimes Reagan's crime rhetoric moved beyond the arena of combat. In 1981 he famously declared police "the thin blue line that holds back a jungle which threatens to reclaim this clearing we call civilization." For some critics of his language, "the jungle" carried racial overtones. In 1985, Reagan noted, "The illegal drug trade . . . is a cancer." The "Just Say No" to drugs campaign of his second term played on volunteerism, individual responsibility, and national uplift to become a "national crusade." But even that campaign pivoted quickly back to war. Proclaiming "Just Say No to Drugs Week," Reagan asserted, "The first thing we did was take down the surrender flag and raise the battle flag." A few weeks later, he described what it would take to vanquish the "enemy," drug use: "We've got to do it as one people, together united in purpose and committed to victory." Wars are usually crusades for Americans, after all, and the war metaphor was irresistible to an administration declaring "drug abuse" to be "a threat to our national security." Reagan trumpeted that metaphor extravagantly. "This is a battle for liberty from the enslavement of drug addiction," he said in 1986 while proclaiming "National Drug Abuse Education and Prevention Week and National Drug Abuse Education Day." "We can win," he continued. "We must win. With God's help and a united people, we shall win."[21]

Such language signaled a notable shift with Reagan: for all his reputation as a crusader against communism, he sounded the alarm on crime at least as often and as loudly. Even before the Mikhail Gorbachev–era détente with the Soviet Union of his second term, Reagan indicated, without explicitly verbalizing, a shift in priorities from communism to crime and the displacement of the communist by the criminal as America's national enemy. It was telling that as his presidency ended, Reagan could say, "There are no Americans braver, and no citizens more precious, than the men and women who guard us— our State and local police." He did not even mention military personnel among those "who guard us." To be sure, Reagan never felt he was choosing between fighting communism and fighting crime. But there was a definite change in his enunciation of national priorities, and it accelerated as the Soviet-American relationship thawed. In 1986, National Security Directive 221 declared, "The international drug trade threatens the national security of the United States by potentially destabilizing democratic allies" (some not so democratic). Not just the drug trade but "drug abuse" itself was a "threat to our national security." "Nothing in our nation's history is more offensive to our fundamental values and national sense of purpose than drug abuse," Reagan proclaimed in September 1986. Neither slavery, nor atheism, nor communism was more distasteful to Reagan, it seemed. "Over the years," he had told Congress a few days earlier, "our country has never hesitated to defend itself against the attack of any enemy." As he explained, "The enemy facing us now—illegal drugs—is as formidable as any we have ever encountered." In that phrasing, communism was no longer—and perhaps had never been—the nation's most "formidable" enemy.[22]

At times that shift in focus was undercut by Reagan's desire to gloat about his presumed successes. By 1987, he was almost consigning the war on crime to the past. "Back in the early days, we faced another crisis . . . the crisis of crime," Reagan reported, taking note of falling crime rates. But of course as he saw it, more of what had already worked was in order. He renewed his case for new tough-on-crime legislation in order to "institutionalize the progress . . . made" and "make . . . recent gains permanent." Resumption of the federal death penalty, new restrictions on the use of habeas corpus, and "a drug free" America were on his wish list as he restated his pitch for the confirmation of Robert Bork as Supreme Court justice.[23] His late-term desire to "make . . . recent gains permanent" also helps explain why the war analogy was by then fading from his rhetoric: war is about emergency and urgency, whereas Reagan wanted his crime-fighting program to become routine. Indeed, in the Reagan-Bush years, many features of a terrifying system of criminal justice and mass incarceration grew.

Rhetorically and functionally, Reagan was less willing to compromise with his political foes on crime than on other major issues like taxes, economic policy, and communism. As he put it amid his failed, angry effort to get Bork's nomination approved, "This battle is all about: the choice between liberal judges who make up the law or sound judges who interpret the law; the choice between liberal judges whose decisions protect criminals or firm judges whose decisions protect the victims; the choice between liberal judges selected by the liberal special interests or distinguished judges selected to serve the people." This was a clash between good and evil, he insisted, and evil included "liberal judges" and their sympathizers, as well as "the gurus of hedonism and permissiveness" (presumably "sixties" types) who gave license to drug taking.[24] For Reagan, there were no honest differences of opinion, only a bright line between good and evil. Likewise, on crime Reagan offered little of the geniality and few of the wisecracks (except when Nancy Reagan was present or when he spoke of her work on "Just Say No") often regarded as trademarks of his public style. Not for him could reasonable men and women have conflicting views on crime.

In the end, the fortieth president had less to boast about than he had hoped for. "No drug network will remain alive," he promised in 1986, but he had not delivered on that promise as he left office. In September 1988, he could only report that "between 1980 and 1987, the overall crime rate fell by nearly 7 percent." While perhaps a comforting trajectory, this was hardly a dramatic reversal, and it was no wonder Reagan now put more emphasis on other statistics. During Reagan's first term "the average sentence handed down by a Federal court per conviction increased dramatically—by over 100 percent for rape, over 100 percent for burglary, and over 60 percent for murder," he reported in 1988. Later that year, he observed, "There are over 12,000 Just Say No clubs," and he belittled "liberals" who "scoffed" at his claim of "winning the war on drugs." In an odd echo of how progress in America's Vietnam War had often been measured, the body count—arrests made, convictions achieved, sentences lengthened, prison beds added, clubs established, cocaine captured—mattered more than the achievement of objectives. Besides, if the crime rate had not gone down much, that was simply a reason to do more of the same to combat it. As Reagan kept repeating on the campaign trail in the fall of 1988, "Make a false move, and the next sound you hear is the clang of a jail cell door slamming shut." Presidents who declare war on enemies as inchoate and pervasive as drug use or crime always find victory elusive, as Johnson had with poverty, Nixon had with cancer, and Reagan himself had with terrorism. Rather than admit failure to win the war on crime, Reagan promised to continue fighting it, as his successors did.[25]

This Reagan—the one of hard-driving, humorless, sometimes ugly rhetoric—is not one that most Americans, even some scholars, recall, perhaps because they were not his victims. (Inmates might recall the president and his language better.) A vague association of the war on drugs with Reagan, or just with the eighties, is often as far as these memories go, as if Reagan the crime-fighter became hidden in plain sight. Historian Daniel Rodgers, for example, shows how Reagan departed sharply from Cold War norms of presidential speech, which had emphasized common responsibility, common danger, common sacrifice. With Reagan, "older rhetorical formulas were overrun by the newer, softer, less demanding ones," including "that ultimate state of boundlessness: dreaming." As the president intoned "freedom" eloquently, "freedom was cut loose from the burdens and responsibilities that had once so closely accompanied it." Indeed, that happened.[26]

Yet regarding crime, Reagan's rhetorical formulas were never "softer, less demanding ones." Urgency and danger infused them; "dreaming" had little place where tough action was to be taken. Even in public, historian David Greenberg notes, Reagan had "an ugly mean streak," evident when he "ginned up bitterness toward welfare queens whose stories he concocted, and played to scorn for liberals whom he called soft on crime." The president's election victories depended not only on "his Hollywood smile" but also on his public meanness, his zest for the punitive. Reagan was not so much "Losing the Words of the Cold War," as Rodgers titles a book chapter, as he was redeploying them to a new war. Rodgers describes "the twin pillars of [Reagan's] domestic policy" as "tax cutting and corporate and environmental deregulation," but there was one more pillar, a big one—the war on crime.[27]

Spreading the Word

Did Reagan's rhetorical work change how Americans regarded crime and wanted to deal with it? Marginally, but less so than Reagan apparently believed and most Americans, taught to hold his rhetorical powers in awe, may assume. Poll-tested concern about crime, though measurable in many ways with conflicting results, remained flat for much of the 1980s, suggesting no quick impact from Reagan's efforts.[28] The major exception was in regard to drugs, agitation over which mounted in the early 1980s. This activism was driven in part by a parents movement and its leading organization, the National Federation of Parents for Drug-Free Youth, which worked closely with Nancy Reagan and the White House. A surge in made-for-TV movies and documentaries further spurred antidrug efforts. While concern about drugs still seemed limited before the spring of 1986, it then spiked after a blitz of administration pronouncements, congressional action, and media stories (themselves often stoked by the administration and law enforcement agencies).[29]

Although a general war on crime elicited only modest public interest, the war on drugs finally did have an effect, in part because it was the front in the fight against crime that most seemed like combat. With the armed forces now ordered to help wage this battle, with police and Drug Enforcement Administration (DEA) agents armed like troops and engaged in spectacular busts, with the president calling these efforts a "war," the late 1980s campaign against drugs was the nearest thing to real war that Americans could indulge. This was especially true since the Reagan presidency was rhetorically bellicose but operationally cautious regarding the diminishing Soviet threat. As one DEA official later put it in boasting of his success stoking media attention to drugs, "Crack was the hottest combat reporting story to come along since the end of the Vietnam War."[30] In a presidency mired in the Iran-Contra scandal and exploring rapprochement with Moscow, it was almost the only "combat reporting story." Poll-measured alarm about crime did climb during George H. W. Bush's presidency, soaring at its end, and perhaps that climb reflected a cumulative effect of Reagan's work. But heightened anxiety also reflected Bush's strident rhetoric on crime during the 1988 presidential campaign and after taking office. Insofar as any president deserves credit or blame for public fears about crime, Bush warranted it as much as Reagan.

Also having a cumulative effect were the "if-it-bleeds-it-leads" local and national television reporting and a wave of TV crime dramas. Both stirred up a generalized fear of crime and encouraged white perceptions of crime in racial terms, as action carried out especially by African Americans. Reporting and crime dramas also distanced public perceptions from crime-rate realities, at least insofar as, in one scholar's words, "the incidence of crime stories in the local news bears no relation to crime in that area."[31] To be sure, "the media, especially television, have been instigators of punitive penal populism in many countries" that experienced no great punitive turn.[32] Like any one factor, television only accounts for so much. Yet it nourished a considerable audience for tough-on-crime politics even if it did little to dictate specific policies. As a scholar had argued in 1963, "The press may not be successful much of the time in telling people what to think, but they are stunningly successful in telling its readers what to think *about*." And as later research indicated, "heavy consumers of violent television crime shows are more likely to see the world as a violent and frightening place and to adopt 'a retributive justice perspective.'"[33]

Meanwhile, decreasing alarm about a Soviet threat allowed other worries to rise in public consciousness, just as it allowed politicians like Reagan to shift focus to crime. Concerns on a poll-driven hit list may rise less because their intensity grows than because competing anxieties fade. The late 1980s spike in poll-measured crime-and-drug fears coincided with a near collapse in fear of war. Similarly, anxiety about crime diminished sharply as the Gulf War loomed in 1990 and then broke out in 1991. In contrast, a 1989 poll showed that "more than two-thirds thought we [Americans] were losing ground on drugs."[34] Public concerns never act solely in hydraulic fashion, one switched with another, but the closeness to each other of the realms of battling enemies abroad and stopping crime at home—both viewed as wars, both involving armed might, both producing languages of fear and contempt, both entwined for decades—strengthened the hydraulic relationship. In the end, disentangling Reagan's rhetoric from the other forces promoting worry about lawlessness is not only impossible but also unnecessary. The point is how those forces converged and met little resistance.

More important than how he moved poll numbers, Reagan's language of war penetrated far beyond the White House. Polls usually tracked the importance that Americans gave to crime as an issue, not how they understood the issue and the policies that should result, beyond a few matters like the death penalty. Less measurable was the diffusion of Reagan's language. Media reports did sometimes convey doubt or cynicism about whether the drug war could be won, whether Reagan was waging it properly, and what motives lay behind it. In July 1981 *Time* was already opining, "Each new war against illegal drugs has seemed . . . as futile as shoving sand from a beach."[35] And given the failed war in Vietnam, some critics took Reagan's war talk where he hardly wanted it to go. *Newsweek* quoted a "Pentagon officer" who said, "We couldn't interdict the Ho Chi Minh Trail [during the Vietnam War]" and "Right now, coming up from the south, we have a Ho Chi Minh Trail 4,000 miles wide." The magazine also noted that "the Pentagon's generals and admirals are not entirely happy about being enlisted in Ronald Reagan's war on drugs."[36] And like most moral campaigns, this one produced its share of silliness. "It was not altogether startling," *Time* reported in 1986, in words that underlined how startling the situation was, "to hear Ronald Reagan offer to take a urine test to determine if he has consumed any narcotics lately—and to ask his entire Cabinet to follow suit." "Across the country," *Time* soon added, "candidates . . . were challenging one another to urinating contests as a demonstration of fealty to the cause."[37]

But the notion that crime-fighting should be prosecuted as a war and with the instruments and mentalities that war brings met little challenge. Politicians and media outlets treated this idea as self-evident and beyond interrogation, no matter how much they haggled over the proper means for battling crime. Hence "war on drugs" and "war on crime" rarely appeared in print media with quotation marks that might have signaled doubt about their reality or authenticity, even in otherwise critical treatments. Television news anchors intoned phrases like "in the war on drugs today"—as they once had uttered phrases like "in the Vietnam War today"—without any hint that the term "war" might be up for grabs.

Likewise, national media rarely challenged the premise behind the drug war—that drug use was surging. Unusual was an assertion in 1986 by *U.S. News* that "there is little evidence to support alarmist claims" about drug use and that even crack use was "barely a blip on the statistical screen."[38] Soon, scattered references to the "war on drugs" crept into federal documents—a congressional bill here, an agency report there—thereby giving the language an official imprimatur beyond its use in political rhetoric.[39] By the late 1980s, criticism of the drug war did emerge, including in some academic circles that condemned the "militarization of drug enforcement" and worried that "questioning the drug war [was] almost subversive."[40] But for the most part, the language of war on crime and drugs circulated widely and uncritically, an achievement by Reagan and his allies more consequential than any nudge they gave to poll numbers.

That accomplishment owed to more than their use of the word "war." It rested on the myriad ways in which crime-fighting was linked imaginatively and operationally to war-fighting. In his national address about drugs on September 14, 1986, Reagan urged Americans to "remember how America swung into action when we were attacked in World War II." He went on at length about that conflict, managing to drag in references to the Holocaust, Soviet gulags, and Lincoln fighting the Civil War. Months earlier, Reagan had declared, "By 1980, illegal drugs were every bit as much a threat to the United States as enemy planes and missiles." He did so just as Democratic senator John Kerry embraced a drug kingpin's claim that "cocaine is the Latin American atomic bomb." Amid the crack frenzy of 1986, *Newsweek* offered one police official's comparison of "little white packets . . . being dropped on this country" to the Japanese attack on Pearl Harbor. The magazine reported, "The war against crack . . . is turning the ghettos of major cities into something like a domestic Vietnam. The analogy is shopworn but apt. The crack trade operates like a guerrilla insurgency," with its purveyors presumably akin to the Vietcong.[41]

There was more. Speaking at the Harpers Ferry, West Virginia, site of John Brown's 1859 uprising, Nancy Reagan said drugs had the "potential of tearing our country apart, just like the Civil War did."[42] A drumbeat of stories and congressional complaints continued about drug addiction among Vietnam-era veterans and current military personnel. Shooting off in another direction were direct analogies to the Vietnam War. The *Miami Herald* editorialized in 1981, "If the War on Drugs is the Vietnam of law enforcement, then South Florida is its Khe Sanh [site of a bloody, inconclusive battle in South Vietnam between U.S. and enemy forces in 1968]—isolated, besieged, almost overrun." For his part, Representative Claude Pepper spotted "a Tet Offensive in South Florida." And in 1986 *Time* commented as follows concerning an explosion of

TV coverage of crack: "The war on drugs, like the war in Viet Nam, has been brought home to the nation's living rooms."[43] Meanwhile, New York mayor Edward Koch "called on the Army, Navy and Air Force to join the war," as *Time* put it.[44] Indicating the cross-racial appeal of such thinking, at least at elite levels, *Ebony* proudly dubbed African American congressman Charles Rangel "the Front-Line General in the War on Drugs" in 1989, as Rangel fulminated, "All these people are talking about protecting the world against communism and the Soviets" instead of protecting America's children.[45]

And then there was the use of armed forces against drug trafficking, so that "by the mid-1980s, the DOD [Department of Defense] had come to employ some of its most sophisticated weaponry, such as Black Hawk assault helicopters and Blue Thunder speedboats, for prohibition purposes."[46] That military deployment had required heavy lifting on the legal front: the Reagan-backed Military Cooperation with Civilian Law Enforcement Agencies Act of 1981 "carved out a huge exception to the Posse Comitatus Act, the Civil War–era law prohibiting the use of the military for civilian policing."[47]

Abroad, the DEA, the Defense Department, and other agencies waged a dirty, expanding quasi war against drug cultivation and trafficking (though sometimes those purposes were a cover for other objectives). That campaign featured abundant talk of "narco terrorists" (Bush was the first president to use the term, on October 19, 1989) and Marxist regimes like the Sandinistas' in Nicaragua, talk that turned the drug war into another front of the Cold War the Reagan administration waged in Central and South America. As one journalist urged the president to say, "These countries"—he identified them as "Colombia, Bolivia, Peru, Mexico, etc."—"are attacking us. They are a far more serious threat to us than terrorism."[48] "War" was not just a metaphor for the campaign against drugs, but a tangled thicket of associations, memories, alarms, and operations. The notion of a war on drugs worked not only because of its thoughtless embrace by Americans or its dogged repetition by political leaders—though plenty of both behaviors went on—but because so much went on in its name that really was akin to war.

The metaphor also worked because many Americans now understood and practiced war as something the United States waged against cultural, racial, and technological inferiors. In the Reagan-Bush years, almost no official declared war on white-collar crimes or high officials' crimes, despite the public outcry about such crimes, and despite a surfeit of them—the junk-bond misdeeds of Michael Milken (indicted in

1989), the savings-and-loan scandal that ensnared banker and anti-pornography crusader Charles Keating, the officials caught up in the Iran-Contra affair. That such lawbreakers fell outside the war-on-crime framework reflected privileges of class, status, and race that usually operate in American criminal justice. For Reagan the "new privileged class in America" was "repeat offenders and career criminals," not wealthy white men in coats and ties.[49]

But something else operated as well. The war invoked by crime-fighters was a timeless category, but also a historically specific one. The world wars had pitted the U.S. against powers of roughly equal might and status. The Cold War had been above all, though not only, a contest between the United States and the USSR. But the hot wars the United States fought from Korea on were against second-rate powers (less so once China entered the Korean War), however much many Americans saw them as proxies for the USSR, that were also non-European and nonwhite. And while the prelude to the 1991 Gulf War featured hype about Saddam Hussein's Iraq—sometimes analogized to Hitler's Germany—it, too, was a second-rate power. Military actions against Grenada in 1983 and Panama's Manuel Noriega in 1989 took on even frailer enemies. Given how Americans now understood real war, it made sense that many also understood their metaphorical war on crime as a campaign against racial and cultural inferiors. That knowledge was borne out in practice through a war on drugs waged disproportionately against black (and often Native American and Latino) subjects, despite evidence that they used and sold drugs no more than whites.

To be sure, no clean white-nonwhite divide defined this understanding. African American and other minority soldiers fought in growing numbers for the United States and sometimes shared the condescension and disgust many white Americans expressed toward their nonwhite enemies (and allies) abroad.[50] Likewise, in cities like Los Angeles, black elites, churches, and activist organizations often joined the chorus demanding "more punitive" responses to drug crime.[51] Way back in 1962, civil rights activist A. Philip Randolph had wanted "a life time sentence without parole" for the "crime of pushing narcotics," and most African Americans in Congress voted (some to their regret) for the Anti–Drug Abuse Act of 1986, with its notorious racialized disparities between powder and crack cocaine.[52] Moreover, the 1980s war on drugs was less the driver of mass incarceration than critics soon judged it to be. "It is a sobering fact that if all drug cases were eliminated, the U.S. imprisonment rate would still have quadrupled over the past thirty-five years," Marie Gottschalk notes.[53] And criminal justice usually hit poor and otherwise marginal populations the hardest. That in itself was not new.

But the way Americans now waged war and carried its language into crime-fighting made that emphasis starker. It was another burden for the many African Americans and other minorities who filled jails and prisons in and after the 1980s, individuals who already bore the burdens of their economic circumstances, the persistence of white racism, the nominally color-blind but racially inflected laws and practices of criminal justice, and the abrupt emptying of mental health hospitals.[54] No wonder that in 1991, "for the first time in American history, there was a greater total number of blacks in prison than whites," even though blacks comprised just "12 percent of the U.S. population."[55] Even specific practices in war making and crime-fighting came to have an eerie similarity: the SWAT teams that burst through doors and pinioned those inside to the floor in drug busts and other actions resembled GIs busting through "hootches" in Vietnam, or later breaking into Iraqi homes in search of "insurgents." Big war making—B-52 carpet bombing, cruise missiles—could not be transplanted home. But much of the grunt work of war making could be.

As Americans usually do during their wars with foreign enemies, they offered a rash of talk about suspending civil liberties and due process in their war against crime. For Florida Democratic congressman Charles E. Bennett, the drug threat demanded "courageous, manly responses" without getting "hung up on something like the Posse Comitatus law."[56] "This is war," after all, said House Republican whip Trent Lott, who backed use of the armed forces at home against the drug scourge.[57] For Los Angeles police chief Daryl Gates, circumstances meant that "the casual drug user ought to be taken out and shot." Drug use was "treason," he told the Senate Judiciary Committee in 1990 in a news-catching statement, one he later defended as "hyperbole to draw attention to a big problem" for him (both his city and his son dealt with drug addiction).[58]

Another palpable consequence of Reagan's performance was its impact on criminal justice agencies, especially at the federal level. Their leaders, then as during other presidencies, took their cues as much from presidential rhetoric as from direct orders sent by the White House. And Reagan targeted these organizations as much as a national audience.[59] He spoke often at gatherings of police chiefs, sheriffs, FBI and other Justice Department personnel, and law-and-order groups like the National Rifle Association with close ties to criminal justice officials. Reagan's "use of rhetoric to send policy signals," argue two scholars, "altered the U.S. Attorneys' prosecution of drug crimes," as those attorneys "translated presidential policy rhetoric into prosecutorial action" by bearing down harder on drug crimes.[60] If that was true of U.S. attorneys, it must have been the case for other officials in the Justice Department, as well as for other agencies focused on crime but at greater literal and institutional distance from the president. Police chiefs, states' attorneys, mayors, and others also had the flow of federal moneys to remind them of the new priorities. Reagan's rhetoric taught them the importance he attached to his war on crime and encouraged them to wage it in that no-holds-barred, rules-must-be-bent spirit that Americans imagine they exercise in war. The message to law enforcement officials was clear: arrest and prosecute more and with fewer constraints, reward those who do so, and tout their achievements publicly.

In turn, those officials' actions amplified a feedback loop with public opinion. As they announced scarier arrest statistics, paraded perps before TV cameras, told frightening crime stories, displayed bristling armaments, and boasted of harsher sentences, they performed their heightened, militarized vigilance against crime, and the apparent pervasiveness of crime itself. The mere fact that prisons bulged ever more with inmates could be taken as a measure of the crime menace; it seemed there could hardly be so many more inmates if they had not committed so many more offenses. In truth, prisons bulged for other reasons, such as greater prosecutorial zeal, longer sentences, mandatory minimum sentences, decreasing parole, and quickened reimprisonment for parole violations. But few people even in law enforcement acknowledged those statistical complexities.

The rising prison population—depending on who is counted, it doubled from a half million in 1980 to over one million in 1990[61]—was like a fever on a thermometer. The higher it rose, the graver the underlying infection appeared to be. As Michelle Alexander puts it, "The average person" could "conclude reasonably (but mistakenly) that when their local police departments report that drug arrests have doubled or tripled in a short period of time, the arrests reflect a surge in illegal drug activity, rather than an infusion of money and intensified enforcement effort."[62] To be sure, public opinion about crime hardened slowly in the 1980s and was never "overwhelmingly punitive." Even in tough-on-crime Alabama, judges overruled jury recommendations for life sentences in favor of the death penalty some one hundred times after 1976, suggesting that some governing elites were more "punitive" than the populace. Nor did poll-measured alarm about crime correlate with crime statistics: "Ironically, the public began to identify crime as a leading problem in the mid-1990s, just as the crime rate was dramatically receding."[63] Still, the alarm sounded by Reagan and amplified by others had its effect.

For politicians, too, Reagan's rhetoric had an impact. They rarely questioned the aptness of his war language, and they felt political pressures similar to those exerted in the Cold War. Appearing "soft" on crime seemed as dangerous as appearing "soft" on communism once had been. Politicians feared getting caught out on the crime issue or saw the chance to one-up the president on it, just as they had regarding communism. The draconian antidrug bill that passed the House by a 392–16 vote in 1986 provoked panic and fear among Democrats. As *Newsweek* reported, "The drug bill was 'out of control,' said Democratic Rep. Dave McCurdy of Oklahoma. 'But of course I'm for it.'"[64] The keystone initiative by Congress in the war on drugs, formulated amid the crack scare, the 1986 Anti–Drug Abuse Act (soon echoed in actions by many state legislatures) turned federal law further away from rehabilitation to punishment, established new mandatory minimum sentences, and included a kitchen sink of other measures. Most legislators felt eager to support it, or at least helpless to resist.

The Reagan administration and Congress advanced the militarization of crime control substantively as well as rhetorically. Action, bounty, and resources accompanied their words. Some state and local officials mistrusted the federal push into local law enforcement that came with Reagan's war on drugs, reflecting the friction that is commonplace among American policing agencies. Among other things, they feared that the feds would hog the limelight, intrude on their autonomy, or divert local forces from more pressing crimes. The solution was "a massive bribe offered to state and local law enforcement by the federal government," as Michelle Alexander puts it, perhaps too baldly. "Incentives" would be the polite word. But bribery was the effective result, if not always the conscious intent. That process had precursors before the Reagan years, but it mushroomed during his administration and expanded even further after it. In 1984 Congress allowed federal law enforcement agencies to seize and use assets from forfeitures, which drug cases increasingly featured, and permitted state and local agencies to retain "up to 80 percent of the assets' value." That was the baldest bribe of all. Federal grant money, Pentagon intelligence and technical support, and formidable firepower found their way to states and localities—planes, copters, weapons in the thousands. As a retired New Haven police chief later commented, "I was offered tanks, bazookas, anything I wanted."[65]

SWAT teams and militarized policing also gained sanction from an erosion of constitutional safeguards against no-knock and warrantless entry, use of dubiously obtained evidence, and seizure of assets without trial. That erosion predated and outlasted Reagan's presidency, and it was the product of Supreme Court and other judicial decisions. But Reagan's administration often prepared the briefs and supported the legislation eroding those safeguards, sometimes with Democrats racing to join them. Democratic senators Daniel Patrick Moynihan and Joe Biden helped shape a 1982 crime bill, passing the Senate 95–1, that included provisions such as expanding the federal government's power to seize assets in drug cases.[66] Court decisions usually deployed legalese, not militarized language. They nonetheless played a powerful permissive role, widening the path on which militarized policing could operate. As one D.C. official put it, "In a war . . . we must give up some rights in order to recapture the streets."[67]

Beyond the White House: "These Guys Get into the Real Shit"

Beyond Reagan, other developments showed the thickening enmeshment of crime-fighting with war-fighting. Those developments advanced during the Reagan-Bush years but also outlasted their presidencies. Neither the White House, nor Congress, nor a compliant national media alone made them happen. They bubbled up from below even as they trickled down from above, as demonstrated by the spectacular rise (and dispiriting outcome) of military-style boot camps for juvenile and young adult offenders. Reagan and Bush never mentioned boot camps publicly, and the federal government had little role in their initiation. With almost no advance planning or pertinent research, Georgia and Oklahoma opened the first such programs in 1983, and Louisiana followed in 1985. But as juvenile crime rates rose, boot camps, especially for young drug offenders, came on fast in the late 1980s and early 1990s, basking in "the bright spotlight of instant celebrity status," a phenomenon few scholars note.[68]

In criminal justice policy, little is entirely new. Boot camps' antecedents included the rural work camps for inmates that California and other states maintained, and the New Deal's army-run Civilian Conservation Corps. But CCC camps were different. Voluntarily entered by recruits, they were designed to keep participants out of trouble rather than rescue them from it, and they were also dedicated to large national purposes (economic recovery, improvement of the natural landscape). In contrast, boot camps were explicitly punitive and more broadly beneficial (repairing roads, collecting trash) only at the margins. Another precedent for boot camps was indirect: the practice by judges, prosecutors, and social workers of allowing young offenders to join the armed forces rather than do jail time. As the armed forces shrank and became choosier and judges' discretion diminished, that option dwindled. Boot camps were an alternative. And like much else, they were distinctly American. The United States was "the forerunner of penal innovations like boot camps for younger offenders, electronic monitoring, and supermax prisons," Marie Gottschalk notes.[69]

Boot camps became fashionable because of hazy memories and vague assumptions about how military service had straightened out troubled youth and nourished their robust, useful citizenship. Those assumptions were embedded in a long tradition of Hollywood films, revived in the 1982 Richard Gere vehicle *An Officer and a Gentleman*, and they had guided Johnson, Moynihan, and others in the 1960s. Indeed, there was a whiff of the old Moynihan report in boot camp proponents' belief that stern male authority would undo the damage done by effeminizing, matrifocal family systems. It was no coincidence that boot camps first arose in southern and border states, where control of presumably undisciplined black youth remained an issue for many whites (as it often did elsewhere as well), and where some black military veterans also extolled the camps' virtues. Those assumptions about military service persisted even when social science research called them into question. As Georgia Democratic governor Zell Miller's spokesperson put it in 1993 regarding one analysis, "We don't care what the study thinks." Georgia would continue with boot camps. Miller was, after all, proud of how marine boot camp at Parris Island had taken him out of an "unstructured environment" and "helped [him] tremendously." "Nobody can tell me from some ivory tower that you take a kid, you kick him in the rear end, and it doesn't do any good," he declared, indicating how boot camp advocacy echoed the era's other tough-love impulses, such as child spanking. New York Democratic congressman Charles Schumer said much the same thing, only more gently.[70]

But military service differed greatly from criminal boot camp. It was an obligation, undertaken voluntarily or under conscription. In turn, it conferred rights and entitlements, some for life, on those who survived with honorable discharges. Boot camp conferred no rights and entitlements, unless avoidance of imprisonment counted, and it provided little or no access to continuing state support and benefits, and little if any of the respect often accorded veterans. Military service mixed dysfunctional youth in with more functional enlistees. Boot camp isolated the dysfunctional together with one another.

Boot camps rode a wave of popular fascination with the military model and the martial past. Quasi or faux camps came into vogue in the 1990s and later: fitness and weight-loss boot camps ("Train like a Marine, with real Marines. Become a Warrior," advertised a New York "Warrior Fitness Boot Camp"), tough-love private academies and programs for troubled youth, and eventually Christian boot camps, culinary boot camps, and boot camps for the digitally challenged, for playwrights, for the retired, and for a host of other constituencies. By this point "boot camp" was more a faddish metaphor than an operating mode. But the attraction to the military model—submission to authority, stripping away the old self to build a new one—was widespread, at least as a marketing tool if not as actual experience. For some organizations, the connection to the military went beyond boot camp. The Elijah Generation later offered a "life-changing Christian boot camp" in which "Some Train for the Army of God" and "Some Train for the Marines."[71] Alongside the boot camp craze, the historical reenactment of war on Civil War battlefields and elsewhere, though hardly new, took off in the 1980s, just as Hollywood films about past and prospective wars enjoyed a revival. While the armed forces were slowly withdrawing from a central place in American life, the impulse to find substitutes like boot camps swelled.

The boot camp craze had a marvelously diverse appeal. It attracted liberals and "save-the-children advocates" seeking "any alternative to juveniles serving hard time," as well as "crime-weary voters" eager for cheap and effective solutions. It appealed to tough-on-crime types who liked the camps' "command-and-control military setting," to veterans engaged in "nostalgic reflections," and even to offenders who might "welcome 'one more chance' to avoid a traditional prison term" or find the martial mode attractive. ("We do everything the Marines do, except stuff with guns," as one inmate put it.) Boot camps, after all, offered "the Marine Method," all the more so since military vets dominated their staffs. As Senator Joe Biden argued in 1993, boot camps would make nonviolent offenders "run, jog, do pushups, sweat their little ears off," and "make sure they actually understand they are paying a price for the crime they committed." Thus boot camps, as imagined, reconciled the rising punitive impulse in American life with the lingering rehabilitative ideal. Hence no consensus emerged about whether the camps were desirable for their toughness (as opposed to prisons) or their leniency (shorter stays with rehabilitation a goal). Here was "something for everyone," one scholar argues. Boot camps seemed to hold the promise that "if widely divergent, rough-around-the-edges military recruits could be transformed into the fine-tuned precision of obedient soldiers, surely the untamed products of urban wilderness could benefit from a similar immersion."[72]

While boot camps offered an eye-catching but minor use of the military model, SWAT teams were a more long-standing, widespread, and impactful example of what critics called "the militarization of American policing."[73] Washington's role in funding and promoting SWAT policing was also more sustained and paramount, even though presidents paid little public attention to SWAT teams. According to one scholar, "Overall activity by paramilitary police units—as measured by total number of 'call-outs'—quadrupled between 1980 and 1995."[74] By the 1990s, 90 percent of cities with more than 50,000 inhabitants had SWAT teams, as well as some smaller towns, resulting in "militarizing Mayberry," as Peter Kraska put it.[75]

SWAT teams expanded far beyond the big-city police forces that pioneered them. They were adopted by county sheriffs and state police forces, and by countless federal agencies, ranging from the improbable (the Department of Education) to the predictable (the Border Patrol and the FBI, with SWAT teams at all of its fifty-six field offices). To be sure, not all SWAT units were alike. "SWAT" was a term of fashion, a glamorizing label, not a single form. Nor were all SWAT team members ("Swatters," the press sometimes dubbed them) the gun-toting warriors of popular imagery. As in most armed forces units, some had duties as medics, drivers, computer operators, negotiators, dog handlers, chaplains, and the like. And some policing units functioned as SWAT teams without a SWAT label—the acronyms mushroomed along with the units themselves—while the influence of SWAT policing extended beyond its official units, shaping the styles and tactics of regular policing. The original LAPD model of the late 1960s had morphed into many forms. At the same time, those many forms underline how far-reaching, covering so many institutional locales, the "militarization of policing" became.

As that happened, a predictable paraphernalia of cultural and political work championed the cause. *SWAT* magazine was established in 1981, for example, and SWAT teams peppered innumerable movies and TV crime shows in the 1980s and after, with *S. W. A. T.* the movie (2003) taking off from the briefly offered TV show of the 1970s. Hollywood's turn to big action films provided numerous opportunities to feature SWAT teams. "Reality" television jumped on the bandwagon in the 2000s: *Dallas SWAT* (A&E) began its three seasons in 2006, also spawning *Detroit SWAT* and *Kansas City SWAT*. A river of online SWAT-oriented games for kids or childish adults to play emerged as well. "Help innocent people and kill terrorists. Survive till the end of the time and rescue the hostages," ran the come-on for the simply named game "SWAT Team."[76] Media treatments usually valorized SWAT units, but even when they did not, they helped normalize their action as a familiar, even commonplace, aspect of American life. Given the media and political atmosphere, one did not have to like SWAT teams to gain a weary sense that they were an irreversible part of American policing.

Why did SWAT teams proliferate in the 1980s and 1990s? Not because of the circumstances that initially justified them, for the urban and campus confrontations of the Vietnam era subsided in the United States and most Western countries. But other forms of disorder, sometimes violent and criminal, persisted or arose, such as drug trafficking and right-wing paramilitarism, and these provided fresh justifications for the SWAT approach. Institutional investment was a key motor of expansion and proliferation. Expensive to maintain, SWAT units were hard to justify if confined to rare, sensational events ("We can't have them like firemen sitting in a firehouse waiting for something to happen," an FBI official explained in 1982).[77] So their members often had other duties, and their units were brought into more routine operations— participating in drug busts, intervening in domestic disputes, serving warrants in dangerous situations, and even enforcing civil regulations and misdemeanor laws. In turn, normalization justified more SWAT teams, the line of reasoning being "Look at how much use they are getting." The war on drugs did much to buttress that thinking, which also drove up costs further.

Then, too, that was where the money was. State governments and the feds would help pay for SWAT teams more readily than they would for beat cops. The biggest pump primer was the 1994 federal law that funded Clinton's campaign promise to put 100,000 more cops onto American streets. The rhetoric of "100,000 more" evoked street cops— the phrase "Cops on the Beat" was enshrined in the language of the sprawling 1994 act. But much of the money flowed to special units, while local agencies sometimes proved adept at tapping federal grants for neighborhood improvement and other purposes to fund SWAT teams. Changes in asset forfeiture laws and regulations made SWAT policing a self-perpetuating machine. Especially in drug cases, state and local agencies could get a slice of assets seized in joint federal-local busts, with the money in turn often used to fund SWAT equipment and operations rather than the police agencies' general budgets. As

President Bush boasted publicly in 1989, "Another shining example of Federal and State cooperation: the seizure and forfeiture of assets from drug dealers. State agencies that cooperate in drug cases will share the benefits from the sale of yachts, planes, and cars used in drug deals." Perhaps one precedent was the seizure of enemy property in war, for as Bush drug "czar" William Bennett said in 1990, "It's a funny war when the 'enemy' is entitled to due process of law and a fair trial." Such policies, according to Radley Balko, were "forging yet another tie between the escalating drug war and hypermilitarized policing."[78]

With money came guns. Dating from the 1960s, the Pentagon practice of supplying police agencies with surplus military equipment expanded. By the end of the Reagan years, it came complete with an 800 number that sheriffs and police chiefs could call and a Pentagon catalog they could peruse.[79] And just as in the Cold War, when branches of the armed forces nervously tried to copy one another or the Soviets, "a kind of masculinity-infused arms race between police agencies" developed.[80] Predictably, private companies spotted a new gravy train, as the German arms manufacturer Heckler & Koch did through subsidiaries that supplied and trained SWAT teams. ("The HK 'SWAT Team' won't be coming to a crack house near you. But they are the best equipped 'team' out there," it boasted in the mid-1990s.)[81] Sensational crimes were cited to cultivate support for SWAT teams, like the 1999 Columbine school shooting, when a unit arrived forty-five minutes after the first shots were fired. As an Associated Press story claimed, "After the tragedy, police across the country developed 'active-shooter' training. It calls for responding officers to rush toward gunfire and step over bodies and bleeding victims, if necessary, to stop the gunman—the active shooter—first."[82]

SWAT-like forces were also an international phenomenon. From the 1970s onward, nearly every country capable of doing so acquired the rough equivalent of SWAT teams. The units' appeal cut across almost every geographical and ideological divide of the post–Cold War world, from Greece to Canada, from Malaysia to Kuwait, from Switzerland to China. For equipment, examples, and tactics, nations learned about, borrowed from, or traded with one another, as the United States did from Israel and West European nations after the bloody 1972 Munich Olympics. At least as justified, SWAT teams responded to the multiple forms of disorder and violence that arose late in the Cold War and after, from the domestic strife and skyjackings of the 1960s through international terrorism and drug trafficking during and after the 1970s. As such, they stepped in as older forms of maintaining order, from conventional policing to welfare systems to conscription to the Cold War itself, faltered. As in the United States, SWAT units helped constitute a new state built on top of the old one, which was apparently discredited and downsized. To a degree, the militarization of policing was nearly global.

Accordingly, it prospered through international conduits of commerce, promotion, and politics that mirrored those within the United States, with a similar valorization of the muscled, armored male body and ego. The SWAT Round-Up International competition in Orlando, Florida, began in 1984. By then, it seemed to observers that "for the first time in history, soldiers and policemen from different societies [had] more in common with each other than the societies from which they come." By the twenty-first century, SWAT teams from much of the world were assembling for annual Warrior Competitions at the U.S.-backed King Abdullah II Special Operations Training Center in Jordan. They strutted their stuff, bonded with (and kept secrets from) one another, and eyed wares peddled by the companies using the competition as an arms bazaar, at what the *New York Times Magazine* labeled "Sleep-Away Camp for Postmodern Cowboys."[83]

Meanwhile, the effectiveness of SWAT teams was hard to monitor. Penologists could measure some dimensions of crime-fighting—recidivism rates for various forms of incarceration, for example—with considerable precision. But SWAT teams operated in so many forms, with so many shifting uses, in so many institutional and geographic settings, and with only a smudgy line between their operations and normal policing, that measurement of their utility was difficult. What would the control group be, and who would run the risk of operating it? The very notion that SWAT teams dealt with the exceptional rather than the routine compounded the challenge of measurement. And just as ICBMs in the Cold War did something presumably immeasurable by deterring nuclear aggression, SWAT units presumably did something unquantifiable by deterring criminals. The lives presumably saved by SWAT policing could hardly be measured. Criminologists, politicians, citizens, advocacy groups, angry libertarians, and others protested, but with anecdotes and incidents, not statistics. And the populations most impacted by SWAT action, such as minorities in drug-war zones, were largely powerless to resist.

Above all, the SWAT phenomenon fed on the same fondness for military models of crime-fighting that buttressed the boot camp craze, the war on drugs, and much else. SWAT teams were not hapless cops on the beat, but soldiers in a war on crime, looking more like servicemen than cops, and analogized to and lionized as warriors. Swatters often described themselves that way for the media, which in turn usually accepted the analogy without question. As one Vietnam veteran and D.C. SWAT team member put it in 1988, antidrug operations were "a lot like combat situations," and the *Washington Post* added, "These days, the battlegrounds are not Southeast Asian jungles but the streets, alleys and apartment houses of the nation's capital."[84] Gun sellers bluntly spelled out the connections between elite soldiering and elite policing, as did the advertising pitch to SWAT police for the Heckler & Koch MP5: "This weaponry will distinguish you, just like the revered Navy Seals, as an elite soldier in the war on drugs."[85]

SWAT policing not only changed police practice, it changed the type of men attracted to policing, in turn further changing practice. Although evidence was more anecdotal and circumstantial than statistical, it made a good case that SWAT policing attracted men who liked war, or at least playing at it. Swatters often mingled with military personnel. One 1990s survey showed that nearly half of police departments had their SWAT teams "training on a regular basis 'with active-duty military experts in special operations,'" with some of those "experts" the "folks who have come right out of the jungles of Central and South America." "These guys get into the real shit," a SWAT commander indicated.[86] New Haven's former police chief complained at the end of the 1990s about "a mind-set that you're not a police officer serving a community, you're a soldier at war." As he worried, "If you think everyone who uses drugs is the enemy, then you're more likely to declare war on the people."[87]

Peter Kraska's ethnographic work with SWAT teams confirmed such impressions, as he observed cops in combat fatigues, spotted a "techno-warrior" image in training sessions, and heard one trainer comment, "Most of these guys like to play war; they get a rush out of search-and-destroy missions instead of the bullshit they do normally."[88] Many were military veterans, strengthening the tie between combat and police work. And with the armed forces shrinking, more tech-oriented, more female, and free from extended war making before 2001, SWAT policing provided an alternative for those seeking macho military adventure. So, too, did paramilitarism, whose growth roughly paralleled that of SWAT policing in the 1980s and early 1990s, for those unqualified for police work or too alienated from the state to pursue it.[89]

To be sure, generalization is risky, for Swatters differed from one another in backgrounds and duties. So, too, did the cohorts of veterans who entered SWAT or other police work. With little U.S. war making before 2001, most ex-servicemen were not combat veterans or even former members of combat units (they might have driven trucks, repaired tanks, handled computers, served as nurses). Veterans after 9/11 were more likely to have had combat experience, even those not in combat units. Still, by the 1980s and 1990s, SWAT policing attracted recruits whose expectations and training differed from those of cops who signed up in 1955 or 1960.

SWAT teams also sustained a masculine image of policing and a male preserve for police just when women were entering law enforcement. (In 1971, 1.7 percent of the nation's police officers were women, but by 2016 over 13 percent were women.[90] The National Association of Women Law Enforcement Executives was founded in 1995.) Women could serve on SWAT teams, but few did, and the public image of SWAT teams in news photos, TV shows, movies, and online content overwhelmingly showcased men, usually stern faced and heavily armed. Women might join the ranks, ran the implicit message, but the law enforcement elite would remain manly and male, just as elite military units usually did.

"SWAT" carried connotations of effectiveness and precision that echoed beyond the arena of policing. As President Clinton commented, "Pension laws . . . are now so utterly complicated that you need a SWAT team of lawyers and accountants to help you fill out the forms and comply with the rules."[91] Members of these teams were the ones who got the job done. As in the boot camp fad, groups far removed from SWAT policing nonetheless traded on the image associated with it: SWAT was the acronym for retired business consultants (Seniors with Amazing Talent).[92] To deal with savings-and-loan failures in the late 1980s, the Resolution Trust Corporation deployed SWAT (Settlement Workout Asset Teams) cadres.[93] In the 1990s, a Virginia swim team was named SWAT (the Southwest Aquatic Team).[94]

Not surprisingly, the language of war pervaded public talk about SWAT teams. It was sometimes employed to criticize their use and more often used to justify it, but in any event, such language placed SWAT in that category of war. In California, originator of SWAT units in the 1960s and epicenter of their later spread, Governor Pete Wilson boasted regarding a new interagency SWAT unit, "California has never seen an army the likes of this."[95] In Fresno, a city hard hit by both crime and SWAT action—raids there might snatch seventy-five or one hundred people in one night—a police spokesperson simply declared, "It's a war." Meanwhile, Fresno's police chief announced he was sending in the "cavalry," a term resonant of earlier wars against a nonwhite population,

Native Americans.[96] The city's district attorney there offered a graphic comparison to the Balkan conflicts in disintegrating Yugoslavia, insisting that "the only difference between the war in Sarajevo and the gang-banging in Fresno was the lack of rocket launchers in the latter."[97] As a Fresno SWAT member wrote in *Police* magazine, "The streets of Fresno have become a war zone for cops."[98]

Such language came easily from SWAT units because SWAT duty appealed especially to military veterans and their members sometimes trained with military units.[99] Meanwhile, in the 1990s special ops military units sometimes engaged in antiterrorism training by having their helicopters descend unannounced on "targets" in cities like Charlotte and Houston. The copters would arrive at night and with guns firing (blanks), frightening residents in what Charlotte's mayor described as "almost like a blitzkrieg operation."[100] Americans who imagined UN "blue helmets" landing to take over the nation had the source wrong but were not altogether paranoid, for helicopters of their own nation were circling above them. There were indeed many plausible ways to connect SWAT policing to war.

SWAT operations went forward against a broad range of targets, from presumed terrorist groups, to abortion clinic bombers, to right-wing militias. Still, insofar as operations were normalized and driven by the war on drugs, they hit minorities hardest, as draconian police action usually does. They bore down not only on African Americans, but also on Latinos, Southeast Asians, and others who were the biggest minority or majority (as in much of California), or the group seen as most engaged in drug and gang actions. In an egregious case in 1990, a heavily armed SWAT team swooped down in a drug raid on a Chapel Hill, North Carolina, neighborhood. "Even amidst the military frenzy the courtesy of the old south prevailed: whites were allowed to leave the area, while more than a hundred African Americans were searched," though none were prosecuted.[101]

To be sure, nonwhites frightened by crime, whether working individually or in neighborhood and advocacy groups, sometimes hailed the arrival of the SWAT cavalry. But they often recoiled once operations ensued. The toll mounted for victims of SWAT policing—those killed, injured, rendered homeless, or deeply scarred as teams hit the wrong house or went out of control. As one police official commented, recalling a 1987 drug bust gone wrong, "God knows how many other times we scared the bejusus out of innocent people."[102] Not a few police officials also worried about the risks posed to Swatters themselves by their no-holds-barred tactics: In no-knock raids, inhabitants had no time to figure out whether it was police, rival gangs, or criminal invaders busting through the door and might open fire or, in their efforts to flee, unleash wild police fire.

The notorious day-scare scandals of the Reagan-Bush years further revealed the hyperbolic quality of American crime-fighting. Starting in 1983, the McMartin Preschool case in Manhattan Beach, California, saw prosecution of the school's owner and teachers on the basis of wild stories coaxed from children as repressed memories recovered by parents and therapists. Defendants were accused, as *Newsweek* uncritically reported, of "sodomy, rape, oral copulation and fondling," of "child pornography and prostitution," of having "terrorized their young charges into silence with threats by example—mutilating pet rabbits or squeezing to death young birds," and even of slaughtering a horse in front of students to shut them up. The fantastical nature of many of the alleged deeds did not keep the case from going forward, with sensational and credulous media coverage, though the charges eventually fell apart. ("No sacrificed babies, no mutilated corpses, no remains of sacrificed animals were ever discovered," nor "any corroborating evidence of satanism," Roger Lancaster reports. Nor could "an archaeological team funded by Gloria Steinem" find the alleged "underground tunnels and dungeons.") Initiated in 1989, the Little Rascals Day Care Center case in Edenton, North Carolina, also presented fantastical and inconsistent charges in a more tense setting where virtually all the accused and the accusers knew one another and their children. The charges yielded convictions, including twelve consecutive life terms for Robert Kelly, that kept people in prison for years before reversals came. Similar cases preceded elsewhere, part of the era's "sex panic."[103]

Rhetoric amid that panic usually sidestepped the language of war. Sex itself, after all, generated its own supercharged language about predatory evil, and the initial arrest of day-care defendants did not entail the militarized policing seen in other arenas (a "global dragnet"[104] for the day-care defendants' nonexistent porn collections came later). But the language of war did creep in. Asked whether Edenton would recover from a case that had torn the town apart, the mayor replied, "Hell, we recovered from the Civil War, from World War II," and "Yeah, I think we'll recover from this."[105] As the Edenton legal case unraveled, *Newsweek* placed it within "the war against child abuse," as it subtitled its cover story, regretting the "fever pitch" over such abuse that it had helped provoke.[106]

More importantly, the sex panic inflamed many of the conditions that made war seem the appropriate mode of action: the belief that the criminal mind could do almost anything and that children are inno-cents vulnerable to the most horrific crimes. And the sex panic estab-lished a template of prosecution and sentencing that worked its way into the treatment of other alleged criminals—corner cutting by zealous prosecutors (the children must be protected), relaxed standards of evi-dence (child victims would be doubly victimized if they had to testify), draconian restrictions on release and residence after felons served their sentences, elaborate measures of electronic surveillance. As Roger Lan-caster summarizes the legacy, "Panic becomes the norm, duty, law."[107] Presidents were not immune from feeling, or at least exploiting, such panic.

Bush, Punisher in Chief

Certainly, Bush was not immune. The aura of moderation and prudence that later hung over his presidency, especially compared to that of his son, obscured his sharp edges on crime, and his postpresidential recollections largely airbrushed away his record and rhetoric on crime.[108] He did at times promote a benign image: "Each of us can make this a kinder and gentler nation just by the way we treat one another each day," he advised Americans on January 30, 1989, repeating a formulation made famous in his GOP nomination speech the previous summer.

But George H. W. Bush had a taste for the political style of Rich-ard Nixon, under whom he had cut some of his political teeth. He had forged his career in Texas, which "reigns supreme in the punishment business," as Robert Perkinson puts it.[109] Bush came to the presidency in part by exploiting a racialized crime politics. His campaign pitches, test-driven before focus groups "monitored electronically and by observation through one-way mirrors,"[110] flogged his opponent, Massa-chusetts governor Michael Dukakis, for opposing the death penalty and supposedly letting a black convicted murderer, Willie Horton, be fur-loughed from prison to commit armed robbery, assault, and rape. Bush had inherited and played a role in Reagan's crime policies. And he had no clear plan to chart a course much different from his predecessor's. With Bush's presidency, writes one scholar, "for the first time since the start of the cold war, Americans found an evil to substitute for commu-nism: drugs."[111] Actually, Reagan had already found that substitute, but his former vice president was happy to follow suit. Bush quickly found the occasion to combine tough-on-crime politics with the militarized assertiveness of America's foreign policy. For him, waging war on crime really did mean waging war. "So, when I talk about a war on drugs, I mean more than a rhetorical war," as he put it soon after taking office.[112]

Only a hint of that came during his inaugural address, an open-hearted celebration of "democracy's big day" and "a Thousand Points of Light." But crime was one of the few issues Bush specifically mentioned: "There is crime to be conquered, the rough crime of the streets." Bush thus reiterated Reagan's assertion that the only crime that mattered was "rough crime," not the white-collar version, though Attorney General Richard Thornburgh did prosecute some figures in the savings-and-loan scandal of the late 1980s. Bush soon made it clear that he intended "to escalate the war against drugs" because "the war must be waged on all fronts," as drug "czar" William Bennett was eager to do.[113]

Like Reagan, Bush was fond of war analogies. If state and local police "represent the infantrymen" in the war on drugs, then DEA agents, he told them, "are something like the Special Forces, the Green Berets." He then threw in analogies to World War II and other "battlefields." Regarding drugs, Bush told state legislators the next day, "It's a war, and it's going to last for years. And perhaps we should take inspiration from a nation at war almost 50 years ago. As Britain faced an adversary that tested the courage and character of its people, Winston Churchill vowed never to surrender. And in today's wars against the pushers, we must draw from these same deep wells of national purpose to summon the spirit of defiance." Since "no war was ever won with two dozen generals acting independently," Bush chose "Bill Bennett to be the commanding general in the drug war" in this "life-and-death struggle against a deadly enemy." If, as one scholar claims, Bennett "pushed him [Bush] to go faster on the issue [of drugs] than he ever wanted to go," Bush expressed no reluctance in his public statements.[114] His rhetoric followed Reagan's playbook—it was so familiar as to be commonplace. Bush meant it literally when he spoke of a war on drugs. That March he approved the use of National Guard forces to help local law enforcement in twelve states enforce drug laws.

Bush accordingly insisted, even more than Reagan, that crime-fighters and drug agents were like soldiers in a war, their lives similarly endangered. He claimed that "it used to be unthinkable to shoot a cop" (this would have been news to earlier generations of law enforcement officers) but "no longer," especially for "narcotics agents . . . targeted by criminals armed with a staggering array of battlefield weaponry." By 1989 their total deaths (many involving no direct contact with criminals) were 30 percent fewer than they had been in the peak years of 1930 and 1974, even though larger numbers were now serving. (Other occupations, from logging to fishing to roofing, had higher casualty rates.) "Undercover narcotics agents," Bush told Orange County officers, "are the unsung heroes in this war, risking your lives almost every single day behind enemy lines." As he spoke, he handed over $10 million, "the bounty of defeated drug criminals," to the local sheriff.[115]

At times Bush suggested that victory in the drug war would be a tribute to those dead or embattled soldiers, a victory owed them for the sacrifices they made, much as victory in America's troubled wars, from Vietnam to Iraq, was justified as the debt owed to the fallen. "I am announcing today—and there is no more fitting place than right here," he told the audience for the 1989 Peace Officers Memorial Day, "a comprehensive new offensive for combating violent crime—for Eddie Byrnes, for every officer we honor here today, and for America."[116] Bush was the first president to attend the Washington observance of Peace Officers Memorial Day, initially proclaimed by John Kennedy, and every president after Bush through Obama did so. Under Bush, the heroization of police, the militarization of their image, and their elevation as the decisive voice on crime proceeded. The punitive turn was accelerating on the public stage, as it did in less visible ways.

What was Bush's—or any president's—political investment in a war that was "going to last for years"? Although showy displays of progress would ensue, the fight against lawbreaking promised no quick victory, and perhaps no distant one as well. Of course, presidents calculate short-term advantage above all: Reagan's war on crime seemed to have worked for him politically, as it did for Bush in 1988. But they also calculate further ahead. Would fighting crime help reelect Bush in 1992, when the war that would "last for years" would still be going on? Making the investment trickier was the fact that in the twentieth century no president and his party had ridden war to long-term political success except for FDR, who died before his war concluded—not Wilson, Truman, Johnson, or Nixon. War is politically treacherous territory for presidents. Did Bush not think about those precedents, or did he regard this war as so different—not a "real" war—that it would defy the historical odds? Was he too caught up in the crime war's momentum and his World War II–borne sense of commanding leadership? Or was crime a leading agenda by default because he struggled with the "vision thing," as he put it, and had little else to offer? (As Bush's chief of staff, John Sununu, announced late in 1990, the president "doesn't need another single piece of legislation unless it's absolutely right. . . . In fact, if Congress wants to come together, adjourn, and leave, it's all right with us.")[117] Few scholars have addressed those questions.[118]

But one plausible answer involves a different political calculation, one about GOP politics. Distrusted or scorned by the rising, angry conservative Republicans eager to wage a culture war, Bush pursued his crime wars in part to placate them. He was, after all, up against the likes of presidential aspirant Pat Buchanan, a former Nixon aide fond of assailing gays, lesbians, and radical feminists. Buchanan declared "culture war" at the 1992 Republican National Convention. He celebrated the troops who swept into Los Angeles when riots erupted that spring over the acquittal of police officers who beat black motorist Rodney King, a beating videotaped for millions to see. In a racially charged climax to his convention speech, Buchanan said, "As those boys took back the streets of Los Angeles, block by block, my friends, we must take back our cities, and take back our culture, and take back our country."[119] It was a call to use military force to subdue crime.

Bush's crime politics were his way to wage a culture war without getting too far into the swamp of the specifics that mobilized conservatives—abortion, AIDS, religion, race. It was his big policy tent (along with being the self-styled "education president"). The war on crime had the added advantage that Democrats were unlikely to resist it; often, they pushed for more. And Bush's tough-on-crime stance shored up an exposed flank regarding his own possible wrongdoing, for he had never convincingly explained his role in the Iran-Contra affair and his association with Panamanian dictator Manuel Noriega. This plan brought him little lasting success in and beyond his party, but one can see why he tried it.

Beyond the insistent war language, Bush helped popularize a related language of "zero tolerance," a term with almost no currency before the 1990s.[120] Reagan was the first president to use the phrase, announcing a policy of "zero tolerance for illegal drugs" on May 18, 1988, and Bush used it often. Their use of the expression indicated its political roots in their "Just Say No" war on drugs. Regarding drugs, Bush pronounced before taking office, "Zero tolerance is becoming a national attitude, and one I mean to encourage."[121] "Zero tolerance" also derived from the "broken windows" argument formulated in the 1980s by James Q. Wilson and others. Tough enforcement against minor infractions, they claimed, would prevent major crimes and create a more orderly environment that itself would deter crime. New York mayor Rudy Giuliani implemented this stance, and it was echoed in policing in other countries as well. As with most of the era's criminal justice fads—boot camps, SWAT teams, supermax prisons—"broken windows" policing found little favor with legal and academic experts: it clogged the system with minor cases, diverted resources from major crimes, poisoned police relations with minority communities, and yielded no evident decrease in lawlessness.

That was neither here nor there for Bush and many others for whom "zero tolerance," a rhetorical snapshot of the "broken windows" theory, was more a moral and political stance than a crime-fighting technique. "Zero tolerance" communicated maximum intolerance for lawbreakers. For Bush, the phrase meant "quite simply, if you do crime, you do time," especially for drug offenses. "I want increased prison sentences for drug-related crimes and, yes, the death penalty for drug kingpins and those who commit these drug-related murders," he declared.[122] His administration argued that cracking down on minor infractions would help dry up demand for drugs, which remained unchecked by prosecution of big-time dealers.

Sometimes Bush hardly bothered to present his initiatives as designed to reduce or deter crime. He gestured to that possibility, pled for drug-free schools and a drug-free America, and supported rehabilitation for low-level users. But death for "drug kingpins" was more the vengeance they were due than a measure to deter them, and more federal prisons for offenders ensured their removal, not their rehabilitation. These were the proper moral stances to take, the proper acts of community indignation. In this regard, Bush was nearer than Reagan to the beating heart of the punitive turn, especially its conservative version. Punishment was a goal in itself, a way to satisfy the call for vengeance regardless of its consequences for crime rates. Bush "defined his executive power in the posture of a prosecutor more than any other previous chief executive of the United States," notes Jonathan Simon.[123] The forty-first president was not the nation's problem solver. He was the prosecutor who secured punishment, and sometimes the scold to Americans for not wanting it enough, at a moment when the prosecutor as political actor and cultural figure (television's *Law and Order* debuted in September 1990) was striding high.

Indeed, Bush had the wind behind his law-and-order sail in many ways. Crime rates approached or topped their post–World War II peaks, with an alarming spike in murder especially (although per capita rates of reported murders did not quite reach the peaks of the mid-1970s and around 1980).[124] If twenty years of more punitive measures had failed to reverse those rates, most politicians reasoned, or simply assumed, that more of those measures were needed. Bush was thus in step with prevalent policymaking and public opinion: death penalty executions rose sharply if erratically in the 1990s, the federal Death Penalty Act of 1994 soon expanded the federal crimes to which the death penalty might apply (though few federal executions took place), and poll-measured approval of the death penalty for murder reached its peak (far above its mid-1960s low) in 1994.[125]

More consequential measures soon arose. Washington voters instituted the a three-strikes-and-you're-out law in 1993, and California voters did the same with a harsher version in 1994. Given the size of California's incarcerated population, that measure had draconian effects. Bush was likewise in step with the steep upward trajectory in incarceration, which he promoted and which soared from over one million inmates in 1990 to nearly two million in 2000.[126] He was also in agreement with the rapid expansion of systems of electronic surveillance and control (the first court-approved use of electronic ankle monitors came in the 1980s). And he concurred with Democrats, who in their 1988 platform promised to "wage total war on drugs" through a national drug czar.[127]

Bush pulled together the strands of his stance on crime in a televised "Address to the Nation on the National Drug Control Strategy" on September 5, 1989. It was a telling marker of shifting agendas and Bush's priorities that he chose this topic for his first prime-time address. That staple of presidential messaging had previously been reserved for (apparently) grave national crises and initiatives—Kennedy addressed the nation during the Cuban Missile Crisis, Nixon spoke amid Vietnam and Watergate, Carter gave a speech concerning energy, and Reagan delivered remarks on the "Star Wars" missile defense system. No crisis spurred Bush's address, though he cited "the gravest domestic threat facing our nation." It was not as if nothing competed for his attention; he could have spoken about matters on which he was more surefooted, including the swift dissolution of communist rule in Eastern Europe and the knotty question of whether the Cold War's end might yield a "peace dividend." He instead chose crime.

The address was a curious affair. It started with Bush as national scold. "Who's responsible?" he asked. He answered by casting a wide net: "Let me tell you straight out—everyone who uses drugs, everyone who sells drugs, and everyone who looks the other way." Bush then moved quickly to a gimmick, holding up a bag of what he said was "crack cocaine seized a few days ago by Drug Enforcement agents in a park just across the street from the White House." To the president's embarrassment, it soon became public that DEA agents had entrapped a teenaged dealer into selling them the drug.

Bush subsequently moved through "four of the major elements of our strategy" to conquer drug use. Most of them were versions of

Reagan-era initiatives and thus so familiar that they hardly warranted public announcement: tougher enforcement and penalties as "we enlarge the criminal justice system across the board" with "more jails, more courts, more prosecutors"; a campaign abroad, especially in Colombia, to destroy drug traffickers; an alarmed and engaged citizenry who would act to protect children. The address also included a coded message about race; nowhere was illegal drug use "worse than in our public housing projects." Finally, the president issued a closing call to arms: "If we fight this war as a divided nation, then the war is lost. . . . Victory—victory over drugs—is our cause, a just cause." It was all over quickly. No soaring orator, Bush seemed awkward, and many observers judged the address a rather out-of-the-blue moment. But it recapitulated in prime time what he had been saying for months.

Bush followed up the speech with war when American forces invaded Panama on December 20, 1989. There, a tangled web of political realities prompted American action, or at least seemed to justify it. Dictator Manuel Noriega had once been a paid CIA agent (including when Bush was CIA director) and a U.S. Cold War ally. He had turned against his patron, and seemingly against his own people, by retaining power after an election the previous spring had apparently anointed a new Panamanian government. Two federal grand juries in Florida had indicted Noriega for drug trafficking in 1988. Moreover, his thugs had run amok against Panamanian opponents and U.S. personnel. Hovering over these particulars was the fate of the Panama Canal, due to pass to Panamanian control in 2000, though with U.S. forces kept nearby. Bush faced added pressure—though it is unclear how much he felt it— from being labeled a "wimp." Would he follow through on his tough talk about drug traffickers?

The ensuing invasion was a standard military action (with nearly 30,000 American military personnel involved, twenty-three of whom died). But it was also a giant SWAT raid against a drug trafficker, carried out as if the stateside version of the units had been enlarged and deployed abroad. When Noriega escaped immediate capture and holed up in the Vatican's diplomatic mission in Panama City, U.S. forces blasted rock'n'roll (the dictator reportedly hated it) and employed other psychological and diplomatic techniques to force him to surrender, as he did on January 3. Taken to Florida, Noriega was convicted on drug-related charges, initially sentenced to forty years, and later denied an appeal he made on the grounds that the trial had barred testimony about his CIA connections. Holding the odd dual legal status of prisoner of war and convicted felon, Noriega got unusually cushy treatment in his American prison, and he later did time in France after extradition from the United States. Meanwhile, he was the biggest felon yet captured in the history of SWAT policing, albeit seized by gentler tactics (the Vatican outpost was off limits) than when SWAT teams in the United States stormed, bulldozed, or teargassed places housing presumed felons.

Bush's televised announcement of the invasion made no mention of war or national security; he simply said he had "ordered U.S. military forces to Panama." The forty-first president resorted instead to a language of criminality long used to justify American interventions south of the border. Noriega's forces had "shot and killed an unarmed American serviceman; wounded another; arrested and brutally beat a third American serviceman; and then brutally interrogated his wife, threatening her with sexual abuse. That was enough." Among Bush's stated goals: to "combat drug trafficking" and "to bring General Noriega to justice in the United States."[128]

The long arm of U.S. law had reached far. Noriega's capture was an anomalous event insofar as it was the first and last time that a foreign leader was dragged off to an American court, rather than being left for punishment in his home country or by an international tribunal. But it was also a powerful sign that the punitive turn was reaching outward from the United States. Noriega's dual status as prisoner of war and convicted felon perfectly captured the meshing of crime-fighting and war-fighting. With war abroad defined as crime-fighting, while crime-fighting at home was defined as war, the distinction between the two realms faded further, while the rhetorical, legal, and operational feedback loops between them multiplied.

Bush soon waged a more old-fashioned war, the Gulf War that vanquished Iraqi dictator Saddam Hussein's forces that had invaded Kuwait. Although the Gulf War featured Bush's denunciations of Hussein's criminality, his administration's rhetoric harked back to World War II and Hitler, and to the appeasement that presumably had unleashed them both. "Iraq's unprovoked aggression is a throwback to another era, a dark relic from a dark time," Bush told the UN on October 1, 1990. The Panama invasion more accurately revealed the enmeshment of war-fighting and crime-fighting that the U.S. state was fostering.

When his poll numbers, soaring amid the Gulf War, then slumped badly, Bush grew desperate to regain his political footing in advance of the 1992 elections, so he trotted out anew the feedback loops between war-fighting and crime-fighting. "Peace in the world, it's fine, but it's not enough," he told a Utah audience in July. "If people don't feel safe in their own backyard, it doesn't seem to matter. What do you say to an elderly woman who watches the Berlin Wall fall on television right before her eyes but is afraid to walk into her neighborhood grocery store? What do you say to kids in our cities who hear of the Russians reducing nuclear weapons but then have to walk through a metal detector at school every single morning? What do you say to these Americans? You say, 'Enough is enough.'"[129] (His rhetoric echoed Ford's in 1975—"Peace on 10th Street in Sacramento is as important to the people who walk and work there as peace in the Sinai Desert.")

With these words, it was as if Bush was insisting that while the Cold War abroad was ending, a cold war at home against crime raged. He summoned victory in the Cold War and the Gulf War to argue that if reelected, he would bring the same spirit and unity that had prevailed in those wars to bear on problems like crime at home. Perhaps because this sort of analogizing was becoming long in the tooth, it did not result in victory when Bush ran against Democrat Bill Clinton and independent candidate Ross Perot. And the Gulf War had such a disheartening aftermath, with Hussein still in power delivering murder and mayhem to Shiites and Kurds, that invoking the conflict to instill confidence in Bush's war on crime could not end well. But if his specific analogies were dated or fraught, Bush kept the rhetorical feedback loops alive. Others would give them a fresher look.

It is easy to see the war metaphor as an airy, weightless thing, or an example of the silly, over-the-top rhetoric of American politics. While one can track and count its uses, a metaphor's influence resists quantification. But when it persists and gains traction through many sectors of society, as the war on crime did, a metaphor performs important work, making natural certain habits of mind, policy, and practice, while excluding other possibilities from consideration. The work of the war metaphor had less to do with the sincerity, calculation, or hypocrisy with which leaders offered it than with its repetition and resonance. That was especially so in the 1980s, when the invocation of war served many other purposes regarding abortion, AIDS, trade, and much else. Those functions of the war metaphor made its use regarding crime seem more unexceptional, unsurprising, but no less malign. As social scientists put it just after the Reagan era, "It takes little acumen to recognize how the metaphor of 'war'—with its emphasis on occupation, suppression through force, and restoration of territory—coincides naturally with the 'new science' of the police targeting and taking control, indeed ownership, of politically defined social spaces, aggregate populations, and social problems with military-style teams and tactics."[130]

That is to say that for many Americans—Reagan and Bush, embattled police chiefs, supercharged Swatters, greedy arms dealers, real and alleged criminals, even crime victims—the war on crime was not simply a metaphor. It seemed like war.

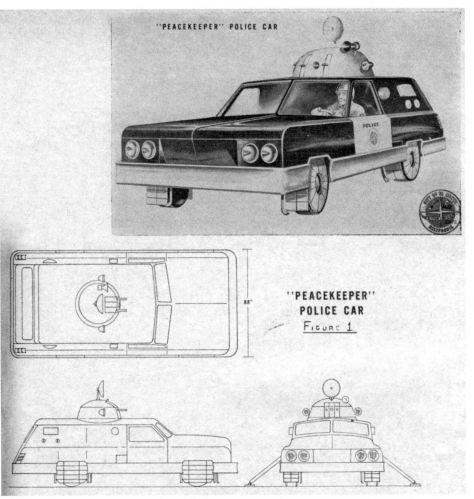

Figure 1. In the Vietnam era, efforts to militarize police equipment advanced, although "the Peacekeeper," designed by rocket maker Aerojet General in response to a federally funded competition, looks quaint in comparison to later equipment. ("The Peacekeeper," *Law and Order*, February 1968)

"Well, Charlie, how does it feel to be back in civvies?"

Figure 2. As suggested by this simple cartoon in the U.S. Army's magazine for its soldiers, readers were so familiar with efforts to turn Vietnam-era veterans into police that even an official publication could have fun with this recruitment. (Cartoon, *Soldiers*, June 1971)

Figure 3. Although he rarely talked about a war on crime, Bill Clinton often embraced warlike systems and settings. On March 1, 1992, Clinton, who was running in the Georgia primary, spoke at the Stone Mountain Boot Camp near the site of notorious white supremacy rallies. This picture features a jarring tableau of soldierlike black inmates fronted by white male politicians. (A.P. Photo/Greg Gibson)

Figure 4. In his challenge to some dimensions of mass incarceration, Barack Obama visited and spoke at a federal prison, the Federal Correctional Institution El Reno in Oklahoma. The visit garnered widespread media and political attention. (White House, 2015)

Figure 5. SWAT teams proliferated across the nation, and not only in big cities. Although not showing a team in action, this photo captures the rugged, ready-for-action, all-male look that even small-city SWAT teams presented. (East Brunswick Police Department, August 2017)

Figure 6. SWAT policing reached far into American life, even to children. In one of many efforts to introduce it to children, Cub Scouts Pack 632 hosted the Tampa FBI in 2019 and awarded the organization with its "Build a Hero" award. The Scouts "then had some fun trying out some cool #FBI gear," per the agency's Twitter account. (FBI Tampa, 2019)

5 THE SPRAWLING PUNITIVE TURN, 1993-2001

The Cold War's end ushered in the third major push to the punitive turn, following the convulsions of the Vietnam era and the crime wars of the Reagan-Bush era. Those earlier phases foreshadowed what happened in the 1990s, the redirection back home of America's militarized institutions and mentalities. But in the Reagan years, the Cold War still had constrained redirection. Its urgencies faded when East Germans clambered past the Berlin Wall in 1989, the Soviet Union disaggregated into Russia and other nations in 1991, and China inched toward market socialism. However, that era's massive accumulation of political, institutional, and imaginative structures geared to war did not vanish. These resources were hardly going to be just tossed away. Some remained within the domain of national security, but many—barracks and bases, personnel and weapons, politics and rhetoric, states of mind and state resources—redeployed to a growing war on crime, and the punitive turn sprawled more widely.

Few Americans foresaw that redeployment in 1989. The Cold War's end brought relief for many Americans, no little triumphalism—their superior systems had presumably won—and eager talk of a "peace dividend." But there were also old scores to be settled and new fears to be imagined. As the conservative patriarch Irving Kristol put it in 1993, "There is no 'after the Cold War' for me," given how "sector after sector of American life has been ruthlessly corrupted by the liberal ethos. . . . Now that the other 'Cold War' is over, the real cold war has begun."[1] The Cold War, now shorn of its former enemies elsewhere, came fully home. The "peace dividend" would go less to "peace" than to a more vigorous war on crime.

President Bill Clinton did little to restrain that process and much to abet it. In line with his hesitantly liberal politics, he sidestepped the rhetoric of a war on crime, but without the intention Carter had (and later Barack Obama would have) to tamp down or reverse the punitive turn or distribute its burdens more equitably. For "war," he substituted "prevention," but that rhetorical shift made little immediate difference. If anything, it made the war on crime more palatable by rendering it less obviously warlike. Meanwhile, the punitive turn was more than ever driven by forces beyond a president's direction, ones that connected the nation's war-fighting machinery to its crime-fighting regime in ever bigger and more complicated ways. Change came through grindingly slow institutional processes, not just high-profile laws and presidential pronouncements. Clinton usually promoted those processes through his eagerness to seize the crime issue and his smooth-talking ways.

Clinton, the Artful Policeman

Clinton's presidency widened the punitive turn even as it jettisoned much of the rhetoric that had justified it.[2] Running for president in 1992, Clinton adroitly managed issues of crime while other problems seemed to loom larger ("it's the economy, stupid!"). His January 1992 return to Arkansas as its governor to preside over the execution of a brain-damaged black murderer insulated him on the death penalty issue. His proposals to fund 100,000 more police and strengthen gun control helped him wriggle free of the tough-versus-soft-on-crime binary that had dominated politics, making prevention his calling card. Clinton "clearly," one scholar later wrote, met "the rhetorical requirement for stealing an issue from the opposition." To the surprise of contemporaries, he outpolled Bush on the crime issue, as he did Robert Dole in the 1996 campaign.[3]

Briefly but loquaciously, Clinton showed a fondness for the military model of crime-fighting by grandstanding about boot camps. Running in Georgia's primary in March 1992, Clinton visited the Stone Mountain Boot Camp, near the site of notorious white supremacy rallies. In an ill-staged tableau (either a "blunder" or a "deliberate subliminal signal"), he and four other "stern-faced white politicians in suits" posed in front of "row after row of prison garbed black inmates [a few were in fact white], stiff and silent at attention" (see figure 3).[4] The scene brought a scathing rebuke from another presidential contender, former California governor Jerry Brown, who thought the inmates "looked like a bunch of Willie Hortons," and who likened Clinton and Georgia senator Sam Nunn to "colonial masters."[5] But it did Clinton no harm insofar as he won the primary. His trip to Stone Mountain echoed Bush drug "czar" William Bennett's embrace of boot camps.[6] And it showcased the tough-on-crime-but-humane (or sometimes, just tough) stance Clinton would strike as president.

He became the first president to champion boot camps publicly—some sixty times in all, though often in passing—and he visited another camp, in Florida, while pushing federal efforts to fund 100,000 more police. Doing so reflected Clinton's effort to claim his affinity for all things military amid post–Cold War defense budget trims and uproar over his gays-in-the-military policy. Reauthorization in 1992 of the Juvenile Justice and Delinquency Prevention Act (1974) had provided for conversion of military bases into boot camps. Clinton also helped open the federal tap with the 1994 Violent Crime Control and Law Enforcement Act, which set aside $150 million to fund state camps, while the federal government instituted its own. But in plumping for the 1994 law, Clinton and his allies performed a classic bait and switch. They touted boot camps as an alternative to prison overcrowding and degradation (they would "give our children a way out of a life of crime and jail," Clinton preached on November 13, 1993). But to get a federal grant for boot camps under the 1994 law, a state had to have "increased the percentage of convicted violent offenders sentenced to prison" and increased the convicts' "average prison time."[7] Though sold as a way to decrease prison overcrowding, boot camps served Clinton as a rhetorical tool to increase prison populations. It was a nifty trick.

Clinton then fell silent about boot camps at mid-decade. They had served his political purposes, and meanwhile a General Accounting Office report, academic studies, and media stories offered dispiriting results about recidivism among boot camp graduates, who fared little if any better after release than former inmates of prisons.[8] Graduates of short stays, who often received little follow-up guidance, reentered "a world where drill instructors are often replaced by drug dealers, where secure confinement is replaced by self-control, and where marching in straight lines is replaced by hanging out on street corners."[9] Reports of inmate and staff abuse at camps, often hastily put together with ill-trained personnel, further tarnished camps' reputation. Many camps, which spread to nearly thirty states, then closed (the Federal Bureau of Prisons, which started boot camps later than many states, shut down its camps in 2005). Even at their peak, boot camps handled a small population of perhaps 7,000 daily, though rapid turnover (with stays as short as thirty days) made the total numbers served much larger. Even at the best camps, in states like New York, recidivism rates were discouraging. As a disillusioned Brooklyn Democratic assemblyman admitted in 1994, "No one should delude themselves that this boot camp, military drill discipline alone is going to straighten everybody out. I thought it would. A lot of us thought it would. But it doesn't."[10]

Still, the popular and political attention boot camps got outweighed their scale, and like most criminal justice innovations, this one persisted, aided by efforts to address the postcamp needs of offenders. (As of 2006, for example, the Cook County, Illinois, sheriff could boast low recidivism rates for his extended program.)[11] For some, the promise endured that boot camp discipline could turn wayward youth into responsible citizens. By the mid-1990s, however, Clinton had backed away from that promise.

Except for his flirtation with boot camps, Clinton tapped on the rhetorical brakes. He rarely used the phrases "war on crime" or "war on drugs" (and in turn, reporters rarely used those phrases in questions to him). As he put it on February 21, 1993, "The people of our country have elected politicians for years who have always talked tough about crime. It's sort of like being for motherhood and apple pie; you've got to be against crime. . . . But there are some things, you know, that work. Drug treatment works. Jobs work. And there are law enforcement strategies that work."[12] Though less forcefully than Carter, Clinton professed to understand crime as an economic and social problem as much as a moral one. Prevention was as important as punishment.

Beyond murder and mayhem, terrorism loomed as an issue, but Clinton and his press aides said little about the February 26, 1993, bombing of the World Trade Center, which killed six and injured many more. Nor did reporters press them hard for comment. In the attack's aftermath, Clinton conveyed reassurance, urged patience, and offered no language of war or anything rabble-rousing, though he did label the bombing "terrorism." Meanwhile, other issues—the implosion of Yugoslavia, aid to Russia, the decommissioning of military bases, the economy, health care, and gays in the military—hogged presidential and media attention. And despite rising crime rates, public opinion, at least as measured by polls, hardly pressed Clinton at the start of his presidency. "Only 7% of those polled identified crime as the nation's most important problem in June 1993," one analysis found, though that number spiked once Clinton and Congress gave crime big-time attention.[13] On crime, Clinton was driven not by public clamor but by his desire to outmaneuver Republicans and legitimize his presidency, all the more so after his other signature initiatives floundered and elicited savage attacks on his leadership.

Clinton outflanked Republicans and helped stoke public outcry about crime by championing passage of the 1994 Violent Crime Control and Law Enforcement Act, a bipartisan omnibus measure spearheaded by Democratic senator Joe Biden and signed by Clinton on September 13.

A "behemoth of a law,"[14] it poured money into the program to employ 100,000 new cops, expanded the federal crimes subject to the death penalty, allocated billions for prison building, provided new funding and prosecutorial powers for a host of federal agencies, "authorise[d] adult prosecution of those 13 and older charged with certain serious violent [federal] crimes," required state registries of violent sex offenders, established a "three-strikes-and-you're-out" rule in sentencing for certain federal crimes, funded boot camps, underwrote "community policing," added antiterrorism measures, incorporated a violence-against-women provision, and banned the manufacture of assault weapons.[15] Most of the bill expanded the Reagan-Bush agenda on crime. "The era of big government is over," Clinton soon declared,[16] but that was hardly the case when it came to crime-fighting. Indeed, it was no more the case for Clinton than it had been for his predecessors, who had offered similar thoughts about big government.

"Prevention" was Clinton's watchword. His January 25, 1994, State of the Union address pledged "to reduce violence and prevent crime," and the 1994 act included provisions like ones to address "at-risk youth." But the mantra of prevention did not extend to rehabilitation of convicts, or to caps on the rising prison population and reduction of race-based inequities. As one Clinton official commented, "You can't appear soft on crime when crime hysteria is sweeping the country. . . . Maybe the national temper will change, and maybe, if it does, we'll do it right later." Of course, the administration, by championing the act and a good deal else, helped stoke the very "hysteria" it now claimed to be trapped by. "By August 1994, a record high of 52% of those polled were most concerned about crime."[17]

In the long and talky run-up to passage of the 1994 bill, Clinton sidestepped war talk, as did Joe Biden ("I don't even like that phrase 'war on drugs'").[18] But such talk peppered congressional and media deliberations on the bill, through generic formulations ("Clearly this is a war which must be fought simultaneously on all fronts," announced Senator Strom Thurmond) and florid adaptations, often ones linking general or specific war zones abroad to those at home. As Democratic senator Ted Kennedy said, "The greatest threat we face is no longer overseas, but here on our streets at home, in every community in America." Supporting the bill, Democratic congresswoman Pat Schroeder argued, "We in America won the cold war and we have lost the war on crime." The political malleability of war talk was on display: it could be used to defend or denounce the bill, to support the assault weapons ban (as Schroeder did) or rail against it. Politicians compared killing on the streets of Sarajevo in the Bosnian War to killing on the streets of America. So, too, did hosts of television news shows: Tim Russert announced on NBC, "Our issues this Sunday morning: war, on the ground in Bosnia and war on crime in America." It was as if both countries were war zones. As telling as the particular uses of war talk was its casual ubiquity, the ready-made framework that war provided. Rare in Congress was an attack on that framework. Congressman Bernie Sanders offered one, then voted for the bill. The alternative language of Senator Mitch McConnell was to claim, "The brutality on our streets perhaps requires the literary skill of horror novelist Stephen King."[19]

Members of the Congressional Black Caucus offered different language, seeking to pair crack-down-on-crime provisions with community improvement. Getting little of the latter but pushed by many black civic leaders, most of them signed on to the 1994 act reluctantly. The Reverend Jesse Jackson Sr., for one, would have none of it, condemning the bill as "criminal" and lamenting, "[When] Jim Crow was a wolf wearing wolf clothes, we were psychologically positioned to fight Jim Crow. But when Jim Crow goes to Yale [as Clinton had] or someplace and disguises his wolf instinct in sheep clothing," people are fooled.[20] As scholars later explained what happened, "Policy makers pointed to black support for greater punishment and surveillance, without recognizing accompanying demands to redirect power and economic resources to low-income minority communities. When blacks ask for *better* policing, legislators tend to hear more instead." Clinton's talk of prevention glided past the war talk without displacing it.[21]

But at a lavish September 13 signing ceremony for the 1994 Violence Act, the administration trafficked in war in softer ways. Building on Reagan/Bush stagecraft and making the old Oval Office signing ceremony (luminaries gathered, a few words spoken, pens handed out) look quaint, the extravaganza on the sun-drenched White House lawn had the look and sound of a patriotic event. A uniformed black female police officer sang the national anthem, a uniformed chaplain offered a prayer (especially for "officers killed in the line of duty"), and big American flags encircled officials and guests, many in police or military garb, and most of them white men. Vice President Albert Gore (on crutches) asserted, "Americans have always known what to do about crime." What they had "always known" was left vague but apparently included the assault weapons ban, three-strikes-and-you're-out laws for violent offenders, more police on the streets, and rapid prison building.

Talkative as usual, Clinton scorned a "system" that had long made "excuses for not punishing criminals and doing the job." Stressing that children were crime's most numerous victims as well as perpetrators, he invoked a mythical past when kids knew that punishment for misdeeds was "swift and certain." Clinton also offered his standard line about deterring lawbreaking. "This is about freedom," he concluded in emotive voice, a "freedom" from fear of attack not unlike the freedom that national defense presumably provided. Finally came the bill signing and handshaking as a military band played upbeat tunes. Making crime-fighting a quasi-patriotic duty, Clinton's stage managers tugged it back toward the arena of war that his words seemed to set aside, although the media mostly ignored the event's theatrics, concentrating on its politics.[22]

Tucked into the omnibus crime bill was a ban on use of federal Pell Grants for the education of prisoners, a telling indication of crime politics. Congressional conservatives had championed a ban since 1982, and North Carolina senator Jesse Helms and Texas senator Kay Bailey Hutchison helped lead the cause in 1994, by which time it had become a bipartisan effort. The Democrat-controlled House approved the ban in April by a 312–116 vote. Unlike many measures Congress approves, this one was not pushed by any well-funded interest group. Indeed, many corrections professionals and advocacy groups opposed it. Instead, the bill was a genuine will-of-Congress measure that reflected the punitive temper of the times. The 1994 Violence Act came after years of hyperbolic attacks on coddled inmates and on "country-club prisons" and "Club Feds," presumably luxurious prisons for the well-to-do and the well connected, places satirized in the slight movie comedy *Club Fed* (1990). The bill was accompanied by politicians' wild exaggerations of the Pell Grants spent on prisoners and wild claims that such grants deprived deserving students of funding, though the Pell funding mechanism prohibited such trade-offs (critics made little of the real abuse of prisoner Pell Grants by for-profit colleges and trade schools). Senators noted in 1993 the complaint of a Pennsylvania police officer that his daughter was denied a Pell Grant while prisoners got theirs. The officer quipped, "Maybe I should take off my badge and rob a store."[23] That many prisoner grantees were black went unmentioned, but that fact was hardly unknown.

Nothing signaled better than the Pell Grant ban that Americans, or at least their political leaders, saw imprisonment as a punitive mechanism providing no glimmer of rehabilitation, however much prison administrators still struggled to provide it. The ban was also another small step toward the privatization of government services, as it left private groups like the Bard Prison Initiative (and some state governments) to slowly pick up the slack on prisoner education. If Clinton objected, he bit his tongue—he wanted too much else in the omnibus bill to veto it over this measure. Soon he signed the 1996 Prison Litigation Reform Act, which sharply curbed prisoners' access to federal courts, as well as those courts' oversight of cruel or incompetent prison practices.

The bombing of the Oklahoma City Federal Building on April 19, 1995, cut deeper than the 1993 World Trade Center attack, eliciting Clinton's first use of the word "evil" in reference to crime and his warning that the death penalty would apply. But he also cautioned against assuming that foreign terrorists had done the deed ("Look at what happened in Japan, where there was no outside influence but a radical group within Japan able to take a little vial of gas and kill large numbers of people, this having happened twice now").[24] Clinton urged "restraint and discipline" among Americans, warned against "incendiary talk," and attended keenly to the 168 dead and their survivors.[25] On this as on other occasions, his rhetoric covered all the bases, but it tilted toward grief and sympathy, patience and procedure, rather than vengeance and quick action. Thus the president became as much mourner in chief as commander in chief. The 1996 election campaign saw a spike in administration use of the term "war on drugs," with the appointment of U.S. Gulf War commander General Barry McCaffrey as drug czar underlining the point. But the administration discarded "war on drugs" after the election. Compared to the war rhetoric that preceded Clinton, his words were tame.

Clinton's key personnel in matters of crime echoed his emphases. Janet Reno, the second-longest-serving attorney general in U.S. history, was called "part social worker, part crime fighter" by Florida senator Bob Graham, *Rolling Stone* reported in June 1993. "To put this in context, think of [Reno's predecessors] William Barr, Dick Thornburgh, Ed Meese, William French Smith. Come across a social worker yet?" As a Florida prosecutor, Reno had introduced a "drug court" to divert nonviolent offenders, and like the White House she avoided "drug-war stunts." "By contrast," *Rolling Stone* pointed out, "eight months into his term, Bush had already reached the point of posing in the Oval Office using an evidence bag of crack as a prop."[26] It was indeed a change. Drug czar McCaffrey sustained the rhetorical shift, rejecting on March 6, 1996, at the start of his appointment, "the whole analogy of a war on drugs" as "probably inadequate," and instead preferring "the notion of cancer."[27]

Yet the rhetorical shift was compromised by other words, images, and actions, as the 1994 Violence Act showed. Reno's record in Florida, where she prosecuted dubious child sex abuse cases, indicated that she was as much "crime fighter" as "social worker." She was in any event at arm's length from the White House, and rarely much of an influence on its crime proposals and budgets. Whatever his words, McCaffrey had worn an officer's uniform for decades, retiring with four stars, and as drug czar he was still addressed as "General." It was his military credentials that got him appointed, the White House made clear: "The appointment of General McCaffrey to that position will now bring . . . a new added element to the arsenal . . . available in fighting the war on drugs."[28] Those qualifications included his efforts while in the army to wage war on drug kingpins in Latin America, a war the administration expanded. Clinton also tried to upgrade the long-running traffic between military service and policing, seeking "a police corps to encourage young people to get an education and pay it off by serving as police officers," and to "encourage retiring military personnel to move into police forces, an inordinate resource for our country."[29]

Retired equipment moved into policing along with retired personnel under the 1033 program Clinton signed into law in 1996. At least as consequential as the 1994 Violent Crime Control Act but less noticed at the time, the 1033 program built on earlier schemes to hand over discarded military equipment to municipal, state, university, and other policing agencies. With the recent Gulf War, and again after the post-9/11 wars, more stuff than ever was available to hand over—anything from discarded air conditioners to armored Humvees. Later critics condemned the giveaway as a post-9/11 phenomenon stoked by fears of terrorism, but it preceded 9/11. Through its Law Enforcement Support Office (LESO), the Defense Logistics Agency advertised its wares widely and sent the leftovers (hundreds of formidable mine-resistant vehicles, for example) to big cities and small towns, to SWAT teams and beat cops. "From Warfighter to Crimefighter," LESO branded its decal, as did state offices that linked it to local police agencies. No other phrase so well captured the historical forces that led to the agency's creation and drove the punitive turn. Politics and policy were stitching war-fighting and crime-fighting more tightly together, as militarized policing advanced in the Clinton era under the guise of prevention.[30]

Though more nuanced and varied than those of his predecessors, Clinton's words, like his policies, did nothing to arrest the punitive turn and much to further militarize it. They might have succeeded "in focusing media attention on his prevention orientation,"[31] but they did not much change the conversation in Congress, statehouses, city governments, prison systems, police forces, and television programming.

His administration never found an ear-catching alternative to war-on-crime rhetoric, as *Rolling Stone* immediately sensed: "The Clinton White House has shut down drug-war demagogy. But lacking direction, it hasn't even attempted to fill the resulting vacuum."[32] As a term, "prevention" had appeal but lacked electricity, especially when given mushy formulation by Clinton and his team. Trying to sideline "war on crime," they put nothing punchy in its place—perhaps none was to be had—so the tone and very words of that phrase still sounded widely and harshly elsewhere. For a piece on New York City police commissioner William J. Bratton, a 1996 *Time* cover proclaimed, "Finally, We're Winning the War Against Crime."[33]

If prevention was the middle ground between being tough on crime and soft on it, or if it was new territory staked outside that binary, it was also opaque and malleable in its implications. On a larger scale, prevention had that all-things-for-all-sides appeal that boot camps had seemed to offer. It might mean more jobs for at-risk youth, or boot camps to stop them from committing more crimes. It might mean better policing, or simply more policing. It might mean smarter incarceration, or simply more of it—what better way to prevent crime than to lock up the criminals? Clinton had pithily captured all those possibilities while touting the crime bill's pending passage in his April 23, 1994, radio address. "[The act] means more police, more punishment, and more prevention"—that is, more capacity for the carceral state. In the 1990s, prevention often meant—for Clinton, Congress, state governments, and other authorities—the punitive option. Prevention encompassed the instruments of a war on crime even as the administration sidestepped the term. The biggest exception to that punitive pattern was the ten-year assault weapons ban pushed by Senator Biden, although even that required more policing to enforce it. And it was a costly exception for Democrats, contributing to the loss of their House majority in the 1994 elections.

In foreign policy, prevention often meant going to war to prevent war, or at least a worse version of it, as it did with U.S./NATO bombing campaigns in disintegrated Yugoslavia in 1995 and 1999. In crime policy, it meant much the same thing, as Clinton proudly acknowledged in his final 1996 campaign address: "We said we need more police and tougher penalties, but we also need effective prevention and fewer guns on the street. So we're putting 100,000 new police officers on the street. We passed 'three strikes and you're out' and the death penalty for drug kingpins and cop killers. We banned assault weapons, passed the Brady bill, and fought for safe and drug-free schools." As Jonathan Simon notes, Clinton "[Clinton] signed every bill extending punishments or contracting rights of prisoners presented to him by Congress, and he promoted many of them."[34]

Clinton and his team recognized that war rhetoric cultivated expectations of victory on which leaders could not deliver, ultimately backfiring on them. Reagan and Bush had promised a victory they could not achieve, and Bush's war on crime did not get him reelected in 1992. Emphasizing prevention, Clinton avoided that rhetorical trap. But the words of war were no longer as necessary because most everything done in their name was now instantiated in governance. The language of war—of emergency, of improvisation, of getting drastic new things up and running—had done its duty, absent the admission, perilous for any politician to make, that the war on crime was permanent. Clinton could escape that rhetorical trap knowing that others would keep the war talk humming. A drug war to be won at the "kitchen table," as McCaffrey put it, hardly could be called a war.[35] But not far from that kitchen table, narcs were still busting into houses, guns were still being brandished, jail cell doors were still clanking shut. "Prevention," then, was a big, leaky rhetorical umbrella under which much good or much bad could happen.

How much its rhetoric, as opposed to the goodies flowing under its name, filtered down is unclear. When William Bratton penned an account of his first go-round as New York's police commissioner in the mid-1990s, he barely mentioned Clinton's rhetoric and policies (beyond appreciating the 100,000 new cops program), and he never mentioned Attorney General Janet Reno. In touting his "turnaround" of the city's "crime epidemic," Bratton made only passing mention of the 1993 World Trade Center bombing, terrorism, and the war on crime. His adoption of "broken windows" and "quality of life" policing fell loosely under the prevention rubric, but he barely acknowledged the connection. (Crime rates fell sharply in New York in the late 1990s, but since they fell nationally as well, the role of Bratton's methods in their fall is hard to assess.) Crime politics in big cities are their own insular worlds, and Bratton detailed the inside world of police politics, operations, corruption, crime-fighting strategies, and his fractious relationship with Mayor Rudolph Giuliani (Bratton did not last long).[36]

The national story of crime rhetoric and politics was distant—permissive of what Bratton wanted to do, but hardly determinative. Even many critics of Giuliani-era policing noted only in passing "the militaristic, crime-fighting ethos of police culture."[37] War rhetoric did pop up in New York. "You can't send the Red Cross onto the battlefield before the infantry," a police spokesman said in defense of aggressive policing. As for firing Bratton, Giuliani commented, "We had a little bit of a Truman-MacArthur problem," alluding to President Harry Truman's dismissal of General Douglas MacArthur during the Korean War.[38] But crime politics are local as well as national matters, limiting how much national talk shapes local developments, although weapons and tactics certainly flow from the federal government to local agencies.

The distance from national politics was even greater in Chicago, farther from the national media's glare and national politicians' attention. As Cook County state's attorney (1980–89) and then Chicago's longtime mayor (1989–2011), Richard M. Daley had no national political aspirations. He stayed exquisitely attuned to local politics, insulted judges and prosecutors he judged soft on crime, and ran roughshod over legal procedure and constitutional norms. In so doing, he practiced "big-tent dictatorship, in which everyone is welcome at the table, as long as nobody forgets who the host is." Given to no lofty rhetoric, and often not even to coherent speech, Daley waged a war on crime while rarely calling it that, with an effort at community policing, funded in part from Washington, added to the mix in the 1990s. Insofar as crime prevention was his goal, it largely meant punishing street-level criminals as harshly as possible. (He pled ignorance about corruption in Chicago politics, just as he did about police detective Jon Burge's torture regime.) Daley got apoplectic about crime, gangs, and the flow of guns into the city. A gun control zealot, he had his closest connection to national politics on that issue. His regime roughly mirrored national patterns in criminal justice, but it felt little direct influence from the prevention talk going on in Washington.[39]

So did Clinton's rhetorical shift make no difference beyond obscuring how the same policies continued and expanded? Did it offer only a kinder, gentler veneer on an ever-harsher system? If rhetoric matters, as this work argues, then surely Clinton's changing language mattered: he distanced crime-fighting from the words of war. Of course, rhetoric can matter in different ways. It can influence politics and policies, or it can obscure them. It can be indicative rather than determinative. It can be fuzzy and inconsequential. Or it can reveal incipient changes slow to emerge. Clinton's rhetoric did foreshadow a trend in the 2000s, when more politicians and activists, including some conservatives, moved to restrain mass incarceration, criticize its racialized foundations, and challenge militarized words and practices. But if Clinton's rhetoric foreshadowed that trend, it probably did not prompt it.

Except rhetorically, Clinton failed to resist the tough-on-crime currents of the time, for the most part because he did not want to, but also because those currents remained strong. They were emboldened by an early 1990s spike in crime rates, and they were scattered across an ever more diffuse, volatile spectrum of issues and events, from "terrorism" (domestic and foreign), to antigovernment militias, to Waco (where the federal siege of a religious sect in 1993 ended disastrously), to Clinton's impeachment. Reagan and Bush could concentrate on "street crime" and their "war on drugs." Clinton had to hopscotch, often on the spur of the moment, across a wider, trickier terrain of crime-related matters, and he had to do so when, with the Cold War over, no other agenda compellingly displaced crime. Even a president more committed than Clinton to downgrading crime on the nation's agenda would have had a tough time achieving that goal. Offering a more spirited resistance to tough-on-crime politics than Clinton ever did, Carter had had little success in that resistance.

"Superpredators" and Much More

Among many obstacles, that resistance faced the mid-1990s hysteria over "superpredators," violent youth whose lack of conscience and restraint presumably had no precedent in the American past, and whose cultural and even biological DNA seemed altogether new. They were another of the "mythical monsters whose apocalyptic threat requires expanding the federal enforcement power," as one historian has put it. The furor gained traction from a sharp rise in juvenile crime in the 1980s and from brutal crimes. "CENTRAL PARK HORROR: WOLF PACK'S PREY: Female Jogger Near Dead after Savage Attack by Roving Gang" ran a *New York Daily News* story on April 21, 1989. New York developer Donald Trump took out newspaper ads proclaiming, "I want to hate these muggers and murderers. They should be forced to suffer and, when they kill, they should be executed for their crimes." (The five young black men convicted had their convictions vacated in 2002.)[40]

Usually understood as nonwhite, poor, and prone to sexual violence, the "superpredator"—so branded in a 1995 article by John DiIulio, a James Q. Wilson student—seemed part of "the biggest baddest generation of criminals any society has ever known," according to the *Washington Times*. DiIulio joined Bill Bennett and John Walters to elaborate that claim in a 1996 book, *Body Count: Moral Poverty . . . and How to Win America's War Against Crime and Drugs*. According to a Northeastern University professor, superpredators were "a teenage time bomb" (a term *Time* embraced) that might unleash a "blood bath of teenage violence." Hillary Clinton chimed in with comments little noticed at the time but savaged as racist during her 2016 campaign. She depicted "superpredators" as having "no conscience, no empathy," as individuals who should be brought "to heel." Yet it was all "a myth," asserts Joseph Margulies. Even as hysteria peaked, juvenile crime rates began declining, while DiIulio was backtracking by 1996. But the image of the "superpredator" stuck, not least because of brutalized victims (often women) of youth crime, and because of a wave of legal changes allowing or requiring some arrested youth to be prosecuted as adults and often housed in adult prisons.[41]

In the 1990s, a hyperbolic assertion of the need to protect children competed with a hyperbolic assertion of the need to constrain them. It was no coincidence that the "superpredator" hysteria erupted after the Cold War's end, which further diminished the chance that young men would go into military service. With the armed forces contracting, pickier about whom they would accept, and taking in more women, presumably violence-prone male youth seemed further beyond the reach of the discipline of military duty. A war on these young men was one response, or as Clinton repeatedly put it in 1997, in a rare foray into war language, a "war on gangs," by which he meant juvenile gangs.[42]

In that way and others, the war metaphor continued to issue new progeny even as the war against drugs retained primacy. For example, Mothers Against Drunk Driving (MADD), founded in 1980, periodically declared war on its enemy as it carried out a "War Against Drunk Drivers," as Newsweek called it in 1982. By 1994 scholars took note of the organization's "war-like rhetoric," and in 1996 MADD's president condemned "a false perception that the war on drunk driving has been won." In 2002 MADD announced in a press release a "plan to jumpstart the war against the most frequently committed violent crime in the nation—drunk driving." Its president worried that "the war on drunk driving ha[d] flat-lined," insisting that "this war is not MADD's war; it's the nation's war." MADD's use of the war metaphor was occasional and reflexive rather than elaborate. But in scholars' opinion, it aligned ideologically with the war on drugs, given a similar emphasis on seeking "retribution from 'criminals'" and on "a punitive system to handle society's problems rather than a public health approach focused on prevention."[43]

MADD's work further indicated how the pressures to be vigilant against and punitive toward crime were manifold and persistent through the Clinton years. To be sure, promiscuous use of war terminology perhaps drained it of much charge in any specific instance. Yet such use also said something—that it was a comfortable, reflexive language to use, one that worked even if little thought went into it, one that often propelled and reflected militarized practices.

More and more Americans, for example, imagined the U.S.-Mexico border as a war zone. They welcomed, or dreaded, a border war against undocumented migrants and drug carriers, ushering in what one scholar calls "the militarization of the U.S.-Mexico border." That process had precedents early in the twentieth century, and it had accelerated under the Reagan-Bush administration ("I mean, we're at war here," explained Senator John McCain in 1988).[44] It sped up further during the Clinton administration, in part to salve fears that the new North American Free Trade Agreement would create a border porous to criminals and migrants as well as goods. The Border Patrol swiftly expanded there (and on a smaller scale, near the Canadian border), eventually to become the largest and most militarized federal law enforcement agency. Companies hawked airplanes, copters, drones, guns, and electronic surveillance for border monitoring, seeking a boom market at a time when the defense spending had plateaued.

As the Border Patrol militarized, U.S. armed forces moved further into border policing, basing this change on their role in drug interdiction but moving beyond it. So, too, did Mexico's armed forces, as coordination between the two militaries ramped up (in 1995 William Perry became the first American defense secretary to visit Mexico). Some military personnel, like Border Patrol officials guarding their turf, disliked the armed forces' policing role. Others saw an opportunity in a post–Cold War world from which the usual enemies had vanished. As a retired officer wrote, "An easily accomplished mission for existing forces would be patrolling the borders. It is, of course, absurd that the most powerful nation on earth cannot prevent a swarming land invasion by unarmed Mexican peasants." Former defense secretary Caspar Weinberger weighed in by imagining a scenario in which 60,000 U.S. troops invade Mexico after a radical leader takes power there. Meanwhile, the border was gradually fortified and walled off (critics noted the irony of American celebration of the Berlin Wall's fall in 1989). National figures presented undocumented immigration and drug trafficking, or just vaguely the border "problem," as threats to national security. As White House aide Rahm Emanuel explained the armed forces' role: "Their actions and involvement are consistent with their mandate in protecting national security. . . . After years of neglect, we are finally restoring the rule of law, locking down the Southwest border."[45]

Immigration policy followed suit. Federal authorities had rarely prosecuted people for unauthorized reentry before the early 1990s, but they now ramped up prosecution, moving to mass incarceration in place of mere deportation. Deportation also escalated as state and local crackdowns on both legal and undocumented immigration resulted in criminal convictions that made immigrants deportable under a 1996 federal law. This legislation had "the effect of importing the priorities of state and local law enforcement into federal immigration control." Almost always, the jailed and deported were Mexicans or other Latinos, some of them escapees from the Central American wars that the Reagan administration had helped stoke.[46]

An explosion of "zero tolerance" rhetoric offered another measure of the pressure to be punitive in the Clinton years, and of how that pressure moved beyond the formal arena of criminal justice. Clinton used the phrase profligately, regarding drugs and a host of other issues (school safety "demands that schools follow a policy of zero tolerance for guns," he declared in December 1997).[47] He consolidated its use in the drug-war context while also applying it to more and more matters, helping to cement the phrase in the political lexicon.

The concept of zero tolerance also spread in administrative law and policy. In 1993 the Department of Veterans Affairs "implemented a 'zero tolerance' policy against sexual harassment," and other government agencies and private employers offered a "zero tolerance" brand for their guidelines concerning harassment, drug use, and other misbehaviors.[48] Moreover, countless public schools announced zero tolerance for various misdeeds, prompted in part by the federal 1990 Gun-Free School Zones Act, which required public schools receiving federal funds to expel for no less than one year any student who brought a firearm to campus. National figures championed zero-tolerance policies in schools. In her book *It Takes a Village* (1996), Hillary Clinton touted "'zero-tolerance' policy for weapons, drugs, and other threats" to school safety, embraced Houston's "'zero tolerance for gangs in the school' policy," and insisted that parents facing such a policy should shout, "'Hallelujah' instead of 'I'll sue!'"[49] In 1998, the Richmond, Illinois, public schools cited such guidelines when it threatened to expel a seventeen-year-old student (taken into police custody) whose rubber band–fired paper clip had struck a cafeteria employee and drawn a little blood. That was only one of thousands of applications of "zero tolerance" in schools over the coming years.[50] Long after the 1990s, government and business officials still cited "zero tolerance" as their reason for firing or disciplining students and employees. Under the banner of this concept, the punitive turn sprawled further.

Why the explosion of "zero tolerance," both as policy and as a faddish term with staying power? (Hillary Clinton was still using the phrase in 2015; as president she would have "zero tolerance for the kinds of abuses and delays we have seen" at the Department of Veterans Affairs.)[51] Top-down action played a role. Presidential statements, federal and state statutes and rules, and local laws and school board decisions encouraged or mandated "zero tolerance" policies. Rules announced by huge agencies like Veterans Affairs provided guidance for other organizations. "Zero tolerance" allowed a posture of toughness, particularly for school boards and administrators besieged by complaints about failing schools infested by gangs and drugs, by talk of superpredators, and by shocking incidents like the 1999 Columbine High School massacre. There was no discretion to exercise, no decision to be made: the policy made the choice for those guided by it. Discretion lurked behind the "zero tolerance" facade, but the facade was a useful shield. Especially for school administrators, it took "a lot of the anxiety out of the exercise of power," Jonathan Simon notes, displacing anxiety onto students instead.[52] Less subject to public scrutiny, private schools and colleges were less likely to embrace "zero tolerance."

For schools, "zero tolerance" also connected closely to militarized words and policing. It was the schoolhouse front of the war on drugs, as schools declared no tolerance not only for illegal drugs, but also for medications (Tylenol, Midol) that might mask or get confused with such drugs. With more and more schoolkid infractions subject to zero tolerance, surveillance and enforcement fell beyond teachers' and administrators' capacity to carry out—another reason for an armed police presence and new regimes of electronic surveillance in schools. Zero tolerance for gang symbols established another vector for the involvement of police and other agencies in schools. As in the war on drugs, zero tolerance in schools bore down hardest on African Americans and other minorities, though its application was widespread and capricious enough to snag others as well.

The phrase became so ubiquitous in so many settings that it often lacked any evident political or ideological charge. But for politicians, public officials, corporate spokespersons, and the like, "zero tolerance" served to parade a posture of unbending, punitive righteousness toward all sorts of ills and threats. Not that posture always led to policy, but often it was not supposed to—the posture was itself the goal. It conveyed an apparent determination to police and punish harshly. At times tolerance itself seemed under attack, since it was to be eliminated. All societies have catchphrases that come and go, and it is foolish to invest too much meaning in them. Still, they say something. This one said something about the rigidity of public institutions and about desires written into law and policy to make them behave rigidly—to have them act with an absolute finality that prevents anything bad happening, or at least expels that bad thing instantly. The notion of zero tolerance measured desperation about these institutions, especially schools, and capitulation by their leaders to that desperation.

The phrase ricocheted in many directions: zero tolerance for drunk driving, for students carrying knives or drugs to school, for drug-using employees in the workplace, for sex criminals, for intimate faculty-student relations in colleges, and for other behaviors. While it often became a cliché, "zero tolerance" was hardly empty of content. It shared with mandatory minimum sentencing and three-strikes-and-you're-out laws the impulse to remove authorities' and systems' freedom to exercise discretion, cut deals, or consider circumstances. The phrase usually applied to relatively powerless groups. There was little talk of zero tolerance for bloated corporate pay, business fraud, or campaign-fund malfeasance. Unintended or ridiculous consequences—the nine-year-old North Carolinian suspended for sexual harassment after calling his teacher "cute" (2011), the twelve-year-old New Yorker cuffed and taken by police for doodling (2010)—were treated as a minor cost in achieving a major good.[53] Despite reversals in courts, state legislatures, and city councils, zero-tolerance policies stuck for decades.

The pressures to be punitive bore their most obvious result in incarceration, which in the 1990s saw its largest modern jump, both in percentage of the total population and in raw numbers. The number of imprisoned Americans almost doubled to nearly 2 million by 2000, with the biggest percentage increase coming in the number of federal prisoners. (As usual, incarcerated people in military jails, immigrant detention facilities, and Native American jails did not fall under standard incarceration statistics.) Those numbers represented the incarcerated population on a single day, but millions more entered jail each year on short-term stays (awaiting trial, serving brief sentences, and so on). One later estimate was that "almost 12 million people cycle through *local jails* each year."[54] Surprisingly, given the superpredator scare, the number of prisoners in juvenile detention budged little, but in part because changing statutes permitted more juveniles to be tried and imprisoned as adults. Unsurprisingly, the number of Americans on probation and parole also increased sharply in the 1990s. Though small, the number of incarcerated women increased more rapidly than that of men through and beyond the 1990s.

The sharp increases for men and women reflected modest growth in convictions. But the surging numbers mainly pointed to lengthened sentences under mandatory minimum laws, and to reimprisonment without an additional conviction for many deemed in violation of probation or parole. In effect, a fairly stable number of convicted inmates filled jails and prisons by serving longer. That circumstance in turn fostered the mistaken impression that there were more convicts. Crime rates had actually taken a sharp downturn (the FBI violent crime rate peaked in 1991 at 758.2 per 100,000 inhabitants and had fallen to 506.5 by 2000).[55] Wide variations among states reflected in part the role of race: states with large minority populations usually jailed far more people. Those variations also indicated that federal policy made by Congress and Clinton was more permissive than compulsory. Often that policy allowed, nudged, and funded what state and local authorities chose to do without dictating it. The federal incarcerated population, far smaller than the state population but increasing more sharply in the 1990s, indicated just how punitive federal policy was, as well as Clinton's role in that policy.

The sharp increase in imprisonment set against the substantial decline in crime rates raised a question rarely posed in the 1990s: Was increased imprisonment a cause of falling crime rates or an indication that imprisonment had gotten out of hand? An unspoken tails-they-lose/heads-we-win logic seemed to apply. Rising crime rates showed mass incarceration was needed, and falling ones showed it was working, in which case more of it was in order.

As the punitive turn made room for more prisoners, shrinking public systems increased the supply of inmates. Uniformed military personnel continued to decline in numbers while women's share of them continued to increase, further narrowing one pipeline of opportunity for young men. Deinstitutionalization of the mentally ill continued as systems for treating them outside of hospital settings frayed further, contributing to an influx of the mentally ill into jails and prisons. Cutbacks in federal and state welfare systems put more poor Americans at risk. Programs for poor mothers and their babies similarly weakened, feeding what critics called a "cradle to prison" or "babies-to-prison pipeline."[56] As usual, change did not tilt all one way. As a growth industry, criminal justice and private security also provided new sources of employment for younger men and women and for veterans, as did some other sectors of the economy, like health care. Still, it was a tough decade for those most at risk of getting arrested and jailed—the poor and the mentally ill, especially young minority males among them.

As the punitive turn accelerated, so too did resistance to it, especially to its most deadly and militarized elements. A spate of innocence projects debuted, starting with Barry Scheck's in 1992 and continuing with others connected to academic sites (the Wisconsin Innocence Project in 1998, the California Innocence Project, and the Northwestern University/ Medill Innocence Project in 1999). These endeavors ran parallel to and often connected with renewed death penalty activism. Such agitation was highlighted by the 1995 Hollywood movie *Dead Man Walking*, about Sister Helen Prejean's anti–death penalty efforts, and by the decision of Illinois governor George Ryan (later to go to the federal pen himself) to put a moratorium on that state's use of execution in 2000 and commute 167 death sentences to life imprisonment in 2003. Meanwhile, a diverse coalition of community and legal activists slowly pried open the secret record of Chicago police detective Jon Burge's torture of African Americans, and of public officials' collusion in his wrongdoing.[57] Adding to its longtime focus on civil rights matters, the American Civil Liberties Union launched its Criminal Law Reform Project (initially called the Drug Law Reform Project) in 1998. Careful scholars assayed the connections among TV crime news, the exploding genre of crime shows like *Law and Order*, and the politics of crime. As schools' zero-tolerance policies led to the expulsion of students for laughable or mystifying reasons, outraged parents and children's advocates pounced, though with little quick success. Critics spotted "Zero Tolerance for Children," as the title of a lawyer's 2001 critique put it, and saw zero tolerance as a motor for the "school-to-prison pipeline" and "the militarization of schools."[58] Well-researched critiques of police militarization came from Peter Kraska and Victor Kappeler, laboring from the relative obscurity of their posts at Eastern Kentucky University.

In particular, SWAT policing met sharper criticism. Some law enforcement officials had long chafed at the outsized resources SWAT teams snared, at their elite status and celebrity, at the poison in police-community relations that SWAT actions might inject, and at the aura of war making that hung over SWAT actions. "It's a very dangerous thing, when you're telling cops they're soldiers and there's an enemy over there," complained the former police chief of San Diego and Kansas City. He concluded, "I don't like it at all." The *Washington Post* summarized many citizens' reactions to such militarization: "[It] led to complaints that an occupying army is marching through

America's streets." Critics suspected that many men attracted to SWAT duty were too attracted to war and to an elite "special ops" status: "The SWAT teams love this stuff," Peter Kraska observed. "It's fun to fire these weapons. It's exciting to train. They use 'simmunition'—like the paint balls and play warrior games. This stuff is a rush."[59] Kraska's work signaled that criticism was moving beyond ad hoc complaints by aggrieved citizens and police officials and into sustained exposition. It strengthened his credibility that Kraska showed a critical sympathy for Swatters gained by direct contact with them, and an appreciation for how warring and policing were converging. He linked "a strengthening of paramilitaristic policing, state tendencies to militarize social problems in the post–Cold War era, and a revitalization of *paramilitarism* in popular culture."[60] Still, criticism made no dint in the SWAT phenomenon, and no president was paying heed.

Such efforts pecked away at various dimensions of the punitive turn, but they did not cohere into a broad-based political project. Nor did they often catch the sympathetic ears of leading officials (Illinois governor Ryan was an exception). Given an apparatus of criminal justice dispersed across an array of international, federal, state, local, and private agencies, and given how much of it was localized, no national target of activism emerged. What mobilized action in one place might seem irrelevant to another. The criminal-industrial complex was everywhere, but no one place in particular; it threaded through American life. Moreover, each action against it had to be prolonged and exhausting. It took decades for Chicago activists to expose Burge's torture regime, secure some legal action against its perpetrators, and win some exoneration and compensation for its victims. Activists and reformers understandably focused on the most egregious practices and incidents—the SWAT raid gone awry, the man wrongly sentenced to death. While they recognized these injustices as the tip of a systemic iceberg, getting to the iceberg was tougher. Tellingly, Peter Kraska's 1997 phrase "militarizing American police" only gained wide use after the Ferguson, Missouri, police shooting of Michael Brown in 2014 and other incidents.[61]

Clinton's impeachment cut bizarrely across this story. After years of criminal accusations against the president and those around him, the House voted on December 19, 1998, to impeach Clinton for perjury and obstruction of justice regarding his statements about his sexual relationship with Monica Lewinsky. The Senate then failed by a narrow margin to convict (no Democrat voted for conviction on either charge). Many accounts of criminal justice in this period simply ignore or passingly mention Clinton's impeachment, as if it were a rogue event disconnected from other punitive currents in American life. It was for sure the product of many forces: bitter partisan politics, GOP revenge for the near impeachment of Nixon, the inflammatory right-wing media's rise to power, contentious struggles over the alleged excesses of the "sixties," and the smarmy, voyeuristic politics of sex.

But Clinton's impeachment was also a measure of how prosecutorial zeal, inflamed by all those forces, was now deeply embedded in American politics. It was a flamboyant example of how the punitive turn—that animalistic, inchoate impulse to punish—could reach beyond its familiar channels. In the late 1990s and 2000s, a long list of political figures faced the media glare, and sometimes criminal charges, for alleged sex crimes or for other sexual misbehavior. (For example, Republican congressman Newt Gingrich resigned his seat in 1998 amid the Clinton impeachment he helped start, in part because of his adulterous relationship with an aide.) For many critics, the report on Clinton that independent counsel Kenneth Starr released on September 11, 1998, embodied that prosecutorial zeal; the prodigiously long document was full of prurient detail and debatable accusations and innuendo.

Clinton's impeachment had no direct connection to the soaring rates of arrest and imprisonment faced by many Americans. Yet it is hard to see the two as merely coincidental, particularly given how the "sex panic" that exploded in the 1990s strengthened the punitive state and made nonnormative sex more suspect. Clinton had played off of a punitive impulse that could go almost anywhere, coming back to bite him. The impeachment story featured many of the hallmarks of routine criminal justice by this point—the de facto perp walk (Clinton's public statements and public humiliation), the leaks from inside (from Starr and zealous members of Congress), the media frenzy (the Starr report was immediately released on the internet), and the molten outrage when sex misbehavior was alleged.

War threaded its way through that drama. Clinton's avoidance of military service during the Vietnam War hovered in the background, as did the missile attacks he ordered on alleged terrorist forces in Sudan and Afghanistan on August 20, 1998, three days after he had been called to testify before a grand jury in the Lewinsky matter. Those attacks became known among critics and in the media as "Monica's War," Clinton's supposed attempt to distract attention from the Lewinsky scandal.[62] And when Clinton unleashed a bombing campaign (Operation Desert Fox) against Saddam Hussein's Iraq regime on December 16, at the height of House deliberations on whether to impeach him, suspicion again erupted that he was using war to escape his legal troubles.

Given the deployment of American forces in most of the world and their recurrent use in the Balkans and the Middle East, war making was an inescapable prism through which to view the story. One can imagine that if Clinton had withheld military action, a different war-related suspicion would have surfaced—that his personal weaknesses and Vietnam-era politics had crippled him in protecting the nation and its interests.

Hillary Clinton declared a "battle" going on against "a vast right-wing conspiracy" out to destroy her husband, and undoubtedly the White House felt warred on by the champions of impeachment. Clinton aide James Carville "declared war" on Starr on national TV. A lengthy *Newsweek* piece was branded "Impeachment Wars," if only to hype the article, which never picked up on the title.[63] Still, words of war only occasionally punctuated the shouting. Rare and scattered, they reflected generic hyperbole rather than a language widely used. Words of war did not frame the impeachment crisis because words of sex, even more provocative, occupied most of the bandwidth. And for decades, the terms "war on crime" and "war on drugs" had mostly referred to anonymous, shadowy criminals, not to powerful white-collar figures.

The words of war were similarly muffled as the United States policed the world more vigilantly in the 1990s, just as it policed more vigilantly at home. These two arenas of the punitive turn were teasingly linked. The United States had played a worldwide policing role long before the 1990s, especially in the Caribbean and Central America, and President Truman had dubbed the United States' role in the Korean War a "police action" under UN auspices. But America's policing role during the Cold War had for the most part been framed in terms of the grand struggle between the Soviet Union and the United States, or between the communist and free worlds, and its military action had been framed in terms of war.

As the Cold War closed, however, the police-action model gained prominence in a series of U.S. interventions—some unilateral, some multinational, some upon invitation, some reluctant—that started with the invasion of Panama in 1989. The 1991 Gulf War fit that model less well because of its scale and because President Bush and others analogized its stakes to those of World War II. Later interventions came closer. A short list includes interventions in Somalia, Bosnia, Kosovo (in the bombing of Serbia), Haiti, Afghanistan, and Sudan, recurrent American and UK bombing of Hussein's Iraqi forces, and operations in Central and South America (and sometimes elsewhere) in pursuit of narcotics agriculture and trafficking. Many actions, especially those against Iraq, were punitive in character, designed to punish bad deeds rather than alter fundamental conditions. They set the stage for the ferociously punitive American response to the 9/11 attacks.

U.S. leaders avoided terms like "world policeman" and "Globalcop," used by critics wanting less intervention or by muscular intervention-ists wanting more. They preferred the anodyne—or as critics saw it, evasive—language of leadership, engagement, and prevention. Asked after the Gulf War whether the United States "should be the world policeman," Bush sidestepped the question, emphasizing multilat-eral cooperation. "But we are the leaders, and we must continue to lead," he added. "We must continue to stay engaged."[64] On this matter, Clinton sounded much like Bush. The closest a leading official came to articulating a Globalcop role was Madeleine Albright. Her sharp comment to Joint Chiefs of Staff chairman General Colin Powell in 1993 while she was UN ambassador circulated widely when Powell later reported it: "What's the point of having this superb military that you're always talking about if we can't use it?"[65] As secretary of state, Albright asserted on NBC's *Today Show*, when queried about further intervention in Iraq, "If we have to use force, it is because we are America; we are the indispensable nation. We stand tall and we see further than other countries into the future, and we see the danger here to all of us."[66] But in official rhetoric, America's status as Globalcop was usually affirmed by denials that revealed how much it was perceived as just such a thing. "The U.S. may not be the 'world's policeman,'" Senator John McCain wrote in 1990, but "its power pro-jection forces will remain the free world's insurance policy." He reas-serted this stance later.[67]

Other leading voices were blunter, sometimes linking policing at home to policing abroad. Columnist Charles Krauthammer saw in 1990 a "unipolar moment" with the disappearance of the Soviet enemy and the rise of "Weapon States" like Iraq. He wrote, "It is slowly dawning on the West that there is a need to establish some new regime to po-lice these weapons and those who brandish them." Krauthammer made clear that the United States, not some vague "new regime," would have to "police these weapons."[68] Closing out a decade of musing along those lines (often from neoconservatives), in 1999 the columnist Thomas Friedman assayed the rush of globalization, spotted an "increasingly dangerous" world at home and abroad, and explicitly linked those are-nas: "Designing ways to avoid that [increasing danger] should be at the heart of American domestic and foreign policy." In curbing that danger, the miracles of new technologies and globalization would not alone suffice. "The hidden hand of the market will never work without a hidden fist," he insisted. "And the hidden fist that keeps the world safe for Silicon Valley's technologies is called the United States Army, Air Force, Navy and Marine Corps."[69] Here was a vision of Globalcop, without Friedman using the word, although its use by others exploded in the 1990s.[70]

The connections between Globalcop and local cop were implicit rather than explicit, though underpinned by rich feedback loops of technologies, policy, and personnel between the two. Political leaders' considerations of their audiences helped to keep these links implicit. Tough war-on-crime rhetoric might work at home, but explicit embrace of a tough-cop posture abroad would inflame enemies, alienate allies, and alarm the many Americans wary of a big policing (or nation building) role for their country. But a nation operating as a vigorous Globalcop could hardly act as a weakling at home, and a nation vigorously policing itself had the ideological and practical resources to play a similar role abroad.

Clinton's rhetoric of prevention linked the two arenas. Just as he packaged his crime-control measures as prevention, he presented America's role abroad as an effort to prevent warring parties from clashing, to forestall (further) genocide, to execute humanitarian missions, and to bring peace to the streets of regions abroad sometimes analogized (by others) to the strife-torn streets of the United States. Also linking the two arenas were the racial and cultural identities of those understood to need the "hidden fist," as Friedman called it: in both cases, those were usually (though not in the Balkans) non–European American peoples and leaders. What was good for warring Somalis and drug-trafficking Colombians was good for African Americans in LA and Latinos in Miami. America's role as global policeman roughly paralleled the role that policing played within the nation.

The Punitive Turn in Culture

Cultural as well as institutional forces undergirded the punitive turn in the 1990s, although they tended to mirror political change rather than instigate it—more lagging indicators than leading ones. The war on crime and drugs only came fully to big and small screens in the 1990s, after presidents and policing forces had long been waging the battle. And given its heterogeneity, culture sometimes offered resistance to the punitive turn or ironic comment on it. The relationship of media representations to political change and public perceptions was indirect and murky. Still, culture differed in the 1990s from what it had offered a few decades earlier.

Hill Street Blues (1981–87), NBC's critically acclaimed police drama (ninety-eight Emmy nominations), indicated how slowly those changes took place. Although set amid urban decay and crime, it was more about its characters' complicated relationships, buffeted by changing norms regarding race, gender, and sexuality, than about criminal catching. The informal dress and casual hierarchy of the show's cops, detectives, and prosecutors hinted that the antiauthority themes of 1970s crime drama persisted. Given their considerable empathy toward each other, toward crime's victims, and even toward its perpetrators, *Hill Street Blues'* main characters strike few postures of vengeance. Episodes frequently end "with Capt. Frank Furillo (Daniel J. Travanti) and public defender Joyce Davenport (Veronica Hamel) . . . discussing how their respective days went," not with a judge pronouncing sentence or a jail door clanking shut.[71]

Rambo pointed toward something else. "Taken in order," Susan Jeffords notes, "the *Rambo* films" of 1982, 1985, and 1988 "narrate the production of the hard body during the Reagan years."[72] Overmuscled and blazingly righteous, Rambo sets forth to defeat not only erstwhile enemies in Vietnam but also the hapless or malevolent government officials who look the other way from the enemies' crimes. The Rambo films presaged crime-fighting series like *Lethal Weapon* (1987, 1989, 1992, 1998), *Die Hard* (starting in 1988), and other films in which the heroes' bodies were only a bit less hardened than Rambo's.

Those hard bodies also surfaced in movies featuring Superman and Batman, ultimate crime-fighters. The Batman of *Batman Returns* (1992) and the later *Dark Knight* movies was more armored and muscular than the slender and sometimes fey Batman played by Adam West in the campy TV series of the 1960s (1966–68). The Superman who re-emerged on-screen in 1978 with Christopher Reeve, and even more so in later iterations like *Man of Steel* (2013), was a more muscular, gloomy figure than the doughy and phlegmatic character played by George Reeves in the forgettable movie *Superman and the Mole Men* (1951) and in television's *Adventures of Superman* (1952–58). To be sure, many hard-bodied films of the 1980s and 1990s were war or science-fiction movies, not crime dramas. But those genres were less distinguishable than ever. The enemies in many war movies were more like supercriminals than conventional combatants, and the crimes committed in Batman and Superman movies took on warlike scale (in *The Dark Knight Rises* [2012], the evildoers threaten Gotham with a nuclear weapon). Collectively, these films suggested that crime-fighting required the warrior's body and the warrior's methods.

Of course, there were many reasons that Hollywood produced the "hard body," and many appeals for it beyond a criminal justice framework. And the hard body was parodied as soon as it began to appear (by the Village People in their 1978 song "Macho Man") and subjected to academic research, which could only go so far in showing links between "hypermasculinity" on-screen and attitudes toward crime and policing.[73] Still, the hard body marched into the 1990s to conquer more space on big and little screens, and its proximity to militarized crime-fighting outlined culture's dominant norms.

Law and Order (NBC, 1990–2010) completed the shift to punitive television drama, though the fact that it debuted in 1990 indicates how much television culture mirrored rather than anticipated real-life changes. The show was literally darker than preceding crime dramas: scant light penetrated the dark streets or the wood-paneled offices where prosecutors gathered. Its lead characters often offer the words and postures of righteous indignation toward criminals — emotive stances far removed from the "just-the-facts" sensibility of Joe Friday in the original *Dragnet*. In addition, the program's villains often were not mere criminals, but embodiments of evil, especially in the spin-off *Law and Order: Special Victims Unit* (1999–), about sex crimes. *Law and Order*'s miscreants were people in whom "criminality" was "a permanent trait, something like personality, present long before a criminal commits the crime and long after the convict does time." And whereas "old [TV crime shows] often portrayed officers determined to stop a crime in progress," in shows like *Law and Order* "the job of the officers is to discover the perpetrator; the television focus is on guilt rather than attempted crime and on punishment rather than prevention." The law enforcement officers assume "that crime cannot be averted; what remains is to deliver the guilty to retribution."[74]

Too much can be read into the giant *Law and Order* franchise. There was variety among its hundreds of episodes, and variety in what its millions of viewers took from it. And while its interpretation of crime might seem distinctively American, it had a large audience beyond the United States, imitators elsewhere, and even (in the case of *Special Victims Unit*) a Russian adaptation. Still, like most police shows airing during the 1990s, *Law and Order* offered assurance that the U.S. criminal justice system worked. As one scholar notes, "[Its] ponderous opening statement about the 'criminal justice system' is a claim for its efficacy."[75] The law enforcers might initially nab the wrong suspect, but they usually end up with the right ones. Indeed, their willingness to move from the wrong suspect to the right one signaled their integrity.

On occasion, a cagey criminal, wily defense lawyer, unreliable judge, or quirk in the law might short-cut the course of justice, but not often.

Notable, too, was a shift in narrative perspective—away from defense lawyers and toward detectives and prosecutors. In *Perry Mason* (1957–66), police lieutenant Tragg and district attorney Burger were minor characters, well-meaning men outwitted by defense lawyer Perry Mason. "What would you think," Steven D. Stark later asked of that show, "of a police force that always accuses the wrong suspects, or a district attorney who unquestioningly prosecutes them?"[76] In *Law and Order*, detectives and prosecutors carried the story and its moral torch, while defense lawyers were minor characters, often nettlesome impediments to justice. (Of course *Perry Mason*, too, was about getting the bad guy, exposed in the witness box by Mason's questioning, but the show's weight was on freeing the innocent, not prosecuting the guilty.)

The principled defense lawyer was a staple of television and movies in the 1950s and 1960s: the clever Perry Mason, the liberal-minded attorneys of the Emmy-winning CBS series *The Defenders* (1961–65), Orson Welles as a Clarence Darrow–like figure in *Compulsion* (1959), Gregory Peck in *To Kill a Mockingbird* (1962), and Jimmy Stewart as a small-town lawyer in Otto Preminger's *Anatomy of a Murder* (1959). *Matlock* (1986–95) faintly echoed *Perry Mason*, but the stalwart defense lawyer from television had largely disappeared by the 1990s. Lawyer-centered programming did persist, but shows like *L.A. Law* (1986–94), *The Practice* (1997–2004), and *Boston Legal* (2004–8) focused on the troubled lives and charged entanglements of the lawyers, not on criminal justice.

By their sheer volume and endurance as well as their content, TV crime shows offered another message long after the sharp decline in crime rates in the mid-1990s—there were an awful lot of criminals out there, and many of them were especially evil. How many viewers grasped that message is hard to say, but as TV networks judged matters, the audience to grasp it was huge and loyal. Crime shows captured big ratings, spawned more progeny (*Law and Order* issued five offshoots, plus video games), and became staples of syndication. By one count, "in one week of police and detective dramas there were 152 murders and 100 attempted murders as well as 239 other B crimes."[77] Already in 1987, it was possible for Steven Stark to conclude that "television melodrama" now "depicted the police as the culture's heroic and effective crime fighters, battling a sea of criminals against overwhelming odds." A few years later, with the advent of *Law and Order*, prosecutors also gained a place among those "heroic and effective crime fighters."

As Stark commented, "If crime shows are about law and order, they are light on the law, and heavy on the order."[78]

Saturation operated. The unceasing reenactment of judgment in crime dramas and in shows like *Judge Judy* and *The People's Court* "anchor[ed] penality in the rituals and background noise of everyday worlds in which television is an ever-present agent," comments one later critic. "Penal iconography . . . is simply too voluminous in its embeddedness."[79] Punishment was normalized—made inescapable, like the weather. Viewers need not like it to regard it as inevitable.

Along with other media treatments of crime, television crime shows also normalized the era's militarized style of policing by presenting it so often as to make it seem routine, inescapable. The imagery of those shows did have a wide range: detectives were lightly armed, sometimes women, or physically unimposing (Jerry Orbach as Detective Lennie Briscoe on *Law and Order*). Many detectives and uniformed cops, however, were more heavily armed and muscled. The body type of *Dragnet*'s detective Joe Friday and his paunchy sidekick in the 1950s had few TV analogs in the 1990s. And SWAT officers (almost all males), with heavy black flak vests and high-powered weaponry, sometimes marching alongside armored vehicles, stormed through many a crime show. Adding another layer to their normalization were competitions, some featured on television or online, among the "best" SWAT teams. By 2015, SWAT Round-Up International was celebrating its thirty-third anniversary, offering "the ultimate SWAT training, competition and vendor show" and promising "brotherhood" and discounts on male enhancement drugs.[80]

Alongside the rise of franchises like *Law and Order* came "reality TV" and its rituals of humiliation and punishment so numerous that scholars identified "humiliation TV" as a major subgenre of reality television.[81] With its presumably unscripted programming and nonprofessional actors, reality TV was not entirely new, and it was too contrived to depict reality. Moreover, it had links both tight and loose to the punitive turn. An early example was *COPS*, a popular show running on Fox from 1989 to 2013 (and on other networks thereafter) and featuring everyday cops' pursuit of presumed offenders. At the end of the 1990s, scholars concluded, "Television reality crime programs are informed by the conservative ideologies that support current crime policies. Crime is seen as a serious problem, and longer prison sentences, not probation and parole, are offered as the solution."[82] It is debatable how conservative those ideologies were and how much audiences saw the messages scholars discerned, but the television shows' law-and-order thrust was undeniable. Critics faulted *COPS'* exploitation of poor, low-level criminals and the humiliating spectacle of their powerlessness, often in physically or psychologically embarrassing circumstances. The message was that criminals deserved not only capture and punishment, but degradation.

Like *COPS*, reality TV generally "tells us empathy has no place in our lives."[83] There had been humiliation in the sunnier era of game-show television, critics noted. Losers, whether on *The $64,000 Question* (1955–58), *The Price Is Right* (1955–65 and later iterations), or *Queen for a Day* (1956–64) were, after all, losers. But the losers' loss was often explained by luck rather than personal failings—they drew the wrong card, or they guessed the wrong price. And even losers usually won something. It was a long way from *Queen for a Day* to, say, *The Biggest Loser*, a show with obese contestants that debuted in 2004.

Punishing bad guys was all the rage on television programming in and after the Clinton era. Defending the good guy had become less common. Whereas *Dragnet* had focused on catching bad guys, *Law and Order* focused on punishing them, concluding "with definitive guilty verdicts, punctuated by a signature sound effect."[84] The judicious conclusions of Katherine Beckett in 1997 seem likely to stand: "Surveys show that heavy consumers of violent television crime shows are more likely to see the world as a violent and frightening place and to adopt a 'retributive justice perspective.'" And "the media's reproduction of the official view of crime and drugs played an important role in generating support for crime and drug policies aimed at punishment rather than prevention."[85] Among "heavy consumers" were not just voters, but politicians and police chiefs, detectives and judges. The "media's reproduction of the official view of crime" did not cause the Clinton-era punitive turn, but it certainly provided another opening for it.

How Bases Became Prisons

Drive on U.S. 31 just north of Kokomo, Indiana, a buckle in the Midwest's Rust Belt, and notice one product of the transfer of resources from the armed forces to criminal justice: an Indiana state prison on the edge of the old, mammoth Grissom Air Force Base, established in July 1942. Where nuke-carrying B-47 and B-58 bombers of the Strategic Air Command once took off, a prison was erected to incarcerate thousands of people. A residual military facility (the Grissom Joint Air Reserve Base), an outdoor museum with a motley collection of Cold War–era aircraft, and an abandoned roadside diner near the base entrance offer reminders of what the base had once been. The state prison, the Miami Correctional Facility, is one of the few structures that look new. Writing under the headline "Battle Plan for Correction," a reporter noted in 2000, after the prison opened, "[It] looks something like a high-tech POW camp."[86] Drive many other places to see something similar. Dozens of downsized or decommissioned military bases became sites for prisons, in a process that revealed the institutional and political underpinnings of the punitive turn, and showed how many hands were at its wheel.

That transfer had a long, messy backstory. In their many expansions, contractions, reorganizations, and adaptations to new technologies, the armed forces had shut down or scaled back hundreds of stateside bases by the 1980s. As an official 1995 report noted, "Excess military property has been a source for new Federal correctional facilities since the late 1890s." The first federal penitentiary opened in 1903 adjacent to Fort Leavenworth, the army base that housed the maximum-security U.S. Military Barracks for military offenders. In the federal system's expansion during the 1930s, military bases "provided the sites for new prisons," and the Federal Bureau of Prisons took over an army prison on Alcatraz Island, in San Francisco Bay, to house felons "possessed of ingenuity, resources and cunning far beyond that of the ordinary offender."[87] After 1945, many wartime bases (some only temporary from the start) closed, while new ones, especially for the air force, went up. By the 1970s, putting prisons on military property had long been in the institutional DNA of American governance.

Yet such use of military property had remained limited. Some 950 military facilities were identified for closure or retrenchment in the 1960s, but virtually none ended up serving criminal justice purposes. Demobilization then was smaller in scale and more gradual in pace than the post–Cold War version, and it emerged in a gentler economic climate, with community and corporate demand for closed facilities and abundant federal support for finding new uses for them. As a 1970 study found, "The economic recovery efforts of these individual communities [where bases closed] in many instances proved to be remarkably successful." Given a robust economy, conversion often involved industrial facilities and commercial aviation, but it extended to "correcting the transportation, educational, recreational, hospital and other public needs of the individual communities." On the site of a former Snark missile base near Presque Isle, Maine, for example, an industrial park with a vocational-technical institute sprang up. Edgemont, South

Dakota, struggled after closure of the Black Hills Army Depot in 1967 but found space for both an ammunition maker and a nursing home for the "retarded."[88]

To a striking degree, demobilized facilities were regarded as opportunities for reinvestment in public or private infrastructures, not as burdens to be bewailed. In 1970, federal officials anticipated that post-Vietnam demobilization would be bigger in scale and harder to manage, but they did not foresee the conversion of bases to prisons. Nor was there yet the rapid growth in the incarcerated population to invite them to do so. Conversion quickened in the late 1970s and early 1980s, when eight former military sites came to house state correctional facilities, according to one survey. But those facilities were mostly small, and other kinds of property, above all mental health facilities, were modified into prison sites more often than military bases were.[89]

Nothing had happened before the 1980s like what soon happened—nothing of the scale, political muscle, and public hype—because never before had so much military downsizing coincided with so much economic decline and so much alarm about crime. It took the convergence of all three circumstances to drive the conversion of bases into prisons. Facing rapid growth in the imprisoned population and hoping for more, Reagan's tough-on-crime administration spotted bases as one place to house inmates. In August 1981 the Attorney General's Task Force on Violent Crime recommended a search for "abandoned military bases for use by states and localities as correctional facilities on an interim and emergency basis only." In October, associate attorney general Rudolph Giuliani followed up, directing U.S. attorneys to "identify any unused military facilities" and other federal property in their districts "that could be utilized as or converted for use as correctional facilities." The new directive dropped the phrase "interim and emergency basis only."[90] "Through our surplus Federal property program," Reagan told the National Sheriffs' Association in 1984, "we've helped States and localities in expanding prison space."[91]

The effort to close bases stalled as Reagan's Cold War placed new demands on the military and Congress resisted the closures, but Bush brought the issue back in his 1988 campaign, urging that bases "not needed" be repurposed as state prisons for the war on drugs. Doing so would be "the single most important thing Congress could do" in that war.[92] And Congress found a way out of its deadlock over base closings that year by turning decisions over to a presumably impartial commission.[93] The BRAC (Base Realignment and Closure Commission) reports in 1988, 1991, 1993, and 1995, coinciding with the end of the Cold War, opened the floodgates for conversion of bases to prisons. Congress could still interfere—members inveighed against the loss of bases in their districts—and the armed services often resisted, but most closings and realignments went forward.

The BRAC process only identified the bases to be closed or "re-aligned" (a euphemism for reduced); it did not designate their use thereafter. That was determined by a tedious pull-and-haul among local and regional interests, politicians, the Department of Defense, and other agencies that sometimes had an eye on the turf, all operating in a difficult economic climate and amid growing concerns about the environmental damage left behind at abandoned bases. The result was a deluge of emptied bases dumped on a faltering economy that produced little private demand for the liberated property. As the General Accounting Office reported in 1994, midway through the process, "Revenues from property sales will be far less than DOD's original and revised estimates," and "the vast majority of the disposed property is being retained by DOD or transferred to other federal agencies and states and localities at no cost."[94] What to do with those "disposed" bases?

There was no master plan to turn bases into prison sites, and many went to other purposes, but prisons were often the outcome. A good example was Fort Dix, established in 1917 and long a giant army base for training enlistees and processing their exit from service. The 1988 BRAC commission slated it for reduction and realignment, moving its basic-training function elsewhere, but it was already more than a gleam in the eye of those seeking new prison sites. In 1982 the federal government had leased the army stockade at Fort Dix to the State of New Jersey for use as a prison housing 500 inmates. The 1988 BRAC report also suggested that abandoned bases might be devoted to "social ends such as . . . drug rehabilitation and prisons."[95]

With BRAC's announcement, coinciding with the apogee of the Reagan-Bush war on drugs, powerful voices sounded off. In February 1989, New York mayor Ed Koch announced his desire to use Dix and other bases to house prisons and treatment centers for drug offenders, and in May he proposed that Dix be a site for "boot camps" for offenders. "I believe," he said, "that the people who have business around Fort Dix would like it." Indeed, the economic fate of nearby communities worried not only locals but also the Justice and Defense Departments, which hardly wanted to be scorned as job-killing machines. The language of war sang at a mayors' conference on crime and drugs, where Koch spoke. For the mayor of Elkhart, Indiana, using troops along

America's borders to stop the flow of drugs fit into "an international effort congruent to the scale of a world war." Meanwhile, a DEA official spoke, not altogether approvingly, of how America was "using the instruments of war" in fighting drugs.[96] By the early 1990s, useful precedents for action at Fort Dix had emerged, since four air force bases in the South had come to host minimum-security federal prisons.[97]

By 1993, inmates were "pouring in[to]" the Fort Dix Federal Correctional Institution. This minimum-security facility became the largest federal prison, housing at times over 4,000 inmates, plus several hundred more in a "satellite" camp nearby, with still more at the existing state facility. The arrangement created what the *New York Times* approvingly labeled a "new growth industry" for New Jersey. Further cementing the link between crime-fighting and national security, "more than 60 per cent of its first 750 permanent inmates" were "aliens," the *Times* noted, coming from sixty-three countries.[98]

Justice Department officials and others like Mayor Koch flagged cost and security as reasons to establish prisons on military sites like Fort Dix. Land costs alone made a big difference—a Fort Dix parcel came virtually free, whereas private property for a site would have to be bought. Yet the savings were limited, for prisons could rarely just take over military buildings unchanged. Planning for the Fort Dix prison included using some barracks but building new facilities as well, plus changing the area infrastructure to provide security. The "five miles of two rows of razor wire–clad chain-link fencing" with "the latest in electronic sensing devices" did not come cheap.[99]

Elsewhere, new prisons were built from scratch on former bases. Beyond cost, an unspoken consideration was simply that federal land on bases was available for the taking, with no need to haggle with private landowners and arouse the ire or envy of their neighbors. Officials also cited the need to offset the economic impact of base closures and reductions. Some 3,100 of 4,000 civilian jobs at Fort Dix were to be axed, but the new prison would replace up to 700 of them.[100] Officials kept careful watch on local opposition, but it seemed minimal in the Dix case, with one local politician providing assurance that while prisoners in state prisons "are killers, rapists, everything," drug offenders at a low-security federal Fort Dix prison would be tame by comparison.[101]

And officials cited the need to reduce overcrowding in existing prisons, which were filling up because of mounting convictions and sentencing provisions that kept inmates in prisons longer. Yet a tail-wags-dog issue lurked in that argument. The addition of new prison beds also facilitated the expansion of arrests and the lengthening of prison terms, crowding prisons once again. Creating more jails was akin to building new highways to alleviate traffic jams: new traffic fills the new highways, which once again become jammed.

Most important, siting prisons on military bases allowed politicians and officials to relate crime-fighting to war-fighting in a tangible way. Such jails gave physical expression to the "war on drugs." Furthermore, they helped garner support for harsher laws and sentencing—politicians could argue that the crime crisis was so grave that the discarded instruments of war had to be used to wage it. Placing prisons on military bases strengthened feedback loops between war-fighting and crime-fighting. Crime-fighters borrowed the cachet and importance associated with the armed forces, whereas prisons had often before been regarded as backwater places run by political hacks and cruel or unskilled jailers. Military bases' reputation for security and their distance from residential areas helped as well. Prisons and military bases were, after all, similar institutions; isolated from the rest of America and walled or fenced off, both were secretive places that few civilians entered. There were obvious differences as well. Most military personnel could come and go from their bases; most inmates could not. But the similarities were sufficient to suggest a logic to the placement of prisons on bases. There was no overarching statement of that logic, no White House or Pentagon directive laying it out. The politics of base closures were too localized and Balkanized for that. But the reasoning emerged in what officials and media said about new prisons on shuttered bases.

A telling omission did run through the rhetoric championing the turnover of Fort Dix and other sites to prisons. "With the hot wars and cold wars fading into the past," the *New York Times* observed in 1993, the Fort Dix "base has found itself at the cutting edge of a growth industry tied to another kind of war—against drugs."[102] Never acknowledged in such statements was the obvious fact that the enemies in the "hot and cold wars fading into the past" were different from those in this new "kind of war." The former were largely people and regimes far away, the latter mostly U.S. citizens. Once "they" were "them." Now "they" were "us." But such rhetoric implicitly left them the same, both enemies. In 1993, when President Clinton touted a new program to turn veterans into police officers, he added, "After defending our freedom abroad, they'll be given a chance to do so at home."[103] How "freedom abroad" was the same as freedom at home, and how freedom's enemies might differ on those two fronts, went unexplained.

The creation of Indiana's Miami Correctional Facility unspooled in a different fashion and on a different timetable than that of the Fort Dix

Correctional Center, though with a similar outcome. Grissom was an air base, not an army depot, distant from the big-city drug wars evident in Dix's creation, and different in its economic underpinnings. Most communities feared the loss of jobs and economic stimulus that came from closing or downsizing bases. But Grissom, the largest employer in its county, dominated the area far more than Fort Dix did populous New Jersey, and that area was already hemorrhaging jobs. Nearby Kokomo was enduring the travails of the auto industry, particularly of Chrysler, as employment and hours shrank at its several plants (in 2008 *Forbes* ranked Kokomo third on its list of America's fastest dying towns, though a turnaround for Chrysler and Kokomo later ensued). The area depended for employment either on Kokomo, a fast-consolidating farm economy, or the Grissom base.

In 1991 BRAC slated Grissom for partial closure, ranking it "below average in the flying-strategic category" (a C grade in its scheme). The base held some 2,000 air force personnel and 450 civilian employees. Local and state politicians protested on economic and strategic grounds ("[its] location deep in the interior of the country makes the base better able to survive cruise missile and submarine-launched missile attacks"), but to no avail. As a full air base it ceased operations in 1994. Also on the chopping block were Grissom's gym, commissary, golf course, hospital, bowling alley, and Randall Elementary School, with some 400 students and several dozen teachers.[104]

As locals debated what to do, few sounded off about a war on drugs or overcrowded prisons—the talk that engulfed the Fort Dix decision. But by the 1990s, every state had a drug war, both in larger cities and in smaller towns and rural areas where it was harder to see or at least to acknowledge, in part because drug use there often involved white people. (A bit later, nearby Elkhart County, with only a small minority population, was sending a higher proportion of people to prison than any other Indiana county, perhaps because all its judges were former career prosecutors.)[105] And the state had to stash the offenders it caught. Its male incarcerated population more than doubled in the two decades after 1982, reaching a total of 19,869, while its smaller female jailed cohort nearly quintupled.[106] A new prison, especially for drug offenders, seemed the solution.

For local voices, the nature of those offenders seemed secondary, although one gubernatorial candidate did tell area Republicans that he "believe[d] in prison chain gangs."[107] Instead, people near the base maintained a laser-like focus on jobs and economic vitality. That focus also reflected national voices distressed over the economic damage wrought by post–Cold War retrenchment. At a lengthy news conference about base closings in July 1993, Clinton and key cabinet members oozed anxiety. Clinton noted "a jarring economic upheaval." Labor secretary Robert Reich pledged to "send . . . jobs SWAT teams into bases" when closings were announced and expressed doubt that companies trying to "deskill and automate" their workers would have much interest in the bases. Commerce secretary Ron Brown felt "the pain of the communities and individuals" going through the base-closing "trauma." No one at that conference mentioned putting prisons on bases, though conversions were already numerous. They instead fumbled ineffectually toward a more uplifting vision for the fate of closed military facilities. Weeks later, Clinton vaguely promised "reusing military bases" for "community centers" and for "revitalizing the economy," assuring a crowd at a naval base in Alameda, California, "The men and women who won the cold war will not be left out in the cold by a grateful Nation." For a president elected in part on his promise to revive the post–Cold War economy, the desperation to find *something* to put on those bases was obvious.[108]

For the Grissom area, that would be a prison, offered by the Indiana Department of Corrections and Democratic governor Evan Bayh. Some thirty-five area businesses formed "Citizens Against the Prison." Opponents feared for "their safe rural landscape" and pointed out that low-paying prison jobs would hardly boost the local economy. But foes were drowned out at a community forum in 1996 that drew 2,200 people to a local high school gym; those detractors "tried futilely to sound as loud" as the much bigger bloc championing a prison. Proponents offered "a passionate plea for the prison" and pointed out that "$10-an-hour [in prison job pay] would be a raise for a lot of people." It was, a local waitress admitted, "not the best tradeoff for a military base," but it was also better than nothing. "I mean, if you look in the paper, there ain't nothing [in the way of jobs] in it." "Project Spells Prosperity," one newspaper headline promised. Those voices underlined another advantage to a prison at Grissom—a local labor force willing to take low-paying and sometimes dangerous prison jobs, for which recruitment could be tough in economically vibrant areas.[109]

Prison backers got their way, and perhaps more than they bargained for. Initial talk was of a 1,000-bed prison, but Miami Correctional eventually reached a capacity of over 3,000 inmates housed in cells and dormitories covering a wide range of security grades. Ground was broken in 1997, with the new facility built from scratch on base land and the first inmates arriving in 1999. With its low-slung concrete buildings and narrow slit windows surrounded by high barbed-wire fences, it looked duly austere, though it at least had windows.

No wonder it made sense for a reporter to see Miami Correctional as "something like a high-tech POW camp," as if its inmates were POWs in America's war on drugs. And despite their differences in climate, landscape, inmates, and purpose, Miami Correctional looked a bit like the later Guantánamo Bay detention camp once it was built up beyond its initial tent phase, with each facility displaying a forbidding white concrete facade. Perhaps that was because prisons from any era resemble each other due to similarities in construction materials, architectural fashion, and security arrangements. But more than coincidence was involved. Miami Correctional's first superintendent, John VanNatta, who helped design the new prison, did double duty while at Miami as a commander of the U.S. Army Reserve's 300th Military Police Command, whose task "in wartime" was to "set up barracks for enemy POWs." He was "as much a war planner as a warden," the *Indianapolis Star* reported, a man with "a bust of Julius Caesar on his desk," who found that "the mixing of prison and military cultures is only natural" and who "thrived" at "designing state facilities for prisoners in Indiana as well as camps for prisoners of war in foreign countries."[110] VanNatta embodied the feedback loops between crime-fighting and war-fighting.

It was no coincidence that most prisons sited on military bases handled drug offenders. There were so many such offenders (though they comprised a minority of the total imprisoned population) that prisons for them were the most needed. At Miami Correctional, inmates, many of them products of the meth epidemic in small-town and rural middle America, could enter its Clean Living Is Freedom Forever (CLIFF) program—a rather Orwellian name for a carefully structured program initiated in 2005. A big banner proclaiming that program was visible to drivers along U.S. 31.[111] As need and numbers drove the use of new prisons placed on bases, the war on drugs was the dimension of criminal justice most closely associated, in rhetoric and operations, with war making.

Though many bases birthed prisons, many others did not due to local opposition and the limits of demand for all the discarded bases. After all, the BRAC commissions had "recommended closure of 98 major bases and hundreds of smaller installations," with many others slated for reduction.[112] When the Federal Bureau of Prisons surveyed some nineteen bases "potentially suitable" as federal prison sites in 1995 (by then, many bases like Fort Dix had already undergone conversion), it struck ten from the list because of "community opposition," scratched several more for other reasons (like "seismic instability"), and marked only three for possible conversion to federal prisons, though other bases came to house state or local prisons.[113] Even at bases selected as prison sites, prisons did not need the vast expanses involved—runways, training fields, recreational facilities. The Miami facility used none of Grissom's buildings; it simply occupied a sliver of land once a part of the base. And even the shrunken air reserve base remained a major enterprise. Its combined military and civilian workforce ranked it "as the largest employer in Miami County [which did not include Kokomo] and the third largest employer in north-central Indiana."[114]

But the transfer of resources was still large, even though no authoritative count exists.[115] From the 1980s to the early 2000s, at least five dozen military bases became sites of criminal justice facilities, among them the Bureau of Prisons' Federal Medical Center Devens, opened in 1999 on land from the army's vast Fort Devens, which was sharply scaled back to become an army reserve base. Meanwhile, a high proportion of prison staff across the nation had done military service—over 40 percent according to a survey released in 2000[116]—and many continued to do so as members of the guard or reserves. Moreover, the base-to-prison movement of the 1990s coincided with the latest federal effort to move military veterans into law enforcement. The Justice and Defense Departments' "Troops to COPS" program "reimbursed agencies up to $5,000 [per individual] to defray the cost of hiring eligible veterans as law enforcement officers." "Military veterans are valuable assets to any potential employer," a Defense Department official noted, but "law enforcement is an extension of a lifestyle they know and understand." The official did not detail which elements of that "lifestyle" he had in mind.[117] The connections between the older purpose of Grissom and the new goals of Miami Correctional kept reworking and expanding, as VanNatta's career showed.

Of course, other prisons were built without tapping military facilities. There were many pathways to mass incarceration, among them the conversion of mental hospitals to criminal justice facilities, as the population of institutionalized mentally ill people plummeted to "negligible levels."[118] For example, the Rochester State Hospital in Minnesota closed in 1982,[119] but its site and some of its facilities became a medical center for the Federal Bureau of Prisons in 1984, a prison for the medically needy and for other, often older, prisoners warranting special protection or lacking other placement in the federal system. In 2002, the facility housed Alfred Taubman, a shopping-mall tycoon and former Sotheby's chairman who was put away for financial crimes;

Justin Volpe, one of the New York City policemen convicted of sodomizing Abner Louima with a broken broomstick; William Hanhardt, a former Chicago police chief of detectives convicted for his role in a jewelry-theft ring; and, until April 2002, Sheik Omar Abdel Rahman, the "blind sheik" sentenced for his role in the 1993 World Trade Center bombing. There, psychiatric staff from the old hospital, many affiliated with the Mayo Clinic, transferred to the Bureau of Prisons, thereby providing better care than most prisons could dream of, with some inmates treated at the Mayo Clinic.[120]

That example underlines how numerous the institutional pathways to mass incarceration were, as well as how diverse the outcomes were. Near a residential area, Federal Medical Center Rochester, with its low-slung brick buildings, playing fields, green lawn, tall trees, and flowers (surrounded by high fencing), looked more like a community college than a prison. Few other jails could sport "predoctoral psychology internships" or assert it was "placing a high priority on the humane treatment of patients," keeping them "in the least restrictive environment for treatment purposes."[121]

Just as the Rochester facility had no direct connection to the military base system, so too did many facilities affording inmates (or arrestees) the harshest treatment. That was the case with many local jail systems operating with little or no state and federal oversight, such as the one that Sheriff Joe Arpaio, an army veteran, ran in Maricopa County, Arizona. The baroquely complex and variegated American incarceration system—no major country's system operated through such a dense network of jurisdictions and political processes—afforded countless ways to treat prisoners badly or well, and to stack up their numbers.

But the conversion of military bases to prison sites made mass incarceration happen more easily, more squarely within the political culture of the time, and in more militarized fashion. Of all the pathways to mass incarceration, it opened with the least resistance and operated with the most robust feedback loops between the realms of war-fighting and crime-fighting. Where soldiers and airmen once marched, inmates and guards often took their place.

The Call of Vengeance

The words used by and about Clinton regarding crime usually set the war framework aside, but they did not displace it, much less its institutional foundations. Word-use tracking suggests that phrases like "war on crime" and "war on drugs" remained in robust use through and beyond the 1990s. The more frequent employment of "war on drugs" hints that for many people, "war on crime" by and large just meant the "war on drugs."[122] Meanwhile, the prison population swelled, new prisons like Indiana's Miami Correctional Facility opened, a drug war at home was enmeshed with one abroad, and the militarization of policing—better thought of as the militarization of criminal justice—continued. Soon, reactions to the 9/11 attacks would further energize the feedback loops between war-fighting and crime-fighting. In 2000, former New York and LA police chief William Bratton expressed hope for a "peace dividend"; falling crime might encourage gentler and perhaps less expensive policing.[123] Like the "peace dividend" imagined at the end of the Cold War, this one did not materialize.

It hardly could given the currents of vengeance now set loose. As the United States pursued vengeance abroad, before 9/11 and more after it, retribution also gained prominence in American criminal justice, especially through the vehicle of victims' rights. Any criminal justice system harbors elements of vengeance, often implicit or voiced outside formal arenas. Revenge hovered at the edges of decades of calls and actions to make sentences mandatory and longer, to reinstate the death penalty, to curb inmates' legal rights, to appoint or elect tougher judges—to execute the punitive turn. Initially, proponents presented victims' rights as a kind of judicial balancing act: Since accused criminals have rights, should not victims, too? Clinton made that case on June 25, 1996, in endorsing a constitutional amendment to enshrine those rights: "Today, the system bends over backwards to protect those who may be innocent, and that is as it should be. But it too often ignores the millions and millions of people who are completely innocent because they're victims, and that is wrong." Victims, it was argued, should have the right to be present at trials even if they are also witnesses. They should also be allowed to testify in the penalty phase of trials and to have a voice in parole and probation decisions.

But by then, victims' rights advocacy had become more strident and explicit about the pursuit of vengeance. It was pushed by groups like MADD, feminist antirape organizations, and criminal justice lobbies and theorists. Victims' rights was "a marriage of feminism and conservatism," asserts Jill Lepore ("a bad marriage," she adds). The goal of punishment, its advocates suggested, was not only to deter, incapacitate, or even punish. It was to weaponize the anger of victims (perhaps individuals, perhaps the whole nation), whose "healing" (therapeutic language was abundant) would then be promoted. Some proponents asserted victims' "right to hate" and argued that a "desire for vengeance is our natural need for retribution." Critics argued, to little avail, that this approach to justice set aside victims' very real tangible needs. The 1997 trial of Timothy McVeigh for the Oklahoma City bombing, with its many child victims, "marked the movement's turning point," notes Lepore. By 1998, one critic thought, victims' rights had come "to focus almost entirely on an individual's right to have an offender swiftly punished, with the punishment based on revenge and incapacitation." Victims' testimony also pushed judges, regarded in the movement as liberal and softhearted, toward harsher sentencing. It was impossible to prove that an exercise of victims' rights actually made victims feel better ("heal"), or even that a primary purpose of justice was to make them feel better. But the movement went forward almost unimpeded through changes in state constitutions, state and federal laws, and court procedures.[124]

"Vengeance is mine, saith the Lord," goes one version of Romans 12:19, but many people claimed the right to seek vengeance or to be conduits for it. It was part of a process whereby "what was once civil society has become a state of war," Lepore concludes.[125] And especially after 9/11, it spilled beyond the nation's borders.

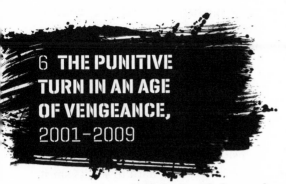

6 THE PUNITIVE TURN IN AN AGE OF VENGEANCE, 2001-2009

Tightly braided together before the September 11, 2001, attacks, war-fighting and crime-fighting became even more so after them—in many countries, but especially in the United States. As they did, the punitive turn moved into new or less developed arenas of control, imprisonment, violence, and torture, even as its core of mass incarceration continued to swell. And the spirit of vengeance nourished during the punitive turn burst forth anew under the horrifying provocation of the 9/11 terrorist attacks, and with new consequences. The age of vengeance had no single starting point; retribution was an element of the punitive turn from its start. But the attacks of September 11 acted like a bomb dropped on already-combustible materials. The fusion of war-fighting with crime-fighting and the pursuit of vengeance were themes of the George W. Bush presidency, ones that he did little to anticipate but much to abet.

American Vengeance Goes Global

Bush had a well-earned reputation as a tough-on-crime Texas governor (1995–2000) who "took over a criminal justice system that was already the largest and arguably harshest in the nation" and made "it tougher still." He served as "Texas's Jailer in Chief" in what "had become America's punishment heartland."[1] Running for election in 1994, he proposed "temporary barracks" for prisoners, saying, "If that's good enough for our military, it's good enough for criminals."[2] As candidate, Bush dwelled on juvenile lawbreaking, liked war-on-crime rhetoric, ridiculed social explanations for criminality, scorned "guilt-ridden thought" about it, advocated trial as adults for many juvenile offenders, and promoted a jail-building spree. "In order to win the war, we've got to make these criminals realize we mean punishment," he stated. "They'll start changing once they realize they're going to get punished every time they screw up."[3]

As governor, Bush echoed right-wing Christian rhetoric regarding young offenders: "Discipline and love go hand in hand."[4] He boasted that Texas had "the highest incarceration rate in the nation" and that "surgical castration [for sex offenders was] now an option in Texas."[5] Furthermore, he vetoed a law that would have spared the death penalty for mentally disabled death row inmates. Indeed, Bush became famous for his simple defense of the death penalty—it would deter crime—and for his dislike of any doubts about its application, ultimately presiding over 152 executions. In this, he echoed his father's 1988 campaign for the presidency and his words as president. The younger Bush avoided an explicit language of vengeance, but it was not hard to see its spirit in his public stance.

But little of that stance emerged in George W. Bush's 2000 campaign or at the start of his presidency. Bush billed himself as a "compassionate conservative," although his campaign's brutal, race-baiting attacks on Senator John McCain before the South Carolina primary exposed his mean streak. Given falling crime rates, Clinton's success in outflanking Republicans on crime, the absence of some horrible incident, and his own greater priorities elsewhere—above all, concerning tax cuts—Bush and his campaign lacked the provocation to say much about crime and the payoff for doing so.

As president, Bush was hardly loquacious, given to terse assertions rather than careful explanations. Attorney General John Ashcroft announced vaguely progressive measures like a challenge to racial profiling in policing and modest initiatives on gun control. Neither offered flame-throwing or moralizing rhetoric on crime—even "war on drugs" and "war on crime" rarely appeared in the Bush administration's rhetoric. Bush was the "new sheriff in town," as his press secretary called him on January 31, but on crime he did not talk like one beyond his formulaic defense of the death penalty. The president touted his education plan ("No Child Left Behind") and "faith-based" initiatives as his chief crime-fighting measures. As he told black law enforcement officials on July 30, "We must have goals beyond just punishment" and make "sure we've got good education systems all around America." Maintaining that "an educated child is one much less likely to commit a crime," Bush challenged the "the soft bigotry of low expectations." He and his press secretary decreed that arrests of his daughters for underage drinking were a private matter.

Nor did Bush link crime-fighting and its machinery to terrorism fighting and its machinery. Instead, the administration initially kept the two separate, in part because it regarded terrorism largely as a state-sponsored threat that enemies like Iran or Iraq would act on through weapons of mass destruction. Thus the danger had to be countered by weapons of war. "We need a missile defense system that prevents the world from being held hostage by terrorism," Bush said on March 26, 2001. Even more than crime, terrorism elicited from Bush and his subordinates frequent but formulaic mention. "We have no higher priority than the defense of our people against terrorist attack," he announced on February 13, but he spoke few words about that priority, whereas tax cuts triggered a tsunami of talk from his administration. For his part, Attorney General Ashcroft, though in charge of the FBI, said almost nothing about terrorism, even in forums inviting attention to the topic.[6]

Administration members' public record mirrored their private deliberations. Abundant evidence indicates that the danger of terrorism rarely reached Bush and his inner circle and got little attention when it did.[7] It is no surprise that the administration issued no warnings of a surprise attack—surprise attacks do not get advance notice. It is startling that Bush and his staff offered little sense of urgency in public about terrorism, and when they did they usually misplaced it, presenting it as a menace sponsored by states rather than nonstate organizations like al-Qaeda. No wonder, then, that Bush and his inner circle (though not counterterrorism "czar" Richard Clarke or the Central Intelligence Agency) were as surprised by the 9/11 attacks as other Americans were. There had been no buildup of alarm, in contrast to December 7, 1941 (a precedent Bush soon cited), when most Americans were surprised that Japan attacked Pearl Harbor but not that Japan had launched an attack somewhere.

In turn, how the United States would regard the 9/11 attacks (as acts of war or as heinous crimes?) and respond to them (with what machinery of state, society, and the international order?) briefly seemed an open matter. A scattering of voices insisted, as one *New Yorker* piece put it, that "the metaphor of war . . . ascribes to the perpetrators [of the 9/11 attacks] a dignity they do not merit, a status they cannot claim, and a strength they do not possess."[8] Others straddled various fences. General Wesley Clark opined about "How to Fight the New War," as his article in *Time* magazine was titled, but a fight "based on deadly accurate police work" at least as much as "force."[9] The philosopher of war Michael Walzer maintained, "We should pursue the metaphorical war" but "hold back on the real thing."[10] Advocates of a criminal justice approach pointed to international law, courts, and peace-keeping—a model that roughly fit the Clinton administration's approach to the

Balkans crisis—but critics scorned this as slow, indecisive, and mired in legalisms.

Louder voices, hardly only conservative or Republican, insisted this was war, as their analogies to Pearl Harbor emphasized. Many were also bent on a unilateral approach, except when alliances could be forged on U.S. terms, and a fast-acting one (although war turned out to be a slow-acting tactic at best). Strategist Eliot A. Cohen sounded the note that dominated the administration and most media chatter: "This is not about cops and robbers, nor about international order. It is, rather, war—hideous, brutal, and merciless war."[11] Those who saw it otherwise were "fifth column" leftists, according to Andrew Sullivan, while the *New Republic's* Lawrence Kaplan lumped Osama bin Laden and Saddam Hussein together with critic Susan Sontag, who found fault with the United States.[12]

Bush had decided on war even before that debate got under way. "We're at war," he told Vice President Dick Cheney by phone on September 11,[13] then told other key officials the same over the next few days, as he did the public on September 15 and Congress on September 20. Fearing worse attacks, humiliated that they had not stopped those on 9/11, and determined to inflict punishment for them,[14] Bush and his team had no hesitation in deciding for war. Defense Secretary Donald Rumsfeld and Senate majority leader Tom Daschle briefly pushed back against Bush's embrace of warfare, but to no avail.[15] Indeed, that embrace was hardly just Bush's impulsive reaction to 9/11: presidents and other officials had designated American responses to terrorism as "war" since the Reagan administration. It was woven into the fabric of national policy and rhetoric that Bush would do so.

But Bush grasped war more loudly, persistently, and operationally in reaction to the greater provocation of the 9/11 attacks. On September 16, he referred to "this crusade, this war on terrorism." By September 20, in his address to Congress, it was "our war on terror." His analogies and references to the Pearl Harbor attack—on September 11 he dictated a message that read, "The Pearl Harbor of the 21st century took place today"[16]—underlined his stance and suggested the presumed stakes and scale of this new war. The president's denunciation of the "axis of evil" (Iran, Iraq, North Korea) in his January 29, 2002, State of the Union address made an implicit comparison to World War II given that "the axis" was a term for America's enemies in that war. As Bush told Congress on February 4, "Americans will never forget the murderous events of September 11, 2001. They are for us what Pearl Harbor was to an earlier generation of Americans: a terrible wrong and a call to action." By June 20, 2002, Bush had publicly named the response to 9/11 a "global war on terror" (others had already introduced the term), which soon became a "global war on terrorism" (with the awkward acronym "GWOT"), a term accorded official status (in March 2003, for example, Bush created the Global War on Terrorism Service Medal). Less apparent to the public, the rush of some in the administration to link Saddam Hussein to the 9/11 attacks and to gin up a war against him showed how fast the war frame gained traction among key officials.

Quickly after 9/11, Congress and most Americans seemed to agree that "war" aptly described both the attacks and the appropriate response. Congress did reject Bush's request that its authorization-of-force resolution, passed on September 14, include a provision "to use all necessary and appropriate force *in* the United States."[17] But the Office of Legal Counsel gave that resolution an unbounded definition, asserting on September 25 that "decisions" regarding it and other legal and constitutional provisions "are for the president alone to make."[18] In 2007, a legal scholar glossed the views of John Yoo, the pivotal Justice Department figure interpreting the president's powers, as follows: "Civil libertarians and human rights advocates make one central mistake, and they make it again and again, on every issue in the war on terror: they regard the struggle against al-Qaeda as a matter of criminal justice, in which all the protections rightly built into our criminal justice system should apply. But according to Yoo, protections that are right for criminal law are dangerously wrong for confronting terrorist threats."[19]

U.S. military action in Afghanistan in the fall of 2001 and in Iraq in 2003 turned the word "war" into reality. "I'm a war president," Bush proudly commented on *Meet the Press*, on February 8, 2004. War was his chosen category, both for his nation and his role in it—he found purpose and self-esteem as the commander in chief. Leaving office, he commented, "You know, I've got mixed emotions. I'm going to miss being the Commander in Chief of the military."[20] This was odd comment given the burdens that role had involved, but Bush seemed to have in mind the pomp and stature involved more than the substance. Being "jailer in chief," the criminal justice model for responding to 9/11, paled in comparison.

The impulse for vengeance in Bush's record as governor erupted after 9/11. His "messianic conviction" followed suit, as he promised on September 14 and on December 20 to do no less than "rid the world of evil." "Bush considered himself the agent of God placed on earth to combat evil," a biographer argues.[21] Dubbing an enemy "evil" was hardly a novel practice, but Bush's use of the term echoed earlier rhetoric that placed criminal evil beyond understanding and cast criminals out of humanity. He hardly invited attempts to understand why the United States' new enemies had attacked it. "Evil" was a substitute for explanation, as in discourses on crime. The death penalty was even more apt for these new "evildoers" (a word Bush used many times, starting on September 13) than it had been for those executed when he was governor. Bush, one scholar argues, "took Texas-style justice to Washington and, after 9/11, to the world," and his time as governor "previewed his punishing response to the attacks of September 11, 2001."[22]

For Bush, the war he proclaimed was a giant exercise in applying Texas-style justice to a new set of evil criminals. He clearly understood that conflict to be retributive, not just defensive. When Defense Secretary Donald Rumsfeld pointed out on 9/11 that international law sanctioned force only to prevent attacks, not to inflict punishment, "Bush exploded. 'No,' the president shouted. 'I don't care what the international lawyers say, we are going to kick some ass.'"[23] An aged and furious Senator Robert Byrd later complained that the president displayed a "kind of retribution-soaked anger."[24] That anger was all the easier to display because the United States had little reason to fear retaliation for acting on it. Though vengeance had underwritten America's bombing of Libya in 1986, U.S. leaders had tempered their words and actions during the Cold War for fear of reprisals by nuclear-tipped Soviet or Chinese missiles. After 9/11, U.S. leaders did fear new, perhaps worse (radiological or bacteriological) attacks. But they seemed unconcerned that their words and actions could trigger such strikes, which in any event could not approach Cold War powers' capabilities. Apparently unrivaled and unbounded, the United States was freer to pursue retribution, not just defense.

By instinct as well as political calculations shaped by Vice President Dick Cheney and senior advisor Karl Rove, Bush tapped into widely felt attitudes connecting vengeance toward criminals with vengeance toward the new enemies. In the dry language of social science offered by a scholar of attitudes about the 1991 and 2003 wars against Iraq, "Otherwise typical strong death penalty supporters were 12 percent more likely than strong opponents to favor the immediate use of force against Iraq in late 1990, and 36 percent more likely to favor war in 2003."[25] That is, an eye-for-an-eye sensibility, widely cultivated before 9/11 regarding crime, strengthened punitive attitudes toward terrorists and toward Iraq's Saddam Hussein, who some officials publicly hinted (despite evidence to the contrary) had sponsored terrorism, possibly even the 9/11 attacks.

Thus America's responses to 9/11 were shaped as much by its values, including those accrued in the punitive turn, as by national security realities, or even the perception of them. The feedback loops between war-fighting and crime-fighting were emotional, visceral, and attitudinal, as well as political and material. U.S. leaders applied their attitudes and postures toward criminal evildoers at home to those who attacked from outside. It was one of the ways in which the United States, as Marilyn Young acidly put it, "became even more itself, almost to the point of caricature," rather than charting some new course after 9/11.[26] The 9/11 attacks were a rupture in history for Americans and much of the world, but the country's response to them fit into established grooves of American belief and practice.

The push for retribution was widely evident in the days after 9/11. "For Many," a *New York Times* headline from September 14 read, "Sorrow Turns to Anger and Talk of Vengeance." Cheney, asked on *Meet the Press* on the sixteenth whether he would like to have bin Laden's "head on a platter," responded, "I would take it today."[27] The Bush administration's use of torture, exposed to the public in 2004 (and taken up in the next section), similarly revealed that desire for vengeance. After 9/11, even more than before, American vengeance went global.[28]

Vengeance works most easily when it is meshed with and shrouded by other motivations with various degrees of plausibility. The eye-for-an-eye approach to criminal justice bundled several arguments: the satisfactions of vengeance, the claim that harsh punishment deters crime, the assertion that nothing else works, and so forth. The same thinking applied to American wars. Incarceration of Japanese Americans during World War II satisfied desires to punish the enemy and allayed unfounded fears of Japanese subversion on the West Coast. President Truman presented the United States' use of the atomic bomb as an act of retribution. "The Japanese began the war from the air at Pearl Harbor. They have been repaid manyfold," he announced, later telling a radio audience, "[The Japanese] have starved and beaten and executed American prisoners of war." But he also presented the bomb as a military means to end the war by attacking "Hiroshima, a military base," as he inaccurately labeled the city.[29]

So too in 2003, when the U.S. war on Iraq not only offered vengeance (of a deflected sort) against the 9/11 attackers, but also satisfied other apparent objectives (taking out Hussein's supposed weapons of mass destruction, freeing Iraqis from tyranny, securing Iraq's oil, shielding Israel, bringing democracy to the Middle East). An advisor to Rumsfeld artfully mixed two of those objectives, vengeance and deterrence, when asked in 2001 why the United States would invade Iraq given its lack of responsibility for the 9/11 attacks: "How do you send the message . . . that we don't allow these things—you inflict damage."[30] The historian does not have to decide which of those aims was paramount. They varied within and beyond policy elites and over time, as some (like weapons of mass destruction) turned out to be unjustified. But vengeance was important among these goals. The desire for retribution emerged in comments Bush made at the time and emotions he later recalled: "My blood was boiling," he wrote later about his first reactions to 9/11. "We were going to find out who did this, and kick their ass." As one sober historian sums up the factors leading to war, "The memoirs" of Bush-era officials "illuminate policy makers scrambling to do something to overcome the shock of 9/11, display American power, and satiate popular American demands for vengeance and 'justice.'"[31] To which we can add policymakers' own "demands for vengeance and 'justice.'"

That meant that the wars the United States waged in Afghanistan and Iraq had the character of punitive expeditions, to use a term employed when American forces invaded Mexico in 1916 in response to Pancho Villa's raids on U.S. soil. That phrase would have seemed quaint in 2001—no one in authority used it—and most war making has a punitive element. But the post-9/11 wars were shot through with retaliatory impulses. "Even if their ultimate consequences are unclear," Max Boot wrote in 2002, rather approvingly of America's "small wars," "punitive raids serve an important function. Much like punishments meted out by the criminal justice system, they satisfy the human impulse to see wrongdoers punished."[32] More than most wars, punitive expeditions target single named villains—Pancho Villa, Noriega in Panama, Hussein in Iraq, Osama bin Laden in Afghanistan—seek their punishment or eradication, and end with failed efforts to remake the countries invaded. And just as American crime-fighters often cast themselves as protectors of women, American war-fighters claimed to be protecting Afghan women from the criminal Taliban, who indeed treated them awfully. To media fanfare in November 2001, Laura Bush, in the first time a First Lady gave a president's entire weekly radio address, asserted, "The plight of women and children in Afghanistan is a matter of deliberate human cruelty, carried out by those who seek to intimidate and control." Accompanying her address, the State Department released a report on "The Taliban's War against Women."[33]

Public and private desires flowed, from Bush on down, to humiliate enemies much as criminals were humiliated. A British journalist reported in December 2003 that he had earlier heard "a U.S. senator . . .

talking to Richard Armitage, Colin Powell's deputy at the State Department, about Osama bin Laden. 'I hope we capture that sonofabitch Bin Laden,' said the senator, 'and parade him through Kabul in a cage.' 'I hope we kill him, tie his bullet-ridden body to the ass-end of a donkey, and parade him through Kabul that way,' replied Mr. Armitage." [34] Of course, the desire to demean enemies was hardly unique to this conflict, or to Americans; after all, that impulse drove al-Qaeda's 9/11 attacks. And given those assaults, it was unsurprising that this desire flourished among Americans and others too. More notable was how often that wish got expressed not just in the language of crime-fighting, but in a vigilante-style version of crime-fighting that, in an echo of lynching, often featured wishes for the degradation of the enemy's body.

War-Fighting or Crime-Fighting?

No wonder, then, that circumstance, rhetoric, and policy kept smudging the line Bush drew between war-fighting and crime-fighting. That the 9/11 attacks featured hijacked civilian airliners, rather than war weapons, muddied that line. Bush himself slipped back into the crime-fighter mode in many remarks. Bin Laden, he told reporters on September 15, was a "prime suspect" in what Ashcroft called "this terrible crime." [35] On September 17, Bush also said of Osama bin Laden, "There's an old poster out west, as I recall, that said, 'Wanted: Dead or Alive.'" This analogy placed the hunt for bin Laden in a crime-fighting mode and made Senator Byrd later excoriate the image of "Sheriff Bush leading a posse after a varmint." [36]

On September 20 came Bush's odd analogy "al Qaeda is to terror what the mafia is to crime." At the start of U.S. military action in Afghanistan on October 7, the president called terrorists "outlaws" and "any government sponsors" of them "outlaws and murderers themselves." On October 10, using crime-fighters' lingo, he announced a "Most Wanted Terrorist List" as part of his effort to "round up"—both cowboy and cop words—"the evildoers." Bin Laden had appeared on FBI "Most Wanted Fugitives" posters in 1999, and the FBI's "Most Wanted Terrorist List" of twenty-two released on October 10 featured each of the twenty-two in an individual poster. [37] In addition, the White House asked Fox Television to feature that list on its popular series *America's Most Wanted*— the beating heart of TV crime culture at the time—in an episode that aired on October 12. [38] In word and action, Bush kept blurring the line between war and crime.

Crime lingo coursed through other channels as well. For the invasion of Iraq, the American armed forces developed a pack of "personality identification playing cards"—widely dubbed "most wanted" cards—to help soldiers identify Saddam Hussein (the Ace of Spades) and other Iraqis sought by the United States. These cards are still online today.[39] In turn, the U.S. government and media treated the capture of Hussein by American forces on December 13, 2003, as if a criminal had been snared. The disheveled, humiliated Iraqi leader was forced out of his "spider hole" or "hideaway" like a fugitive felon and paraded before cameras while medics poked in his mouth and checked his hair for lice. This spectacle was the war criminal's version of the "perp walk" shown so often in crime news coverage (reporters later compared Hussein's appearance in an Iraqi court to a "perp walk"). Hussein deserved "a felon's death on the gallows," a British commentator opined. "The world is better off without you, Mr. Saddam Hussein," Bush said on December 15. He added, "I find it very interesting that when the heat got on, you dug yourself a hole, and you crawled in it."[40]

Although U.S. forces gave Hussein prisoner-of-war status, Bush publicly framed his fate as a matter of criminal justice in a December 15, 2003, press conference. "And of course we want it to be fair. And of course we want the world to say, 'Well, this—he got a fair trial,' because whatever justice is meted out needs to stand international scrutiny." Iraqis soon executed Hussein. Because bin Laden's execution by U.S. special forces in Pakistan in 2011 yielded no authoritative video the public could see, was announced by a president whose language was more circumspect, and produced no humiliated or degraded body, the playful caught-the-bad-guy circus that arose about Hussein was largely absent after bin Laden's death. Still, Americans were given many ways to understand the war against terrorism as a criminal-catching operation, not—or not just—a war. The very fact that the Bush administration refused to accord its captives (Hussein aside) prisoner-of-war status also clouded matters. If these individuals were not prisoners of war, what were they prisoners of? Even as the administration insisted that the nation was at war, it often acted like a cop on a beat or a warden in charge of the world's inmates.

That the war was hard for Bush to define muddied things further. Was it a war against al-Qaeda? Terrorists? Terrorism? Evil itself? For the White House, the vagueness was perhaps deliberate; it wanted to avoid sounding as if the United States was waging war on Islam. But the ambiguity was still a problem. Critics pointed out that terrorism was a tactic, not a definable enemy. It was hard to maintain clarity about a conflict whose named enemy was an abstraction, even if playing cards and other imagery filled in the blanks. Often Bush's words made this war seem to encompass most everything, and therefore nothing in particular. "We fight a war at home, and part of the war we fight is to make sure that our economy continues to grow," he told employees of the Dixie Printing and Packaging Plant on October 24. Meanwhile, some voices singled out fellow citizens as the enemy. In much-noted comments that he quickly retracted, the Reverend Jerry Falwell claimed that "the pagans and the abortionists, and the feminists, and the gays and the lesbians" and others had triggered God's wrath against America.[41] Such comments sowed confusion about who was the enemy and whether the country was engaged in war as usually understood.

Adding to the confusion, the term "war" had lost conceptual clarity. In the preceding years, various Americans had promiscuously and often loudly declared war on so many things—poverty, disease, cancer, AIDS, smoking, drunk driving, drugs, abortion, trade deficits, illiteracy, terrorism, and crime itself, to name only some. In the process, they had undercut the word of its power to define. In this swirl of war talk, the "global war on terror" stood out for its scale and stakes while drifting on a murky linguistic sea. When almost everything was a "war," no particular war held the charge and specificity the term once had, leaving space for the terminology of crime-fighting.

Action also drew on the techniques and institutions of crime-fighting. In the fall of 2001, the roundup, and often deportation, of alleged Arab or Muslim "suspects" was a Justice Department, primarily FBI, operation conducted in concert with local police agencies. That roundup snared, among others, some 762 men illegally in the United States. Apparently, none of them was linked to terrorism in the end, but they were held for up to eight months, often in solitary confinement, and they were sometimes beaten (treatment that by some standards amounted to torture).[42] As U.S. and allied forces failed in December to trap Bin Laden at Tora Bora in Afghanistan, the effort to disrupt his finances fell to the Treasury Department (its Terrorist Finance Tracking Program). The campaign to track terrorists on or entering American soil linked a multitude of local and state policing agencies to the federal apparatus of intelligence and defense. Of course, civilian agencies usually play a role in war—nearly all of them did in World War II—since war is never just about shooting. Still, the balance in this conflict often tilted toward those agencies.

Bush's rhetoric in the aftermath of 9/11 also set up a sharp tension between war zone urgency and home front comfort. His calls for Americans to resume their normal lives, be spared the burden of wartime taxes, and be freed of wartime duties—beyond being alert to possible terrorist threats and subject to far-reaching surveillance—undermined his call to war. "Get down to Disney World in Florida," Bush was already urging Americans on September 27. "Take your families and enjoy life, the way we want it to be enjoyed." If this was war, it would not involve the sacrifices many Americans associated with war, especially those made after Pearl Harbor, the precedent the commander in chief often cited. When Bush called the response to the September 11 attacks a "war unlike any we've ever had" (as any war is) on June 11, 2002, he presumably had terrorism in mind. But he inadvertently was right in a different way. As the historian Richard Kohn put it years later, "Missing was any rhetoric of sacrifice, leading to the normalization of war: 'the military at war and America at the mall.'"[43]

Symbolically, too, the arenas of crime-fighting and war-fighting seemed to collapse together. The police and fire personnel who responded to the 9/11 attacks—"first responders" became a widely circulated term for them, and soon for others—were remembered as soldiers at war, while the war in Afghanistan at first produced few American military casualties to showcase. The conflation of soldiers and "first responders" proved tenacious in venues both conspicuous and obscure. The America's Response Monument near the site of the World Trade Center "forever links first responders, [and] Special Forces," according to the American Legion in 2016. The little Almira Township Veterans Memorial near Lake Ann, Michigan, groups military veterans with civilian police and emergency personnel.[44]

The new Department of Homeland Security (DHS) created by Congress in November encapsulated the ambiguous relationship between war-fighting and crime-fighting and the thickening feedback loops between them. Absorbing agencies from a host of bailiwicks, and soon to become the third-largest (as measured by employees) cabinet department after Defense and Veterans Affairs, DHS performed a plethora of duties—airport and other transportation security, immigration and border control, disaster relief, and more. The department carried out a confusing amalgam of humanitarian, policing, and warring functions. And the term "homeland" seemed curious. It was first deployed in the context of terrorism by the Clinton administration, and the Bush White House was fond of using it, even as critics winced at the term's apparent evocation of Nazi/German use of the word "heimat" and its whiff of ethnonationalism. It was also a term whose meaning few could agree on.

Bush gave the term a criminal justice tilt when he attempted to appoint former New York police commissioner Bernie Kerik as DHS secretary after Tom Ridge (a former Pennsylvania governor) stepped down from the position in 2005. Kerik fell victim to scandal, and Bush then appointed former prosecutor and judge Michael Chertoff as secretary. "The President loves cops," one Republican insider insisted after the Kerik's nomination unraveled. Cops are "not pretentious, they do a hard job, they don't get paid a lot of money, they're real people and they live in a world that is fairly black and white, with good guys and bad guys. And that's the way President Bush looks at the world."[45] No wonder that the public face of this war was often civilian crime-fighters like Attorney General Ashcroft and DHS secretary Ridge issuing color-coded warnings about the danger of terrorist attacks, not just the defense secretary and multistarred generals. It did not help that Bush exercised unsteady, ill-informed control over the swelling leviathan of defense, intelligence, and crime-fighting agencies. Unlike most governors, Bush had "had no real executive responsibility" in Texas, where state agencies were headed by elected officials, and he "did not read newspapers." Hence Vice President Dick Cheney and others often exercised "executive responsibility," though Bush was the final "decider," as he called himself.[46]

But even a genius might have had trouble guiding that leviathan. Ever more diffuse, as responsibilities spilled across a growing pile of public agencies and private contractors, and ever more secretive, it could not be monitored and managed, its parts at cross-purposes with each other. Virtually every federal agency had a security-related duty, from Agriculture to the Voice of America, as did any local police force, charged to look out for terrorists as well as drunks and murderers. Much of this apparatus was out of sight, not only for citizens but for official managers. At the height of American war making, for example, few knew about "the Pentagon's invisible army," some "seventy thousand cooks, cleaners, construction workers, fast-food clerks, electricians, and beauticians from the world's poorest countries" working in Iraq and Afghanistan. "Filipinos launder soldiers' uniforms, Kenyans truck frozen steaks and inflatable tents, Bosnians repair electrical grids, and Indians provide iced mocha lattes."[47]

Critics imagined a National Security Agency efficiently gobbling up bits of information about everyone and everything, which was apparently NSA's aspiration. "In the words of an NSA PowerPoint slide disclosed by [Edward] Snowden," David Cole reported, "the agency's goal is to 'Collect It All,' 'Process It All,' 'Exploit It All,' 'Partner It All,' "Sniff It All,' and "Know It All.'"[48] But managing and assessing this data and coordinating the findings with myriad other agencies in the United States and abroad was impossible. To "Know It All" was to risk getting lost in all that was known.

Once punitive impulses were exhausted, insofar as they ever were, through the invasions of Afghanistan and Iraq and the capture of Hussein, the U.S. wars settled into a variant of the crime-fighting model—killing or capturing as many terrorist fighters as possible. This was an incapacitation approach similar to the thrust behind mass incarceration: lock up enough miscreants, and crime—or terrorism—will recede. At its peak use under American control in March 2004, Iraq's Abu Ghraib prison held some 7,500 inmates, though not all were regarded as terrorist suspects. That summer the army estimated "that over 50,000 detainees [had] been captured or processed," apparently a figure for both Iraq and Afghanistan.[49] As with mass incarceration, policymakers gave remarkably little thought to rehabilitating captured terrorists or to luring prototerrorists away from their destination. True, administration figures seemed to hope that whole nations like Afghanistan and Iraq might be rehabilitated, but their efforts at recovery turned out to be extravagantly expensive, deeply corrupt, badly managed, and perhaps doomed from the start. It was as if the United States had given little thought during World War II about what to do with Germany and Japan once they were defeated.

Instead, in the absence of strategic thinking, "whack-a-mole," as critics called it, prevailed. Aided increasingly by drone technology, regular and clandestine U.S. forces targeted terrorists in a widening array of places, from Pakistan west through the Middle East and into Africa. That was the policy ("strategy" the White House sometimes called it) through the presidency of Barack Obama, who, as the Islamic State presented a new threat, asserted on September 10, 2014, that his plan was for the United States and its "friends and allies to degrade and ultimately destroy the terrorist group known as ISIL." As the *National Interest* characterized it: "The 'new' policy: blowing up the bad guys and hoping they get tired of it eventually."[50] "It's whack-a-mole all over again," commented Andrew Bacevich.[51] This approach was oddly similar to how American policing authorities chased after alleged criminals, like growers and purveyors of illegal drugs, though often to little success. As former CIA official Michael Morrell commented, "For every 100 hours I spent in the Situation room talking about how to deal with terrorists that already exist, maybe we spent 10 minutes talking about winning hearts and minds and deradicalization."[52] The ratios were not much different in crime-fighting. State secrecy also defined both arenas, especially drone warfare, whose expansion the Obama administration worked hard to deny, disguise, and dissemble about.[53]

Of course the stakes were higher, or at least different, in the war on terrorism. But the thrust of policy seemed similar: capture (or kill) enough "bad guys" and a measure of victory would ensue, sometime. In the process, U.S. terrorism fighters and their allies arguably produced—there was no control experiment to prove it—as many terrorists as they subdued. In the same way, mass incarceration often seemed to produce criminals, given how prisons hardened inmates, circulated knowledge about lawbreaking, and released prisoners marked for life with few options.

It was the global version of what Texas governor Bush and others had long practiced in American criminal justice. Both versions of policy had racial underpinnings. Both had similar assumptions. Just as many Americans regarded crime as inexplicable except as the product of evil, even more regarded terrorism as inexplicable except as the product of its perpetrators' evil. And they shared a sense of the dogged futility of combating both phenomena. Crime might be punished and contained, but it never ended; terrorism would persist into some ill-defined, perhaps endless, future. Indeed, insofar as Americans thought of wars as having definite beginnings and endings, this war's open-ended nature, which national leaders repeatedly emphasized, made it seem less like a war than like something else (that no one seemed able to define or label). It seemed to float free of time itself.

This fact also helps explain the pessimistic, nontriumphal manner in which the Bush and Obama administrations presented the war on terror as stretching into an indefinable future, into "forever wars," as they were dubbed. Of course, seeing the war as endless served many purposes. It was a writ for the endless assertion of power by the presidency and the United States and a way to guard against expectations of victory that might backfire. Presumably, this interpretation was also a response to the nature of terrorism. But it made sense in another way too. Wars are to be won and concluded, but no one thinks that policing crime ever ends. Criminality is like death and taxes (and evil), and policing is a permanent obligation of government. As a giant policing action for Globalcop, the war on terror need not and could not have an end. "Unfortunately a cop's work is never done," wrote Max Boot in 2003, asserting that "America's destiny is to police the world" as a "Globocop."[54]

There was perhaps no way for Bush and others to draw a sharp line between war-fighting and crime-fighting, as other countries also found out. But the president and his colleagues also made strikingly little effort to do so, as if it were natural that the two were almost one and the same. *New York Times* reporter Charlie Savage later noted, "Perhaps the most fundamental question that faced the United States after the 9/11 attacks . . . was whether what Bush liked to call the 'global war on terror'—counterterrorism efforts beyond the invasion and occupation of Afghanistan—was, for legal purposes, a literal war or just a metaphor for rallying public support behind a difficult effort, like the 'war on drugs' or the 'war on poverty.'"[55]

But judging by the accounts of Savage and others, the Bush administration never addressed that question squarely (although individuals like Richard Clarke thought about it), much less formulated an answer to it. Instead, the Bush White House slid back and forth between the war and the crime models for fighting terrorism. But even if the president and his staff had recognized that "war" was more of a "metaphor"—more "like the 'war on drugs'"—doing so would have clarified little. That war on drugs had itself long been militarized. The boundaries between war-fighting and crime-fighting had already eroded; 9/11 simply produced their further collapse. Even if Bush had squarely labeled the 9/11 attacks a "crime," the engines of war would have swung into action, though perhaps less destructively. In any event, Bush was neither inclined nor equipped to ponder how metaphors work.

Perhaps American responses to 9/11 would not have been altogether different had punitive culture not gained force. Some military reaction to the attacks would have been likely no matter who was president. The United States' warlike responses to terrorism were already inscribed in precedent, policy, and presidential rhetoric, as well as in the behavior of Israel, on whose policies America often leaned. Large-scale incarceration, resettlement, and other policing practices evident in Iraq had been endemic in neoimperial wars, as in America's Vietnam War. The same was true of the torture of captives (British soldiers, too, were charged with mistreating Iraqi prisoners). By the same token, U.S. responses to terrorism were not as distinctly American as critics often found them to be. Other countries developed their own lumbering, complex security systems and war language; in 2015, France's prime minister declared "war against terrorism and radical Islamism" after the Charlie Hebdo attack in Paris.[56] The United States' use of torture was distinctive, and its power to act was unrivaled, but much that Western European nations soon did resembled what the United States was doing. And leaders in most wars have sent mixed messages about their nation's values and purposes as they catered to different constituencies and groped through their own confusion.

Indeed, by the 2010s the punitive turn was a global phenomenon in which the United States was both an outlier—its mass incarceration alone made it stand out—and a leader. Much depends on the points of comparison chosen.[57] Most scholarship and activism compared the United States to Western Europe and Japan, which left U.S. criminal justice looking harsh and repressive. Comparisons to, say, Turkey, much of Central and South America, or Russia and China would yield a muddier picture. Many nations underwent punitive turns as the authority of central governments frayed, the social welfare of populations declined, and the challenges to authority increased internally and from transstate networks often dubbed "terrorist."[58]

But the United States sometimes led the way, or at least tried to. It did so by example, though one that many people and institutions elsewhere recoiled from. It did so by peddling weapons, crime-control technologies, and practices, especially in the Global South, usually in the name of fighting communism or terrorism, and by training other nations' police forces. It did so by offering its "soft power" (Russian versions of *Law and Order*!). It did so by resisting international norms that other states, the United Nations, and nonstate organizations tried to establish. It did so by trying to police much of the world. America's influence can also be exaggerated. Just as it exercised waning authority in other realms after the Cold War's end, so it probably did in the realm of the punitive, especially since criminal justice is more rooted in a given country's culture, politics, and history than many arenas where the United States wielded power. And flows of ideas, weapons, and practices were multidirectional, hardly set by the United States alone. For example, Israel's methods of policing and walling off hostile populations influenced U.S. practices along its southern border, and U.S. police forces and their chiefs trained with Israeli security forces.[59] Antiterrorism efforts bred a plethora of bilateral and international arrangements, and multinational corporations offered weapons, tactics, and personnel to buttress the security of states, companies, and other institutions.

But America's punitive culture made a difference. It further sanctioned the country's role as Globalcop, informed the Bush administration's rhetoric, underwrote the invasion of Iraq, and legitimated dubious practices of incarceration and torture—that is, the punitive character of official policy. Once again, American values were projected outward, but these were not the values of Progressive uplift, New Deal liberalism, or Cold War management. They were the values of religious vengeance and punitive treatment of those whom Bush called "evildoers."

Torture in Two Silos

As vengeance went global, so too did torture, its handmaiden. But most Americans regarded torture as something that Americans did "over there"—whether as a rogue, necessary, or reprehensible practice—not as something that happened here. With torture, the feedback loops between home and abroad ran underground, secret and serpentine. They were hard to see, or at least easy to avoid seeing, just as torture itself was easy to avoid seeing.[60]

In the immediate wake of 9/11, no chorus arose to demand torture of alleged terrorist suspects (not least because there were initially few such suspects). In the same way, there had been little apparent support for torture before 9/11. Diverse voices—liberal and conservative, inside and outside the administration, elite and ordinary—initially rejected the practice as anathema to American values or as a bad way to extract information. Attorney General Ashcroft, for one, publicly ruled out "interrogation that would violate [terrorist suspects'] rights" and asserted, "When you force someone . . . they're likely to tell you something that's not true." Noted lawyer Alan Dershowitz was an exception, offering, on November 8, 2001, his conditional acceptance of torture, which he based on Israel's practice. Torture will happen anyway, he reasoned, so it is best carefully regulated and constrained ("limited to the rare 'ticking bomb' case"), as banning it would be a fruitless fiction. But Dershowitz "was widely condemned for his views."[61]

More Americans (especially conservatives and Republicans) came to embrace torture later, when the war on terror ground on inconclusively and when there was actual torture, not its theoretical prospect, to debate. In the war on terror, as in most wars, attitudes and practices later attributed to initial shock and fury over surprise attacks in fact took months to emerge. Actual torture of a fictionalized sort greeted viewers of the popular Fox TV series *24*, which debuted November 6, 2001, and popularized the ticking bomb scenario in which counterterrorist Jack Bauer is forced to torture suspects to prevent mass destruction (a scenario rarely, if ever, present in the torture practices of the United States). That program helped move popular culture from presenting torture "as a tool used by the demonic 'Other'" to portraying it as a tool in "the American hero's arsenal." "Just as opinions about Islam have grown more negative as we move farther from September 11, opinions about torture have grown more positive," Joseph Margulies observed in 2013.[62]

Despite earlier rumors, leaks, and reports, most Americans first confronted torture by U.S. military and intelligence forces (and by their allies, handed prisoners by the United States under "extraordinary rendition") when CBS's *60 Minutes II* reported on April 28, 2004, about Abu Ghraib prison in Iraq, showing American personnel's jarring photos of their abuse and torture of prisoners. Almost simultaneously, Seymour Hersh published an exposé in the *New Yorker*.[63] Those revelations and later ones showed that the administration, despite resistance from the uniformed armed forces and their military lawyers, and from the Defense and State Departments and the FBI, had decided not to give POW status to captives in its war on terror. The president and his staff authorized torture of prisoners at Abu Ghraib, as well as of others captured in the war on terror. Regarding the U.S. prison at Guantánamo, Bush had promised on October 14, 2003, "We don't torture people in America. And people who make that claim just don't know anything about our country." (Perhaps "in America" was an intended hedge, allowing the possibility that "we" might torture elsewhere.) The spring 2004 revelations challenged Bush's assertion.

In the ensuing media and political firestorm about those revelations, administration figures variously acknowledged, condemned, trivialized, and evaded torture. At an April 30 news conference, Bush commented, "I shared a deep disgust that those prisoners were treated the way they were treated. Their treatment does not reflect the nature of the American people." He stated at a May 5 press conference with Jordan's king that "the actions of those folks [American forces who committed torture] in Iraq do not represent the values of the United States of America," and he said later (in a June 26 statement) that the United States was committed to "the worldwide elimination of torture," and would "continue to lead the fight to eliminate it everywhere" ("We are leading this fight by example," he had said a year earlier). On January 27, 2005, Bush assured the *New York Times*, "Torture is never acceptable. . . . Nor do we hand over people to countries that do torture." Meanwhile, on May 4, 2004, Deputy Defense Secretary Paul Wolfowitz had observed, "It's such a disservice to everyone else, that a few bad apples [the low-level personnel who tortured at Abu Ghraib] can create some large problems for everybody."[64]

Multiple investigations by various official bodies (one by the army before the story broke) sought to explain why torture had occurred and who was responsible for it. However, no investigation had the writ to run fully up the chain of command to the White House. The most media-grabbing of inquiries' findings came from former defense secretary James Schlesinger, chair of the Independent Panel to Review DOD Detention Operations, who commented publicly in August 2004, "There was sadism on the night shift at Abu Ghraib, sadism that was certainly not authorized. . . . It was kind of '*Animal House*' on the night shift."[65] As the emergence of secret "torture memos" showed, perhaps "sadism" was not authorized, but torture—illegal under U.S. and international law—was. The distinction between it and "sadism" was hard to parse. The thrust of statements by Schlesinger and by administration figures was to confine torture to Abu Ghraib and to rogue figures there. Since no photographs surfaced that showed torture elsewhere, the logic seemed to be that it did not exist. Seymour Hersh reported one official saying that prison guards from the Army Reserves at Abu Ghraib included "recycled hillbillies from Cumberland, Maryland."[66] Senator Mark Dayton caught the thrust of the administration's various statements when he commented on May 18, "We have a general acceptance of responsibility, but there's no one to blame, except for the people at the very bottom of one prison."[67]

The administration's stance denied both official culpability and the past. In 2004 there was rarely any public recognition of America's long record of torture in earlier wars, although historians, military officials, and torturers themselves already knew about it. Like many warring nations, the United States had committed torture, especially on non-Europeans, in campaigns against Native Americans, in the Filipino-American War, and in the Vietnam War. Indeed, America's Phoenix Program of torture and assassination in Vietnam dwarfed anything under Bush, a fact that Bush might have paraded to defend himself ("we're not nearly as bad as we used to be"). Yet doing so would have involved an admission that torture did represent "the values of the United States of America," or at least a frequent practice by it.

Even more troubling, there was little mention, even by critics and scholars of Bush-era torture, of torture stateside. Dershowitz had acknowledged it in his defense of limited "torture warrants." As he noted, "Throughout the years, police officers have tortured murder and rape suspects into confessing—sometimes truthfully, sometimes not truthfully," and "[The] 'third degree' [often a euphemism for torture] is all too common . . . in the back rooms of real police station houses."[68] But that acknowledgment got little notice in public debate about his proposal. White House press secretary Scott McClellan claimed on May 5, 2004, "We do not tolerate that kind of activity in America," presumably referring to torture abroad but also at home. That claim went unchallenged, at least by those in position to do so, even though a history of past and recent abuse was widely available in 2004.

By then, vigilante torture in the form of lynching (often with state complicity) was a well- known story, as was police use of the "third degree." Also by then, Jon Burge's long-running torture regime in Chicago had been exposed, and Governor George Ryan's reaction to it widely publicized. How much torture had recently occurred in other police and prison systems was less apparent, since public authorities almost never went looking for it or listened to those who complained about it. But if Burge's practices had been distinctly egregious, they were not unique. Torture (and murder) of inmates by New York State troopers and corrections personnel retaking Attica Correctional Facility in 1971 was later exposed in a series of well-publicized criminal and civil proceedings, with the word "torture" forcefully used in a 1997 case.[69]

By 2004, Chicago journalist John Conroy's jarring examination of torture in Belfast, Israel, and Chicago had appeared to considerable, if sometimes dismissive, attention. (Conroy, a *New York Times* reviewer sniffed, "gives little credit to the free institutions that shine light on the abuses." According to *Salon's* reviewer, Conroy had failed by "examining the cruelties of just one side.")[70] By then, activist groups were also reporting on police and prison torture. Amnesty International had been "extremely concerned" in 1997 "at reports indicating that the spread of hand-held electro-shock weapons [tasers, stun belts, and the like] amongst law enforcement officers [was] contributing to the incidence of torture and such ill-treatment" in many countries, including the United States.[71]

A good deal else was known by 2004. Congress's passage of the Prison Rape Elimination Act in 2003 signaled awareness of sexual abuse and assault in prisons and policing—some forms of it regarded as torture under international law and by legal and activist organizations. (Widespread sexual abuse of inmates by staff, particularly against juveniles and often by women, was fully exposed later through studies overseen by the Department of Justice.[72]) During the 2000s, prolonged solitary confinement, a practice derived in part from Cold War–era "military experiments," was spreading fast, and it was readable as torture, especially when used for juvenile and mentally ill inmates.[73] So, too, was the death penalty, especially when faultily administered. By this time, published reports and legal proceedings had emerged about beatings and other abuse at stateside facilities housing detainees (Israeli as well as Arab) caught in the post-9/11 dragnet. A lot was known that might have led observers and critics to connect torture "over there" to torture "back here." In the United States, constitutional lawyer David Cole claimed in 2009, "discussions [of torture] were generally confined to philosophy classrooms before the terrorist attacks of September 11, 2001."[74] But that claim was only true as it pertained to torture of captives America held abroad. Both before and after 9/11, "discussions" of torture stateside had been robust in journalism, legal circles, courts, and elsewhere.

Moreover, by 2004 government officials, journalists, and activists knew how American negotiators had dodged and weaved for years about U.S. ratification of the Convention against Torture, lest its provisions expose the country's police and prison abuse and torture. Initially backed by the United States, the convention had been adopted by the United Nations in 1984. American negotiators had quibbled about how to define torture. They had proposed "certain reservations" (nineteen, later dropped to twelve). They had sought to restrict the role of the UN Committee against Torture within the United States, insisting that only nation-states, not individuals, could make claims before it. U.S. negotiators worried, as one Justice Department lawyer put it, that America's "aggressive law enforcement response to . . . terrorism and drug trafficking" would leave its officials open to complaints, even to extradition. The U.S. Constitution and Americans' values sufficed to protect people within the nation from torture, the negotiators asserted. "The country and its Constitution [are] the beacon of human rights," one lawyer told a Senate committee, noting that this status rendered the convention unneeded for the United States. It was torture in or by other nations—by the Pinochet regime in Chile after its overthrow of Salvador Allende in 1973, for example—that must be stopped.

The paradoxical stance of many officials and politicians was that while torture in the United States did not exist, the nation's laws and institutions would stop it if it did. The Senate did finally ratify the convention in 1994—it would have been embarrassing for the United States to have done otherwise—but with robust guardrails against outside interference in its "aggressive law enforcement response." As one legal analysis asserts, "In ratifying the Torture Convention, the United States, in effect, reserved the right to inflict inhuman or degrading treatment (when it is not punishment for crime), and criminal punishment when it is inhuman and degrading (but not 'cruel and unusual')." As one historian puts it, the United States "hoped to maintain the country's human rights credentials abroad, while exempting itself from the law at home." The country's efforts might have alerted critics in 2004 to a stateside story of torture.[75]

And quickly in 2004, alert observers knew about bread crumbs on the trail from Abu Ghraib back to American prisons, bread crumbs few pursued.[76] Two leading guards at Abu Ghraib, Charles Graner and Ivan L. "Chip" Frederick II, had worked as correction officers in those U.S. prisons, having gained knowledge about and perhaps participated in abusive practices similar to those at the overseas facility. Two former administrators of prisons in Utah and elsewhere, the *Salt Lake Tribune* reported in May, elicited suspicion after they were recruited to help supervise the Abu Ghraib prison. The paper noted, "[Their critics] say the pictures of abuse and humiliation at Abu Ghraib are eerily similar to video and written records that detail the plight of bound and naked Utah prisoners in the former isolation chamber at Utah's Point of the Mountain prison."[77]

Numerous other guards and officials at Abu Ghraib and other U.S. prison sites abroad had come from (and then sometimes rotated back to) American prison and police facilities. At least "5000 civilian prison guards," and probably more, were "called up to active duty" after 9/11, and still more volunteered for service, though not all ended up doing prison work abroad. As members of the Army Reserves or the National Guard, often in military police units, they were the obvious personnel to call up for prison or policing duties abroad. However, they were usually ill prepared for such duties and poorly supervised, as were many prison guards in the United States. Not that most such personnel participated in torture at home or abroad, but many were familiar with and inured to abusive practices in U.S. prisons and policing. At least for Graner, "Abu Ghraib was a familiar environment."[78]

Perhaps alarmed observers had good reasons for their singular focus on torture abroad. That abuse carried the imprimatur of the U.S. government and the president. However much mayors, prosecutors, police chiefs, wardens, and governors turned a blind eye to torture at home, it carried no evident presidential approval (at least until Donald J. Trump won the presidency). Torture abroad represented the nation in a way that torture under Burge did not. The practice found defenders in the top levels of national government, whereas almost no voices defended torture at home (though Arizona sheriff Joe Arpaio came close)— ignoring it, winking at it, or letting it continue was not the same as defending it.

Torture abroad appeared to involve bigger stakes. It seemed singularly to jeopardize the nation's interests and safety if it harvested bad intelligence, inflamed Muslim radicals, and alienated American allies. Torture was presumably designed to extract information that would forestall attacks on American and allied forces, on friendly civilians, or on the United States itself. Torture at home often seemed to have little purpose other than gratification of the torturers. Victims of torture abroad had almost no legal redress or personal support, whereas those at home had some recourse (many of Burge's victims eventually had their convictions overturned) and some access to families, friends, and lawyers. There were reasons to regard torture abroad as more dangerous, offensive, and shameful.

Meanwhile, defenders of "enhanced interrogations"—Bush administration officials never admitted they constituted torture—employed a related set of distinctions, admirably summarized by Joseph Margulies. The United States tortured "only when absolutely necessary" and "only to gather lifesaving intelligence, and not simply to gratify [Americans'] sadistic nature," while terrorists "tortured for any reason or no reason—simply because they were savages" (or "very smart subhumans," according to one Fox News guest). U.S. torture was regulated, constrained, and purposeful in defense of the nation and civilization. "In short, we [Americans] tortured *because* we were civilized; they [non-Americans] because they were not." Besides, as Bill O'Reilly of Fox News said, "every nation in the world does 30 times worse than we do."[79]

Most of those distinctions wither upon examination. They certainly made little difference to many of the victims. Military officials' admission that Abu Ghraib housed "large quantities of detainees with little or no intelligence value" undercut the extraction-of-information rationale, as did many officials' and experts' suspicion that torture produced bad information.[80] Critics who traced torture abroad through the CIA and "torture memos" assumed that the tactic's purpose was instrumental, as its defenders claimed, however much it went awry. But that assumption was naive about human nature, politics, and war. One wellspring of torture abroad, from the White House down to the "hillbillies" committing it, was a desire to punish people for the 9/11 attacks and the deaths suffered by U.S. forces.

Whatever its rationale, whether in Abu Ghraib or at Jon Burge's headquarters, torture, either from the start or once it got going, served many purposes, often ones not wholly known by the torturers: creating the spectacle of pain, asserting power, imposing punishment, pleasing superiors or comrades, unleashing the torturer's own demons, and so forth. And secrecy was its own source of thrills. None of those satisfactions required that the victims be guilty of something or harbor useful information. Rarely is torture only about extracting information. Stateside torturers did offer that rationale; they wanted to find out what awful act a suspect or his accomplices might do next, and indeed, in murderous patches of cities, police sometimes felt they were facing their own little ticking time bombs. But they also took sadistic pleasure in their work, as torturers did abroad, and they regarded their victims as subhuman, usually for racial reasons. Furthermore, the legal redress for stateside victims was often more theoretical than actual, taking decades when it occurred at all. Torture abroad and torture at home had much in common. They were both products of "American values."

So if torture at home was hardly unknown in 2004, why did so few connect the dots between it and torture abroad? One explanation involves how Americans had learned to see human rights as a problem only in the international, non-U.S. sphere. "Almost everywhere else in the world the focus of human rights advocacy was on violations of rights happening at home. . . . But in the United States human rights were almost never imagined to have resonance for domestic rights questions in the 1970s," according to historian Mark Bradley. In America, "It was the suffering of strangers, rather than one's neighbors, that animated the movement."[81] Americans engaged in vigorous discourse about civil rights, legal rights, prisoners' rights, and the like, but they rarely framed them as human rights. Burge's challengers had sometimes linked his torture to torture overseas, presenting Chicago police as guilty of "real torture in the Third World sense." But those challengers later backed off such comparisons, and the habit of locating abuse elsewhere remained strong.[82]

And that is where it usually stayed after 2004. Venerable peace groups like the War Resisters League trained their sights almost exclusively on torture done abroad. By then that organization was also taking on "police militarization" and prison abuse, but it declined to declare the latter "torture" or to connect either to U.S. torture abroad.[83] When distinguished jurists and lawyers contributed to *Terrorism: A Collection* (2004), they dwelled on whether torture might be justified to prevent a "catastrophe," framing the tactic as a matter of choice, not practice. One contributor referred in passing to Chicago torture, but most ignored torture at home. Jerome H. Skolnick seemed to break ranks from his fellow contributors, tracing the history of the "third degree" in American policing and suggesting that torture "is there, hidden by other labels." But then he dismissed it as an ongoing problem, as police chiefs and others had been dismissing it for a century. "The whippings of the Jim Crow era, and the fists and blackjacks of the early twentieth-century period of the third degree, have largely disappeared in U.S. interrogation rooms," replaced by "psychological pressure as an alternative to physical brutality." "Contemporary cases of known American police brutality are usually retributive or self-aggrandizing, not motivated by the enforcement of criminal law," Skolnick added. *Terrorism: A Collection* offered little admission that torture might spring from American soil, not just from officials' agonized decisions about terrorism.[84]

That admission was also absent in the first wave of investigative journalism and scholarship about torture abroad. When Mark Danner issued his probing examinations of the sources, consequences, and official dishonesty about torture for the *New York Review of Books* in 2004 (republished with additional material as a book), he made no mention of the practice on American soil.[85] When historian Alfred W. McCoy researched *A Question of Torture* (2006), he traced the practice to the CIA and to "a script written over fifty years ago during the depths of the Cold War," when "a distinctive American form of torture" was foreseen by "brilliant scholars" and "distinguished professors" and "great universities" and all those "good Americans who acquiesced."[86] When Jane Mayer wrote *The Dark Side: The Inside Story of How the War on Terror Turned Into a War on American Ideals* (2008), she traced torture to the apocalyptic fears and insidious manipulations of figures like Vice President Dick Cheney. Offering remarkable depth in their fast-produced work, Danner, McCoy, and Mayer were right about the operational sources of post-9/11 torture. But it was still for them an "over there" practice.

Other voices occasionally offered something different. Although professional journals about criminal justice said little,[87] *Justice Quarterly* had in 1999 squarely identified practices of torture in U.S. prisons.[88] Journals about prison life and administration sometimes weighed in,[89] and the president of the American Society of Criminology bluntly asserted in 2007, "In human-rights terms, American governments treat their own citizens nearly as badly in the name of domestic security as the American national government treats its foreign 'enemies' in the name of national security."[90] But religious figures, though too varied and voluminous to track fully, rarely made that point. When they did, they often expressed their opinions only obliquely, in passing, or belatedly.[91] The liberal Unitarian Universalist Association, for example, loudly condemned U.S. torture abroad, sponsoring billboards of protest along Connecticut highways, but did not address abuse of prisoners at home.[92] Some evangelical groups questioned torture, but only its use abroad. It was "the torture of military prisoners," as *Christian Century* put it 2006, that concerned most religious groups, with the implication that it was a rogue "over-there" practice.[93]

Nearer the fringes of American life, others weighed in. The journal *Muslim World* belatedly tackled connections between home and abroad. Some radical scholars and writers protested, if in tortured prose. Alongside "gasps at the carceral torture of the distant racial other," observed a contributor to *Radical History Review*, was "a relative silence and sanction around the everyday racial terror of the intimate domestic," part of "the very life force of the U.S. prison regime as a truly earthly mobilization of torture/terror."[94] Views like that were exceptions, scarcely noticed beyond their core audiences.

"For many prisoners, human rights advocates, and some corrections officials, the shock was that the public and media were so shocked" by the Abu Ghraib revelations, Marie Gottschalk notes.[95] But not everyone was shocked. In 2005, the United Kingdom's Channel 4 documentary *Torture: America's Brutal Prisons* offered a graphic, if unavoidably sketchy, survey of its subject, much of it focused on Sheriff Arpaio's Maricopa County. Not broadcast in the United States, the program did find its way to U.S. activist organizations and to various tertiary outlets online. In words and images it pointedly linked torture abroad to torture at home. "Once you know how America runs its prisons at home, then the obscene abuses at Abu Ghraib are no less shocking, just less surprising," the film concluded.[96]

Notable, too, were efforts by Reed College political scientist Darius Rejali to flag how torture circulated between home and abroad. As an Iranian American, he demonstrated again that those with a perspective from outside the United States often engaged with torture in more complex—and with Rejali, pungently phrased—ways. In his mammoth 2007 book, *Torture and Democracy*, containing chapters like "Prods, Tasers, and Stun Guns," Rejali probed practices that constituted torture or charted a path to it. He did much the same in a volume that emerged from a 2006 Princeton University conference, *Torture Is a Moral Issue: Christians, Jews, Muslims and People of Conscience Speak Out* (2008). Rejali showed that prisoner abuse was hardly some relic of a barbaric past, stating, "I grew up in Iran at a time when the Shah's secret police, the SAVAK, did not hesitate torturing Islamic and Marxist insurgents. No one thought torture was something incompatible with cars, fast food, washing machines, and other parts of modern life." Rejali also insisted, "There is no bright line between domestic and foreign torture; the stuff circulates." He knew about Burge's torture regime in Chicago and other practices, and about how past U.S. torture abroad had returned home: "I think we need to understand that torture doesn't just hide in a vault in the CIA. It hides in all the dark pockets of society—military barracks, schools, frat houses, our supermax prisons, and immigration lockups." He was at pains to stress that democratic states can torture, albeit often by "clean tortures" that leave little evidence. But it was telling that for all the attention paid to Rejali by other contributors to *Torture is a Moral Issue* and an interviewer for *Harper's*, they slighted his emphasis on the circulation of torture and kept their focus on post-9/11 torture.[97]

Jimmy Carter, the most prominent figure, both political and religious, to engage torture, shared this focus. Carter's grasp of the punitive turn in American life was wide ranging and his disdain for it full throated. Writing in 2005, at the peak of public controversy over torture, he condemned "the transformations . . . taking place in our nation's basic moral values, public discourse, and political philosophy." He singled out mass incarceration, "our fascination with the death penalty," the torture of post-9/11 captives, and the abuse and forced deportation of Arabs and Muslims in the United States. The former president deplored how America had "completely abandoned and reversed" its effort to rehabilitate prisoners, instead training "almost total focus . . . on punishment, not rehabilitation." There, perhaps, was an implicit acknowledgment that torture abroad sprung from values and practices at home, but if so, Carter stopped short of explicitly addressing the circulation of torture.[98]

That circulation was no surprise to Anne-Marie Cusac, a Chicago-based journalist and scholar who by 2004 "had been reporting on abuse and mistreatment in our nation's jails and prisons for eight years." For her, "the images from Iraq looked all too American." As she asked, "Why were we surprised when many of these same practices were already occurring at home?"[99] First writing about "Abu Ghraib, USA" for *Progressive* magazine in July 2004, she went on to make post-9/11 torture the final chapter of her 2009 book, *Cruel and Unusual Punishment*, showing how that abuse flowed out of American thinking and practice. A few academics, especially those with a vantage point abroad, took a similar line, insisting that "the revelations of extreme brutality perpetrated by allied soldiers represent the inevitable end product of domestic incarceration [especially but not only in the United States] predicated on the use of violence up to and including lethal force."[100]

Responses to Cusac's book underlined the very problem she emphasized—a widespread tolerance of, or looking away from, torture. Major newspapers and magazines ignored *Cruel and Unusual Punishment*, as did most academic journals, and reviews were confined largely to small-bore outlets for professional and political groups. Even when appearing, many reviews downplayed the connections she drew between torture abroad and at home. This scantiness of attention might be explained by circumstances. Cusac drew on her reporting for the *Progressive*, a once mighty but now marginal voice of Left liberalism. She was not a big name, nor did she promote the book as big names often do.

More reportorial and idiosyncratic than academic in approach, *Cruel and Unusual Punishment* fell outside standard disciplinary boundaries. Released in 2009, it appeared after the initial wave of media and investigatory interest in torture abroad and at a time when Obama's repudiation of torture perhaps led many Americans—and book review editors—to assume that the sun had set on torture as a public issue. Yet here was a big book from a major academic press concerning matters that had consumed Americans. The bigger obstacle was that few Americans were willing to think about torture.

The posture of surprise about Abu Ghraib that Cusac tried to counter had shielded observers from thinking about what also happened at home. Americans could be surprised by torture abroad only if they claimed ignorance about torture in their own country. That stance made brutality toward prisoners overseas seem rogue, bizarre, and exceptional, thus insulating most Americans from acknowledging how far-reaching the practice was in America. As Cusac put it, "The revelations at Abu Ghraib shock us because our soldiers seem to have acted out behaviors that we condone, yet don't face up to, at home."[101]

Other Bush-era practices also seem less surprising upon examination, such as extraordinary rendition, the practice of sending captives to "black sites" in other countries where the CIA or local interrogators could operate beyond the reach of U.S. law. Rendition had long occurred within the United States in enforcement of the Fugitive Slave Act of 1850. The rendition of American-held prisoners to other countries, and vice versa, had a long history; thousands of Latin Americans of Japanese ancestry had been forcibly taken to the United States during World War II.

In and after the 1990s, rendition of prisoners within the United States had exploded. State and local jail authorities, facing rising costs and bulging inmate populations (and sometimes court orders to reduce them), shipped prisoners out of state, far from their lawyers and families, to facilities that bid to house them at lower cost. (National by definition, the Federal Bureau of Prisons long sent inmates far from their places of residence or conviction.) In the prison market, inmates were commodities duly commodified. No one called that practice "rendition," which had a technical meaning in national and international law. But the cavalier way that prisoners were moved about within the United States resembled the practice of moving U.S.-held "terror" prisoners around the world, with one big difference: Bush-era rendition operated outside the courts, in secret, and with the intent to allow torture, which was what made it "extraordinary."

The determination to see torture as an "over there" problem appeared anew when the Senate Select Committee on Intelligence released its "torture report" in December 2014. To be sure, that committee had no writ to range widely, for it was charged with preparing a *Committee Study of the Central Intelligence Agency's Detention and Interrogation Program*, as its final (redacted) report was subtitled. Committee members were not entrusted with writing a report on torture beyond the CIA's boundaries. And on that score, it was a damning document. But aside from brief nods to the role of the Justice Department and the Federal Bureau of Prisons in the history it traced, neither the report nor Senator Dianne Feinstein's foreword hinted that abuse and torture had been or might still be practices in U.S. criminal justice.[102] Activist organizations also ignored such practices at times. Responding to the "torture report," the ACLU did declare, "Accountability today is critical to stopping torture tomorrow." But the organization clearly had in mind torture by the CIA or other national security agencies.[103] The ACLU found in 2006 that "U.S. violations of the Convention Against Torture are not limited to actions by military personnel overseas in the 'war on terror,' but in fact are far too ubiquitous at home."[104] But the impulses— bureaucratic, political, imaginative—to keep torture at home and torture abroad in separate silos kept returning, even with the ACLU.

Torture kept sliding out of view. After the MacArthur Foundation assembled an impressive group of scholars in April 2015 for a round-table entitled "Why Is America So Punitive?"—the group's conference "may have been the first of its kind"—its report contained no mention of torture. Perhaps that was because the discussion "was limited to incarceration," not "other expressions of punitiveness," but of course "other expressions" like torture occurred during incarceration. Likewise, despite long-standing critiques of "police militarization," the foundation's report made no mention of feedback loops between war-fighting and crime-fighting. Sometimes those loops seemed to pop up spontaneously: when a California official sought to discredit prisoners on a hunger strike in Pelican Bay's solitary confinement (branded as "torture" by a UN special rapporteur), she declared in 2013, "They are terrorists," signaling that they deserved the same treatment that terrorists abroad presumably deserved. But such moments were few and perhaps inadvertent. The inability to see connections between torture abroad and torture at home persisted.[105]

This lack of discernment continued despite fresh efforts to see those connections. In 2015, Britain's *Guardian* newspaper published a story about torture allegations against Chicago detective Richard Zuley.

Reposted by the Marshall Project and taken up later by Rachel Maddow on MSNBC, the article asserted that Zuley, having practiced torture and abuse (apparently unconnected to Burge's torture) in Chicago, employed remarkably similar tactics on prisoners at Guantánamo, where he went in 2003 as a navy reservist, and then once more in Chicago. Zuley's record underlined how "the use of torture against enemy combatants and as part of the criminal justice system converged," as one historian notes.[106]

Such stories gained limited traction because most people maintained separate silos for imagining torture, and because large numbers—often majorities in polling—accepted, endorsed, or welcomed torture, whatever the locale, especially when the tortured were nonwhite. Still, obliviousness to abuse of prisoners at home made it easier to accept the same practices abroad. Torture was done to mysterious, faraway others, not to fellow Americans; it was carried out when Americans went rogue abroad, not in expression of American values; it was performed in the name of the nation's safety, not the cop's authority.

As president, Bush never squarely repudiated torture, hemming and hawing to the end. In 2005, he bitterly resisted Senator John McCain's legislation outlawing U.S. torture. "Basically," McCain complained, "he [Bush] told me that if our legislation passes, I am going to have planes flying into buildings." And when the legislation passed Congress, the president's signing statement indicated he "would interpret the new anti-torture law as he saw fit."[107] Sometimes Bush seemed to disavow mistreatment of prisoners. He said on October 5, 2007, "This Government does not torture people," but that formulation left open whether Americans might outsource torture to other governments. Days later, on November 1, Bush responded to a question about waterboarding by saying, "It doesn't make any sense to tell an enemy what we're doing." He repeatedly waffled. About to leave office, he insisted on January 7, 2009, in an interview with Fox News, "You know, I firmly reject the word 'torture.'" But he did not regard "enhanced interrogation techniques" as torture. "Everything this administration did was—had a legal basis to it; otherwise, we would not have done it." As he maintained, "The techniques were necessary and are necessary to be used on a rare occasion to get information necessary to protect the American people." In contrast, President Obama's renunciation of prisoner mistreatment seemed unqualified. "I can stand here tonight and say without exception or equivocation that the United States of America does not torture. We can make that commitment here tonight," he told Congress on February 24, 2009.

Yet when these presidents repudiated torture—Bush wafflingly, Obama forthrightly—they did so on the assumption that it only occurred abroad. That was the context of all their comments, and they offered no suggestions that the practice might occur in the United States. On the presidential stage, and hence by and large the national stage, torture remained in separate silos, one abroad visible but apparently dismantled, the other at home but supposedly nonexistent. By presumably banning torture abroad, Americans could pretend that it no longer existed, least of all on their soil.

It is hardly surprising that many Americans confronted torture evasively, defensively, and selectively, even as some did so boldly. Short of a political rupture that forces confrontation, most nations hesitate to confront such topics. In the American case, a long history of slavery, Jim Crow, lynching, mass killing in war and conquest, and torture in war and policing shadowed the post-9/11 reckoning. To confront torture in the present also meant confronting that past. Imagining the abuse of inmates as an "over there" practice preserved the fiction of American innocence, just as it protected politicians, police chiefs, prison wardens and the like from nasty inquiries and legal action questioning what they had allowed, sanctioned, or ignored in the way of torture at home. And in response to 9/11, most Americans were scared, or at least told by leaders to be scared. Perhaps it is a wonder that Americans addressed torture at all. Had the rogue release of photos about Abu Ghraib not occurred, most might never have acknowledged as much torture as they did. How they addressed torture warrants as much attention as the extent to which they addressed it. By and large, Americans kept home and abroad neatly separate, even as similar political and emotional currents undergirded torture in both arenas.

Meanwhile, the number of people incarcerated still grew for most of the Bush years, harsh police practices persisted, reality cop shows flourished, and much else continued, although law enforcement policies also faced mounting resistance, a subject taken up in the final chapter. Although this era's spirit of vengeance did not alone account for these practices, or for torture, it certainly buttressed them.

7 REVERSAL OR REDIRECTION?
2009-2017

The punitive turn appeared to be waning in the 2010s. Years of war against terrorist enemies had seemingly diverted energies away from stateside wrongdoers, opening space for new attitudes and practices toward them. As if displaced by the war on terrorism, talk of a war on crime and a war on drugs diminished, though all those wars overlapped. The Barack Obama administration pushed slowly and cautiously against racialized mass incarceration and militarized policing, pressed to do so by new waves of activism and legal action. But Obama also met fierce opposition, and by the end of his presidency it remained unclear whether the punitive turn would reverse, plateau, or simply be redirected, above all against undocumented immigrants and against terrorists targeted in "forever wars."

Two public moments highlighted Obama's efforts to push back against the punitive turn. On July 16, 2015, he became the first sitting president to visit a federal prison, Oklahoma's Federal Correctional Institution El Reno (with cattle grazing nearby, a less forbidding facility than most jails and prisons) (see figure 4). It was an extraordinary, eye-catching initiative that even governors and mayors rarely undertook (except for the goodly number sentenced to prison). Meeting with six "nonviolent" drug offenders, Obama offered them sympathy and tough questions. In calibrated comments outside the meeting (he thanked prison guards and officials for their service), he recounted for the cameras the dreadful statistics about mass incarceration and made a reasoned case for reducing it, at least for "nonviolent" offenders, especially drug offenders and "young people of color." He also made a case, as did some of the inmates, for rehabilitation of those behind bars.

Some of Obama's words echoed those of President Jimmy Carter decades earlier, but the visit and its stagecraft were without precedent. As the *New York Times* reported on the El Reno visit, in reference to the forty-fourth president's youthful drug use: "As it turns out, Mr. Obama noted, there is a fine line between president and prisoner. 'There but for the grace of God,' he said somberly after his tour. 'And that, I think, is something that we all have to think about.'" His suggestion that inmates shared a humanity, even a record of misbehavior, with other Americans challenged understandings of criminal evil that had dominated the punitive turn.

Days earlier, on June 26, Obama had delivered his memorable eulogy for the Honorable Reverend Clementa Pinckney and eight others killed in Dylann Roof's massacre at a black Charleston, South Carolina, church. He celebrated "Christian faith"—"That's what the black church means. Our beating heart"—led the crowd in singing "Amazing Grace," and read the names of the victims. He made no case on this occasion or others for criminal evil, a war on crime, righteous vengeance, or bristling police armaments, although he did flag "our nation's original sin," slavery. In his words, Obama offered as sharp a break from his predecessors as Carter had from his.[1]

Push and Pull

Pushback against the punitive turn came in many forms, some direct and some indirect, some sharp and others slow moving. As always during the punitive turn, war making played a role. During World War II, huge demands for manpower led to relaxations on incarceration and the treatment of inmates as assets in a national cause rather than threats to it. Shards of that historical experience reappeared after 9/11, especially with the 2003 U.S. war in Iraq. Desperate for personnel, the armed forces used their "moral waivers" program to take in more recruits with criminal convictions past or pending, some for serious crimes. By 2007 "the military has allowed more than 100,000 people with such troubled pasts to join its ranks over the past three years," Palm Center director Aaron Belkin reported, with more than half of marine recruits in 2006 needing a waiver of some sort (for criminal, medical, educational, or other reasons). Belkin added, "The same vulnerable populations that are getting channeled into the prison-industrial complex are also high on the list for military recruiters."[2]

Most likely but impossible to track, prosecutors and judges waived more young defendants on to enlistment in return for suspending convictions or sentences. "Okay," muses the fictional soldier Billy Lynn about these recruits in Ben Fountain's novel, "so maybe they aren't the greatest generation by anyone's standard, but they are surely the best of the bottom third percentile of their own somewhat muddled and suspect generation."[3] Although on a smaller scale than in World War

II, young people headed toward or convicted for crimes were again an asset to be tapped rather than stashed away in prisons.

Other policies unrelated to the post-9/11 wars showed similar effects. As climate change amplified California's natural disasters, the state expanded its use of prisoners to fight fires and other calamities. Only about 1,000 inmates performed these duties in 1976, but some 4,000 performed them in 2017, including many women, making up "anywhere from 50 to 80 percent of total fire personnel." Inmates resented the low pay, but they also expressed self-respect for meeting challenges, gratitude for their experience bonding with others, pleasure at living on campsites far from prison walls, and pride when civilians hailed them as quasi-military heroes who saved lives and property. "The conservation camps are bastions of civility," one reporter noted. The camps "smell[ed] of eucalyptus, the ocean, [and] fresh blooms," and they sometimes offered "civilian food cooked by other inmates," like "rib-eye steak and lobster."[4]

In that practice, the state treated prisoners as a resource to be tapped rather than a burden to be feared. Similar practices popped up elsewhere. When storms "ripped through" Tipton County, Indiana, in 2015, and "the county couldn't handle the clean up on its own," Miami Correctional Facility inmates "donated 16,570 hours of labor to area projects." Even so, one newspaper reader complained, "It isn't donated time. . . . It is return payment to taxpayers for their gym, cable, air conditioning, heat, bed, hygiene products, and food."[5]

Crime rates—sharply declining in some categories and places—also provided an opportunity to soften the punitive turn. New York City, for example, had 295 recorded murders in 2018, barely over 10 percent of the 2,262 recorded for 1990 (some other cities were less fortunate).[6] National violent crime rates also fell far below 1990s peaks, before experiencing upticks in 2015 and 2016.[7] The ups and downs of crime rates are always the products of so many forces, often slow-moving ones of demography, that experts argue over them endlessly. Among those forces, heightened action by "ordinary citizens" and civic groups to patrol and improve crime-prone neighborhoods might have contributed to the reduction in lawbreaking.[8] Those declines after the late 1990s served opposing arguments: To some, they showed that warehousing millions in prisons worked and should be sustained. For others, they indicated that mass incarceration was less needed or even counterproductive. Still, it became harder to point to crime rates as a reason to build more prisons, arm more police, and deny more defendants' rights.

Prison population growth stalled around 2008 and then slightly reversed as resources shifted to the war on terrorism, state budgets sagged, resistance to incarceration mounted, some acts like marijuana possession were decriminalized in some places, and the Obama administration challenged practices linked to mass incarceration. According to Bureau of Justice Statistics, the "total adult correctional population"—those in jails and prisons, those on parole and probation—began a slight but persisting decline after peaking in 2007 at 7,339,600 individuals under correctional control. The number of people behind bars peaked in 2008 at 2,310,000.[9]

Those figures excluded a good deal, like people held by tribal agencies (perhaps 2,390 persons at a given point in 2014)[10] and in juvenile detention. The numbers of youth arrested and coming before juvenile courts decreased significantly in the Obama years.[11] Still, the ACLU states, "Each year, an estimated 250,000 children—some not yet in their teens—are prosecuted in adult criminal courts and subjected to the consequences of adult criminal convictions"; those who went to adult prisons were presumably counted in standard statistics.[12] Those statistics appeared to exclude perhaps 10,000 people (no public agency kept track) committed to forensic mental hospitals after verdicts of not guilty by reason of insanity. Such verdicts dictated open-ended commitments that might last longer than a sentence under criminal conviction.[13]

Prison population statistics also excluded thousands who were done with prison but on sex crime registries. Because many could never leave those registries, the numbers on the registries had to keep growing, while others in that category remained indefinitely incarcerated in mental hospitals. The number of people in jails and prisons excluded armed forces personnel in military jails—1,400 in 2016, a number that excluded service members convicted in civilian courts. Above all, prison population numbers excluded those in immigration detention facilities. Moreover, the on-a-given-day method of measuring the imprisoned population did not capture the "enormous churn" of the system, whereby "people go to jail over 11 million times per year."[14] Although total numbers were uncertain, this huge population was scattered over an ever-shifting array of jurisdictions and institutions. The prison population declined only slightly after 2008 even as crime rates fell sharply, but the decline did constitute a break from decades of rising populations.

While imprisonment numbers stabilized, employment in the justice and security fields grew, amplified by post-9/11 policies and long-term trends. Having swelled in the 1980s and 1990s, private security–related employment appeared to level off after 2000, with perhaps 2 million people holding such positions as of 2013, in one estimate. As of 2007, the Bureau of Justice Statistics reported, federal, state, and local governments had 2.45 million "justice employees," double the number in 1982. Over that same twenty-five-year period, the number of active-duty military personnel shrank by about 750,000 to 1.379 million, which suggests that the larger sphere of "security" employees (military and otherwise) had seen not so much growth in personnel as shifts in their function toward stateside ("homeland") security. "Penal Keynesianism," Marie Gottschalk calls this phenomenon. To a degree, it displaced the military Keynesianism that underwrote so much employment in an earlier era.[15]

But numbers also became harder to ascertain. Certain categories fell outside standard criminal justice statistics, like information technology workers who did security-related tasks. Long fuzzy, the lines between public and private, and domestic and foreign, further blurred as public agencies ranging from the U.S. military to state prison systems to local sheriffs contracted with private agencies—some 100,000 private security guards worked for the United States in Iraq in 2006, at the peak of the American war there—and as more private personnel gained arrest powers. The best indices of growth come from institutionally stable agencies. For example, Border Patrol agents increased in number from 4,139 in fiscal year 1992 to over 20,000 by the second Obama administration, and more growth occurred thereafter. To be sure, not all of the combined 4 million or more private and public security employees snatched criminals or guarded prisoners; many had jobs far from the formal arena of criminal justice. All, nonetheless, had some tie to a huge apparatus of punishment and surveillance.[16]

These mixed statistics on the punitive turn did not tell the full story. Practice also mattered, and some punitive practices receded. A federal court ruling and police reforms sharply curtailed New York City's use of "stop and frisk," by which police stopped thousands of people, usually nonwhite, on city streets. Some county jail systems, like Cook County's in Illinois, underwent real reform at the behest of court orders or in-house reformers. The notorious rule of Sheriff Joe Arpaio in Arizona came to an end when he was voted out of office in 2016 and convicted of criminal contempt of court in a federal case in 2017 (and then pardoned by President Donald Trump). Elected reform prosecutors in big cities (Philadelphia and Chicago among them) sought to curtail or end abusive policing, prosecutorial overcharging, cash bail for those awaiting trial on lesser charges, and much else, bumping up against the entrenched practices and attitudes of many police and veteran prosecutors in the process.[17] Unfolding over several years, federal investigation into and monitoring of the sexual abuse of prisoners made a real difference. Moreover, use of the death penalty continued its uneven decline. The list of curtailed punitive practices was considerable.

Some credit for that curtailment owed to the Obama administration and Attorney General Eric Holder, a major voice of reform. The administration's research reports, like those on prison sex abuse, exposed a good deal. The Justice Department initiated many consent decrees with policing agencies, including those in big cities like Chicago and little ones like Ferguson, Missouri, decrees that allowed the department to monitor and curb abusive practices. The Justice Department also banned the use of private prison companies in the federal system. In the spirit of helping those "deserving of a second chance," Obama issued more commutations and pardons (and received more requests for them) than any president since Truman—1,927, nearly ten times the number George W. Bush issued, and more per year than Carter.[18] These actions could barely dint the total imprisoned population. But like Obama's words at El Reno and Charleston, they sent a powerful message that punishment was not the only measure of justice, that second chances might be possible. Reconsideration of sentences for drug-related crimes led to a significant trickle of federal inmates leaving prison (that reconsideration did not affect those sentenced under state or municipal laws). Those words and actions also bolstered the efforts of many activist organizations.

Growing resistance to the punitive turn seemed poised to curb some of its most pernicious elements. Just as the punitive turn arose from many sources, so did the resistance to it. It drew on the maturation of academy-based legal clinics; a turn toward criminal justice issues in scholarly work; the persistence of organizations like the American Civil Liberties Union; the wealth of resources from George Soros via the Open Society Foundations; and many religious groups—some, like the American Friends Service Committee, long active, and others recently mobilized.[19] Occasional successes, like that in Illinois regarding the Burge torture regime, galvanized further action. Though the connection was indirect, resistance also drew on the suspicion of state authority unleashed by Bush-era torture practices, suspicion that helped fuel challenges to solitary confinement, especially for juveniles.

More than before, resistance also drew on civic action, mobilized not only by specific incidents but also by the impact of Michelle Alexander's

2010 book, *The New Jim Crow*. Civic action included the Black Lives Matter movement that began in 2013 and mushroomed after the police shooting of Michael Brown in Ferguson, Missouri, in 2014. It further included a rush to join the ACLU in the wake of Donald J. Trump's election; membership more than quadrupled to 1.6 million, much of that increase driven by the ACLU's criminal justice and immigration work. Prisoners' activism also expanded, manifested in part in a burgeoning production of penal journalism similar to the sort that flourished in the mid-twentieth century, and other prisoners' writing. Inmates' protests included hunger strikes by thousands of California prisoners in 2011 and 2013 undertaken in support of their counterparts stashed away in the state's Pelican Bay solitary confinement unit. Pelican Bay was one of the places where "supermax prisoners" were "physically isolated, mostly invisible, and literally untouchable for more than two decades."[20]

Rising numbers of imprisoned women nourished another line of resistance. Michigan inmates had filed the first class-action lawsuit by female prisoners back in 1977 (*Glover v. Johnson*). The case spun out in federal court for decades and undergirded activism about female incarceration, while gender norms positioned women inmates more readily as victims of incarceration.[21] At the visionary end of the reform spectrum, a loose network of activists, scholars, and groups championed the abolition of prisons, often pointing to far lower rates of incarceration in other countries.[22] A mighty chorus of complaint and critique about the punitive turn—it now included some disillusioned law-and-order conservatives—had found a voice.

Beyond overt resistance, other developments, some initiated by prison administrators and others by outsiders, fostered the resilience and resistance of some prisoners. These included education (often provided by nearby colleges) for inmates, programs for them to train service and security dogs, and arts and theater activities, including music-and-arts therapy programs for juvenile offenders. Even the U.S. prison facility at Guantánamo Bay, once a site of torture, started art classes in 2009 for its dwindling cohort of prisoners (forty-one by 2017), with some of the resulting art exhibited in 2017 at the John Jay College of Criminal Justice.[23] That program illustrated the enormous variety of prison practices—there were no art classes for the thousands in solitary confinement and "supermax" prisons—and their shifting content. It also underlined how blurry the lines were between resistance, rehabilitation, and pacification, and it pointed to a revival of the rehabilitative ideal, one Obama gave voice to. At least for some inmates, the lock-'em-up-and-throw-away-the-key approach now seemed less appropriate.

The "worst of the worst," numbering in the hundreds of thousands, were another matter.

There is also a simpler explanation for growing resistance to the punitive turn: there was more to resist. As prison conditions worsened in many places, as the number of people in jail continued to rise into the 2000s, as the numbers serving life without parole skyrocketed, as the number in solitary confinement "for days, weeks, months, years, or even decades" reached at least 80,000 by 2015,[24] as shoot to kill (dogs as well as people) seemed to displace shoot to wound,[25] and as practices like civil asset forfeiture expanded, punitive regimes reached even more harshly into the lives of even more Americans, arousing fury and resistance. The punitive turn had been stacking up people for decades, and it now had reached a tipping point. The number jailed at any one time was hardly the only measure of punitive practices. Even as that number leveled off, the number of those who had cycled in and out of punitive regimes, often enduring sharp restrictions on their rights and opportunities after serving their sentences and facing what critics called "civil death," kept mounting.

Yet the punitive turn churned on, invigorated in some arenas even as it was trimmed in others, so that additions canceled out subtractions. Underwritten by the federal government in the name of fighting terrorism, militarized policing continued to expand. A new influx of veterans, many of them war hardened, sought jobs in security forces. New York City's cops, like most any city's cops, could plausibly claim that they, not the armed forces or the FBI, were "the first line of defense for the nation's top terror targets," especially given how "the new breed of terrorist will strike anywhere and at any time."[26]

A new surge of high-tech gadgets and hardware left over from wars abroad also juiced up militarized policing—every police force seemed to covet the armored Humvees used in Iraq. Modest efforts to roll back federal provision of military equipment to policing agencies came late in the Obama presidency. For 2014 and 2015, one organization still "found a federally-sponsored 'gun show' that never ends: small town police [were] armed with M16 and M14 rifles, night-vision goggles, bayonets and armored trucks; junior colleges and county sheriffs procured mine-resistant vehicles (MRVs); even local park districts and forest preserves stocked up on military-style equipment." As the *South Bend Tribune* reported under a photograph of police exiting a Mine Resistant Ambush Protected vehicle, "[Such] equipment looks as if you might find it on a battlefield in Afghanistan—not the streets of Mishawaka, North Liberty or Bourbon," towns in northern Indiana.[27] And then the Trump administration canceled Obama's rollback initiative. Tougher practices mirrored tougher hardware and tougher men. Burly male SWAT teams continued to proliferate, with children urged to emulate them (see figures 5 and 6). Police shootings of civilians remained numerous or increased, despite the absence of any crime wave and the decreasing vulnerability of police to death on duty.[28]

Beyond those carried out by uniformed personnel, other punitive practices continued or expanded. They included the "breathtaking power" and immunity to punishment for illegal or unprofessional conduct that most prosecutors enjoyed,[29] and the cruelties of the plea-bargaining system. They included the abuse of bail, civil asset forfeiture, faulty or rigged drug tests,[30] and traffic tickets, all used less to control crime than to enrich public and private authorities (in an antitax era, proceeds from these sources and from drug busts paid for police officers, SWAT teams, and armored vehicles). They also included the indeterminate sentences of sex crime offenders, often incarcerated long after their formal sentences ended, and the distribution of scarlet letters by sex crime registries for both serious criminals and teenagers engaged in consensual sex, who then faced severe legal, residential, and employment consequences.

Meanwhile, the school-to-prison pipeline remained busy, even as catchphrases like "zero tolerance" lost their novelty. Prison conditions, shielded from public scrutiny, if anything worsened,[31] while claptrap private van services hauled prisoners across the nation at their peril.[32] In particular, the medical neglect of prisoners (often those awaiting trial) remained appalling. This situation was made worse by the growing use of private medical providers and prison operators, often even less accountable than public authorities and no cheaper than state-provided care. All these practices operated along highly racialized lines, though they were hardly confined to nonwhites. Even as some practices receded, others persisted or expanded, so that their overall bulk remained largely unchanged. Reformers' gains were offset by the reinvigoration of old practices or the institution of new ones.

The punitive turn reached more women as well, especially poorer ones. Women had always been affected by crime, most awfully as its victims (often in sex crimes), and also as witnesses to fathers, brothers, sons, and partners falling victim to it or becoming party to it. Families and support for children were devastated as men entered jails and children entered highly policed schools. (The punitive turn did much to foster the very "matrifocal" quality of African American family life that worriers like Daniel Patrick Moynihan had lamented in the early

1960s.) Now, women themselves were increasingly in prison: their incarceration numbers grew by 20 percent between 1999 and 2008, to 114,852, and by a staggering 750 percent between 1980 and 2017.[33] (Women's imprisonment still got little attention in journalism, and scholarship largely focused on men in trouble with the law.) Mounting efforts to criminalize abortion threatened worse; already, poorer mothers faced fresh efforts to criminalize actions deemed harmful to their fetuses and to remove their children if they were deemed unfit parents. Women bore other burdens, too; they provided much of the leadership and grassroots support for activist and protest groups, just as they contributed much of the journalism and scholarship on the punitive turn.

Gains notched against the punitive turn were offset above all by a stunning rise in punitive practices toward undocumented immigrants and border crossers, and by a further militarizing of the U.S.-Mexico border (with private vigilante groups often weighing in). It was as if, in hydraulic fashion, any retrenchment in punitive practices toward "Americans" had to be offset by a rise in such practices toward others. Indeed, "hydraulic" may be the apt word, because many of the interests—weapons makers, prison builders and operators, unions, Beltway consulting firms, politicians—that had sustained the punitive turn found new opportunities as its older form flatlined. As the official prison population leveled off, the number of immigrants in detention facilities (and in federal prisons) and the number of those who were deported—in both cases, Central Americans and Mexicans above all— soared to new heights in the Obama years.

Precision in that regard is difficult, given the shifting categories employed by Immigration and Customs Enforcement and the conflicting figures offered by nonstate observers. But the "number of immigration detainees" reported by ICE more than doubled between 2001 and 2011, reaching 429,000. The number of immigrants in detention facilities (a motley mix of federal and poorly monitored private housing that held "nearly half of all immigration detention beds" as of 2011)[34] reached 352,882 over the course of the year 2016 (perhaps a tenth of that number on any given day, given how fast most detainees cycled in and out of facilities, either released or deported).[35]

Deportations more than doubled between 2001 and 2012, to over 400,000. Thousands more entered federal prisons on criminal convictions, destined to be deported if they ever got out, helping to make Hispanics "the largest ethnic or racial group in federal prisons and courts." The Border Patrol grew, and the southern border became more surveilled, trip wired, fenced, and walled—militarized—even before Donald Trump promised a new "wall" along that border. All in all, Marie Gottschalk reported in 2015, "The amount that the federal government spends on immigration enforcement exceeds funding for all principal law enforcement agencies combined," although, she also notes, the distinction is becoming artificial since "the line between immigration enforcement and law enforcement is rapidly disappearing."[36] These developments were sometimes justified as antiterrorism measures (explicitly in the Secure Fence Act of 2006) and funded through antiterrorism budgets, but no terrorist action crossing the southern border surfaced as of 2017. Instead, anti-immigrant and anti-Latino sentiment drove those developments. The result was a lateral spread of punitive energies, rather than some vertical decline or increase.

The Limits of Resistance

Why did the punitive turn not roll back, given all the resistance and indignation it unleashed and America's new focus on external enemies? External and internal enemies could not be neatly distinguished, as the intense focus on undocumented immigrants underlined. The systems for both were embedded in each other, the feedback loops between them robust. The war on terror also produced new criminals even if it downgraded fears of older ones—small numbers of terrorists and terrorism funders, larger numbers of war-damaged, sometimes crime-prone veterans of Iraq and Afghanistan. Swelling systems of policing and surveillance, justified as measures to catch terrorists, caught others in their nets. Enhanced airport security, for example, nabbed not only potential shoe bombers and terrorism plotters, but also unwary people carrying drugs, contraband goods, or guns. And the war on terror mostly involved distant, faceless enemies, ones usually killed (often by their own actions) rather than paraded in perp walks or court appearances. It provided only intermittent satisfaction of the impulses for vengeance and the thrills of criminal catching that coursed through American life. Above all, deeply embedded and crudely manipulated fears of undocumented immigrants and porous borders led to an expansion of those facing deportation, offsetting small declines in the population housed under criminal convictions and parole violations.

Other obstacles obstructed any rollback of the punitive turn. For one thing, the war on terrorism was hardly World War II redux, despite politicians' and pundits' efforts to draw the analogy (or to see it as World War III or World War IV). It did not entail that conflict's huge demands for military personnel and industrial workers, and hence its pressures to regard criminals as a resource to be tapped, rather than a threat to be warehoused. Any post-9/11 downshifting also had to start from a far bigger punitive apparatus than in 1941. It was harder to redirect a giant ocean liner than a small cruiser. Powerful public and private interests guarded what they had acquired and sought to expand it. Corporate interests, a minor player in instigating the punitive turn, now played a large role in sustaining it. Floundering briefly in the 1990s, they were rescued when "the federal government emerged as a financial godsend" by turning to private companies for immigrant detention.[37]

Closely tied to local and state politicians and prosecutors, unions for police, parole officers, and prison guards fiercely resisted curbs on their behavior, punishment for their bad deeds, and closings of their facilities. At least union leaders resisted; their members were often more diverse in their demographics and politics than their leadership. Even programs like California's firefighting camps tapped the punitive turn as much as they softened it. Because inmate firefighters were cheaper than the civilian version, California's attorney general's office in 2014 opposed reductions in the state's imprisoned population because it wanted a robust supply of inmates to work the front lines of disaster.[38]

If anything, the Great Recession aggravated punitive impulses. Despite expectations at the time that recession-damaged budgets would force states to shrink prisons and policing systems, lawmakers and prison authorities instead simply cut resources for prisoners' (and staffs') well-being, and extracted more revenue from fines, court costs, and practices like civil asset forfeiture. Stoked by politicians, public perceptions that crime rose during hard times, even though it did not, gave ballast to these trends.[39]

Even efforts at reform and leniency often yielded punitive results, Marie Gottschalk explains. The classic case was death penalty activism. Foes of the death penalty presented life without parole as a humane — or, as some argued, worse-than-death — alternative to execution. In doing so, they contributed to an explosion in statutes and court decisions mandating life without parole. Capital punishment's opponents also accorded life sentences a legitimacy they had rarely had before the 1980s, so that those serving them "increased a hundredfold" thereafter, including several thousand "juvenile lifers." As a result, Gottschalk notes, "one out of every nine persons imprisoned in the United States is serving what some critics call 'the other death penalty,'" and "prisons are becoming maximum security nursing homes."[40] It was another way in which retreats in the punitive turn got zeroed out by fresh advances. Other reform efforts posed similar risks. As states, cities, and judges moved to cut back cash bail for persons awaiting trial for low-level offenses, the alternative seemed to be electronic monitoring devices (especially favored by the companies that produced and administered them), but these devices imposed costs and restrictions on the accused arguably as severe as jail time, creating a new "digital jail."[41]

And although heartfelt and sometimes vigorous, Obama's challenge to the punitive turn was also cautious and compromised. Inadvertently sending the message that punishment was for the powerless, his administration declined to prosecute any major figures in the banking/finance/insurance meltdown that ushered in the Great Recession, abandoning past Justice Department practice and instead pursuing civil litigation (sometimes with whopping fines) against companies and new regulations to rein them in.[42] Sending a similar message, Obama declined to prosecute, or even criminally investigate, the officials and private contractors who had authorized, condoned, or practiced torture in violation of U.S. and international law during the Bush years. Obama asked for "reflection, not retribution," rejecting "spending our time and energy laying blame for the past."[43] He was not going to open that can of worms. His embrace of drone warfare against presumed terrorists moved him onto legally and morally fraught ground. Insofar as such warfare replaced torture, it was hardly clear that such killing was more justified.

Above all, Obama's consistent emphasis on how "nonviolent" offenders deserved rehabilitation and sentencing reconsideration greatly narrowed the scope of his reform efforts, since "violent" offenders comprised the bulk of the imprisoned population (and drug offenders only a minority). He asserted that he had "no tolerance" and "no sympathy" for "violent" offenders, squeezing into one homogenous category a population greatly varied by motivation and by action. (Simply brandishing a gun or knife in the commission of a crime might be judged a violent crime even if the weapon was never used.) For him, all violent offenders seemed to be "murderers, predators, rapists, gang leaders, drug kingpins."[44] To be sure, resistance to Obama's efforts was mighty, even as some conservatives and born-again law-and-order types now joined the reform choir. And he had done more on this front than any predecessor. But what he did still had sharp limits.

A historical comparison may be useful. After the Vietnam War and again after the Cold War, the scaling back of America's militarization turned out to be modest and partial, despite lavish hopes invested in it. It featured lateral redeployment of resources (to criminal justice among other places) as much as vertical downsizing. Some elements of militarization receded—the shift to an all-volunteer force shrank the number of uniformed personnel. Others grew, such as a force of civilian contractors who did work that uniformed personnel had once done, and the resources poured into high-tech warfare. Similarly, twenty-first-century downsizing of the "criminal-industrial complex" was fitful and partial at best.

If anything, challenging the criminal-industrial complex was harder than challenging the military-industrial complex had been, for the former was far more dispersed and localized. National security work was diffused through elaborate institutional networks, as President Dwight Eisenhower's famous 1961 address pointed out (he did not flag a military-industrial "complex" for nothing). But at least the realm of national security had symbolic and substantive capitals—the Pentagon, the presidency, Congress—against which critics and antiwar agitators could readily and sometimes literally mobilize. But who or what headed up the criminal-industrial complex? Who or what guided the punitive turn at a time when, as one congressman noted, "every agency want[ed] to be involved in counterterrorism and intelligence,"[45] and even staid old institutions like the Department of Agriculture and the U.S. Post Office had roles to play. At times the Department of Justice, and the president above it, seemed in charge. But Justice hardly had the centralized power that the Defense Department had—one reason there was no mass march on it—and the president was no commander in chief of the many criminal justice systems.

Against whom or what could aggrieved foes of the punitive turn direct their ire? The president? The attorney general? The governor? The mayor? The police chief? The prosecutor? The prison warden? The sheriff? The corrections-corporation chieftain? The judge? The Congress? The state legislature? The police union? The cop? The school superintendent? James Forman wrote of America's "almost absurdly disaggregated and uncoordinated criminal justice system," one in which "nobody has to take responsibility for the outcome, because nobody *is* responsible—at least not fully."[46] Even the singular noun "system" was misleading: the criminal justice apparatus was a system of systems, an archipelago of agencies.

That disaggregation made it hard even to see what was going on. The intricate connections between the institutions of defense and criminal justice—the Department of Homeland Security alone was unfathomable in this regard—made it still harder to see the component parts, let alone to disentangle the myriad tentacles of this beast. So, too, did the secrecy and invisibility (attributes shared with the national security apparatus) of many punitive systems, which resisted reporting and transparency, let alone oversight. As at Pelican Bay, dreadful places like supermax prisons were often a "local innovation," the products of "prison officials" carrying out projects funded by the state but so secret that even interested parties, (legislators, judges, scholars, activists) struggled to gain knowledge of them.[47]

Entrenched systems often perpetuate themselves for no good reason, or even no bad one, but simply because they can, because it is in the nature of systems and the self-interest of their people to do so. They usually have to offer some reason, internally or for the outside world, for their perpetuation, but it may have little to do with why they perpetuate themselves. This is not always a bad thing insofar as beneficial systems carry on, even grow—there are self-perpetuating forces within the system of Social Security, for example. But systems that are secretive, shielded from public scrutiny, and byzantine easily perpetuate themselves in malign ways, or at least with high social and moral costs. As Anne-Marie Cusac comments regarding "punishment creep," "Punishment wanders in many directions, and its vectors are often unclear."[48] Critics offered reasons for why criminal justice systems should reform, retrench, or dismantle. But it was hard for such reasons to make a dint in the self-perpetuating nature of those systems. As a case in point, even as prisoner, activist, and legal efforts produced some rollback in the use of solitary confinement in California and other states in the 2010s, they fell short of its abolition and saw many systems create its rough equivalent under other names.[49]

The forces of resistance did find villains, like Burge in the Chicago police, Arpaio in Arizona, and the cops in Ferguson, Missouri. But with so many targets scattered over a vast institutional and political map, resistance unavoidably took on a scattershot quality, scoring victories but overwhelmed by the larger task. Just as the U.S. government pursued terrorists in whack-a-mole fashion, foes of the punitive turn were stuck with whack-a-mole tactics. They faced a terrain sketched in 2011 by Richard Cohen, a senior *Washington Post* columnist:

> We live in a soft police state. It's not a film-noir one, based on ideology and punctuated by the crunch of hobnailed boots, but one created in response to terrorism and crime. Cameras follow us. Our travels, our purchases, are recorded. Our computers and cellphones snitch on us. There's no Orwellian Big Brother, just countless little ones, all of them righteously on the lookout for the bad guys. It's necessary, I suppose. It will be abused, I don't suppose.[50]

It was hardly a "soft police state" for many, of course, and it had an ideology: the preference for warlike responses to crime (and to many other problems), especially when nonwhite people were involved. It was an ideology, just not one nested inside the conventional Left/Right, conservative/liberal definitions of the term. But Cohen's depiction suggested why it was hard to locate or resist that "police state."

Earlier efforts at reform of police and punitive practices had produced changes, though not always beneficial ones (the penitentiary was a reform innovation). However, these modifications involved systems of far smaller scale. By 2017 punitive systems were too vast, variegated, and embedded to allow much change. They were "no longer just the creation of the larger political, social and economic forces that shape U.S. society," Gottschalk concludes. They had "become 'one of those causal or shaping forces.'"[51] The recognition that the punitive turn was embedded in larger structures of racial and economic inequality only made the task more difficult. If the evils of criminal justice could not be ended until those structures were demolished—a daunting task indeed—then the path to ending those evils was likely a dead end. But also, as Gottschalk argues, "the package of penal policies based on the three-R model that prevails in elite circles today—reentry, justice reinvestment, and reducing recidivism—is not up to the task."[52] Squeezing the prison pipeline at its entry point—by decriminalizing some acts, reducing punishment for others, and finding humane alternatives to incarceration—held more promise than helping people stagger out of the pipeline at its other end. Except for modest rollbacks in municipal, state, and federal penalties for lower-level drug offenses, which only accounted for a fraction of the imprisoned population, efforts to narrow that entry point met with little success.

Texas illustrated the limits of reform, especially the version driven by the cost-cutting goals of an emerging conservative "right on crime" movement. The state had led the nation's prison-building boom, but in 2007 its legislature, trying to reduce the enormous costs of its prison system, rejected a bill to spend billions more on new prisons. Texas legislators also authorized redirection of some arrested people to community supervision and added moneys for drug abuse and mental health treatment. These efforts were hailed for producing a system both more humane and cheaper. The state's imprisoned male population (not its women's population) modestly shrank, by about 6 percent, a few prisons closed, and reform politicians took office in several cities. Yet other elements of the state's punitive politics offset those changes. "The war on sex offenders" intensified, brutal prison conditions remained, "the number of new felony cases filed in Texas reached a near all-time high" in 2018, and prison privatization advanced. The cost-cutting impulse that closed a few prisons also worsened conditions in remaining ones (weekend lunch ended for many inmates in 2011). Meanwhile, Governor Rick Perry "racked up a breathtaking record of execution in his eleven years in office: 234 and counting" as of 2011, with Perry remaining in office until 2015. There were so many nodes—political, corporate, attitudinal—in Texas's elite-driven punitive system that major overhaul proved elusive.[53]

But just as there were so many nodes in the system to attack, there were also so many places to attack it. No such ingrained system would be dismantled, but it might be whittled down through all sorts of measures. With so many attacking the prison system from so many vantage points, by 2020 it seemed possible to chip away at it seriously. If not death by a thousand cuts, at least serious injury by hundreds. Prosperity also chipped away at mass incarceration. As long as it lasted—until the pandemic of 2020—a tighter though patchy labor market diverted some people into jobs rather than prisons, encouraged prisons and allied groups to train inmates for postincarceration jobs, and provided prisoners more opportunities upon their release. A modestly smaller and more humane system seemed about to emerge, at least for those directly caught up in it, though not for those caught up in the burgeoning system of immigrant detention and deportation. How much it would be whittled down, in whose interests, with what consequences, and with what countervailing results (still more electronic surveillance? still more policing of the borders?) remained in question. So, too, did the ways in which crime-fighting and war-fighting would continue to spool into each other.

And so, too, the ways in which vengeance would continue to course through American and global culture, as it did in minor but revealing ways. When Kenneth Branagh directed and starred in a 2017 remake of the 1974 movie *Murder on the Orient Express* (based on the Agatha Christie novel), he changed its ending. Detective Hercule Poirot discovers that all the survivors on the train had a role in murdering the man responsible for the killing of a baby (a fictionalized version of the kidnapping and murder of Charles and Anne Morrow Lindbergh's baby in 1932). Rather than merely wrapping up the plot, Poirot sermonizes that the culpable parties were seeking revenge, that they were justified in seeking it, and that it promoted their healing—an ending simply not present in the earlier version. Branagh knew what he was doing. He "felt that he needed to switch things up by giving Poirot an actual moral quandary to wrestle with," reported one critic. "'We need someone more morally absolute than we are. Poirot,' he says. 'There is right; there is wrong; there's nothing in between.'" Branagh's ending encapsulated years of political and cultural endorsement of vengeance as an act of healing.[54]

The Twilight of War Talk

At that, there were also signs that some of the ideological and linguistic propellants of the punitive turn, captured in war talk, were continuing to fade. Beginning in the Clinton years, rhetoric from presidents and other national leaders about a war on crime and a war on drugs dissipated, virtually ending with Obama. The movement to legalize marijuana cultivation and use helped undercut talk of a "war" on drugs, as did the opioid crisis of the 2010s. Victims of opioid abuse were seen as largely white and often poor and rural, thus depleting the racial charge embedded in the war on drugs. A medical rather than punitive framework for that crisis emerged, at least in op-ed columns and experts' pronouncements, and it was sometimes applied by police chiefs and their departments, who had once been frontline troops in the war on drugs. And insofar as the terrorist displaced the criminal, "war on terrorism" marginalized "war on crime." Stabilizing or receding crime rates perhaps also made a difference, although attitudes about lawbreaking never correlated closely with the ups and downs of crime's incidence.

The shift was marked not only by diminished use of war talk but also by redeployment of that talk to challenge the punitive turn. Used in reference to Soviet prison camps, "gulag" alone gained considerable favor. Mark Dow used it for his 2005 book, *American Gulag: Inside U.S. Immigration Prisons*. Ruth Wilson Gilmore tapped it for her important 2007 book, *Golden Gulag: Prisons, Surplus, Crisis, and Opposition in Globalizing California*. And in one of many more obscure examples, a Michigan attorney charged in 2015 that his state was holding "Prisoners of War in the Michigan Gulag." The United States, critic Tom Engelhardt argued that year, had created an "American Gulag, a vast carceral archipelago that no other country can match and into which millions of human beings are simply deep-sixed."[55] Political cartoonists suggested something similar, as when the *Buffalo News* depicted a fearsome character labeled "war on drugs" dumping "prisoners of war" into a deep pit.[56]

War had been deployed before to resist the punitive turn, whose skeptics had drawn on the Vietnam War to ask whether the war on crime was to be a similarly hapless venture. Since war was such a multi-faceted historical experience, it could be tapped for many political purposes. The twenty-first century saw a proliferation of counterpunitive uses of the language of war and the use of different kinds of war-related historical experience. Meanwhile, America's flailing wars in Afghanistan and Iraq hardly made war an enticing model for state action in crime-fighting.

It was also striking how, in the wake of Michael Brown's death in Ferguson, Missouri, and other incidents, terms like "the militarization of policing" and "militarized policing" erupted into activist, pundit, and political circles. The words were hardly new, dating in academic and policy circles to the 1990s, and they were rather stiffly academic, hardly tripping off the tongue as "war on drugs" had. Nonetheless, they gained considerable cachet as an explosion of video technology attached more images to them. Obama himself publicly warned against "building a militarized culture inside our local law enforcement" and found fault with local officers' "militarized gear."[57] The use of such terms reconfigured discrete incidents, like Brown's death, as parts of a long historical and institutional process, even if most users traced that process back only to the post-9/11 era, not to its 1960s jumping-off point. This rhetoric concerning law enforcement also reconfigured such incidents as products of state policy, especially the federal largess of armaments and training that had done much to militarize policing agencies and the flow of veterans into police work, rather than as products only of racist cops and police chiefs. In that vein, the Marshall Project stressed "the impact of military veterans migrating into law enforcement. Even as departments around the country have attempted a cultural transformation from 'warriors' to 'guardians,' one in five police officers is literally a warrior, returned from Afghanistan, Iraq or other assignments."[58]

For sure, war talk hardly disappeared, sometimes popping up in unexpected places. In 2016, the *New York Times* billed an editorial "Governors Unite In the War against Opioids," urging a crackdown on "dispensing prescription painkillers." By then, articles, op-eds, and letters to the editor in the *Times* had called for a medical rather than militarized approach to addiction and had explicitly rejected war language. But there that rhetoric was again, as if on autopilot. This remained the case even though, as often happened when such language was used, the *Times* editorial made no mention of it beyond the headline aside from a passing reference to "front lines." This was "war" by political habit—evidence of the tenacity of war talk.[59]

Of course, the rhetoric of a war on crime had never been the sole cause of the punitive turn. It was more the linguistic vessel on which the punitive turn rode. Nonetheless, words had mattered: "war on crime" had sent signals to prosecutors, police officers, and a host of others about how to act, and it had sanctioned quasi-military approaches to crime. That such language diminished early in the twenty-first century perhaps only indicated that warlike approaches to crime were now so entrenched that the words were hardly needed any longer. Yet they were not replaced by any new language justifying the punitive turn that was equally robust, stable, and appealing. By 2017, the punitive turn was impelled by its inertia more than by its compelling rhetoric, or so it seemed.

EPILOGUE: THE ENDURING PUNITIVE TURN

The "twilight of war talk" in the Obama years turned out to be a false sunset. By 2017, the punitive turn seemed to have reached a standstill, having done its work of creating a punitive nation and having met mounting resistance. But it was hardly static. Thanks in part to President Donald J. Trump, war-fighting and crime-fighting continued to intersect, often in new and dangerous ways, with the spirit of vengeance running through them. And police and the military were called on to do more of the work that a fraying state otherwise struggled to accomplish.

Gun advertisements, similar to those with which this book began, suggested as much. FN America hawked its pistols during TV coverage of the 2017 U.S. Open tennis tournament (perhaps an improbable audience for such ads). In one ad, a tough-looking man in uniform ("for over 125 years, his entire family has served on the front lines") appears on a battlefield pointing an FN 509 pistol, and then in civvies holding the same weapon. In another ad the man appears on "the battlefield where tyranny is laid to rest," then in civvies pointing the pistol, and then gun-toting women appear in similar poses. These commercials narrated a seamless transition from war abroad to a "battlefield" at home. So, too, did ads flagged by the *New York Times* in 2015: "As Close as You Can Get Without Enlisting"—that is, as close as the civilian could get to war.[1] Unsurprisingly, the National Rifle Association echoed those ads, insisting that in a country run by "cowards," Americans needed guns to battle Islamist terrorists and to abide by "the rule of war"—"the weak get slaughtered, and we are at war." It was as if the line between war-fighting and crime-fighting had vanished. Earlier, many men had been invited to obtain "proof of [their] manhood" by buying an AR-15 rifle, advertised by Bushmaster Firearms in its "man card" campaign, which posed manhood questions to buyers like "Have you ever watched figure skating on purpose?" The company's official campaign continued until Adam Lanza used an AR-15 in his massacre at the Sandy Hook Elementary School in 2012, but its "man card" words and images remained online.[2]

Mass shootings, some likely carried out by men who had seen such ads, also fed new feedback loops between war-fighting and crime-fighting. The massacres had come in shocking waves for decades, with another crescendo at El Paso and Dayton in the summer of 2019. Shooters, usually young, white, and male, often regarded their massacres as warlike acts of vengeance against immigrants, racial and religious minorities, women, and gay people. In turn, those acts elicited fear among others that innocent Americans were being warred on. And they generated talk of warlike responses, as when some officials and gun control advocates insisted that the term "domestic terrorism" be applied to mass shootings. That term had echoes of the war against terrorism that the United States had long waged.

That insistence suggested how ingrained the war framework was even among those determined to stop mass shootings, including some stalwart liberals and progressives, as well as how capacious and slippery the term "terrorism" had become. "Although the body count is smaller than 9/11, a domestic 'war on terror' is urgently needed," claimed one presumed expert. "We can and must apply some of the lessons from the post-9/11 period to our domestic terror problem." Proponents of that view seemed to have forgotten how that earlier response had been repressive and taken the form of war.[3] To be sure, for gun control advocates, what better way was there to stop war at home than to take away the weapons that made war possible? However, no "war" on mass shooters emerged. Gun control advocates met well-funded resistance, embraced by Trump, from those who insisted that shooters had problems concerning their mental health, not their access to guns. But the moods and words of war hung over it all.

Gun advertisements, gun massacres, and the impulse to replay "the post-9/11 period" were grim reminders that the punitive turn had long been propelled by visceral emotions of fear and vengeance, ones stoked by war talk. Those sentiments were on full display in the 2016 presidential campaign, when the talk by and around Trump's campaign prized vengeance. The glee with which many supporters greeted his calls to resume torture of presumed terrorists suggested the persistent appeal of retribution. "They're chopping off our heads in the Middle East," Trump told one audience. "And don't tell me it doesn't work. Torture works, okay, folks?" He urged something "much stronger" than waterboarding.[4] Trump's paeans to torture were paired with his references to Mexicans as "rapists," his denigration of other groups, his embrace of cries to "lock her [Hillary Clinton] up," and his winking endorsement of audiences' chants demanding to "kill the bitch" (old rumors resurfaced that Clinton was a lesbian and a murderer).[5]

In that mind-set, it was irrelevant that torture might be ineffective, or worse, counterproductive when it inflamed hatred of America. Indeed, a malign outcome might enhance its appeal, as if its moral purity swelled in proportion to the self-harm it caused. "Our vengeance is so righteous," torture's supporters seemed to be saying, "that we inflict it even if it means shooting ourselves in the foot." That outlook mirrored the one held by many death penalty supporters—its efficacy as a deterrent to crime often seemed irrelevant. It made little difference whether torture was useful in fighting terrorism, any more than it mattered whether most elements of the punitive turn were useful in limiting crime. Vengeance trumped efficacy.

Few among Hillary haters probably expected that she would be locked up or killed, or even cared whether she was. That Trump's venom spewed in so many directions and at so many groups suggested that the actions taken were less important than the display of hatred. Those Americans who embraced Trump's calls for vengeance were asserting their and their nation's right to treat foes vengefully more than the value of doing so, although a fine line separated declaration of the right from its implementation. Trump voiced a shrill American exceptionalism: we have the right to be vengeful and to thumb our nose at norms others might wish to impose.

Were those just empty, though ugly, words uttered in 2016? For one thing, they suggested that the feedback loops between war-fighting and crime-fighting at the institutional, political, and rhetorical levels had an emotive core: many of those who endorsed torture also appeared to endorse "kill the bitch," as Trump and surrogates like Michael Flynn invited them to do.[6] Impulses for vengeance easily swished back and forth between the arenas of home and abroad. "For decades," Gottschalk argues, "retribution has been a guiding principle, if not the preeminent philosophy of the criminal justice system in the United States."[7] So it also was in Trump's public stances (except when retribution might touch his inner circle). The ugly words also offered an emotive foundation for the Trump administration's reversal of Obama's initiatives to moderate the punitive turn.

Trump tapped animal spirits that had operated, usually just beneath the surface, during America's half-century war on crime. A striking shrinkage in presidential and gubernatorial pardons and commutations (except under Obama) also reflected those spirits, suggesting that for numerous Americans, "many crimes remain eternally unforgivable and unforgettable," with "their perpetrators . . . forever defined by the crime."[8] It could not have been otherwise since war, either as fact or as idea, is always a venue for such attitudes. But Trump helped bring those animal emotions further to the surface, stripping away the veneer of policy talk and rhetorical codes that had obscured them. As Joseph Margulies commented in 2016 regarding Clinton, "The frenzied blood-lust in the cry to 'lock her up' conjures not so much the ideal of the law as the specter of a lynching, complete with the degradation and humiliation spectacles that routinely accompanied those savage affairs."[9]

Fickle and explosive, those animal spirits were not easily controlled. They could veer off in many directions. "Lock her up" was occasionally countered by "lock him up," in reference to Trump. That many Americans wanted Trump impeached or jailed suggested the range of these currents of vengeance, though hardly the equivalence of them in emotive ugliness and public display. There were no big rallies in which crowds chanted, "Lock him up" to the approval of a leading politician, but "lock her up" still was shouted at Trump's rallies in 2019.

In office, Trump bypassed "war on crime" and "war on drugs," the shopworn phrases of the past, although Attorney General Jeff Sessions often declared a "winnable war" against drugs and a "multi-front war against rising crime."[10] Instead, Trump came up with a different version of war talk. He and his supporters engaged in near-endless claims of an "invasion" by migrants from Mexico and Central America crossing the southern border of the United States.[11] "Invasion" was the language of war, even though there was no war to wage. The word signaled the fusion of war-fighting and crime-fighting, all the more so since Trump presented those migrants as agents of horrific crime within the United States. So, too, did his decision to widen the spigot, which Obama had narrowed, carrying surplus military weapons and equipment to police forces.

And there was Trump's bolder if capricious use of military forces to patrol the border. In an election eve ploy that did Republicans no good in November 2018 congressional voting, he dispatched several thousand more troops to the border, where they had little to do. More gravely, his administration moved to corral asylum seekers and "unaccompanied alien children" (an odd term indeed) on military bases.[12] In the past, the United States had used bases to house Hungarian, Vietnamese, Cuban, and other refugees, but those bases were usually way stations for their admission into the country, not for their deportation.[13]

In another warlike move, in February 2019, Trump declared a "national emergency," a term often associated with war, to siphon funds Congress authorized for other purposes into his floundering effort to build a "border wall." Most of the president's actions had some precedent, but their scale was larger, their heartlessness more transparent, their warlike apparatus more robust, their constitutional legitimacy more suspect, and their words uglier, for they involved the denigration of an imagined enemy that is common in war. While hardly over, the long-running wars on crime and drugs were yielding to a new war on migrants (at least poor and dark-skinned ones).

The fusion of crime-fighting and war-fighting took on new life, albeit on the odd terms of Trump's persona and presidency. Trump turned to the armed forces to patrol the border and house border crossers in part because the barren cupboard of the U.S. state, whose shelves he did much to empty, provided few alternative mechanisms. Despite his extravagant praise for the military, especially those men who joined his administration, his stance toward the armed forces was so transparently exploitative, condescending, and shallow (on November 11, 2018, he skipped a trip to an American cemetery in France to honor U.S. troops who died in World War I) as to undercut any sense that he had respect for the institution or the people in it. He seemed more interested in the atmospherics of war and boasts about threatening it than in waging it.

Trump added much else to the mix. He designated various people and institutions as enemies, often along racial and gender lines, including four congresswomen of color critical of Israel in 2019. In reaction to his tweets and rants, critics sensed that Trump seemed to be sanctioning war on dark-skinned people in the United States and elsewhere (in the "shithole" countries he once referred to). According to Trump, American Jews who did not vote for him showed "great disloyalty" to Israel (and presumably to him and the United States).[14] He also said the "fake news media" were "enemies of the people." In addition, Trump's embrace of "trade wars" poured more war talk into the national discourse. His man bonding with law-breaking, war-loving thugs—Putin in Russia, Duterte in the Philippines, Erdoğan in Turkey, and others—added to worries that he was a menace to the law.

But presidents' and other leaders' words and deeds do not alone set national patterns. Punitive practices also follow long-running historical trajectories at state, municipal, and institutional levels. There remained striking variations in that regard, with southern states leading the way in jailing people. As of 2012, Louisiana incarcerated people at more than four times the rate of Minnesota, six times the rate of Massachusetts and Maine, and eight times that of Rhode Island.[15] Race was a factor in those variations, but class, history, and geography were factors as well. Despite their large minority populations, California, Illinois, New Jersey, and New York jailed people at far lower rates than Deep South states. Yet southern states tended to have "the lowest black-white ratios in incarceration," in part because their white populations also tended to be poor.[16] Despite all the huffing and puffing at the national level, these variations persisted. They pointed toward a further disaggregation of punitive practices—sharper differences among states and regions—perhaps along the much-touted "blue/red state" lines of U.S. politics.

Or perhaps along lines now hard to predict. The differential impacts of climate change and of responses to it might be a wild card. Changes in criminal justice often occur not because people or governments plan them but because something poorly foreseen, like climate change, knocks systems off balance. The widespread use of legal and undocumented immigrant labor to clean up and rebuild after Hurricane Katrina pointed to one possibility if climate-related crises worsened. "Natural disasters" may provide new opportunities to exploit or to liberate (the line between the two is fuzzy and shifting) undocumented migrants. Bring 'em in might override kick 'em out. As global warming causes more forest fires, burns up more pastures, floods more coastlines, and melts more glaciers, the need for whopping numbers of people to avert or fight those effects will grow. The country might look to immigrants or to youth conscripted into some form of national service. But inmates might be an obvious, available, and exploitable labor pool whose use had robust historical precedents. Prisoners may be deemed not a threat but an asset to be released from jail in order to battle climate change, just as they often had been during World War II and in California's inmate "forest army." Addressing climate change, states and cities may differ sharply from one another in their needs for such labor and their ways of securing it.

Which is another reason that disaggregation may prevail. Minnesota and Louisiana may diverge further in incarceration rates, and Minneapolis still further from New Orleans. Some prison systems may abandon solitary confinement while others cling to it, just as the death penalty still holds its grip in some states. Some localities may continue to lock up low-level drug offenders, while others seek to divert them to social support services or to treat their behaviors as misdemeanors rather than felonies. Some may dispatch them to burning forests and crumbling shorelines, while others keep them behind bars. Generalization about them all may become more difficult. Since federal prisons house less than 10 percent of all inmates (excluding undocumented immigrants), what states, municipalities, sheriffs, and local prosecutors do still makes a difference. Trump and other federal officials did nudge these entities and officials with leftover war equipment, calls to crack down on crime, signals to treat arrested people rough, and tirades about immigrants (whether illegal or not seemed to make no difference—where they came from was what mattered to the president). But nudge was a long way from control.

Trump also undercut the very law enforcement apparatus he would need to wage war on crime. He castigated his first attorney general, Jeff Sessions, whose Justice Department saw experienced prosecutors, administrators, and FBI agents fired or retiring in disgust. Trump declared the FBI was "in tatters." He also decimated other agencies whose law enforcement responsibilities were less obvious but still real, like the State Department, the Environmental Protection Agency, and the National Park Service—parts of the "deep state" that Trump supporters often deplored. The Trump administration shredded (except when courts said no) protections and regulations for climate, the environment, public lands, gas mileage, workplace safety, consumer protection, for-profit colleges, corporate honesty, and much else. It shrank the ranks of agency professionals (career administrators, scientists, lawyers, economists), putting political hacks in charge. Notably for this book, Trump named such a hack to head the Justice Department's Bureau of Justice Statistics, a valuable resource for researchers and policymakers.[17] More often civil than criminal in its operations, the administrative state was nonetheless an arm of law enforcement. Its disarray was another sign that the Trump administration was selective, capricious, and often just ineffective (except for the private interests it served) in enforcing laws and regulations.

Even more than Nixon, Trump cared more about the postures he struck and the strutting he could do than about the policies that would implement his postures. His dog whistles about race and crime did make a difference to those police, prosecutors, judges, and legislators who liked them. It was no coincidence that in 2019, Florida Republicans tried mightily to nullify a voter-approved constitutional amendment enfranchising the state's huge ex-felon population. And where federal policy was paramount, pernicious change did occur, as in immigration policy and the administration's gutting of criminal justice reforms undertaken under Obama. Trump's signature in December 2018 on the First Step Act, a motley collection of modest reforms on sentencing, prison operations, and reentry programs, was only a passing nod in the other direction.

But it was hardly clear that Trump had the capability, even the desire, to redirect the engines of law enforcement, except to turn them against his political enemies, as Attorney General William Barr tried hard to do. And his efforts to undercut the rule of law made it hard for others to impose that rule. It was difficult for a serial liar and lawbreaker to be a credible exponent of vigorous law enforcement, though goodness knows he was not the first to try. It was difficult for a regime determined to uproot the "deep state" also to harness it toward law-and-order purposes. Of course, regimes do not have to be competent to be brutal (history is littered with examples), and Trump's zeal to inflict vengeance on people and organizations in the United States and abroad that crossed him seemed unlimited. But how far that zeal would penetrate the workings of criminal justice remained to be seen. One possible outcome: not a tougher punitive state, but simply a more chaotic, capricious, and lawless one.

The coronavirus pandemic of 2020 posed that possibility, making it even more of a wild card than climate change. Reactions to it cut in many directions. Quick efforts to reduce prison populations slightly and an abrupt slowdown in the criminal justice system suggested one path. Indicating another, public health mandates to shelter and close up shop imposed policing authority on a vast scale, although arrests were few and resistance substantial. A prolonged crisis would likely unleash passions taking violent form and inviting harsh action against it. Extended hardship rarely promotes social harmony and benign public policy (the New Deal was a partial exception to that rule), neither in evidence while President Trump reigned. Hardship invites increased crime and a search for scapegoats (China and the Obama administration, among many others, in Trump's view). The result might be a still more chaotic, but still more punitive, criminal justice system. Florid if unconvincing comparisons of the pandemic crisis to World War II indicated how easily war's language resurfaced amid the pandemic.

It also resurfaced amid another crisis in late spring of 2020. The powerful mass response to George Floyd's death by a police officer's chokehold—in many ways also a reponse to the whole course of the punitive turn—augured major changes in policing. In contrast, defense secretary Mark Esper's claim that cities seeing protests accompanied by violence were a "battle space" flagged anew, and alarmingly, the associations many Americans made between war-fighting and crime-fighting. It was if the Trump administration was contemplating war against protesting Americans.

The seepage between war abroad and at home continued, with local variations, twists, and turns that in turn influenced national patterns. At Indiana's Miami Correctional Facility, built in the 1990s on the edge of a once-giant air force base, its superintendent, army reservist John VanNatta, went to Guantánamo after 9/11 as superintendent of its terrorist detention facility. There, in his words, he "designed [and] supervised construction of several state-of-art facilities, namely Camp Delta." He then rotated back to Miami Correctional. Subsequently, VanNatta served as the director of detainee operations in Afghanistan while consulting on prison operations in Iraq, then returned again to his position as Miami Correctional superintendent.[18] Though caught up in controversy about Guantánamo—he insisted "that he never said guards had put Korans in toilets"[19]—VanNatta was no flame-thrower. If Guantánamo inmates yielded valuable "information," he said, their detention "[would] be viewed as one of the smartest moves ever made," but if not, "then [it would] be viewed as a superpower using its power unchecked."[20] But VanNatta continued to embody the feedback loops knitting together war abroad and war at home. By 2017, Miami Correctional's superintendent was Kathy Griffin, the first woman and African American in charge and another product of the military, a retired army first sergeant.

Indiana politics reflected the nation's conflicting impulses. The legislature in 2012–13 "drastically curtailed one of the country's largest higher education programs for prisoners,"[21] but when Governor Mike Pence proposed expanding Miami Correctional to house 512 more inmates, legislators balked, questioning the wisdom and cost of mass incarceration.[22] Soon the Indiana corrections commissioner touted the state's efforts at "diverting low-level inmates from prison," enrolling "qualified inmates" into Medicaid and challenging the notion that prison staffing is "a male dominated field."[23] But a daily population of over 9,000 men still resided in Indiana maximum-security facilities in 2019 (Miami Correctional held the biggest number), as did 840 women.[24] And traces of Miami Correctional's militarized connections remained literally visible. Prisoners might glimpse the outdoor Grissom Air Museum displaying old warplanes, where prison staff volunteered, or the long runways of the Grissom Air Reserve Base, the remnant of the former Strategic Air Command installation.[25] That is, prisoners, like staff and visitors, could see the connection between war-fighting and crime-fighting.

That connection appeared on a national scale as well. According to a 2016 study, 762,000 veterans were serving as police, sheriff officers, detectives, and criminal investigators. About a quarter of all police patrol officers were veterans, and a fifth of all detectives or criminal investigators. Male veterans were three times more likely to be employed in "protective service occupations" than male nonveterans. For male veterans of the Gulf War and post-9/11 eras, "protective services" was the second most likely occupational destination.[26] Many veterans retained a place in the armed forces as members of the National Guard or the Reserves. Fitting long-term patterns, those numbers were hardly surprising, and by some measures veterans' share of police and protective service workers may have declined from earlier peaks, when veterans' cohorts had been much larger. Those numbers remained robust enough to keep the soldiers-to-cops pipeline flowing.

That connection between war-fighting and crime-fighting was painfully visible to Patrick Skinner, an ex-CIA officer with extensive experience in Iraq and Afghanistan who joined the police force of Savannah, Georgia, in 2017. He came there disillusioned that counterterrorism abroad was "creating more problems than it solved," only to find that "American police forces were adopting some of the militarized tactics that Skinner had seen give rise to insurgencies abroad." "We have to stop treating people like we're in Fallujah," he commented, referring to the Iraqi city that in 2004 saw the bloodiest fighting of the war for U.S. forces. "It just doesn't work," he said, though he was skeptical that it would stop. Skinner added, "You sometimes hear cops talk about people in the community as 'civilians,' but that's bullshit. . . . We're not the military." Making his task harder, as a reporter commented, "police officers [were] increasingly filling the gaps of a broken state," operating as an emergency social service agency but getting little support for doing so. This was yet another burden added to the many that police personnel faced. In parts of Savannah and elsewhere, it seemed like not just a "broken state" but a broken nation, one patrolled by an occupying force at great expense but to little benefit, or worse, "creating more problems than it solved."[27]

The United States still had a war on crime, even though fewer Americans called it that, forged in part by crime-fighting's past and present connections to war-fighting. Likely to persist, it was attenuated in some dimensions, magnified in others. How much and in what ways would depend on politics—on whether civic activism against the punitive turn and its racial injustices gained further traction; on whether ger-rymandered districts, political dysfunction, and the corrupting tide of money kept those who resisted change in power; on whether the secrecy and invisibility of many criminal justice institutions were challenged; and on what forces controlled state governments, prison systems, and prosecutors' offices. And the fate of the war on crime would depend on whether Trump's presidency would end through his removal, res-ignation, death, disability, or defeat in the 2020 elections. If he had a Republican successor, many of his policies might remain in place, but at least some of the venom and vengeance spewing from the White House might dissipate.

But the war on crime also depended on something else this book has underlined but Americans pay less attention to: war. The punitive turn began in the wake of two big wars and in the midst of another, and its twisting path thereafter ran through the linkage of crime-fighting to war-fighting. Remember that President Lyndon Johnson had asserted on September 22, 1965, "The policeman is the frontline soldier in our war against crime." The future of the punitive turn would hinge in part on how and where the United States waged war. For the moment, Trump's apparent aversion to large-scale war making pointed one way. If sustained by him and his successors, that aversion would constrict the pipeline that for decades had sent leftover armaments and war-hardened veterans into policing and criminal justice (and left no few of those veterans prone to crime). It might, too, dry up the river of words, advertisements, movies, TV shows, and online games that rendered cops as soldiers at war and buyers of guns as warriors against crime. It would, that is, constrain the militarized dimensions of the punitive turn.

But given Trump's ignorance of a volatile world, his impulsiveness, and his zeal for vengeance, he might well lead the nation into major com-bat despite his aversion to it. Bullies are often cowards afraid of a real fight, but they can still stumble into one. Given how the nation's quasi war against terrorism seemed endless and how deeply rooted its history of going to war was, the spillover of war making into crime-fighting and vice versa is likely destined to continue under Trump or his successor.

Acknowledgments

Inspiration for this book arose on September 11, 2001, when I anticipated a repressive and warlike American response to the attacks of that day. Inspiration grew further after someone close to me encountered the criminal justice system and I made visits to jails and prisons. Essays and lectures ensued, and serious work began in 2009, although it dragged on as each year added more history (often scary or depressing) and more material to cover. My previous scholarship on war, politics, and culture informed my approach to this project.

Audiences at several institutions gave helpful responses to my early talks on this project: Columbia University, Oberlin College, Brown University, the University of Cincinnati, Miami University, the American Anthropological Association, the Triangle Seminar in the History of the Military, War, and Society, and the Northwestern University Humanities Institute. At this book's early stage, the late Marilyn Young offered invaluable criticism, suggestions, inspiration, and encouragement. Numerous exchanges with Roger Lancaster were very useful. Two reviewers for the press, Marie Gottschalk and Beth Bailey, generously provided thoughtful critiques of the manuscript and numerous corrections. My colleague Michael Allen did likewise with the manuscript in its near-final stage. And Henry Binford was also available for brainstorming.

Northwestern University students have been essential to this project. In classes related to this book's subject, undergraduates provided insights and challenging questions. Through the History Department's Leopold Fellows Program, which funds undergraduates to assist faculty, several provided important research, fresh leads, and good ideas: Jack Neubauer, Richard Murphy, Lee Mason, Logan Koepke, Daniel Barlava, Aleksandr Sverdlik, Jeremy Seah Jun En, Will Kirkland, Will Corvin, and Daniel Fernandez. In the final stages of the book's preparation, Fernandez provided further research, meticulous fact-checking and quote checking, shrewd editorial suggestions, historical insights, proofing of the manuscript, technical assistance, and an ear for my frustrations; I could not have finished this book when I did without his help. Graduate students Michael Green, Charlotte Cahill, Kyle Burke, Matthew June, Andrew Baer, and Bonnie Ernst did research for me or shared their own research findings; Alex Hobson provided further research, insight into the workings of vengeance, and a smart vetting of the manuscript. Endowed research funds from the Richard W. Leopold Professorship at Northwestern University provided major support for this project. An editor on all my books since my first in 1977, Charles Grench provided his trademark soft-spoken encouragement and counsel. Essential help came from his assistant, Dylan

White, and other staff at the University of North Carolina Press. Errors in the book are, of course, my responsibility (they may be more numerous than normal because this book was finalized during the coronavirus pandemic, blocking my access to many materials and technical support and leaving me infected for a time).

The History Department's longtime administrator, Paula Blaskovits, deserves special thanks for her personal support and her navigation of the bureaucracy. Even more thanks go to my partner, James Beal, for enduring my absences and frustrations with this project, and for sparking some of the ideas in it.

Notes

A Note on Citations

Quotations from presidents and their subordinates are taken from the online American Presidency Project (presidency.ucsb.edu) unless another source is cited. When a date in the text suffices to lead readers to the relevant document in the Presidency Project, I usually do not provide a citation or give a full title for the document if I do. Page references to nonscholarly magazines and newspapers are not given except for advertisements, for which digital searching may be impossible.

Abbreviations

BJS   Bureau of Justice Statistics, U.S. Department of Justice
FBI   Federal Bureau of Investigation
JAH   *Journal of American History*
L&O   *Law and Order* (trade journal)
NYT   *New York Times*
NYTM *New York Times Magazine*
PC   *Police Chief*
WP   *Washington Post*

Introduction

1. Quoted in *NYT* editorial "War Profiteering on the Home Front," December 11, 2015. These advertisements, along with many others, are reproduced with extensive analysis, in a June 2011 Violence Policy Center report entitled "The Militarization of the U.S. Civilian Firearms Market," http://www.vpc .org/studies/militarization.pdf. "As Close as You Can Get . . ." with a photo of the gun in question, also appeared on the website Gentlemint (offering "the manliest content on the Web"), http://gentlemint.com/tack/7096/, with the notation that it had been taken earlier from the website www.fnhusa. com. The manufacturer, FN International, was headquartered in Virginia (with manufacturing in South Carolina) as of 2016, when the gun in question seemed no longer for sale; see http://www.fnamerica.com/about.

2. Michael Sherry, "Dead or Alive: American Vengeance Goes Global," *Review of International Studies* 31 (2005): 245–63. At least one scholar, and perhaps more, used the phrase "the punitive turn" before I did, though in a passing way; see David Garland, *The Culture of Control: Crime and Social Order in Contemporary Society* (New York, 2001), 142. Since my article appeared, some scholars have used the term, apparently on their own initiative. They usually do so in regard to some specific aspect of criminal justice rather

than in the broad way I use it. See, for example, John Muncie, "The 'Punitive Turn' in Juvenile Justice: Cultures of Control and Rights Compliance in Western Europe and the USA," *Youth Justice* 8 (2008): 107–21; Eduardo Batista, "Immigration Control and the Punitive Turn," *Themis: Research Journal of Justice Studies and Forensic Science* 2 (2014): Article 1; Deborah E. McDowell, Claudrena N. Harold, and Juan Battle, eds., *The Punitive Turn: New Approaches to Race and Incarceration* (Charlottesville, VA, 2013).

3. "Statement by the President Following the Signing of Law Enforcement Assistance Bills," September 22, 1965.

4. See Michael S. Sherry, *In the Shadow of War: The United States Since the 1930s* (New Haven, CT, 1995); for FDR's first inaugural, see pp. 15–17.

5. Even superb historical work treats the language of a war on crime as a given warranting no analysis or comment, as if it were natural or its meaning self-evident and uncontested. Thus Heather Ann Thompson refers to "a historically unprecedented War on Crime," capitalizing the term as if it were an official designation, and to "waging a major War on Crime in America's most fragile communities," and to "America's new War on Crime," all without comment on the terminology or exploration of where it came from. See Thompson, *Blood in the Water: The Attica Prison Uprising of 1971 and Its Legacy* (New York, 2016), 18–19; see also other references to a "War on Crime" in her treatment.

6. Michelle Alexander, *The New Jim Crow: Mass Incarceration in the Age of Colorblindness* (New York, 2010), 2.

7. Scholarship especially influential on me includes: Alexander, *The New Jim Crow*; Radley Balko, *Rise of the Warrior Cop: The Militarization of America's Police Forces* (New York, 2013); Katherine Beckett, *Making Crime Pay: Law and Order in Contemporary American Politics* (New York, 1997); Anne-Marie Cusac, *Cruel and Unusual: The Culture of Punishment in America* (New Haven, CT, 2009); Marie Gottschalk, *The Prison and the Gallows: The Politics of Mass Incarceration in America* (New York, 2006); Marie Gottschalk, *Caught: The Prison State and the Lockdown of American Politics* (Princeton, NJ, 2015); Philip Jenkins, *Decade of Nightmares: The End of the Sixties and the Making of Eighties America* (New York, 2006); Peter B. Kraska, ed., *Militarizing the American Criminal Justice System: The Changing Roles of the Armed Forces and the Police* (Boston, 2001); Joseph Margulies, *What Changed When Everything Changed: 9/11 and the Making of National Identity* (New Haven, CT, 2013); Robert Perkinson, *Texas Tough: The Rise of America's Prison Empire* (New York, 2010); Keramet Reiter, *23/7: Pelican Bay Prison and the Rise of Long-Term Solitary Confinement* (New Haven, Conn., 2016); Jonathan Simon, *Governing through Crime: How the War on Crime Transformed American Democracy and Created a Culture of Fear* (New York, 2007). Among agenda-setting overviews, see Heather Ann Thompson, "Why Mass Incarceration Matters: Rethinking Crisis, Decline, and Transformation in Postwar American History," *JAH* 97 (December 2010): 703–34; and Peter B. Kraska, "Militarization and Policing–Its Relevance to 21st Century Police," *Policing: A Journal of Policy and Practice*

1 (January 2007): 501–13, which in social science terms outlines arguments I make about "the police/military blur" and provides a guide to Kraska's detailed work.

8. See Sherry, *In the Shadow of War*, which hints at some of the themes explored in this book.

Chapter 1

1. Do so even if Ted Gest begins his account by stating, "Barry Goldwater started it." See Ted Gest, *Crime and Politics: Big Government's Erratic Campaign for Law and Order* (New York, 2001), 5. An exception to the tendency to blame Goldwater is Elizabeth Hinton, "'A War within Our Own Boundaries': Lyndon Johnson's Great Society and the Rise of the Carceral State," *JAH* 102 (June 2015): 100–112, which argues that "Johnson and his radical domestic programs laid the foundation of the carceral state" (102).

2. Lyndon B. Johnson, "Remarks to the Members of the President's Commission on Law Enforcement and Administration of Justice," September 8, 1965.

3. Not surprisingly, given what else went on during his presidency, studies of LBJ, his administration, and the 1960s paid little attention to his views and efforts on crime until recently. Prior analyses tended to present Johnson's stance on crime as reactive and tactical rather than an expression of basic impulses, and these works ignored or noted only in passing the "war on crime" metaphor and its link to administration policies. LBJ's presidency has a larger, though still secondary, place in scholarship on the history of crime control and incarceration. Among general treatments of the Johnson-Nixon years, Rick Perlstein offers episodic but extensive treatment of crime and the related presidential politics in his three volumes, *Before the Storm: Barry Goldwater and the Unmaking of the American Consensus* (New York, 2001); *Nixonland: The Rise of a President and the Fracturing of America* (New York, 2008); and *The Invisible Bridge: The Fall of Nixon and the Rise of Reagan* (New York, 2014). For recent treatment, see Elizabeth Hinton, *From the War on Poverty to the War on Crime: The Making of Mass Incarceration in America* (Cambridge, MA, 2016).

4. Doris Kearns, *Lyndon Johnson and the American Dream* (New York, 1976), 350.

5. FBI, "Uniform Crime Statistics for the United States, National and State Crime, 1960–2014," compiled using the FBI's online data tool, https://perma.cc/6VEM-CGZQ. Homicide rate noted in Marie Gottschalk, *Caught: The Prison State and the Lockdown of American Politics* (Princeton, NJ, 2015), 146. See also BJS, *Homicide Trends in the United States, 1980–2008* (November 2011), https://www.bjs.gov/index.cfm?ty=pbdetail&iid=2221, which despite its title has data back to 1950. Among many assessments of crime rates during the 1960s, see Elaine Tyler May, "Security against Democracy: The Legacy of the Cold War at Home," *JAH* 97 (March 2011): 944. FBI Uniform Crime Reports assemble data only on *reported* crimes and did so in the 1960s by a dated methodology.

6. See Garrett Felber, "'Shades of Mississippi': The Nation of Islam's Prison Organizing, the Carceral State, and the Black Freedom Struggle," *JAH* 105 (June 2018): 71–95.

7. James Q. Wilson, "Crime in the Streets," *National Affairs* 5 (Fall 1966), 26–35.

8. Murray Lee, *Inventing Fear of Crime: Criminology and the Politics of Anxiety* (Portland, OR, 2007), 51 ("explosion"); on misleading polling, see pp. 59–61. Dennis D. Loo and Ruth-Ellen M. Grimes, "Polls, Politics, and Crime: The 'Law and Order' Issue of the 1960s," *Western Criminology Review* 5 (2004): 60 (poll phrasing), 59 ("recorded concerns"). On polls, see also William J. Chambliss, *Power, Politics, and Crime* (Boulder, CO, 1999), 15, 17, 18–19. On mid-1960s crime stories, see also May, "Security against Democracy," 947.

9. Robert Dallek, *Flawed Giant: Lyndon Johnson and His Times, 1961–1973* (New York, 1998), 406.

10. Marie Gottschalk, *The Prison and the Gallows: The Politics of Mass Incarceration in America* (New York, 2006), 27; Peter K. Enns, *Incarceration Nation: How the United States Became the Most Punitive Democracy in the World* (New York, 2016), 14. Enns offers careful analysis but does not adequately engage how elites shaped as well as responded to public opinion and chose among the many concerns polls revealed. Nor does he sufficiently explain why punitive policies intensified after the mid-1990s despite "recent decreases in the public's punitiveness" (17). See also Enns, "The Public's Increasing Punitiveness and Its Influence on Mass Incarceration in the United States," *American Journal of Political Science* 58 (October 2014): 857–72.

11. Radley Balko, *Rise of the Warrior Cop: The Militarization of America's Police Forces* (New York, 2013), 28.

12. John Morton Blum, *Years of Discord: American Politics and Society, 1961–1974* (New York, 1991), 210.

13. Robert Alan Goldberg, *Barry Goldwater* (New Haven, CT, 1995), 221–22.

14. Stephen E. Ambrose, *Nixon: The Triumph of a Politician, 1962–1972* (New York, 1989), 201.

15. Goldberg, *Barry Goldwater*, 223.

16. Balko, *Rise of the Warrior Cop*, 64.

17. Quoted in Blum, *Years of Discord*, 215.

18. Quoted in Ambrose, *Nixon*, 184.

19. Noted in Gest, *Crime and Politics*, 21–22.

20. That is an argument in Hinton, *From the War on Poverty to the War on Crime*.

21. Hruska to Attorney General Nicholas Katzenbach, August 19, 1965, quoted in Hinton, "'War within Our Own Boundaries,'" 103.

22. Jonathan Simon, *Governing through Crime: How the War on Crime Transformed American Democracy and Created a Culture of Fear* (New York, 2007), 96.

23. June 19, 1968, statement.

24. Simon, *Governing through Crime*, 97.

25. For use of the phrase "war on crime" from the 1920s and 1930s, see "Thompson Starts War on Crime Asks All Chicagoans to Aid," *NYT*, January 20, 1922; Joseph Gollomb, "The War on Crime," *American Journal of Police Science* 2 (May–June 1931): 262–67, reprinted from a July 1931 article in *Vanity Fair*. Ernest Jerome Hopkins devoted a chapter to lamenting the consequences of policing cities with a war mentality; see "The War Theory of Crime Control," chap. 21 in *Our Lawless Police: A Study of the Unlawful Enforcement of the Law* (New York, 1931).

26. *WP*, October 3, 1908; "Spurs War on Peddlers," *Los Angeles Times*, January 9, 1923.

27. Sarah Siff, "Exposing the Narcotics Racket: The West Coast Kefauver Hearings and California's Drug Wars" (paper delivered at the Organization of American Historians annual conference, April 7, 2017).

28. See Lisa McGirr, *The War on Alcohol: Prohibition and the Rise of the American State* (New York, 2016), though McGirr does not explain and historicize her use of the term "war."

29. I elaborate this war-as-model argument in *In The Shadow of War: The United States Since the 1930s* (New Haven, CT, 1995).

30. As Alfred W. McCoy argues, the United States' "clandestine innovations" in policing when it pacified the Philippines "migrated homeward, silently and invisibly, to change the face of American internal security"; see *Policing America's Empire: The United States, the Philippines, and the Rise of the Surveillance State* (Madison, WI, 2009), 8. See also Alfred W. McCoy and Francisco A. Scarano, eds., *Colonial Crucible: Empire in the Making of the Modern American State* (Madison, WI, 2009).

31. Daniel Fernandez, "'Essentially and Ordinarily Human': The Legacy of America's Penal Press as Viewed through the *Atlantian*" (senior thesis, Northwestern University, May 2019). I owe to this thesis many of the observations and sources in this and the following paragraphs.

32. Quoted in Fernandez, "'Essentially and Ordinarily Human.'"

33. No recent scholarship comprehensively examines the role of convicts, parolees, and ex-convicts in military service and war production. For the figure of one hundred thousand serving, see W. H. Burke, "The Prison War Program," *Journal of Criminal Law and Criminology* 35 (July–August 1944): 79. For the nearly three thousand paroled in Illinois in order to serve in uniform, see, by a sociologist, Hans W. Mattick, "Parolees in the Army during World War II," *Federal Probation* 24 (1960): 49–55. From the success of the Illinois program, this article concludes "that a comprehensive concept of national defense, designed to protect the nation from the enemy within as well as the enemy from without, could well include a program of absorbing selected former prisoners on parole into various military services" (55). Mattick also authored an exhaustive study, "Parole to the Army: Military Experience as a Factor in Parole Success" (master's thesis, University of Chicago, 1956), dealing with Illinois but usefully laying out wartime regulations on the national level and reaffirming the rehabilitative ideal: "The theory that punishment of

the offender leads to the deterrence of further crime by the offender, or other potential offenders, is flatly contradicted by historical evidence and contemporary observation," and "the theory of retribution, which still has powerful support, must resort to increasingly desperate stratagems to survive" (2). For a generally positive view of the experience of 3,565 New York state parolees who served, see David Dressler, "Men on Parole as Soldiers in World War II," *Social Service Review* 20 (December 1946): 537–50.

34. See the account of the film and short (silent) clips from it in "CDCR Time Capsule (Video) 1942: Archived Footage Was Ending of Film Noir Tale," *Inside CDR*, the newsletter of the California Department of Corrections and Rehabilitation, February 9, 2017, https://www.insidecdcr.ca.gov/2017/02 /cdcr-time-capsule-video-1942-archived-footage-was-ending-of-film -noir-tale/. The full film with sound is available on YouTube at https://www .youtube.com/watch?v=VYYh4FcK.

35. Quoted in Fernandez, "'Essentially and Ordinarily Human.'"

36. Burke, "Prison War Program," 79.

37. BJS *Bulletin, Prisoners 1925–1981* (1982), https://www.bjs.gov/content /pub/pdf/p2581.pdf.

38. J. Edgar Hoover, "Battlefield," *Army Digest* 23 (October 1968).

39. J. Schaeffer quoted in in Christian Appy, *Patriots: The Vietnam War Remembered from All Sides* (New York, 2003), 317.

40. Volker Janssen, "From the Inside Out: Therapeutic Penology and Political Liberalism in Postwar California," *Osiris* 22 (2007): 116–34 (quotation, 117), on which I have relied for much of this paragraph.

41. That story is told, or at least asserted, in many online and print sources, but to my knowledge it has not been systematically examined. For a careful treatment of radiation experiments on prisoners, see Eileen Welsome, *The Plutonium Files: America's Secret Medical Experiments in the Cold War* (New York, 1999), which also charts some officials' resistance to such experiments.

42. For political surveillance before World War II, for example, the U.S. apparatus "was fragmented and localized, with limited coordination among local and federal authorities and private agencies competing for business"; Jennifer Luff, "Covert and Overt Operations: Interwar Political Policing in the United States and the United Kingdom," *American Historical Review* 122 (June 2017): 740.

43. Janssen, "From the Inside Out," 133.

44. Office of Policy Planning and Research, U.S. Department of Labor, *The Negro Family: The Case for National Action* (Washington, D.C., March 1965; repr., Westport, CT, 1981), 30 ("matriarchy"), 35 ("Negro children"), 38 ("disastrous"), 42 ("service," "training and experience").

45. *Negro Family*, 42, 43.

46. Christian Appy, *Working-Class War: American Combat Soldiers and Vietnam* (Chapel Hill, NC, 1993), 31, 32.

47. For the LBJ-McNamara exchange, see Geoffrey W. Jensen, "A Parable of Persisting Failure: Project 100,000," in *Beyond the Quagmire: New Interpretations of the Vietnam War*, ed. Geoffrey W. Jensen and Matthew M. Stith

(Denton, TX, 2019), 148, 149. For McNamara on the "subterranean poor," see Appy, *Working-Class War*, 32, and "McNamara's Salvation Army," *New Republic*, September 10, 1966.

48. Jensen, "Parable of Persisting Failure," 155. Jensen offers a more favorable assessment of Project 100,000 than its many critics did at the time.

49. "Annual Message to Congress: The President's Manpower Report," May 1, 1967.

50. Quoted in Charlotte Cahill, "Fighting the Vietnam Syndrome: The Construction of a Conservative Veterans Politics, 1966–1984" (PhD diss., Northwestern University, 2008), 47.

51. Volker Janssen, "When the 'Jungle' Met the Forest: Public Work, Civil Defense, and Prison Camps in Postwar California," *JAH* 96 (December 2009): 702–26; for quotations, see pp. 708 ("transformed"), 705 ("forest camps"), 717 ("praised"), 716 ("turning").

52. See John Prados, *Vietnam: The History of an Unwinnable War, 1945–1975* (Lawrence, KS, 2009), 275 (for seventy thousand desertions), and 274–76 (for other figures alluded to here).

53. John Whiteclay Chambers II, ed., *The Oxford Companion to American Military History* (New York, 1999), 753.

54. "Helping the GI's Get New Start," *U.S. News and World Report*, February 5, 1968.

55. "Special Message to Congress—'Our Pride and Strength: America's Servicemen and Veterans,'" January 30, 1968 ("disadvantaged").

56. "Remarks at the Swearing in of the Members of the New District of Columbia Council," November 3, 1967.

57. Neil Sheehan, "U.S. Freeing G.I.'s to Be Policemen," *NYT*, November 22, 1967; "From Uniform to Uniform," editorial, *WP*, November 27, 1967.

58. "Special Message to the Congress," January 30, 1968.

59. "Statement by the President upon Signing the Departments of State, Justice, and Commerce, the Judiciary, and Related Agencies Appropriation Act, 1968," November 9, 1967.

60. See Cahill, "Fighting the Vietnam Syndrome," 36–46.

61. Johnson, "Special Message to the Congress," January 30, 1968.

62. Chief Bernard C. Brannon, "News and Views," *PC* 27 (February 1960).

63. Metcalf Brothers advertisement, *PC* 23 (January 1956), 7; Simpson advertisement, *PC* 27 (January 1960), 21.

64. Raeford advertisement, *PC* 32 (February 1965), 23 (the ad ran for several years); Klopman Mills advertisement, *PC* 35 (January 1968), 26–27.

65. Badger Uniforms advertisement, *L&O* 15 (August 1967), 94; Klopman advertisement, *PC* 36 (January 1969), 11.

66. "The New High Standard Police Shotgun," *L&O* 15 (October 1967).

67. Applied Electro Mechanics advertisement, *L&O* 16 (May 1968), 105.

68. "Armored Vehicles," *L&O* 15 (November 1967).

69. "A Design Concept for a Riot Control Vehicle," *L&O* 16 (February 1968).

70. B&H Enterprises advertisement, *L&O* 12 (December 1968), 43.

71. Smith & Wesson advertisement, *PC* 37 (October 1970), 7.

72. National Law Enforcement Officers Memorial Fund, "Office Deaths by Year," www.nloemf.org. Like all crime-related statistics, police officer deaths are measured in different ways by different agencies.

73. As one critic has put it, "In one sense, the paramilitarism in today's police departments is a consequence of the increasing professionalism of police in the 20th century." See Diane Cecilia Weber, "Warrior Cops: The Ominous Growth of Paramilitarism in American Police Departments," *CATO Institute Briefing Papers* No. 50 (August 26, 1999), www.cato.org/pubs/briefs /bp50.pdf, 5.

74. Unattributed quotation read by the actor Efrem Zimbalist Jr. while addressing the graduating class of the FBI National Academy, November 2, 1966, in "New Communications Will Improve Law Enforcement," *FBI Law Enforcement Bulletin*, January 1967.

75. Federal Laboratories advertisement, *PC* 35 (October 1968), 75; untitled editorial, *PC* 35 (August 1968).

76. Lieutenant Colonel Theodore J. Newman, U.S. Air Force, "The Role of the Police in Counter-Insurgency," *PC* 33 (March 1966).

77. "50 Million to Fight Local Crime in 1968; 300 Million in 1969!," *L&O* 15 (June 1967).

78. Gottschalk, *Prison and the Gallows*, 86.

79. "Preparation through Training," *FBI Law Enforcement Bulletin* (December 1967).

80. Micol Seigel, "Objects of Police History," *JAH* 102 (June 2015): 152.

81. "Armored Vehicles"; Hughes Aircraft advertisement, *L&O* 15 (October 1967), 71; "Design Concept."

82. Sherwood Dist. advertisement, *PC* 44 (January 1977), 69.

83. Though skimpy on the origins of SWAT teams, an excellent treatment is Peter B. Kraska and Victor E. Kappeler, "Militarizing American Police: The Rise and Normalization of Paramilitary Units," *Social Problems* 44 (February 1997): 1–18. See also Weber, "Warrior Cops."

84. Kraska and Kappeler, "Militarizing American Police," 3–4.

85. Daryl Gates with Diane K. Shah, *Chief: My Life in the LAPD* (New York, 1992), 115 ("to no avail"), 109, 115 ("regularly"), 115 ("quasi"), 136 ("war zone"), 110 ("foreign territory"); New Jersey spokesman quoted in Balko, *Rise of the Warrior Cop*, 63; Edward J. Escobar, "The Dialectics of Repression: The Los Angeles Police Department and the Chicano Movement, 1968–1971," *JAH* 79 (March 1993): 1496.

86. For "post–Cold War," see Kraska and Kappeler, "Militarizing American Police," 2.

87. Keramet Reiter, *23/7: Pelican Bay Prison and the Rise of Long-Term Solitary Confinement* (New Haven, CT, 2016), 180.

88. Victoria Hattam, "Imperial Designs: Remembering Vietnam at the US-Mexico Border Wall," *Memory Studies* 91 (2016): 32.

89. Joy Rohde, *Armed with Expertise: The Militarization of American Social Research During the Cold War* (Ithaca, NY, 2013), 116–17 ("checked in"), 139 ("used the same"), 118 ("enmity"), 140 ("the relationship").

90. Rohde, *Armed with Expertise*, 137 ("I have"), 141 ("military's experts").

91. Here I rely on Christian Parenti, *The Soft Cage: Surveillance in America From Slavery to the War on Terror* (New York, 2003); on FBI use of Social Security records, see p. 86. Parenti makes little mention of surveillance technologies' origins in space and defense programs. For closed-circuit television and Olean, see Gary C. Robb, "Police Use of CCTV Surveillance: Constitutional Implications and Proposed Regulations," *University of Michigan Journal of Law Reform* 13 (Spring 1980): 571–602 (572n5, on Olean).

92. Quoted in Jennifer Light, *From Warfare to Welfare: Defense Intellectuals and Urban Problems in Cold War America* (Baltimore, MD, 2003), 1.

Chapter 2

1. Rick Perlstein, *Nixonland: The Rise of a President and the Fracturing of America* (New York, 2008), 588 ("hippie lynchings"), 339–40 ("keeping score"), 589 ("berserk," "harbored"), 462 ("embodied"), 237 ("a pattern").

2. Robert Sam Anson, *McGovern: A Biography* (New York, 1972), 165.

3. Stephen E. Ambrose, *Nixon: The Triumph of a Politician, 1962-1972* (New York, 1989), 394; see also 396.

4. Michelle Alexander, *The New Jim Crow: Mass Incarceration in the Age of Colorblindness* (New York, 2010).

5. "Remarks at the 17th Annual Republican Women's Conference," April 16, 1969; "Remarks on Arrival at Lancaster, Pennsylvania," October 17, 1970.

6. Ambrose, *Nixon*, 393 (Ambrose's summary of the commission's finding and Nixon on smut); Nixon, "Statement on Campus Disorders," March 22, 1969 ("civilizations").

7. "Radio Address about the State of the Union Address on Law Enforcement and Drug Abuse Prevention," March 19, 1973 ("soft-headed").

8. Jeremy Kuzmarov, *The Myth of the Addicted Army: Vietnam and the Modern War on Drugs* (Amherst, MA, 2009), 113 (on tenfold increase), and chap. 6 for practices pioneered abroad.

9. Jonathan Simon, *Governing through Crime: How the War on Crime Transformed American Democracy and Created a Culture of Fear* (New York, 2007), 72.

10. Black, quoted in Francis A. Allen, *The Decline of the Rehabilitative Idea; Penal Policy and Social Purpose* (New Haven, CT, 1981), 5. Allen offered a brief, smart treatment of his subject, which is yet to receive comprehensive historical examination.

11. Quoted in Joseph Margulies, *What Changed When Everything Changed: 9/11 and the Making of National Identity* (New Haven, CT, 2013), 92.

12. Richard A. Chappell, "What Did the War Services Develop in Techniques in Corrections?," *Prison Journal* 27 (1947): 299–305. When he spoke to the National Conference of Social Work in April 1947, Chappell was chief of the U.S. Probation System but reflecting on his wartime service in the navy.

13. Quoted in Margulies, *What Changed*, 94 (Humphrey), 95 (Democrats).

14. Anne-Marie Cusac, *Cruel and Unusual: The Culture of Punishment in America* (New Haven, CT, 2009), 172–73; Keramet Reiter, *23/7: Pelican*

Bay Prison and the Rise of Long-Term Solitary Confinement (New Haven, CT, 2016), 82 ("prison critics"); Robert Martinson, "What Works?—Questions and Answers about Prison Reform," *Public Interest* 35 (Spring 1974): 22–54.

15. Good accounts of Martinson are in Joseph F. Spillane, *Coxsackie: The Life and Death of Prison Reform* (Baltimore, MD, 2014), 197–206, quotation from 204 (*New Republic*); and in Timothy Crimmins, "Incarceration as Incapacitation: An Intellectual History," *American Affairs* 2 (Fall 2018): 144–66. See also Martinson. "New Findings, New Views: A Note of Caution Regarding Sentencing Reform," *Hofstra Law Review* 7 (1979): 243–58.

16. Allen, *Decline of the Rehabilitative Ideal*, 54. Allen explores at greater length many considerations treated in this paragraph. See also Reiter, *23/7*, chap. 3. For a recent overview of the history and its literature, see Anthony Grasso, "Broken beyond Repair: Rehabilitative Penology and American Political Development," *Political Research Quarterly* 70 (June 2017): 394–407.

17. For example, Michigan state prison director Perry Johnson vigorously, though not always successfully, pursued rehabilitative programming. He did so on his own initiative and while under pressure in federal court from (among others) female inmates and their attorneys, despite the state government's crack-down-on-criminals politics. See Bonnie Ernst, "Women in the Age of Mass Incarceration: Punishment, Rights, and Resistance in Michigan" (PhD diss., Northwestern University, 2018).

18. Quoted in Allen, *Decline of the Rehabilitative Ideal*, 8.

19. Marie Gottschalk, *Caught: The Prison State and the Lockdown of American Politics* (Princeton, NJ, 2015), 94.

20. I draw on numbers offered in Heather Ann Thompson, *Blood in the Water: The Attica Prison Uprising of 1971 and Its Legacy* (New York, 2016), especially p. 187; on Guadalcanal comparison, see pp. 204–5.

21. For long-term impact, see Thompson, *Blood in the Water*, 558–63.

22. See BJS, Table 2, in *Race of Prisoners Admitted to State and Federal Institutions, 1926–1986* (Washington, D.C.: Department of Justice, May 1991), https://www.ncjrs.gov/pdffiles1/nij/125618.pdf.

23. Ernest van den Haag, *Punishing Crime: Concerning a Very Old and Painful Question* (New York, 1975). 40; Tony Platt and Paul Takagi, "Intellectuals for Law and Order: A Critique of the New 'Realists,'" *Crime and Social Justice* 8 (Fall 1977): 12 ("street crime"), 1 ("candor"); Michael Ignatieff, "Punishing Criminals," *New Republic*, May 22, 1976 ("liberals"). See also Jack P. Gibbs, "Punishment: The Controversy Goes On," *Journal of Criminal Law and Criminology* 67 (1976): 244–48.

24. "State of the Union Address," January 22, 1970; "Remarks on Arrival at Lancaster, Pennsylvania," October 17, 1970; "Remarks on Arrival at Teterboro, New Jersey," October 17, 1970.

25. "Remarks at Graduation Exercises of the FBI National Academy," June 30, 1971; "Radio Address on Crime and Drug Abuse," October 15, 1972.

26. Nixon used the phrase "terrorized by crime" five times in 1970. For "rising rate," see "Remarks on Arrival at Grand Forks, North Dakota," October 19, 1970.

27. Ambrose, *Nixon*, 395.

28. Nixon quoted in Michael S. Sherry, *Gay Artists in Modern American Culture: An Imagined Conspiracy* (Chapel Hill, NC, 2007), 6.

29. "War on Drugs Law and Legal Definition," US Legal website, https://definitions.uslegal.com/w/war-on-drugs/ ("the term"); Kuzmarov, *Myth of the Addicted Army*, 1 (citing the June 17 "Special Message" and the *NYT*, June 18, 1971, neither of which shows Nixon using the term "war on drugs" or uses the term in reference to his address); Kuzmarov repeats this claim on p. 109. See also Matthew D. Lassiter, "Impossible Criminals: The Suburban Imperatives of America's War on Drugs," *JAH* 102 (June 2015): 134, which refers to "Nixon's formal declaration of war on drugs" without quoting the alleged declaration, and Donna Munch, "Crack in Los Angeles: Crisis, Militarization, and Black Response to the Late Twentieth-Century War on Drugs," *JAH* 102 (June 2015): 162, which claims that "Nixon coined the phrase *war on drugs*," without providing a direct quotation or citation. While this point may seem like nit-picking, the phrase "war on drugs" later had such political resonance and legal implications that it is important to get the history of its use right, and not attribute it literally to Nixon. For a typical claim of Nixon's importance, see Ron Milam, "Myths of the Vietnam War," *Reviews in American History* 39 (2011): 374 ("thus President Nixon launched the modern 'War on Drugs'").

30. For Nixon statements quoted here and in the following paragraph, see "Special Message to Congress on Drug Abuse Prevention and Control," June 17, 1971; "Remarks about an Intensified Program for Drug Abuse Prevention and Control," June 17, 1971; "Statement about Drug Abuse Law Enforcement," September 22, 1972; "Campaign Statement about Crime and Drug Abuse," October 28, 1972; "Message to the Congress Transmitting Reorganization Plan 2 of 1973 Establishing the Drug Enforcement Administration," March 28, 1973 ("all-out global war").

31. Kuzmarov, *Myth of the Addicted Army*, 100 (for an example of use of the phrase "War on Drugs" to criticize Nixon), 110 ("support"). On White House efforts to scuttle federal support for drug rehabilitation, see Memo ("Drug Bill—Background for Leadership Meeting"), John Dean to Attorney General John Mitchell, September 10, 1970, Folder "Administration Drug Bill [II] [8 of 8]," Box 29, White House Special Files, Staff Member and Office Files, John Dean, Richard Nixon Presidential Library, Yorba Linda, CA (document provided by Matthew June). For "the forthright view" and state-level decriminalization, see Lassiter, "Impossible Criminals," 135.

32. Radley Balko, *Rise of the Warrior Cop: The Militarization of America's Police Forces* (New York, 2013), 105, 72. Dean quoted in Robert Perkinson, *Texas Tough: The Rise of America's Prison Empire* (New York, 2010), 298.

33. Quoted in Elizabeth Hinton, *From the War on Poverty to the War on Crime: The Making of Mass Incarceration in America* (Cambridge, MA, 2016), 25.

34. Video of McGovern 1972 campaign commercial, Museum of the Moving Image, The Living Room Candidate: Presidential Campaign

Commercials 1952–2008, www.livingroomcandidate.org/commercials/1972 /crime-and-drugs; Kuzmarov, *Myth of the Addicted Army*, 82 (*Ramparts*), 100 (Kuzmarov); Lester L. Wolff introducing a hearing of the House Select Committee on Narcotics Abuse and Control, September 29, 1976, in *Oversight Hearings on Narcotics Abuse and Current Federal and International Narcotics Control Effort* (Washington, D.C., 1976), 469.

35. Kuzmarov, *Myth of the Addicted Army*, 102, quoting Rockefeller. On Rockefeller, see the summary of evidence and scholarship in Heather Ann Thompson, "Why Mass Incarceration Matters: Rethinking Crisis, Decline, and Transformation in Postwar American History," *JAH* 97 (December 2010): 707–8, 731 (Thompson's words). See Michael Javen Fortner, *Black Silent Majority: The Rockefeller Drug Laws and the Politics of Punishment* (Cambridge, MA, 2015), 3 ("committing"); for criticism of Fortner's claims, see the review by Jessica Neptune, *Journal of Social History* 50 (June 2017): 748–50, and Donna Murch, "Who's to Blame for Mass Incarceration?," *Boston Review*, October 16, 2015. On Washington, D.C., see James Forman Jr., *Locking Up Our Own: Crime and Punishment in Black America* (New York, 2017), chap. 2, quotation from p. 10.

36. See Sherry, *Gay Artists*, 218.

37. Marie Gottschalk, *The Prison and the Gallows: The Politics of Mass Incarceration in America* (New York, 2006), 10, 32.

38. See Simon, *Governing through Crime*, especially chap. 2.

39. "The President's News Conference," June 1, 1971.

40. J. Edgar Hoover, "Battlefield," *Army Digest* 23 (October 1968).

41. Lieutenant Robert W. Engelhardt, "Policing Up Recruits," *Army Digest* 24 (January 1969). For on-base recruiting, see "U.S. Defense Department Expands Its Assistance in Police Recruiting," *PC* 35 (June 1968).

42. "For Viet Nam Veterans: New Skills and Better Jobs," *Nation's Business*, October 1968; "Los Angeles Ad Agency to Help Recruit Police," *NYT*, February 22, 1970.

43. "From Uniform to Uniform," editorial, *WP*, November 27, 1967; "Police Sign Up 186 among GIs," *WP*, December 19, 1967; "Negro Police Recruits Now Outnumber Whites," *WP*, December 21, 1969; "Crime Package Backed," *WP*, January 24, 1970.

44. Memo, Alfred B. Fitt to Paul Nitze, December 3, 1968, "Correspondence: General 10/1/68–1/30/69," Box 2, Papers of Alfred B. Fitt, Lyndon Baines Johnson Presidential Library, Austin, TX, as provided to the author by Charlotte Cahill; Forman, *Locking Up Our Own*, 126 ("Bunker Bunny"), 80 ("police executives," etc.); similarities between white and black cops' attitudes toward policing are a theme of Forman's book.

45. No precise number is available because official standards for disability shifted over time, some forms of disability were not officially recognized, and some only became manifest years after the Vietnam era. The Census Bureau estimated that of the 19.3 million veterans alive in 2014, of whom the 7 million Vietnam-era vets were the biggest cohort, 3.8 million had service-connected disabilities, many severe; see "Veteran's Day 2015," U.S.

Census Bureau Newsroom, https://www.census.gov/newsroom/facts-for
-features/2015/cb15-ff23.html.

46. On the army's rehabilitative model, see SP4 Chuck Noland, "New Start on the Road Back," *Soldiers* 28 (March 1973), and Noland, "Taking Stock," same issue.

47. SP4 Chuck Noland, "Army Crime Preventers," *Soldiers* 28 (January 1973). *Soldiers* was the successor to *Army Digest*.

48. For these incidents and their media coverage, see Andrew J. Huebner, *The Warrior Image: Soldiers in American Culture from the Second World War to the Vietnam Era* (Chapel Hill, NC, 2008), 234–37.

49. Quoted in Huebner, *Warrior Image*, 268.

50. See Michael J. Allen, *Until the Last Man Comes Home: POWs, MIAs, and the Unending Vietnam War* (Chapel Hill, NC, 2009).

51. Huebner, *Warrior Image*, 269; on Calley, see 210–17.

52. See Jeremy Kuzmarov, "The Myth of the 'Addicted Army': Drug Use in Vietnam in Historical Perspective," *War and Society* 26 (October 2007), 121–41; "G.I.'s in Vietnam High on Hope's Marijuana Jokes," *NYT*, December 23, 1970 (Hope); see also Huebner, *Warrior Image*, 231–32.

53. "The Nation: The New Public Enemy No. 1," *Time*, June 28, 1971; Nixon, "Special Message to the Congress on Drug Abuse Prevention and Control," June 17, 1971.

54. On fears of black veterans' violence and the *Newsweek* quotation ("De Mau," *Newsweek*, October 30, 1972), see Charlotte Cahill, "Ghetto Guerrillas," chap. 2 in "Fighting the Vietnam Syndrome: The Construction of a Conservative Veterans Politics, 1966–1984" (PhD diss., Northwestern University, 2008).

55. On the appeal of military service for African Americans, see Michael Cullen Green, *Black Yanks in the Pacific: Race in the Making of American Military Empire after World War II* (Ithaca, NY, 2010).

56. Huebner, *Warrior Image*, 233.

57. Paul Starr, *The Discarded Army: Veterans after Vietnam: The Nader Report on Vietnam Veterans and the Veterans Administration* (New York, 1973).

58. Volker Janssen, "When the 'Jungle' Met the Forest: Public Work, Civil Defense, and Prison Camps in Postwar California," *JAH* 96 (December 2009): 722 (Reagan), 707 ("prisons").

59. BJS Special Report, *Veterans in State and Federal Prison, 2004* (Washington, D.C.: Department of Justice, May 2007), https://www.bjs.gov /content/pub/pdf/vsfp04.pdf. "When compared to other men in the U.S. resident population," however, "male veterans have had consistently lower incarceration rates."

60. BJS, "Employment and Unemployment among Vietnam-Era Veterans," *Monthly Labor Review*, April 1990, 22–29. The 4.6 percent figure would have been much higher if measured against the actively working population of Vietnam-era veterans, since 10 percent of Vietnam-era veterans were officially regarded as disabled, and others had dropped out of the workforce for various reasons.

Chapter 3

1. Ford, "Address before a Joint Session of the California State Legislature," September 5, 1975. Hereafter, this source is cited as Ford, California Legislature address, September 5, 1975.

2. Ford, "Yale Law School Address," April 25, 1975; Robert Goldwin, Memorandum through James Connor to Donald Rumsfeld, Folder "President—Speeches—Yale Law School, 4/25/75 (1)," Box 13, Robert A. Goldwin Papers, Gerald R. Ford Presidential Library (hereafter Ford Library) Ann Arbor, MI; Gerald R. Ford, *A Time to Heal: The Autobiography of Gerald R. Ford* (New York, 1979), 269. Ford's memoirs give limited attention to this speech and almost no attention to the general issue of crime. The work presents his phrasing as an alternative to the Nixon administration's "law and order" rhetoric and the "public perception that Washington felt the federal government—and only the federal government—could do something about crime" (269).

3. Memo, Jim Cannon to Dick Parsons, June 5, 1975, summarizing "Don Rumsfeld's thoughts on what the crime message should accomplish," Folder "1975/06/13—Crime Message Memorandum," Box 47, James M. Cannon Files, Ford Library.

4. James Q. Wilson, *Thinking about Crime* (New York, 1975), 5, 209 (Wilson's book was circulated among White House staff before Ford's Yale Law address). Robert A. Goldwin, "Memorandum of a Conversation with James Q. Wilson—Harvard University November 29, 1974," memo dated December 6, 1974, in Folder "Wilson, James Q.," Box 28, Robert A. Goldwin Papers, Ford Library; James Q. Wilson, "Lock 'Em Up and Other Thoughts on Crime," *NYTM*, March 9, 1975.

5. Ford, California Legislature address, September 5, 1975.

6. Marie Gottschalk, *The Prison and the Gallows: The Politics of Mass Incarceration in America* (New York, 2006), a valuable book substantially focused on the 1970s, mentions Ford in two sentences. Philip Jenkins, *Decade of Nightmares: The End of the Sixties and the Making of Eighties America* (New York, 2006), one of the best books on the decade and one with a focus on crime, hardly mentions Ford in this context, while James Q. Whitman, *Harsh Justice: Criminal Punishment and the Widening Divide between America and Europe* (New York, 2003), does so once in passing. Katherine Beckett, *Making Crime Pay: Law and Order in Contemporary American Politics* (New York, 1997), asserts that "the salience of the crime and drug issues declined dramatically" after Nixon left office, noting that Ford never "mentioned crime-related issues" in his State of the Union addresses (44). These assertions are untrue—Ford's January 19, 1976, address took up "violent crime" and at length offered his standard prescriptions—and they ignore everything the president said on other occasions. Among other treatments of the Ford presidency and the period that neglect or wholly ignore crime are: Yanek Mieczkowski, *Gerald Ford and the Challenges of the 1970s* (Lexington, KY, 2005); Bernard J. Firestone and Alexej Ugrinsky, eds., *Gerald R. Ford and the Politics of Post-Watergate America*, 2 vols. (Westport, CT, 1993); John Robert Greene, *The Presidency of Gerald R. Ford* (Lawrence, KS, 1995); Bruce

J. Schulman, *The Seventies: The Great Shift in American Culture, Society, and Politics* (New York, 2001); Bruce Schulman and Julian E. Zelizer, eds., *Rightward Bound: Making America Conservative in the 1970s* (Cambridge, MA, 2008); Sean Wilentz, *The Age of Reagan* (New York, 2008); Jefferson Cowie, *Stayin' Alive: The 1970s and the Last Days of the Working Class* (New York, 2010); Daniel T. Rodgers, *Age of Fracture* (Cambridge, MA, 2011); Laura Laman, *Right Star Rising: A New Politics, 1974-1980* (New York, 2010); Scott Kaufman, *Ambition, Pragmatism, and Party: A Political Biography of Gerald R. Ford* (Lawrence, KS, 2017). Insofar as the standard literature treats law and crime in Ford's presidency, it usually focuses on little besides Watergate and Ford's pardon of Nixon.

7. Michael W. Flamm, *Law and Order: Street Crime, Civil Unrest, and the Crisis of Liberalism in the 1960s* (New York, 2005), 10; Jonathan Simon, *Governing through Crime: How the War on Crime Transformed American Democracy and Created a Culture of Fear* (New York, 2007), 54.

8. The citations here are all to versions of stateside reports and columns reprinted in *Pacific Stars and Stripes*: Carl Rowan, "Psychiatry as a Crime-Fighter," April 22, 1975 ("serious"); "School Violence at a 'Crisis Level,'" April 11, 1975 (Bayh); "Kid Gangs Answer the Bell Again," April 19, 1975 ("martial or quasimilitary"); "On the Collapse of South Vietnam," April 13, 1975 (Buckley); "Aide: Some Cons Can't Be Rehabilitated," April 15, 1975 (Carlson); "The Weekend Pass for Convicts," May 21, 1975 ("we recognized"); Andrew Tully, "Get Criminals off the Streets," June 6, 1975 ("demagogic").

9. "The Attorney General Speaks Out" (interview with Edward H. Levi), *U.S. News & World Report*, June 30, 1975.

10. Ford, "Remarks at the Sixth Circuit Judicial Conference in Mackinac Island, Michigan," July 13, 1975; Ford, California Legislature address, September 5, 1975; Ford, "State of the Union Address," January 19, 1976.

11. Ford, "Remarks to the White House Conference on Domestic and Economic Affairs in Portland, Oregon," November 1, 1974.

12. Gottschalk, *Prison and the Gallows*, offers a valuable account of many of these changes. For incarceration statistics, see BJS *Bulletin: Prisoners 1925-1981* (December 1982), https://www.bjs.gov/content/pub/pdf/p2581.pdf.

13. Ford, California Legislature address, September 5, 1975.

14. Ford, California Legislature address, September 5, 1975. Ford's words about war and peace did not appear in drafts dated September 3. See Folder "Crime, April 25,–September 25, 1974," Box 9, James Cannon Files, Ford Library. See also Folder "Sp 3–179, 9/5/75," Box 71, White House Central Files, Ford Library, where the "too negative" comment appears in an undated, unsigned, handwritten comment on a near-final speech draft.

15. BJS, "Arrests for Violent Crimes, 1970–2003" (Washington, D.C., December 15, 2004), http://www.bjs.gov/index.cfm?ty=pbdetail&iid=2028. On employment, I rely mainly on Kathleen Maguire and Ann L. Pastore, eds., *Sourcebook of Criminal Justice Statistics 1994* (Washington, D.C.: U.S. Department of Justice, BJS, 1995), which appears to tally only public

employees, not private ones. Reliable data on juvenile arrests and incarceration would also shed light on these shifts, but it is hard to come by because different agencies have collected it over time and legal definitions of "juvenile" have changed. It is possible that juvenile arrest and incarceration rates were static in the 1970s; see BJS, section 5, in *Historical Corrections Statistics in the United States, 1850–1984* (December 1986), https://www.bjs.gov/content/pub/pdf/hcsus5084.pdf. The massive data-gathering machine of the BJS, empowered especially by the 1994 Violent Crimes Act, often tracks data only back to the early 1990s.

16. But see Anne E. Parsons, *From Asylum to Prison: Deinstitutionalization and the Rise of Mass Incarceration* (Chapel Hill, NC, 2018), which cautions against exaggerating the scale of the "hospital-to-prison pipeline" and argues that "the overincarceration of people with psychiatric disabilities in prisons has stemmed in large part from the rapid growth of the criminal legal system itself" (5).

17. Memo, Robert Goldwin to James Cannon, September 8, 1976 [misdated: internal evidence and folder context indicate 1975], summarizing telephone call with Wilson, Folder "President—Speeches—Message on Crime, 6/19/75," Box 30, Robert A. Goldwin Papers, Ford Library.

18. "The Governor's Message," *Detroit Free Press*, January 8, 1863.

19. See his comments at August 25, 1975 news conference.

20. Quotations: Beth Bailey, "The Army in the Marketplace: Recruiting an All-Volunteer Force," *JAH* 94 (June 2007): 63. On slow aging, see Pew Research Center, "6 Facts about the U.S. Military and Its Changing Demographics," (Washington, D.C., April 13, 2017), http://www.pewresearch.org/fact-tank/2017/04/13/6-facts-about-the-u-s-military-and-its-changing-demographics/. "The average military officer was roughly 34.5 years old in 2015, up from 32.1 in 1973. And the average enlisted member was just over age 27 in 2015, compared with age 25 in 1973."

21. Department of Defense, Table 7-6, in *National Defense Budget Estimates for FY 2003* (March 2002), https://comptroller.defense.gov/Portals/45/Documents/defbudget/Docs/fy2003_greenbook.pdf.

22. Alex Lichtenstein, "Flocatex and the Fiscal Limits of Mass Incarceration: Toward a New Political Economy of the Postwar Carceral State," *JAH* 102 (June 2015): 115–16.

23. Schulman, *Seventies*, 249, 239, though Schulman also notes, "On Reagan's watch, the federal government grew larger and larger; it cost more dollars, employed more bureaucrats, sustained more agencies, departments, and programs" (239). On distrust and a sense of betrayal, see especially Michael J. Allen, *Until the Last Man Comes Home: POWs, MIAs, and the Unending Vietnam War* (Chapel Hill, NC, 2009). On U.S.-Europe comparisons, see Whitman, *Harsh Justice*, and Gottschalk, *Prison and the Gallows*.

24. As Marie Gottschalk puts it, "Intensification of crime-control activities is an attractive way for the state to burnish the image of its competence and restore its sense of purpose." *Prison and the Gallows*, 35.

25. Simon, *Governing through Crime*, 25, 45.

26. See James Q. Wilson, note to Robert A. Goldwin, June 20, 1975, in which Wilson reported, "Gov. Brown's office ordered my book, air mail" and "If he were a scholar, I'd accuse him of plagiarism!" Wilson attached an undated news article (newspaper name not indicated), "Gov. Brown's Hard Line on Crime Shocks Audience," from which the Brown quotations are taken. Both in Folder "Wilson, James Q.," Box 28, Robert A. Goldwin Papers, Ford Library. California's 1976 law is quoted in Julilly Kohler-Hausmann, "Guns and Butter: The Welfare State, the Carceral State, and the Politics of Exclusion in the Postwar United States," *JAH* 102 (June 2015): 98.

27. Quoted in Gottschalk, *Prison and the Gallows*, 169.

28. FDR, "Fireside Chat," December 9, 1941.

29. James Q. Wilson, "Crime in the Streets," *National Affairs* 5 (Fall 1966): 26–35.

30. See also William J. Novak, "The Myth of the 'Weak' American State," *American Historical Review* 113 (June 2008): 752–72.

31. Beckett, *Making Crime Pay*, 51, 106.

32. Gottschalk, *Prison and the Gallows*, 4.

33. Schulman, *Seventies*, 122 (Scheer); "Ford News Conference," August 28, 1974 ("no amnesty"); "Presidential Campaign Debate," September 23, 1976, available in the American Presidency Project.

34. "Remarks at the 100th Anniversary Luncheon of the Los Angeles County Bar Association," May 4, 1978.

35. White House statement later inserted into the record of "The President's News Conference," March 24, 1977.

36. "Interview with Editors and News Directors," July 29, 1977 ("major," "waste," etc.); Kenneth E. Morris, *Jimmy Carter: American Moralist* (Athens, GA, 1996), 222.

37. "Drug Abuse Message to the Congress," August 2, 1977 ("penalties"); "Drug Abuse Remarks on Transmitting a Message to the Congress," August 2, 1977 ("strong concern"); "Democratic Party Platform," August 11, 1980, in the American Presidency Project. For the mutual entanglement of the Columbian and U.S. governments in an escalating drug war, see Lina Britto, chap. 5 in *Marijuana Boom: The Rise and Fall of Colombia's First Drug Paradise* (Berkeley, CA, 2020).

38. Jenkins, *Decade*, 11; Wilson, "Lock 'Em Up."

39. Anne-Marie Cusac, *Cruel and Unusual: The Culture of Punishment in America* (New Haven, CT, 2009), 124, quoting "The Youth Crime Plague," *Time*, July 11, 1977. On murder rates, overall crime rates, and related matters, see the useful compilation of official data by the Justice Research and Statistics Association, *Historical Data* (undated), http://www.jrsa.org/projects/Historical.pdf.

40. Jenkins, *Decade*, 111, 13, 116.

41. Peter Braunstein, "'Adults Only': The Construction of an Erotic City in New York during the 1970s," in *America in the 70s*, ed. Beth Bailey and David Farber (Lawrence, KS, 2004), 130, 152, 153.

42. Gottschalk, *Prison and the Gallows*, 115.

43. Jenkins, *Decade*, 120–21.

44. Jerry Falwell, *Listen, America!* (Garden City, NJ, 1980), 185.

45. Roger N. Lancaster, *Sex Panic and the Punitive State* (Berkeley, CA, 2011), 41.

46. See "National Commission on the Observance of International Women's Year, 1975: Remarks at a Reception Honoring the Commission," March 22, 1978.

47. Margot Canaday, *The Straight State: Sexuality and Citizenship in Twentieth-Century America* (Princeton, NJ, 2009); David K. Johnson, *The Lavender Scare: The Cold War Persecution of Gays and Lesbians in the Federal Government* (Chicago, 2004).

48. On this point, see Lancaster, *Sex Panic*.

49. See especially Jenkins, *Decade*.

50. Of course what I see as hapless or pathetic others may now see, or might have at the time seen, as something darker—like any cultural fiction, these characters can be read differently. But when I have shared episodes like these in classes, students of very different generational and cultural sensibilities than mine almost always see these characters as I do and pick up, on their own initiative, the differences between shows like *Dragnet* and later series like *Law and Order*.

51. Cusac, *Cruel and Unusual*, 189.

52. On the matter of which phrase Friday used, see "Dragnet: 'Just the Facts,'" Snopes, December 2008, https://www.snopes.com/radiotv/tv /dragnet.asp.

53. Cusac, *Cruel and Unusual*, 195. One viewer's 2009 comment about "The Big Crime" episode suggests the shift in attitudes: "I have twin girls who are four years old right now, and this story hits me right between the eyes. If someone raped either/both of my girls, I would not rest until that person was dead." Posted on "Dragnet—The Big Crime 1/5 (1954)," YouTube, https://www.youtube.com/watch?v=UvBqg_A8Yqk (read July 8, 2010; unavailable May 2020).

54. A characterization of the program given to me by a research assistant who examined many of the crime shows described in this paragraph.

55. Michael Ryan and Douglas Kellner, *Camera Politica: the Politics and Ideology of Contemporary Hollywood Film* (Bloomington, IN, 1990), 87, 45. Their surveys involved only several dozen subjects and were done in 1987; see p. 303.

56. The observation of a research assistant, who examined the music surveyed in this paragraph.

57. Cusac, *Cruel and Unusual*, 114.

58. Cusac, *Cruel and Unusual*, 139, 144–45, 140, 158; see generally chaps. 6–7.

59. Cusac, *Cruel and Unusual*, 155, 158–59.

60. Christopher Lasch, *The Culture of Narcissism: American Life in an Age of Diminishing Expectations* (New York, 1979), 229, 235, 232.

61. William Graebner, *Patty's Got a Gun: Patricia Hearst in 1970s America* (Chicago, 2008), 179. Graebner offers a sharp, complicated reading of the many ways in which Hearst and her case were understood.

62. "The Criminal Mind," *Newsweek*, February 27, 1978, also discussed in Cusac, *Cruel and Unusual*, 8–9, 111; see 123 on reactions to Gilmore. Graebner, *Patty's Got a Gun*, 109, 110.

63. Gottschalk, *Prison and the Gallows*, 15.

64. Jenkins, *Decade*, 138.

65. The surge of such reporting in the 1970s is more widely asserted than carefully examined in scholarship and criticism, which more often focus on the 1980s and after. A useful introduction to the issue is Marc Mauer and The Sentencing Project, *Race to Incarcerate* (rev. and updated ed., New York, 2006), chap. 10.

66. Jenkins, *Decade*, 138.

67. The conversion of demobilized military bases and arsenals into prisons, for example, was not even a glimmer in the eyes of Defense Department planners. See John E. Lynch, *Local Development after Military Base Closures*, with a foreword by Seymour Melman (New York, 1970), which catalogues the wide range of uses to which facilities demobilized during the 1960s were put. Virtually none of the uses involved or foreseen for the 1970s pertained to criminal justice.

68. Jenkins, *Decade*, 133.

Chapter 4

1. Katherine Beckett, *Making Crime Pay: Law and Order in Contemporary American Politics* (New York, 1997), 55, 25. As other scholars make the point, "Between 1979 and 1984, drug use and abuse did not appear at all in the Gallup polls among the most often mentioned problems facing the country, indicating a relatively and consistently low level of concern about the issue." Erich Goode and Nachman Ben-Yehuda, *Moral Panics: The Social Construction of Deviance* (Cambridge, MA, 1994), 206.

2. August 1, 1986 ("drug dealers"); September 28, 1981 ("very prone"). That last comment does not appear in the American Presidency Project, but it does appear in the prepared text in the Reagan Presidential Library files. Reagan had trouble with the teleprompter on this occasion and might have skipped over this phrase, which was nonetheless widely quoted in reports based on the advance text; see Ronald Reagan Presidential Library Digital Library Collections, Collection: Blackwell, Morton: Files, Folder Title: "American Law Enforcement Officers Association," Box 1, document marked "President's Backup Copy," https://www.reaganlibrary.gov/sites/default/files/digitallibrary/smof/publicliaison/blackwell/box-001/40_047_7006969_001_014_2017.pdf.

3. September 28, 1981 ("arrogance," "stark"); October 14, 1982 ("repeat"); March 11, 1983 ("sustained"); December 5, 1983 ("crime statistics").

4. March 30, 1981 ("first duty"); September 28, 1981 ("we've learned," "massive").

5. See Office of Management and Budget, Table 5.1—Budget Authority by Function and Subfunction: 1976–2017, in *The Budget for Fiscal Year 2013, Historical Tables* (Washington, D.C.: Office of Management and Budget, 2012), www.whitehouse.gov/sites/default/files/omb/budget/fy2013/.

6. Beckett, *Making Crime Pay*, 47, on repudiation of Carter's "preoccupation."

7. September 28, 1981.

8. February 20, 1984 ("liberal"); February 28, 1984 (radio address).

9. December 4, 1987.

10. February 26, 1982 ("great moral"); October 9, 1985 ("music").

11. Barr quoted in Marie Gottschalk, *The Prison and the Gallows: The Politics of Mass Incarceration in America* (New York, 2006), 88; see also 86–91.

12. In his first term, he used the phrase on September 28, 1981, June 15, 1982, September 11, 1982, January 14, 1983, June 20, 1984, and July 18, 1984. Those are only instances where he used that specific phrase, not the many variations on it that he also employed ("war on drugs" being the most common).

13. Cover, *War on Drugs*, 1 (August 1980). See the June, July, and August 1980 issues for other claims by the magazine noted here. The magazine ceased publication in 1981 amid a sea of legal troubles for the National Anti-Drug Coalition and other LaRouche organizations.

14. See James Forman Jr., *Locking Up Our Own: Crime and Punishment in Black America* (New York, 2017), especially chaps. 2, 5.

15. October 2, 1985 ("the war against"); October 16, 1987 ("a war of abolition"); November 2, 1986; June 20, 1984 ("this administration"); October 21, 1985 ("war to the end"); June 24, 1982 ("the situation"); September 22, 1986 (Lincoln).

16. June 21, 1985 ("the other"); July 2, 1986 ("the line"); August 4, 1986 ("military forces").

17. Radley Balko, *Rise of the Warrior Cop: The Militarization of America's Police Forces* (New York, 2013), 147, 148 ("blaring"); Beckett, *Making Crime Pay*, 53, quoting Stockman's memoirs.

18. "Individual Commissioners Statements, Personal Comment by Commissioner James Dobson," part 1, chap. 3 in *Attorney General's Commission on Pornography: Final Report* (July 1986), http://www.porn-report.com/personal-comments-commissioner-james-dobson.html.

19. Andrea Dworkin, *Letters from a War Zone: Writings, 1976–1989* (New York, 1989), 234.

20. On that promiscuous use, see Michael S. Sherry, *In the Shadow of War: The United States Since the 1930s* (New Haven, CT, 1995), chaps. 8–9, and Michael Sherry, "The Language of War in AIDS Discourse," in *Writing AIDS: Gay Literature, Language, and Analysis*, ed. Timothy F. Murphy and Suzanne Poirier (New York, 1993), 39–53.

21. September 28, 1981 ("thin blue"); April 4, 1985 ("illegal drug"); August 4, 1986 ("national crusade," "to defeat"); May 20, 1986 ("first thing"); October 6, 1986 ("We can").

22. September 22, 1988 ("there are"); August 4, 1986 ("the international"); September 22, 1986 ("nothing"); September 15, 1986 ("over the years"). Redacted versions of NSD 221 are available online; see the Homeland Security Digital Library, www.dhs.gov/xabout/laws/gc_1219263961449.shtm.

23. October 16, 1987 ("back in," "institutionalize").

24. September 30, 1987 ("this battle"); July 30, 1986 ("liberal judges").

25. September 25, 1986 ("no drug"); September 9, 1988 ("Between"); January 25, 1988 ("the average"); September 9, 1988 ("there are"); October 19, 1988, and other times campaigning ("Make a").

26. Daniel T. Rodgers, *Age of Fracture* (Cambridge, MA, 2011), 28, 29, 40.

27. Rodgers, *Age of Fracture*, 35; "Losing the Words of the Cold War" is the title of chapter 1. David Greenberg, "The Man, The Myths," *Slate*, June 9, 2004 ("an ugly"); David Greenberg, "Bygone Bipartisanship," *NYT Book Review*, November 24, 2013, 31 ("Hollywood").

28. See Gottschalk, *Prison and the Gallows*, 28, on "Percentage of Americans Identifying Crime as Most Important Problem Facing the Nation." In contrast, Peter K. Enns, assessing "the public's punitiveness"—a related but more complicated and diffuse measure—finds that punitiveness arose steadily through the 1970s and 1980s; see *Incarceration Nation: How the United States Became the Most Punitive Democracy in the World* (New York, 2016), chap. 2, especially figure 2.6, p. 38.

29. See Beckett, *Making Crime Pay*, 58.

30. Quoted in Beckett, *Making Crime Pay*, 56.

31. Among many treatments of this issue, especially careful and comprehensive, though more focused on the 1990s, is Sara Sun Beale, "The News Media's Influence on Criminal Justice Policy: How Market-Driven News Promotes Punitiveness," *William and Mary Law Review* 48 (2006): 397–481; quotation, 430. Enns, *Incarceration Nation*, on the other hand, without specific reference to local TV news, argues that "shifts in news coverage of crime and shifts in the public's punitiveness track the actual crime rate" (96).

32. Gottschalk, *Prison and the Gallows*, 26.

33. "The press may not be" as quoted in Maxwell E. McCombs and Donald L. Shaw, "The Agenda-Setting Function of Mass Media," *Public Opinion Quarterly* 36 (Summer 1972): 177, citing Bernard C. Cohen, *The Press and Foreign Policy* (1963), 120; Beckett, *Making Crime Pay*, 62 (her words).

34. On the late 1980s collapse in fears of war see, Robert T. Schatz and Susan T. Fiske, "International Reactions to the Threat of Nuclear War: The Rise and Fall of Concern in the Eighties," *Political Psychology* 3 (March 1992); 1–29. On "losing ground," see Pew Research Center, "Interdiction and Incarceration Still Top Remedies," March 21, 2001, https://www.people-press.org/2001/03/21/interdiction-and-incarceration-still-top-remedies/. See also Beckett, *Making Crime Pay*, chap. 2.

35. "Reinforcements in the Drug War," *Time*, July 20, 1981.

36. "Reluctant Recruits," *Newsweek*, July 28, 1986.

37. "Crack Down," *Time*, August 18, 1986. "Rolling Out the Big Guns," *Time*, September 22, 1986.

38. Brian Duffy, "War on Drugs: More Than a 'Short-Term High'?," *U.S. News & World Report*, September 29, 1986.

39. See, for example, the Joint Congressional Resolution (PL 100-87), August 11, 1987, referring to "the Nation's war on drugs"; H.R. 1065, submitted to the House on February 23, 1993, with numerous references to "the war on drugs"; and the Accounting Office report *War on Drugs: Federal Assistance to State and Local Drug Enforcement* (Washington, D.C., April 1993). My conclusion here also draws on assistance from Matthew June and a search of the Federal Digital System.

40. Morris J. Blachman and Kenneth E. Sharpe, "The War on Drugs: American Democracy Under Assault," *World Policy Journal* 7 (Winter 1989/1990):148, 156.

41. September 14, 1986; May 5, 1986 ("by 1980"); Kerry at a hearing of a Senate Foreign Relations subcommittee, August 29, 1989, HRG-1989-FOR-0012, 3; "Crack and Crime," *Newsweek*, June 16, 1986.

42. Quoted in "Rolling Out the Big Guns," *Time*, September 22, 1986.

43. *Miami Herald* and Pepper as quoted in Jeremy Kuzmarov, *The Myth of the Addicted Army: Vietnam and the Modern War on Drugs* (Amherst, MA, 2009), 173; "America's Crusade," *Time*, September 15, 1986.

44. "America's Crusade," *Time.*

45. Balko, *Rise of the Warrior Cop*, 168, citing *Ebony*, March 1989.

46. Kuzmarov, *Myth of the Addicted Army*, 173.

47. Michelle Alexander, *The New Jim Crow: Mass Incarceration in the Age of Colorblindness* (New York, 2010), 76.

48. James Mills, interviewed for "America's Best Weapon Is Political Pressure, Says an Expert," *U.S. News and World Report*, August 25, 1986.

49. October 14, 1982.

50. See Michael Cullen Green, *Black Yanks in the Pacific: Race in the Making of American Military Empire after World War II* (Ithaca, NY, 2010).

51. Donna Murch, "Crack in Los Angeles: Crisis, Militarization, and Black Response to the Late Twentieth-Century War on Drugs," *JAH* 102 (June 2015): 170.

52. Randolph quoted, and African American support for the 1986 act noted, in Kelefa Sanneh, "Body Count," *New Yorker*, September 14, 2015, which examines new books about black support for punitive measures. See also David Cole, "The Truth about Our Prison Crisis," *New York Review of Books*, June 22, 2017.

53. Marie Gottschalk, *Caught: The Prison State and the Lockdown of American Politics* (Princeton, NJ, 2015), 128.

54. See especially Alexander, *New Jim Crow.*

55. Robert Perkinson, *Texas Tough: The Rise of America's Prison Empire* (New York, 2010), 337. See also BJS, *Correctional Populations in the United States, 1991* (Washington, D.C., August 1993), https://www.ncjrs.gov /pdffiles1/bjs/142729.pdf.

56. "Saddling Up for the War on Drugs," *National Journal*, September 6, 1986.

57. "Government by Gimmick," *Time*, October 13, 1986.

58. "Casual Drug Users Should Be Shot, Gates Says," *Los Angeles Times*, September 6, 1990; Daryl Gates with Diane K. Shah, *Chief: My Life in the LAPD* (New York, 1992), 287.

59. A purpose of presidential rhetoric often overlooked, as in Daniel Rodgers's sketch of how "presidents use their modern fount of words for many purposes." See Rodgers, *Age of Fracture*, 15–16.

60. Andrew B. Whitford and Jeff Yates, "Policy Signals and Executive Governance: Presidential Rhetoric in the 'War on Drugs,'" *Journal of Politics* 65 (November 2003): 999.

61. BJS, *Correctional Populations in the United States, 1993* (Washington, D.C., October 1995), https://www.bjs.gov/content/pub/pdf/cpop93bk.pdf

62. Alexander, *New Jim Crow*, 77.

63. Gottschalk, *Prison and the Gallows*, 27. On Alabama, see the summary of a report by the Equal Justice Initiative in "Lawyers Stumble, and Clients Take Fall," *NYT*, January 8, 2013.

64. "Drug Fever in Washington," *Newsweek*, September 22, 1986.

65. Alexander, *New Jim Crow*, 73 ("massive bribe"), 78–80 (on forfeitures), 73–74 (on federal resources), 74 (New Haven police chief).

66. Balko, *Rise of the Warrior Cop*, 146; Balko mistakenly attributes sponsorship to Hubert Humphrey, who had died in 1978.

67. Quoted in Forman, *Locking Up Our Own*, 171, citing *WP*, December 15, 1991.

68. Jeanne B. Stinchcomb, "From Optimistic Policies to Pessimistic Outcomes: Why Won't Boot Camps Either Succeed Pragmatically or Succumb Politically?," in *Rehabilitation Issues, Problems, and Prospects in Boot Camp*, ed. Brent B. Benda and Nathaniel J. Pallone (Binghamton, NY, 2005), 28. Criminologists have paid attention to boot camps, but scholars offering more general surveys of the period have not.

69. Gottschalk, *Prison and the Gallows*, 22.

70. "'Shock' Punishment, New Doubts: A Special Report. As Boot Camps for Criminals Multiply, Skepticism Grows," *NYT*, December 18, 1993 (Miller, Schumer). For summaries of research on the effects of military service and boot camps, see, Francis T. Cullen, Kristie R. Blevins, Jennifer S. Trager, and Paul Gendreau, "The Rise and Fall of Boot Camps: A Case Study in Common-Sense Corrections," in Benda and Pallone, *Rehabilitation Issues*. For a summary of research offering "mixed results," see "Correctional Boot Camps: Lessons from a Decade of Research," *Research for Practice* (Washington, D.C.: Department of Justice, National Institute of Justice, June 2003). For later research that offered a more sympathetic view of boot camps, see Lauren O'Neill, Doris Layton MacKenzie, and David M. Bierie, "Educational Opportunities within Correctional Institutions: Does Facility Type Matter?," *Prison Journal* 2007 (87): 311–27.

71. http://www.warriorfitnessbootcamp.com/program [2018]; similar ads with similar slogans ran for years prior to 2018. Elijah Generation—Boot Camp, Teen Missions, Masters Commission, www.elijahgeneration.org/

[inactive in 2019]; that website for the organization, based in Oklahoma City, and other online sources do not reveal when its boot camp began, but a 2005 copyright suggests before that year. See also Jeff Birkenstein, Anna Froula, Karen Randell, eds., *Reframing 9/11: Film, Popular Culture and the "War on Terror"* (New York, 2010), 49.

72. Stinchcomb, "From Optimistic Policies to Pessimistic Outcomes," 28–30; "We do everything" quote from Chi Sileo, "Abuse, Absolution Found at Boot Camp," *Insight on the News*, June 27, 1994; "The Marine Method," *WP*, February 28, 1987; 139 *Congressional Record* 27464 (November 4, 1993) (Biden).

73. This term had so many variants that it is difficult to track its first use, but Peter Kraska's work in the late 1990s jump-started its widespread adoption.

74. Christian Parenti, *Lockdown America: Police and Prisons in the Age of Crisis* (New York, 1999), 113.

75. Kraska, quoted in William Booth, "Exploding Number of SWAT Teams Sets Off Alarms; Critics See Growing Role of Heavily Armed Police Units as 'Militarization' of Law Enforcement," *WP*, June 17, 1997.

76. "Police Quest Games," Flash Arcade Games website, www.flasharcade-gamessite.com/police-swat-team-online-game.html.

77. "SWAT Teams Belie Their Shoot-'Em-Up TV Image," *Christian Science Monitor*, February 18, 1982.

78. Bush, March 10, 1989; Balko, *Rise of the Warrior Cop*, 165 (Bennett), 154.

79. Balko, *Rise of the Warrior Cop*, 156.

80. Balko, *Rise of the Warrior Cop*, 210.

81. HK International Training Division, n.d., featuring promotional materials of the mid-1990s, www.hkpro.com/index.php?option=com_content&view=article.

82. Fox News (reprinting an Associated Press story), "Shoot First: Columbine High School Massacre Transformed U.S. Police Tactics," April 18, 2009, https://www.foxnews.com/story/shoot-first-columbine-high-school-massacre-transformed-u-s-police-tactics.

83. R. R. Kothari, et al., *Towards a Liberating Peace* (1988), as quoted in Peter B. Kraska and Victor E. Kappeler, "Militarizing American Police: The Rise and Normalization of Paramilitary Units," *Social Problems* 44 (February 1997): 2; Josh Ellis, "Sleep-Away Camp for Postmodern Boys," *NYTM*, July 21, 2013.

84. "SWAT Teams Becoming the Big Guns against Drugs," *WP*, September 26, 1988.

85. Quoted in Peter Kraska, "Enjoying Militarism: Political/Personal Dilemmas in Studying U.S. Police Paramilitary Units," *Justice Quarterly* 13 (September 1996): 412.

86. Kraska and Kappeler, "Militarizing American Police," 12. See also Balko, *Rise of the Warrior Cop*, 208.

87. Quoted in Balko, *Rise of the Warrior Cop*, 191, from a 1999 *NYT* article.

88. Peter B. Kraska, "Playing War: Masculinity, Militarism, and Their Real-World Consequences," in *Militarizing the American Criminal Justice System*, ed. Peter B. Kraska (Boston, 2001), 143.

89. The classic work is James William Gibson, *Warrior Dreams: Paramilitary Culture in Post-Vietnam America* (New York, 1994).

90. Peter Horne, "Policewomen: Their First Century and the New Era," *PC*, July 2006. See also "Crime in the United States 2013: Full-Time Law Enforcement Employees," FBI Uniform Crime Reports, https://ucr.fbi.gov /crime-in-the-u.s/2013/crime-in-the-u.s.-2013/tables/table-74.

91. "Conference on Small Business," June 2, 1995.

92. "Tapping a Source of Business Acumen; Consultants' Group Markets Expertise of Older Clients," *Orange County (CA) Register*, May 25, 1989.

93. "SWAT Teams Are Working Out Largest, Most Troubled Loans; SAMDAs Are Dead," *RTC Watch*, July 6, 1992.

94. "Swimming Youths Converge on Tech for Big Meet," *Roanoke (VA) Times*, December 27, 1995.

95. Quoted in Parenti, *Lockdown America*, 121, drawing on a February 2, 1998, *Los Angeles Times* article.

96. Parenti, *Lockdown America*, 112, 114.

97. Parenti, *Lockdown America*, 114, Parenti's paraphrase of a 1994 comment by the district attorney.

98. C. D. Smith in *Police* magazine in 1995, as quoted in Booth, "Exploding Number of SWAT Teams Sets Off Alarms," *WP*, June 17, 1997.

99. For a legal defense of such cross-training, albeit one resting heavily on the simple claim that it is needed, see Karan R. Singh, "Treading the Thin Blue Line: Military Special-Operations Trained Police SWAT Teams and the Constitution," *William and Mary Bill of Rights Journal* 9 (2001): 673–717.

100. Dana Priest, "Inside America: Manoeuvres in the Dark," *Guardian* (UK), April 15, 1997, on joint training and on special ops exercises.

101. Parenti, *Lockdown America*, 125.

102. Quoted in Balko, *Rise of the Warrior Cop*, 150.

103. For the Edenton case, I've relied on three episodes of PBS's *Frontline* that played a major role in reversal of the convictions and generated enormous commentary: "Innocence Lost" (1991), "Innocence Lost: The Verdict" (1993), and "Innocence Lost: The Plea" (1997). For daycare cases generally and analysis of them, I have relied on Roger N. Lancaster, *Sex Panic and the Punitive State* (Berkeley, CA, 2011), 52–60; 51 for *Newsweek* quotation; 53 for "no sacrificed."

104. Lancaster, *Sex Panic*, 53.

105. Quoted on the Little Rascals Day Care Case website, littlerascalsday-carecase.org/Archive/13Q3/130807Dowd.htm?, which attributes the quotation to Kathy Dobie, "The Little Town of Horrors," *McCall's*, June 1992.

106. "Rush to Judgment," *Newsweek*, April 19, 1993.

107. Lancaster, *Sex Panic*, 62.

108. In his major memoir *A World Transformed*, cowritten with Brent Scowcroft (New York, 1998), Bush focused on foreign policy, barely mentioned the invasion of Panama, and made little mention of crime or drugs.

109. Perkinson, *Texas Tough*, 4.

110. Herbert Parmet, *George Bush: The Life of a Lone Star Yankee* (1997; repr., New Brunswick, NJ, 2001), 336.

111. Parmet, *George Bush*, 327.

112. "Remarks to Members of the Woodrow Wilson International Center," March 7, 1989.

113. January 20, 1989 (inaugural); February 9, 1989 ("to escalate").

114. March 9, 1989 ("represent"); March 10, 1989 ("it's a war");March 13, 1989 ("no war"); John Robert Greene, *The Presidency of George Bush* (Lawrence, KS, 2000), 71.

115. March 9, 1989 ("it used"); April 25, 1989 ("undercover").

116. May 15, 1989 ("I am announcing").

117. Quoted in Michael S. Sherry, "George W. Bush," in *The American Presidency*, ed. Alan Brinkley and Davis Dyer (New York, 2004), 493.

118. Among the better standard sources, Greene, *Presidency of George Bush*, offers minimal though reliable treatment of Bush's record and rhetoric on crime, implicitly leaving them as a minor aspect of his presidency, and does not address the questions I raise here. Parmet, *George Bush*, does likewise.

119. Patrick Buchanan, "Address to the Republican National Convention," August 17, 1992, Voices of Democracy: The U.S. Oratory Project, https://voicesofdemocracy.umd.edu/buchanan-culture-war-speech-speech-text/.

120. Many sources indicate that Congress's 1958 Delaney Amendment, concerning food safety, established "the first 'zero-tolerance' standard in American governance," but the specific phrase does not appear in the amendment; see Jonathan Simon, *Governing through Crime: How the War on Crime Transformed American Democracy and Created a Culture of Fear* (New York, 2007), 88. Judith Kafka traces zero-tolerance policies back to "a U.S. Customs Service antidrug program implemented in the 1980s"; *A History of "Zero Tolerance" in American Public Schooling* (New York, 2011), 2. Among early uses of a related term was a 1990 reference to the Evanston, Illinois, police chief's "'zero-based' tolerance for gang members"; see Irving A. Spergel and Ron L. Chance with the assistance of Candice Kane, Phyllis Garth, and G. David Curry, *Community and Institutional Responses to the Youth Gang Problem* (Chicago: School of Social Service Administration University of Chicago, January 1990), https://www.ncjrs.gov/txtfiles/d0029.txt.

121. January 12, 1989 ("zero tolerance").

122. March 22, 1989 ("quite simply").

123. Simon, *Governing through Crime*, 58.

124. James Alan Fox and Marianne W. Zawitz, section on "Long term trends," in *Homicide Trends in the United States* (Washington, D.C.: Bureau of Justice Statistics, 1999), https://www.bjs.gov/content/pub/pdf/htius.pdf.

125. See Gallup poll entitled "Death Penalty" summarizing poll responses from 1937 to 2017, http://news.gallup.com/poll/1606/death-penalty.aspx.

126. See BJS, excel table entitled "Estimated Number and Rate of Persons Supervised by U.S. Adult Correctional Systems, by Correctional Status,

1980–2016," in "Key Statistic: Incarceration Rate" (n.d.), https://www.bjs
.gov/index.cfm?ty=kfdetail&iid=493.

127. Quoted in Joseph Margulies, *What Changed When Everything
Changed: 9/11 and the Making of National Identity* (New Haven, CT,
2013), 97.

128. December 20, 1989.

129. July 18, 1992.

130. Kraska and Kappeler, "Militarizing American Police," 14.

Chapter 5

1. Quoted in Michael S. Sherry, *In the Shadow of War: The United States
since the 1930s* (New Haven, CT, 1995), 496.

2. As with other recent presidents, many sources about Clinton and his
presidency pay little attention to his record on crime, despite the attention
he gave it at the time, other than to attend to the impeachment scandal
and related matters. Clinton's memoirs are unrevealing, scarcely going beyond this rhetoric and positions at the time; see Bill Clinton, *My Life* (New
York, 2004). The best and most critical accounts are those, most cited in his
chapter, about criminal justice. For a recent example in the public sphere,
see Donna Murch, "The Clintons' War on Drugs: When Black Lives Didn't
Matter," *New Republic*, February 6, 2016, which extends the criticism to
Hillary Clinton.

3. David B. Holian, "He's Stealing My Issues! Clinton's Crime Rhetoric
and the Dynamics of Issue Ownership," *Political Behavior* 26 (June 2004):
95–123 (quotation, 106). But Holian begins with an inaccurate premise, that
"Republican rhetoric about and newspaper accounts of crime in the 1980s
overwhelmingly concerned the death penalty and issues related to narrowing
judicial discretion" (100). As chapter 4 of this book shows, it "overwhelmingly
concerned" the war on drugs, the subject of Bush's first TV address, and the
broader war on crime.

4. Frank LoMonte, "Poor Ideas Capture Bill Clinton's Inexperience,"
Savannah News-Press, March 8, 1992.

5. Martin Nolan, "Brown Calls Clinton 'Slick,' Cites 'Deception' in Statements on Civil Rights," *Boston Globe*, March 8, 1992; Jack Germond and Jules
Witcover, "Clinton Must Deal with Brown Irritant," *Baltimore Sun*, March
23, 1992.

6. See John Robert Greene, *The Presidency of George Bush* (Lawrence, KS,
2000), 72.

7. Violent Crime Control and Law Enforcement Act (1994), Sec. 20102.

8. A measured official study is National Institute of Justice, *A National
Study Comparing the Environments of Boot Camps with Traditional
Facilities for Juvenile Offenders* (Washington, D.C.: Department of Justice,
August 2001), www.ncjrs.gov/pdffiles1/nij/187680.pdf. Much of the research
was later gathered into two volumes: Brent B. Benda and Nathaniel J.
Pallone, eds., *Rehabilitation Issues, Problems, and Prospects in Boot Camp*
(Binghamton, NY, 2005).

9. Jeanne B. Stinchcomb and W. Clinton Terry III, "Predicting the Likelihood of Rearrest among Shock Incarceration Graduates: Moving Beyond Another Nail in the Boot Camp Coffin," *Crime and Delinquency* 47 (April 2001): 240.

10. "Prison Boot Camps Prove No Sure Cure," *NYT*, April 10, 1994.

11. Statement by Cook County Sheriff Michael Sheahan, October 12, 2006, Cook County Boot Camp website, http://www.digibridge.net/bootcamp /BootCamp_stats.pdf.

12. Clinton, "Remarks on the Economic Program in Santa Monica, California," February 21, 1993.

13. Katherine Beckett, *Making Crime Pay: Law and Order in Contemporary American Politics* (New York, 1997), 25.

14. Jonathan Simon, *Governing through Crime: How the War on Crime Transformed American Democracy and Created a Culture of Fear* (New York, 2007), 102.

15. The 1994 act as summarized and quoted in U.S. Department of Justice "Fact Sheet," https://www.ncjrs.gov/txtfiles/billfs.txt.

16. Clinton, "State of the Union Address," January 21, 1996.

17. Michael Kramer, "From Sarajevo to Needle Park," *Time*, February 21, 1994, 29, which does not name the official; Beckett, *Making Crime Pay*, 25.

18. *Senate Judiciary Committee, Hearing on "Reviewing Strategies for Controlling National Drug Problems"* (February 10, 1994) (statement of Senator Joe Biden, Senate Judiciary Committee), http://babel.hathitrust.org/cgi /pt?id=mdp.39015042564149;view=1up;seq=6.

19. *Senate Judiciary Committee, Hearing on "Reviewing Strategies for Controlling National Drug Problems"* (February 10, 1994) (statement of Senator Strom Thurmond), http://babel.hathitrust.org/cgi/pt?id=mdp.3 9015042564149;view=1up;seq=6; Senator Ted Kennedy speech on Senate floor, 103rd Congress, *Congressional Record* (daily edition, August 25, 1994), http://congressional.proquest.com.turing.library.northwestern.edu /congressional/docview/t17.d18.c4b49b8e17003e59?accountid=12861; Representative Pat Schroeder speech on House floor, 103rd Congress, *Congressional Record* (daily edition August 16, 1994), http://congressional .proquest.com.turing.library.northwestern.edu/congressional/docview/t17 .d18.c4b521881a0036b0?accountid=12861; Tim Russert, *Meet the Press*, NBC, April 17, 1994, Guests: Sen. Joe Biden and Sen. Orrin Hatch, Republican of Utah, http://search.alexanderstreet.com.turing.library.northwestern.edu /media-studies/view/work/2409076; Senator Mitch McConnell, Senate floor speech, 103rd Congress, *Congressional Record* (daily edition November 20. 1993), http://congressional.proquest.com.turing.library.northwestern.edu /congressional/docview/t17.d18.c4b49b8e170028f5?accountid=12861.

20. Rev. Jesse Jackson Sr., July 7, 1994, on C-SPAN, https://www.youtube .com/watch?v=7pQfKeHtsfo.

21. For reluctant black support, see, among much analysis prompted by Hillary Clinton's 2016 campaign, Elizabeth Hinton, Julilly Kohler-Hausmann,

and Vesla M. Weaver, "Did Blacks Really Endorse the 1994 Crime Bill?," *NYT*, April 13, 2016. See also James Forman Jr., *Locking Up Our Own: Crime and Punishment in Black America* (New York, 2017), especially 194–98.

22. Video of the complete September 13, 1994, ceremony is available on C-SPAN's website, https://www.c-span.org/video/?60148–1/crime-bill -signing-ceremony.

23. J. M. Taylor, "Pell Grants for Prisoners Part Deux: It's Deja Vu All Over Again," *Journal of Prisoners on Prisons* 8 (1997), is one of the most careful pieces among many on the Pell Grant issue. The article circulated widely online, as in *Straight Low Magazine* ("Louisiana's Official Prison Magazine") 9 (2008), under the title "Pell Grants for Prisoners: Why Should We Care?," http://www.realcostofprisons.org/writing/Taylor_Pell_Grants.pdf. See also Jim Zook, "Effects of Ban on Pell Grants for Inmates, *Chronicle of Higher Education*, November 9, 1994. For later developments, see Nick Anderson, "Advocates Push to Renew Pell Grants for Prisoners, Citing Benefits of Higher Education," *WP*, December 3, 2013. On "country club prisons," see "Famed 'Country Club Prison' Is to House Violent Inmates," *NYT*, July 31, 1990.

24. "The President's News Conference with President Fernando Cardoso of Brazil," April 20, 1995.

25. Clinton on *60 Minutes*, CBS, April 23, 1995.

26. Francis Wilkinson, "Can Janet Reno Bust the War on Drugs? The New Attorney General Tries to Change the Debate on Drugs and Crime," *Rolling Stone*, June 10, 1993.

27. "Press Briefing by General Barry McCaffrey," March 6, 1996.

28. "Press Briefing by Mike McCurry," February 12, 1996.

29. Clinton, "State of the Union Address," January 25, 1994.

30. On 1033, LESO, and its decals, see ACLU, *War Comes Home: The Excessive Militarization of American Policing* (June 2014), https://www.aclu .org/sites/default/files/assets/jus14-warcomeshome-report-web-rel1.pdf; Radley Balko, *Rise of the Warrior Cop: The Militarization of America's Police Forces* (New York, 2013), 301–3. It is unclear when the phrase "From Warfighter to Crimefighter" first appeared on LESO decals, but it happened well before the media took notice of it in 2014; see, for example, "This Is Why Your Local Police Department Might Have a Tank," *Time*, June 24, 2014. The decals can be found in promotional literature by or about LESO, and on websites for images, such as https://www.google.com/search?q= LESO+from+warfighter+to+crimefighter&source=lnms&tbm=isch&sa=X&ved =0ahUKEwjdxqKomtblAhXKY98KHf-OCZQQ_AUIESgB&biw=1344& bih=740#imgrc=v33I5LaqYiaiFM:&spf=1573064609726.

31. Holian, "He's Stealing My Issues!," 116.

32. Wilkinson, "Can Janet Reno?"

33. *Time*, June 15, 1996.

34. "The President's Radio Address," November 2, 1996; Simon, *Governing through Crime*, 59.

35. "The Two General McCaffreys," editorial, *NYT*, July 5, 1997.

36. William Bratton, *Turnaround: How America's Top Cop Reversed the Crime Epidemic* (New York, 1998). For brief mention of "war on crime," see p. 273.

37. Andrea McArdle and Tanya Erzen, eds., *Zero Tolerance: Quality of Life and the New Police Brutality in New York City* (New York, 2011), 11. The critiques in this volume emphasize neoliberalism, a framework I find useful but incomplete.

38. Both quotations (the first by John S. Miller) in "Bratton, Who Shaped an Era in Policing, Tries to Navigate a Racial Divide," *NYT*, July 26, 2016.

39. Evan Osnos, "The Daley Show: Dynastic Rule in Obama's Political Birthplace," *New Yorker*, March 8, 2010. See also David Jackson, "The Law and Richard M. Daley," *Chicago Magazine*, September 1988.

40. Joseph Margulies, *What Changed When Everything Changed: 9/11 and the Making of National Identity* (New Haven, CT, 2013), 98 ("mythical"), 99 (Central Park). For Trump and his ads, see Oliver Laughland, "Donald Trump and the Central Park Five," *Guardian* (UK), February 16, 2016.

41. Margulies, *What Changed*, 100 (1995 article), 102 ("the biggest"), 101 (1996 book), 103 ("myth"). Anne-Marie Cusac, *Cruel and Unusual: The Culture of Punishment in America* (New Haven, CT, 2009), 174 ("teen-age time bomb" and *Time*). C-SPAN's website provides the full text of Hillary Clinton's comments, https://www.c-span.org/video/?69606-1 /mrs-clinton-campaign-speech.

42. Clinton, "State of the Union Address," February 4, 1997. He publicly repeated this phrase on April 11, May 8, May 10, May 15, and June 11.

43. "War against Drunk Drivers," *Newsweek*, September 13, 1982; Katherine Prescott, MADD president, quoted in "Drunken Driving Deaths Rising, Again MADD Gives Nation an Overall C Grade for Efforts to Crack Down," *USA Today*, November 27, 1996; "MADD Unveils 8-Point Plan to Jump-start Stalled War on Drunk Driving," press release, June 8, 2012, http://www .safetyalerts.com/new.02/madd8pt.html; Mac Marshall and Alice Oleson, "In the Pink: MADD and Public Health Policy in the 1990s," *Journal of Public Health Policy* 15 (Spring 1994): 54 ("war-like rhetoric"), 59 ("retribution," "punitive").

44. Timothy J. Dunn, *The Militarization of the U.S.-Mexico Border, 1978–1992* (Austin, TX, 1996); Peter Andreas, *Border Games: Policing the U.S.-Mexico Border* (Ithaca, NY, 2000), 44 (McCain).

45. Andreas, *Border Games*, 150 (retired officer and Weinberger's scenario) l; Emanuel quoted in "U.S. Strengthening Patrols along the Mexican Border," *NYT*, January 13, 1996.

46. See Torrie Hester, "Deportability and the Carceral State," *JAH* 102 (June 2015): 41–51 (quotation from p.149).

47. "The President's Radio Address," December 6, 1997.

48. Department of Veterans Affairs Employment Discrimination Resolution and Adjudication Act, House Report No. 105–292 (October 2, 1997), https://www.congress.gov/congressional-report/105th-congress/house -report/292/1.

49. Hillary Rodham Clinton, *It Takes a Village: And Other Lessons Children Teach Us* (New York, 1996), 138, 257, 256.

50. "'Zero Tolerance' Strikes Again In Richmond: Flying Paper Clip Lands Pupil in Trouble," *Chicago Tribune*, May 12, 1998; "Richmond Student Expelled for Flying Paper Clip Incident," *Chicago Tribune*, May 13, 1998.

51. "Hillary Clinton: U.S. Is 'Failing to Keep Faith with Our Veterans,'" *WP*, November 10, 2015.

52. Simon, *Governing through Crime*, 222–23.

53. For such cases, see the "ongoing archive of zero tolerance stories run amok" called "Brain Dead," www.suspensionstories.com/brain-dead/?, which emphasizes ridiculousness but is fun and useful nonetheless.

54. Prison Policy Initiative, *Mass Incarceration: The Whole Pie* (March 12, 2014), http://static.prisonpolicy.org/images/lockedup_pie.jpg?v=6. See also BJS, *Jail Inmates at Midyear 2012—Statistical Tables* (May 2013), 3, http://www.bjs.gov/content/pub/pdf/jim12st.pdf.

55. Table 1 in *Crime in the United States, 2009* (September 2010), FBI Uniform Crime Reports, https://www2.fbi.gov/ucr/cius2009/data/table_01.html.

56. See Report of the Children's Defense Fund, *America's Cradle to Prison Pipeline* (2007), http://www.childrensdefense.org/library/data/cradle-prison-pipeline-report-2007-full-lowres.pdf. For "birth to prison pipeline," see Jill Lepore, "Baby Doe: A Political History of Tragedy," *New Yorker*, February 1, 2016.

57. Andrew S. Baer, *Beyond the Usual Beating: The Jon Burge Police Torture Scandal and Social Movements for Police Accountability in Chicago* (Chicago, 2020). See also W. Fitzhugh Brundage, *Civilizing Torture: An American Tradition* (Cambridge, MA, 2018), 320–31.

58. Bernardine Dohrn, "'Look Out, Kid / It's Something You Did': Zero Tolerance for Children," in *Zero Tolerance: Resisting the Drive for Punishment in Our Schools—A Handbook for Parents, Students, Educators, and Citizens*, ed. William Ayers, Bernardine Dohrn, and Rick Ayers (New York, 2001). Terms like "the militarization of schools" appeared later, often promoted by organizations like the National Network Opposing the Militarization of Youth, whose focus was on military recruitment and training in schools; see, for example, its *NNOMY Reader: Voices from the U.S. Counter-recruitment Movement* (January 2015), https://nnomy.org/index.php/en/resources/downloads/trainings-trainers/557-nnomy-reader-2015/file.html.

59. Quotations from William Booth, "Exploding Number of SWAT Teams Sets Off Alarms; Critics See Growing Role of Heavily Armed Police Units as 'Militarization' of Law Enforcement," *WP*, June 17, 1997.

60. Quotation from the abstract for Peter Kraska, "Enjoying Militarism: Political/Personal Dilemmas in Studying U.S. Police Paramilitary Units," *Justice Quarterly* 13 (September 1996): 406.

61. Peter B. Kraska and Victor E. Kappeler, "Militarizing American Police: The Rise and Normalization of Paramilitary Units," *Social Problems* 44 (February 1997).

62. See, for example, "Clinton's Airstrike Motives Questioned. Many Wonder If Attack Was Meant to Distract from Lewinsky Matter," *Baltimore Sun*, August 23, 1998.

63. "First Lady Launches Counterattack," *WP*, January 28, 1998; James Carville, *Meet the Press*, NBC, January 25, 1998, https://search .alexanderstreet.com/view/work/2318448; "Impeachment Wars: The Clintons Now and Then," *Newsweek*, October 18, 1998.

64. "The President's Press Conference," March 11, 1992.

65. Colin L. Powell with Joseph E. Persico, *My American Journey* (New York, 1995), 576–77. For later references, see, for example, Walter Isaacson, "Madeline's War," *Time*, May 17, 1999.

66. Secretary of State Madeleine K. Albright, interview by Matt Lauer, *Today Show*, NBC, February 19, 1998, Columbus, Ohio, https://1997–2001. state.gov/statements/1998/980219a.html.

67. John McCain, "The Need for Strategy in the New Postwar Era," *Armed Forces Journal*, January 1990, quoted in Michael Klare, *Rogue States and Nuclear Outlaws: America's Search for a New Foreign Policy* (New York, 1995), 235n25. See also McCain, "Should the United States Be the World's Policeman" (address, 24th Annual Conservative Political Conference, March 7, 2007), https://www.mccain.senate.gov/public/index.cfm /speeches?ID=542F0A7C-3529–4F3F-B807-AF9A816E8205.

68. Charles Krauthammer, "The Unipolar Moment," *Foreign Affairs: America and the World* 70 (1990/91): 22–33.

69. Thomas L. Friedman, "A Manifesto for the Fast World," *NYTM*, March 28, 1999.

70. A Google Ngram for "global cop" (it does not track the truncated "globalcop" version) indicates the term had almost no use before the end of the Cold War but skyrocketed in use in the 1990s, partly in reaction to the role the United States played in the Gulf War. Use of a familiar similar term, "world policeman," was much older, peaked in the 1960s and early 1970s, and remained in considerable use thereafter.

71. A useful, sympathetic retrospective is Todd VanDerWerff, "Hill Street Blues Transcends Its Era to Remain Tremendous TV," TV Club website, April 29, 2014, http://www.avclub.com/review/hill -street-blues-transcends-its-era-remain-tremen-203893.

72. Susan Jeffords, *Hard Bodies: Hollywood Masculinity in the Reagan Era* (New Brunswick, NJ, 1994), 28.

73. For a number-crunching attempt, see Erica Scharrer, "Tough Guys: The Portrayal of Hypermasculinity and Aggression in Televised Police Drama," *Journal of Broadcasting and Electronic Media* 45 (Fall 2001): 615–34.

74. Cusac, *Cruel and Unusual*, 195–96 ("criminality"), 194–95 ("old" shows).

75. Laura Quinn, "The Politics of *Law and Order*," *Journal of American and Comparative Cultures* 25 (Spring 2002): 131. Quinn offers a substantial, complicated reading of the show.

76. Steven D. Stark, "Perry Mason Meets Sonny Crockett: The History of Lawyers and the Police as Television Heroes," *University of Miami Law Review* 42 (1987): 230.

77. Scharrer, "Tough Guys," 625. Scharrer does not give dates, or a year, for this week.

78. Stark, "Perry Mason Meets Sonny Crockett," 282.

79. Michelle Brown, *The Culture of Punishment: Prison, Society, and Spectacle* (New York, 2009), 72, 76.

80. See the competition's website, https://web.archive.org/web/20151026090003/http://www.swatroundup.net/.

81. See, for example, Nico Carpentier, "Post-Democracy, Hegemony, and Invisible Power: The Reality TV Media Professional as *Primum Movens Immobile*," in *Trans-Reality Television: The Transgression of Reality, Genre, Politics, and Audience*, ed. Sofie Van Bauwal and Nico Carpentier (Plymouth, UK, 2010), 111; Nicolaus Mills, "Television and the Politics of Humiliation," *Dissent*, Winter 2016.

82. Gray Lavender and Mark Fishman, "Television Reality Crime Programs: Context and History," in *Entertaining Crime: Television Reality Programs*, ed. Gray Lavender and Mark Fishman (New York, 1998), 7.

83. Mills, "Television and the Politics of Humiliation."

84. Lisa Kern Griffin, "The True Lessons of True Crime," *NYT*, January 12, 2016.

85. Beckett, *Making Crime Pay*, 62, 78. Among much cultural analysis, Jonathan Nicholls-Pothook, *TV Cops: The Contemporary American Television Police Drama* (New York, 2012) is one of the best studies, unfolding the complex ways in which the TV programs can be understood. However, the work is not much interested in how those programs intersected with politics and influenced public attitudes.

86. Scott Miley, "Battle Plan for Correction," *Indianapolis Star*, May 15, 2000.

87. Department of Justice and Department of Defense, *Report to Congress: Conversion of Closed Military Installations into Federal Prison Facilities* (Washington, D.C., February 1995), 1-1, 1-2. Report prepared by the Federal Bureau of Prisons.

88. John E. Lynch, *Local Economic Development after Military Base Closures*, with a foreword by Seymour Melman (New York, 1970), ix, 301. Although privately published, the study was effectively sponsored by the air force—Lynch was an air force analyst on loan to the Institute for Defense Analyses.

89. Extrapolated from Barbara Krauth and Clyde W. Dickerson, *Converting Other Facilities into Prisons* (Boulder, CO: Library Information Specialists, May 1984), static.nicic.gov/Library/001617.pdf?. The authors listed some facilities still undergoing conversion in 1984.

90. *Attorney General's Task Force on Violent Crime: Final Report* (Washington, D.C., August 17, 1981), 10, https://www.ncjrs.gov/pdffiles1/Digitization/78548NCJRS.pdf; Memorandum, Rudolph W. Giuliani,

Associate Attorney General, to All United States Attorneys, October 6, 1981, Folder "John G. Roberts Jr. Misc.," Box 30, Accession #60–89–372, Record Group 60, National Archives and Records Administration.

91. June 20, 1984.

92. "Bush Calls for Turning Some Bases into Prisons," *NYT*, June 27, 1988.

93. A useful account is David Lockwood and George Siehl, "Military Base Closures: A Historical Review from 1988 to 1995," *Congressional Research Service Report* (Washington, D.C.: Library of Congress, October 18, 2004), https://digital.library.unt.edu/ark:/67531/metacrs7095/.

94. General Accounting Office, *Military Bases: Reuse Plans for Selected Bases Closed in 1988 and 1991* (Washington, D.C., November 1994), 3.

95. *Report of the Defense Secretary's Commission on Base Realignment and Closure* (Washington, D.C.: December 1988), 27. For later perspectives and statistics, see Congressional Research Service, *Base Closure and Realignment (BRAC): Background and Issues for Congress* (Washington, D.C., April 25, 2019), https://fas.org/sgp/crs/natsec/R45705.pdf.

96. "Among Mayors, a Tide of Drugs Brings Forth Desperation and Ideas," *NYT*, February 12, 1989; Edward J. Koch, op-ed, "For Anti-Drug Boot Camps," *NYT*, May 24, 1989.

97. "Fort Dix May Become Federal Prison," *NYT*, August 30, 1992.

98. "Fort Dix Finds New Growth Industry: Housing U.S. Prisoners," *NYT*, August 8, 1993.

99. "Fort Dix Finds New Growth Industry."

100. "Fort Dix May Become Federal Prison."

101. "Fort Dix May Become Federal Prison."

102. "Fort Dix Finds New Growth Industry."

103. August 11, 1993.

104. *Defense Base Closure and Realignment Commission, Report to the President, 1991* (Washington, D.C., 1991), 5–36; Representative James Jontz (Ind.), "Grissom Air Force Base Is Important to Indiana, Nation," *Northwest Indiana Times*, June 23, 1991.

105. "Unequal Justice? Similar Crime, Similar Counties, Different Punishments," *South Bend (IN) Tribune*, September 24, 2006.

106. Figures offered by the state administration as reported in "Crime Bills to Get Cost Scrutiny in House," Associated Press State & Local Wire, February 9, 2003.

107. Rex Early paraphrased in "Early Sets Forth Goals at GOP Dinner," *South Bend (IN) Tribune*, March 11, 1996.

108. "Press Conference," July 2, 1993, that included the heads of the Departments of Defense, Labor, Transportation, Commerce, and Housing and Urban Development, as well as the head of the Environmental Protection Agency. Clinton, "Remarks to the Community in Alameda, California," August 13, 1993.

109. "Hearing to Gauge Views on Prison Site," *South Bend (IN) Tribune*, January 21, 1996; "Prison Draws Support for [from] Peru Residents, Project Spells Prosperity," *South Bend (IN) Tribune*, January 23, 1996; "For Peru-Area

Residents, New State Prison Means Jobs," *South Bend (IN) Tribune*, March 7, 1996.

110. "Battle Plan for Correction." "Grissom Turned Into Reserve Base," *South Bend (IN) Tribune*, October 2, 1994.

111. For a favorable view of the CLIFF program, see "Programs Allow Inmates to Grow, Give Back," *Pharos Tribune* (Logansport, IN), March 26, 2010.

112. Lockwood and Siehl, "Military Base Closures," unpaginated "Summary."

113. Department of Justice and Department of Defense, *Report to Congress: Conversion of Closed Military Installations into Federal Prison Facilities* (Washington, D.C.: February 1995), 2-16 to 2-17. Report prepared by the Federal Bureau of Prisons.

114. "Grissom Air Reserve Base," Wikipedia, https://en.wikipedia.org/wiki/Grissom_Air_Reserve_Base. This undocumented claim is apparently based on 2010 census data.

115. It does not exist because transfer occurred over so many years and under so many federal, state, and local auspices. In addition, those counts that were made usually excluded certain facilities—juvenile and immigrant detention centers and boot camps—because they were not officially designated as prisons. The guess offered here is pieced together from fragmentary reports and may well be an undercount.

116. Mary K. Stohr et al., "We Know It, We Just Have to Do It: Perceptions of Ethical Work in Prisons and Jails," *Prison Journal* 80 (June 2000): 134.

117. Undated item from Department of Justice Community Oriented Policing Services, "Troops to COPS (1995 and 1999)," www.cops.usdoj.gov/default.asp?Item=76?. U.S. Department of Defense News Release, May 2, 1995, http://www.defense.gov/Releases/Release.aspx?ReleaseID=475.

118. For a careful data-heavy study, which found a real though limited shift from hospitals to prisons, see Dae-Young Kim, "Psychiatric Deinstitutionalization and Prison Population Growth: A Critical Literature Review and Its Implications," *Criminal Justice Policy Review* 17 (August 13, 2014): 3–21. For "negligible" and other considerations, see Bernard E. Harcourt, "An Institutionalization Effect: The Impact of Mental Hospitalization and Imprisonment on Homicide in the United States, 1934–2001," *Journal of Legal Studies* 40 (January 2011): 39–83, which ranges more widely than its subtitle's focus on homicide suggests.

119. See the report *Governor's Task Force 1982—Rochester State Hospital Site*, mn.gov/mnddc/past/pdf/80s/82/82-gov-task-force-roch-st-hosp.pdf.

120. Description based on my visits to the facility in 2002 and 2003, which included conversations with psychiatric staff and all inmates identified here except the "blind sheik." On the sheik's presence, see "Police Step Up Security Near Federal Prison in Rochester," *StarTribune* (Minneapolis–St. Paul, Minn.), September 13, 2001.

121. Federal Medical Center Rochester, announcement of internships for 2014–15, www.bop.gov/jobs/students/cpdiprch2.pdf; *Doctoral Psychology Internship Program, Federal Medical Center Rochester*, June 1, 2017, https://www.bop.gov/jobs/docs/rch_internship_brochure.pdf. Many state

and local prisons, jails, and forensic hospitals hosted interns in psychology and other fields selected and paid for by external institutions (universities, nonprofits). It was less common for them to recruit and pay for such interns themselves.

122. Here I draw on a research assistant's unpublished November 2015 report, "War on Drugs, War on Crime: Language Usage Frequency, 1981–2005," which created Google Ngram graphs for those two phrases. I also draw more briefly on an *NYT* internal language frequency search called Chronicle. Google Ngrams draw largely on books, leaving the word usage this book mainly tracks—in newspapers, magazines, and electronic and online media—poorly represented. And tracking says nothing about content—about whether, for example, the phrase "war on drugs" might have become used more to criticize it, not support it.

123. Bratton in 2000 as quoted in "Bratton, Who Shaped an Era in Policing, Tries to Navigate a Racial Divide," *NYT*, July 26, 2016.

124. Jill Lepore, "Sirens in the Night: How the Victims'-Rights Revolution Has Remade American Justice," *New Yorker*, May 21, 2018; Lynne Henderson, "Co-Opting Compassion: The Federal Victim's Rights Amendment," *Scholarly Works (St. Thomas Law Review)* (1999): 595, 596, 592 (Henderson's words).

125. Lepore, "Sirens in the Night."

Chapter 6

1. Robert Perkinson, *Texas Tough: The Rise of America's Prison Empire* (New York, 2010), 340, 343.

2. 1994 campaign TV ad, quoted in R. G. Ratcliffe, "Richards: Pull Plug on Bush Ad," *Houston Chronicle*, August 23, 1994.

3. Skip Hollandsworth, "Born to Run," *Texas Monthly*, May 1994.

4. Quoted in Clay Robinson, "Bush Signs 'Tough Love' Juvenile Crime Bill," *Houston Chronicle*, June 1, 1995.

5. Quoted in Rad Sallee, "Lanier, Bush Applauded for Crime-Fighting Efforts," *Houston Chronicle*, August 19, 1997.

6. Ashcroft's speeches and press conferences are available at https://www .justice.gov/archive/ag/speeches/2001/021201agpressconf1.htm.

7. Jean Edward Smith, *Bush* (New York, 2016), chap. 9 ("Asleep at the Switch") offers a biting distillation of the mountain of evidence on this score. See also Melvyn P. Leffler, "The Foreign Policies of the George W. Bush Administration: Memoirs, History, Legacy," *Diplomatic History* 37 (April 2013): 192–93.

8. Hendrik Hertzberg, "Talk of the Town," *New Yorker*, September 24, 2001.

9. General Wesley K. Clark, "How to Fight the New War," *Time*, September 24, 2001.

10. Michael Walzer, "First, Define the Battlefield," *NYT*, September 21, 2001.

11. Eliot A. Cohen, "Make War, Not Justice: How to Fight," *New Republic*, September 24, 2001.

12. Lawrence Kaplan, "Foreign Policy after September 11: No Choice," *New Republic*, October 1, 2001. For Sullivan, see Eric Alterman, "The Uses of Adversity," *Nation*, September 20, 2001.

13. Smith, *Bush*, 219, citing Bob Woodward, *Bush at War* (New York, 2002), 17.

14. Leffler, "Foreign Policies" summarizes the evidence from memoirs about these emotions.

15. See Smith, *Bush*, 230–32 on this point.

16. Smith, *Bush*, 226, citing Woodward, *Bush at War*, 37.

17. Smith, *Bush*, 255.

18. Smith, *Bush*, 257.

19. David Luban, "The Defense of Torture," *New York Review of Books*, March 15, 2007, is a valuable assessment of the constitutional issues involved in the administration's invocation of war and use of torture.

20. George W. Bush, interview by Brit Hume, Fox News, January 7, 2009.

21. Smith, *Bush*, 227 ("messianic"), 233.

22. Perkinson, *Texas Tough*, 343, 349.

23. Smith, *Bush*, 225, citing Richard A. Clarke, *Against All Enemies: Inside America's War on Terror* (New York, 2004), 24.

24. Robert Byrd, *Losing America: Confronting a Reckless and Arrogant Presidency* (New York, 2004), 90.

25. Peter Liberman, "An Eye for an Eye: Public Support for War against Evildoers," *International Organization* 60 (Summer 2006): 687–722 (quotation, 689).

26. Marilyn B. Young, "Ground Zero: Enduring War," in *September 11 in History*, ed. Mary L. Dudziak (Durham, NC, 2003), 11.

27. Blaine Harden, "For Many, Sorrow Turns to Anger and Talk of Vengeance," *NYT*, September 14, 2001; Cheney, interview by Tim Russert, *Meet the Press*, NBC, September 16, 2001 (for transcript, see "The Vice President Appears On Meet the Press with Tim Russert," September 16, 2001, https://georgewbush -whitehouse.archives.gov/vicepresident/news-speeches/speeches/vp20010916. html). Scholars have not fully explored how much vengeance was felt across a diverse nation. The national media, given their location in and focus on New York City and Washington, D.C., the sites of the 9/11 attacks, might have exaggerated the currents of vengeance. My treatment of vengeance is indebted to Alex Michael Hobson, "Chains of Vengeance: The United States and Anti-Imperialism in the Middle East" (PhD diss., Northwestern University, 2017).

28. I first worked out this argument, in slightly different phrasing, in "Dead or Alive: American Vengeance Goes Global," *Review of International Studies* 31 (2005): 245–63.

29. Michael S. Sherry, *The Rise of American Air Power: The Creation of Armageddon* (New Haven, CT, 1987), 349, 350.

30. Quoted in Lloyd C. Gardner and Marilyn B. Young, eds., *Iraq and the Lessons of Vietnam, or How Not to Learn from the Past* (New York, 2007), 10.

31. George W. Bush, *Decision Points* (New York, 2010), 128; Leffler, "Foreign Policies," 216.

32. Max Boot, *The Savage Wars of Peace: Small Wars and the Rise of American Power*, rev. ed. (New York, 2014), 361.

33. "Laura Bush Addresses State of Afghan Women," *Los Angeles Times*, November 18, 2001. Her November 17 address is in the American Presidency Project. U.S. State Department *The Taliban's War against Women* (November 17, 2001), https://2001–2009.state.gov/g/drl/rls/6185.htm.

34. Bruce Anderson, "The Only Penalty: A Felon's Death on the Gallows," *Independent* (UK), December 14, 2003.

35. "Remarks in a Meeting with the National Security Team and an Exchange with Reporters at Camp David, Maryland," September 15, 2001.

36. Byrd, *Losing America*, 83.

37. See "FBI Most Wanted Terrorists," Wikipedia, https://en.wikipedia.org/wiki/FBI_Most_Wanted_Terrorists.

38. For Bush on "evildoers," see "Remarks Announcing the Most Wanted Terrorists List," October 10, 2001. Although extensive efforts failed to locate the October 12 episode, numerous sources indicate that it aired. See "America's Most Wanted: Season 15, October 12, 2001," tv.com, http://www.tv.com/shows/americas-most-wanted/october-12-2001-381852/, and "'Most Wanted' Targets Terror's Top 22," *New York Post*, October 12, 2001.

39. See, along with many commercial sites, "Most-Wanted Iraqi Playing Cards," Wikipedia, https://en.wikipedia.org/wiki/Most-wanted_Iraqi_playing_cards.

40. Among others to refer to a "spider hole," U.S. Lt. General Ricardo Sanchez did so in a press conference on December 14; see "The Capture of Hussein; 'We Got Him,' and Then a Call by American and Iraqi Officials for Reconciliation," *NYT*, December 15, 2003. Many media outlets referred to a "hideaway." Anderson, "The Only Penalty." For an example of "perp walk" characterizations, see "Chained Beast—Shackled Saddam Dragged to Court," *New York Post*, July 3, 2004. "Bush Press Conference," December 15, 2003.

41. Quoted in Patrick Allitt, *Religion in America since 1945* (New York, 2003), 253. Allitt surveys a range of such responses.

42. Among the extensive reporting, see "Justices Consider Lawsuit over Post-9/11 Detentions," *NYT*, January 19, 2017.

43. Richard H. Kohn, "The Danger of Militarization in an Endless 'War' on Terrorism," *Journal of Military History* 73 (January 2009): 298. No one dwelled more frequently and forcefully on the absence of sacrifice than Andrew Bacevich. See, for example, *Breach of Trust: How Americans Failed Their Soldiers and Their Country* (New York, 2013), and for a short version, "Unequal Sacrifice," *New Republic*, September 20, 2010.

44. "9/11 Monument Forever Links First Responders, Special Forces," September 15, 2016, American Legion website, https://www.legion.org/honor/234102/911-monument-forever-links-first-responders-special-forces. I observed the Almira Township memorial in July 2017.

45. Elisabeth Bumiller, "In Kerik, Bush Saw Values Crucial to Post-9/11 World," *NYT*, December 19, 2004.

46. Smith, *Bush*, 152, 169. Although Bush had used the term "decider" before, his use of the term on April 18, 2006, in casual comments defending his retention of Rumsfeld as defense secretary, particularly caught the media's attention.

47. Sarah Stillman, "The Invisible Army," *New Yorker*, June 6, 2011.

48. David Cole, "Must Counterterrorism Cancel Democracy?," *New York Review of Books*, January 8, 2015.

49. Department of the Army, The Inspector General, *Detainee Operations Inspection* (July 21, 2004), 23 (7,500), v (50,000), http://hrlibrary.umn.edu /OathBetrayed/Mikolashek%20Report.pdf.

50. "Whack-a-Mole: Obama's Real ISIS Strategy," *National Interest*, September 12, 2014. Use of the phrase "whack-a-mole" to describe U.S. policy in the Middle East goes back at least to December 9, 1996, when a national security advisor used it to depict U.S. policy toward Saddam Hussein; see William Safire, "Whack-a-Mole," *NYT*, October 29, 2006.

51. Andrew Bacevich, "Obama's Strategy against Islamic State? Whack-a-Mole," *Los Angeles Times*, September 15, 2014.

52. Quoted in Micah Zenko, "A Familiar, Failed Afghanistan Strategy," *NYT*, August 26, 2017. Morrell's comments were made at a Washington Institute for Near East Policy session, "Israel vs. al-Qaeda: Emerging Challenges on Two Fronts," April 29, 2014, with a recording of the event at http://www.washingtoninstitute.org/policy-analysis/view/israel -vs.-al-qaeda-emerging-challenges-on-two-fronts.

53. Of many sources on drone warfare and secrecy about it, see Lloyd Gardner, *Killing Machine: The American Presidency in the Age of Drone Warfare* (New York, 2013).

54. Max Boot, "America's Destiny Is to Police the World," *Financial Times*, February 18, 2003.

55. Charlie Savage, *Power Wars: Inside Obama's Post-9/11 Presidency* (New York, 2015), 60.

56. "French Prime Minister: 'We're Fighting a War . . . against Terrorism and Radical Islamism,'" *WP*, January 11, 2015.

57. A valuable cautionary note about the tendency to regard the United States as singularly headed for a punitive system is suggested in an article comparing British and U.S. political policing in the interwar era: Jennifer Luff, "Covert and Overt Operations: Interwar Political Policing in the United States and the United Kingdom," *American Historical Review* 122 (June 2017): 727–57.

58. Mirroring striking diversity among U.S. states, incarceration rates elsewhere diverged widely, as did their trends. Many nations had increases in those rates between 2000 and 2016, some modest, others (Turkey) large. But the exceptions are also notable: Ireland, Japan, and Singapore, for example, had stable or declining rates. See the comprehensive figures in Institute for Criminal Policy Research, "World Prison Brief Data," 2016, http://www .prisonstudies.org/world-prison-brief-data.

59. For a critical appraisal, see Alice Speri, "Israel Security Forces Are Training American Cops despite History of Rights Abuses," *Intercept*, September 15, 2017.

60. For the long history of torture and its discourses in an American context, see the valuable treatment by W. Fitzhugh Brundage, *Civilizing Torture: An American Tradition* (Cambridge, MA, 2018).

61. This and the following paragraph draw on the careful tracking and analysis of public and elite opinion in Joseph Margulies, *What Changed When Everything Changed: 9/11 and the Making of National Identity* (New Haven, CT, 2013) chaps. 9–10. Quotations from pp. 194 (Ashcroft), 197 (Margulies on Dershowitz), 207 (Margulies), 210 (Margulies). For Dershowitz quotation, see Alan M. Dershowitz, "Is There a Torturous Road to Justice?," *Los Angeles Times*, November 8, 2001.

62. Margulies, *What Changed*, 207, 210.

63. Seymour Hersh, "Torture at Abu Ghraib," *New Yorker*, May 10, 2004 (posted online on April 30), with follow-up articles by Hersh.

64. "News Transcript, Deputy Secretary Wolfowitz Interview on the Pentagon Channel, Presenter: Deputy Secretary of Defense Paul Wolfowitz, May 04, 2004," U.S. Department of Defense, http://archive.defense.gov /Transcripts/Transcript.aspx?TranscriptID=2970.

65. Quoted in many places, but see Jared Del Rosso, *Talking about Torture: How Political Discourse Shapes the Debate* (New York, 2015), 92, in a book with excellent analysis of rhetoric at the time about torture.

66. Seymour Hersh, "The Gray Zone," *New Yorker*, May 24, 2004.

67. Quoted in Mark Danner, *Torture and Truth: America, Abu Ghraib, and the War on Terror* (New York, 2004), 10.

68. Alan M. Dershowitz, "Want to Torture? Get a Warrant," *San Francisco Chronicle*, January 22, 2002.

69. See Heather Ann Thompson, *Blood in the Water: The Attica Prison Uprising of 1971 and Its Legacy* (New York, 2016), 486, and the book's many other references to torture. On the difficulties of uncovering police torture, see Andrew S. Baer, "The Men Who Lived Underground: The Chicago Police Torture Cases and the Problem of Measuring Police Violence, 1970–2016," *Journal of Urban History* 44 (March 2018): 262–77.

70. David Bosco, review of *Unspeakable Acts, Ordinary People: The Dynamics of Torture*, by John Conroy, *NYT*, May 19, 2000; Patricia Kean, review of *Unspeakable Acts, Ordinary People: The Dynamics of Torture*, by John Conroy, *Salon*, March 15, 2000.

71. "Arming the Torturers: Electro-Shock Torture and the Spread of Stun Technology," Amnesty International, March 4, 1997, https://www.amnesty. org/en/documents/ACT40/001/1997/en/. The organization's later reports can be found at http://www.amnestyusa.org/.

72. For summary and analysis of the findings, see David Kaiser and Lovisa Stannow in the *New York Review of Books*: "The Rape of American Prisoners," March 10, 2010; "Prison Rape and the Government," March 23, 2011; "Prison Rape: Obama's Plan to Stop It," October 11, 2012.

73. Keramet Reiter, *23/7: Pelican Bay Prison and the Rise of Long-Term Solitary Confinement* (New Haven, CT, 2016), 180 ("military experiments").

74. David D. Cole, *The Torture Memos: Rationalizing the Unthinkable* (New York, 2009), 7. Cole discusses court cases about torture by U.S. police and other officials, but he does not connect them to torture authorized by "the torture memos."

75. Louis Henkin, "U.S. Ratification of Human Rights Conventions: The Ghost of Senator Bricker," *American Journal of International Law* 89 (April 1995): 342 ("in ratifying"). The preceding paragraph and the rest of this paragraph gloss and quote from an unpublished manuscript: Jonathan Ng, "Violent Contradictions: The United States, Human Rights, and the Convention against Torture" (paper prepared for Michael Sherry, March 15, 2016). "Hoped to" is Ng's conclusion.

76. For an example of how much was quickly exposed, see the extensive profile of Charles Graner by David Finckel and Christian Davenport, "Records Paint Dark Portrayal of Guard," *WP*, June 5, 2004.

77. Greg Burton, "Utahns Who Rebuilt Prison Are in Hot Seat," *Salt Lake Tribune*, May 16, 2004.

78. For the numbers, see Avery F. Gordon, "The United States Military Prison: The Normalcy of Exceptional Brutality," in *The Violence of Incarceration*, ed. Phil Scraton and Jude McCulloch (New York, 2008), 169, in an article that extensively examines links between home and abroad. Anne-Marie Cusac, *Cruel and Unusual: The Culture of Punishment in America* (New Haven, CT, 2009), 250; see generally chap. 12, "Abu Ghraib, USA," 244–52.

79. Margulies, *What Changed*, 220, 221, 22. Distinctions like those made by the administration and its supporters between torture and "enhanced interrogation" and between civilization and savagery, as well as efforts to challenge those distinctions, have a long history laid out in Brundage, *Civilizing Torture*.

80. Danner, *Torture and Truth*, 31.

81. Mark Philip Bradley, *A World Reimagined: Americans and Human Rights in the Twentieth Century* (New York, 2016), 223, 224.

82. Andrew S. Baer, "From Law and Order to Torture: Race and Policing in De-Industrial Chicago" (PhD diss., Northwestern University, 2015), 116. For the backing off, see p. 292.

83. See, for example, "WRL Peace Awardees Challenge Torture," *WIN Magazine*, Winter 2008, https://www.warresisters.org/win/win-winter-2008/wrl-peace-awardees-challenge-torture.

84. Sanford Levinson, ed., *Terrorism: A Collection* (New York, 2004), 105, 116–117 (Skolnick). For the brief reference to Chicago torture, see p. 27. On the history, back to the early twentieth century, of dismissing "the third degree" as an "archaic practice" passing out of existence, see Brundage, *Civilizing Torture*, 214–21.

85. See Danner, *Torture and Truth*.

86. Alfred W. McCoy, *A Question of Torture: CIA Interrogation from the Cold War to the War on Terror* (New York, 2006), 6. Also leaving torture at

home virtually unmentioned were the ten contributors to this lengthy treatment, "Are Our Highest Officials Guilty of Torture?," *The Long Term View: A Journal of Informed Opinion* 6 (Spring 2006).

87. This was the case with the American-based *Criminal Justice Studies, Journal of Criminal Justice,* and *Journal of Contemporary Criminal Justice,* and with the international journal *Punishment and Society,* judged by electronic indices for "torture." That is a selective look at a few journals—there were dozens more in this category, not to mention those in law and legal studies.

88. Michael S. Vaughn and Linda G. Smith, "Practicing Penal Harm Medicine in the United States: Prisoners' Voices from Jail," *Justice Quarterly* 16 (1999): 175–231.

89. See the lengthy review, although mainly about Abu Ghraib, by Arthur Lurigio, "The Rotten Barrel Spoils the Apples: How Situational Factors Contribute to Detention Officer Abuse Toward Inmates, a Review of *The Lucifer Effect,* by Philip Zimbardo," *Prison Journal* supplement to 89 (March 2009). On the other hand, a search for "torture" in the U.S.-based *Corrections: Policy, Practice and Research* yielded nothing.

90. Michael Tonry, "Crime and Human Rights—How Political Paranoia, Protestant Fundamentalism, and Constitutional Obsolescence Combined to Devastate Black America," American Society of Criminology 2007 Presidential Address, *Criminology* 46 (February 2008): 3.

91. This section draws on a November 14, 2017, report prepared by Alex Hobson that includes most of the citations that follow.

92. See "United States–Sponsored Torture Must End: 2005 Action of Immediate Witness," Unitarian Universalist Association, n.d. [2005], https://www.uua.org/action/statements/united-states-sponsored-torture-must-end. On billboards, "Unitarian Universalists Condemn 'Torture' Law," UU World: Liberal Religion and Life, October 20, 2006, https://www.uuworld.org/articles/unitarian-universalists-condemn-torture-law.

93. John M. Buchanan, "Shame on Us," *Christian Century,* April 18, 2006.

94. Dylan Rodriguez, "NonScenes of Captivity: The Common Sense of Punishment and Death," *Radical History Review* 96 (Fall 2006): 11. See Amey Victoria Adkins, "From Crib to Cage: The Theological Calculus of Solitary Confinement," *Muslim World,* April 1, 2013, and Mohammad Fadel, "Theology, Torture and the United States: Do Abrahamic Religions Have Anything Meaningful to Say?," *Muslim World,* April 1, 2013.

95. Marie Gottschalk, *Caught: The Prison State and the Lockdown of American Politics* (Princeton, NJ, 2015), 135.

96. *Torture: America's Brutal Prisons,* directed by Nick London (UK Channel 4, 2005), http://crimedocumentary.com/torture-americas-brutal-prisons-2005/.

97. Darius Rejali, *Torture and Democracy* (Princeton, NJ, 2007), 3 ("clean" tortures); George Hunsinger, ed., *Torture Is a Moral Issue: Christians, Jews, Muslims and People of Conscience Speak Out* (Grand Rapids, MI, 2008), 253 ("I grew up"), 261 ("there is no"), 260 ("I think we need"); Scott Horton, "Six

Questions for Darius Rejali, Author of *Torture and Democracy*," *Harper's*, February 13, 2008 ("I grew up").

98. Jimmy Carter, *Our Endangered Values: America's Moral Crisis* (New York, 2005), 1, 80, 79. See also Jimmy Carter, "A Cruel and Unusual Record," *NYT*, June 24, 2012.

99. Cusac, *Cruel and Unusual*, 248.

100. Scraton and McCulloch, *Violence of Incarceration*, 4; see especially Gordon, "The United States Military Prison," 164–86. The editors were based in Belfast (Scraton) and Melbourne (McCulloch); Gordon was based at the University of California, Santa Barbara.

101. Cusac, *Cruel and Unusual*, 252.

102. Senate Select Committee on Intelligence, *Committee Study of the Central Intelligence Agency's Detention and Interrogation Program, Foreword by Senate Select Committee on Intelligence Chairman Dianne Feinstein, Findings and Conclusions, Executive Summary* (released December 9, 2014).

103. ACLU, *The U.S. Torture Program: A Blueprint for Accountability* (n.d. [December 2014]), https://www.aclu.org/other/us-torture-program -blueprint-accountability.

104. ACLU, *Enduring Abuse: Torture and Cruel Treatment by the United States at Home and Abroad* (April 2006), https://www.aclu.org/files/safefree /torture/torture_report.pdf.

105. *Why Is America So Punitive? A Report on the Deliberations of the Interdisciplinary Roundtable on Punitiveness in America, Held at John Jay College of Criminal Justice, April 2015* (March 2016), quotations on 33, 5, http://thecrimereport.s3.amazonaws.com/2/12/4/3478/monograph_ final_3_22_16__1_.pdf; Reiter, *23/7*, 196.

106. "Bad Lieutenant: American Police Brutality, Exported from Chicago to Guantánamo," *Guardian* (UK), February 18, 2015. For the Marshall Project's link to that story, see https://www.themarshallproject.org /records/306-guantanamo-bay#.IZXvsIBkv. For the story on *The Rachel Maddow Show*, MSNBC, August 26, 2016, see https://www.youtube.com /watch?v=de4OPaNO174. Brundage, *Civilizing Torture*, 292 ("the use").

107. Smith, *Bush*, 458 (McCain), citing Peter Baker, *Days of Fire: Bush and Cheney in the White House* (New York, 2013); 470 (Smith's words).

Chapter 7

1. "Obama, in Oklahoma, Takes Reform Message to the Prison Cell Block," *NYT*, July 16, 2015. The visit received enormous print and visual coverage. It was also usefully framed in a Vice News (HBO) documentary, *Fixing the System*, released in September 2015, https://www.youtube .com/watch?v=QgJPYJoJno4. The official version of Obama's remarks in Charleston is the White House press release, "Remarks by the President in Eulogy for the Honorable Reverend Clementa Pinckney," June 26, 2015, https://obamawhitehouse.archives.gov/the-press-office/2015/06/26 /remarks-president-eulogy-honorable-reverend-clementa-pinckney.

2. Aaron Belkin quoted in "Military Accepting More Ex-Cons," Military.com, February 14, 2007, http://www.military.com/NewsContent /0,13319,125220,00.html, and in the Palm Center's newsletter, *Blueprints for Sound Public Policy* 2 (Summer 2008), http://archive.palmcenter.org /newsletters/volume2_number2_Summer2008. A higher figure of 125,000 moral waivers was reported in "Moral Waivers and the Military," *NYT*, February 20, 2007. See also Michael Boucai, "Balancing Your Strengths against Your Felonies: Considerations for Military Recruitment of Ex-Offenders," *University of Miami Law Review* 61 (July 2007): 997–1032.

3. Ben Fountain, *Billy Lynn's Long Halftime Walk* (New York, 2012), 166.

4. Jamie Lowe, "The Incarcerated Women Who Fight California's Wildfires," *NYTM*, August 31, 2017. Useful historical background and statistics can be found in Philip Goodman, "A Brief History of California's Prison Camps," June 2010, https://web.archive.org/web/20170201045200/http:/www.cdcr .ca.gov/Conservation_Camps/docs/History_of_firecamps.pdf.

5. "Offenders at Miami Correctional Donate Time, Money," *Kokomo (IN) Tribune*, January 22, 2016.

6. Police Department, City of New York, "Historical Perspective," in *CompStat: Report Covering the Week 8/5/2019 Through 8/11/2019*, https://www1.nyc.gov/assets/nypd/downloads/pdf/crime_statistics/cs-en -us-city.pdf.

7. Congressional Research Service, *Recent Violent Crime Trends in the United States* (June 20, 2018), reporting and analyzing FBI Uniform Crime Reports data, https://fas.org/sgp/crs/misc/R45236.pdf; FBI, Table 3, in *Preliminary Semiannual Uniform Crime Report, January–June, 2018*, https://ucr.fbi.gov/crime-in-the-u.s/2018/preliminary-report/tables /table-3/table-3.xls/@@template-layout-view?override-view=data -declaration.

8. See "The Unsung Role That Ordinary Citizens Played in the Great Crime Decline," *NYT*, November 9, 2017, drawing on the work of sociologist Patrick Sharkey at New York University.

9. BJS, "Key Statistic: Total Adult Correctional Population, 1980–2015," https://www.bjs.gov/index.cfm?ty=kfdetail&iid=487.

10. BJS, *Jails in Indian Country, 2014* (October 2015), https://www.bjs .gov/content/pub/pdf/jic14.pdf.

11. See C. Puzzanchera, A. Sladky, and W. Kang, "Easy Access to Juvenile Populations: 1990–2016" (2017), http://www.ojjdp.gov/ojstatbb/ezapop/.

12. ACLU, "Youth Incarceration," (n.d.), https://www.aclu.org/issues /juvenile-justice/youth-incarceration.

13. See Mac McClelland, "They'll Be Here Till They Die," *NYTM*, October 1, 2017.

14. For a recent attempt to break down and aggregate all forms of imprisonment and detention, and for "enormous churn," see Prison Policy Initiative, *Mass Incarceration: The Whole Pie 2019* (March 19, 2019), https://www .prisonpolicy.org/reports/pie2019.html.

15. For employment numbers, I draw on a report by a research assistant, May 28, 2014, on BJS, *The Private Security Industry: A Review of the Definitions, Available Data Sources, and Paths Moving Forward* (2010), https://www.ncjrs.gov/pdffiles1/bjs/grants/232781.pdf, and on BJS, *Justice Expenditures and Employment, FY 1982–2007—Statistical Tables* (December 2011), https://www.bjs.gov/content/pub/pdf/jee8207st.pdf; Marie Gottschalk, *Caught: The Prison State and the Lockdown of American Politics* (Princeton, NJ, 2015), 32.

16. On Border Patrol staff, see U.S. Customs and Border Protection, *U.S. Border Patrol Fiscal Year Staffing Statistics (FY 1992–FY 2016)* (October 2016), https://www.cbp.gov/document/stats/us-border -patrol-fiscal-year-staffing-statistics-fy-1992-fy-2016.

17. Ben Austen, "In Philadelphia, a Progressive D.A. Tests the Power—and Learns the Limits–of His Office," *NYTM*, October 30, 2018; Jennifer Gonnerman, "Larry Krasner's Campaign to End Mass Incarceration," *New Yorker*, October 29, 2018.

18. Pew Research Center, "Obama Used Clemency Power More Often Than Any President Since Truman," January 20, 2017, https://www.pewresearch.org/fact-tank/2017/01/20/obama-used-more-clemency-power/. On "deserving," see White House press release, "President Obama Grants 153 Commutations and 78 Pardons to Individuals Deserving of a Second Chance," December 19, 2016, https://obamawhitehouse.archives.gov/blog/2016/12/19/president -obama-grants-153-commutations-and-78-pardons-individuals-deserving -second.

19. See, for example, work by the General Commission on Religion and Race of the United Methodist Church, as sketched in "Mass Incarceration and Race: How Must Christians Respond?," January 28, 2016, http://www.gcorr .org/mass-incarceration-and-race-how-must-christians-respond/.

20. See, for example, "San Quentin News Editor Is Remembered for His Legacy In and Out of Prison," KQED News, October 6, 2017, https://www. kqed.org/news/11621561/san-quentin-news-editor-is-remembered-for-his -legacy-in-and-out-of-prison. Keramet Reiter, *23/7: Pelican Bay Prison and the Rise of Long-Term Solitary Confinement* (New Haven, CT, 2016), 30.

21. See Bonnie Ernst, "Women in the Age of Mass Incarceration: Punishment, Rights, and Resistance in Michigan" (PhD diss., Northwestern University, 2018).

22. On prison abolition, see Rachel Kushner, "Is Prison Necessary? Ruth Wilson Gilmore Might Change Your Mind," *NYTM*, April 21, 2019. On the range of abolition efforts, see The Marshall Project, "Prison Abolition: A Curated Collection of Links," updated June 18, 2019, https://www .themarshallproject.org/records/4766-prison-abolition.

23. "'I can get my soul out of prison': the art made by Guantánamo detainees," *Guardian* (UK), October 2, 2017. "Who Owns Guantanamo Art? Not Prisoners, the U.S. Says," *NYT*, November 28, 2017; as that headline indicates, ownership of the art was claimed by the U.S. government and the object of another round of legal wrangling regarding the facility.

24. Gottschalk, *Caught*, 136.

25. So critics speculated, but the scantiness of available statistics makes validation of such speculation difficult. What seems clear from a scan of many online sources on this subject is that police authorities and policing experts vigorously defended shoot to kill (though not all uses of it) for operational, psychological, and crime-prevention reasons, that they rarely compared U.S. practices to practices elsewhere, and that they ignored how police had become more heavily armed, more accustomed to militarized policing, and more inclined to view policing as a warlike operation. The most persistent, well-placed critic of shoot-to-kill policing was Radley Balko in blogs and in his articles for the *WP* and *Huffington Post*, with his statements picked up or quoted by many media outlets.

26. Patrick J. Lynch, New York City Patrolmen's Benevolent Association president, "NYC Cops Not Equipped for New Terror Threats," paid opinion piece, *NYT*, November 10, 2014.

27. Adam Andrzejewski, "War Weapons for America's Police Departments: New Data Shows Feds Transfer $2.2B in Military Gear," *Forbes*, May 10, 2016; "Local Police Acquire More Firepower," *South Bend (IN) Tribune*, July 21, 2014.

28. Whether fatal police shootings–or all police shootings–of civilians increased after 2000 is another statistical minefield, in part because police agencies are urged but not required to report them to the FBI. In addition, no private institution has the wherewithal to assemble the statistics reliably. On the likelihood of serious "underreporting" on this score, see Catherine Barber et al., "Homicides by Police: Comparing Counts from the National Violent Death Reporting System, Vital Statistics, and Supplementary Homicide Reports," *American Journal of Public Health* 106 (May 1, 2016): 922–27. For good guesses of an alarming increase, as well as an account of the political and statistical obstacles to any definitive statement, see Daniel Bier, "How Many Americans Do the Cops Kill Each Year?," *Newsweek*, July 16, 2016. More detailed number crunching suggesting a sharp increase is in Sarah DeGue, Katherine A. Fowler, and Cynthia Calkins, "Deaths Due to Use of Lethal Force by Law Enforcement: Findings from the National Violent Death Reporting System," *American Journal of Preventive Medicine* 51 (2016): S173–87, and in a source on which that article draws: Joanna Drowos, Charles H. Hennekens, and Robert S. Levine, "Variations in Mortality from Legal Intervention in the United States–1999 to 2013," *Preventive Medicine* 81 (2015): 290–93. The reported increase may have been due in a small way to increased provocation of police in "suicide-by-cop" incidents. National patterns, even if accurately counted, often do not reflect what happens in given jurisdictions, among which there were wide variations on this front, as on others.

Statistics on police officers "feloniously killed" are similarly partial and contested. In recent years, half or more of those who died in the line of duty did so from "[non]felonious" causes, accidents among them. But the numbers killed from all causes and "feloniously" declined greatly from a peak in the 1970s (with year-to-year wobbles, especially in 2001). Given a sharp increase over those years in the numbers of police serving (nearly doubling between 1975 and 2013), the per capita decline was even sharper. See, among many sources, "U.S. Police Shootings: How Many Die Each Year?," *BBC News Magazine,* July 18, 2016, http://www.bbc.com/news/magazine-36826297.

29. Emily Bazelon, *Charged: The New Movement to Transform American Prosecution and End Mass Incarceration* (New York, 2019), xxv. See also David Cole, "The Truth about Our Prison Crisis," *New York Review of Books,* June 22, 2017.

30. See Ryan Gabrielson and Topher Sanders, "Proof Negative: Widespread Evidence Shows That Roadside Drug Tests Routinely Produce False Positives. Why Are Police Departments and Prosecutors across the Country Still Using Them?," *NYTM,* July 20, 2016.

31. See the careful, depressing assessment in Gottschalk, *Caught,* chap. 2.

32. See Eli Hager and Alysia Santo, "Private Prisoner Vans' Long Road of Neglect," *NYT,* July 18, 2016.

33. Appendix Table 4, in *BJS Bulletin: Prisoners in 2008* (December 2009), https://www.bjs.gov/content/pub/pdf/p08.pdf; The Sentencing Project, *Incarcerated Women and Girls,* (June 6, 2019), https://www.sentencingproject .org/publications/incarcerated-women-and-girls/.

34. Gottschalk, *Caught,* 68.

35. Numbers drawn from *Report on ERO Facts and Statistics,* U.S. Immigration and Customs Enforcement, December 12, 2011, www.ice.gov /foia/library/, and from "United States Immigration Detention," Global Detention Project, https://www.globaldetentionproject.org/countries /americas/united-states. These numbers hardly represent all who were caught up in various immigration dragnets, many of whom did not pass through formal detention facilities. See also Migration Policy Institute, *Immigration Enforcement in the United States: The Rise of a Formidable Machinery* (January 2013), https://www.migrationpolicy.org/research /immigration-enforcement-united-states-rise-formidable-machinery.

36. Gottschalk, *Caught,* 219, figure 10.1; 215.

37. On this point, see Gottschalk, *Caught,* especially chap. 3; quotation, 67.

38. Lowe, "The Incarcerated Women Who Fight California's Wildfires."

39. See Gottschalk, *Caught,* chap. 2.

40. Gottschalk, *Caught,* 174, 179–80, 170, 171.

41. Ava Kaufman, "Digital Jail: How Electronic Monitoring Drives Defendants Into Debt," *NYTM,* July 3, 2019.

42. For an introduction to this issue, see Jed S. Rakoff, "The Financial Crisis: Why Have No High-Level Executives Been Prosecuted?," *New York Review of Books,* January 9, 2014.

43. Fitzhugh Brundage, *Civilizing Torture: An American Tradition* (Cambridge, MA, 2018), 317. For Obama's full statement, see "Statement on the Release of Department of Justice Office of Legal Counsel Memos Concerning Interrogation Techniques," April 16, 2009.

44. James Forman Jr., *Locking Up Our Own: Crime and Punishment in Black America* (New York, 2017), 230, 221; Forman's epilogue offers an

extended critique of the narrowness of the Obama administration's reform efforts.

45. Representative Rush Holt (Democrat-New Jersey), quoted in James Risen and Matt Apuzzo, "Getting Close to Terror, But Not to Stop It," *NYT*, November 9, 2014.

46. Forman, *Locking Up Our Own*, 14.

47. Reiter, *23/7*, 5, 7.

48. Anne-Marie Cusac, *Cruel and Unusual: The Culture of Punishment in America* (New Haven, CT, 2009), 72, in a chapter titled "Punishment Creep."

49. See Reiter, *23/7*, 203–5.

50. Richard Cohen, "Who Signed Anwar al-Awlaki's Death Warrant?," *WP*, October 10, 2011.

51. Gottschalk, *Caught*, 242,

52. Gottschalk, *Caught*, 259.

53. Robert Perkinson, "Rick Perry, Criminal Justice Reformer? The Governor's Surprisingly Complicated Record," *New Republic*, September 16, 2011 (on executions); Marie Gottschalk, "The Prisoner Dilemma: Texas Fails to Confront Mass Incarceration," *Baffler*, July 2019 (other quotations).

54. Ryan Britt, "Why Kenneth Branagh Changed the Ending of 'Orient Express.' Different Times Demand Different Endings," *Inverse* website, November 10, 2017, website, https://www.inverse.com/article/38311-murder-on-the-orient-express-kenneth-branagh-ending-twist-agatha-christie.

55. Grant Parsons, "Prisoners of War in the Michigan Gulag," *Northern Express Weekly* (Michigan), August 24, 2015, 4; Tom Engelhardt, "The American Gulag," *HuffPost* (blog), *Huffington Post*, January 18, 2015, http://www.huffingtonpost.com/tom-engelhardt/the-american-gulag_b_6497920.html. The term "gulag" also had currency in the visual media, as in interviews with Mark Dow and reports on his book. It also had some usage before 9/11.

56. *Buffalo News*, August 20, 2013.

57. December 1, 2014, and May 18, 2015.

58. The Marshall Project, "When Warriors Put on the Badge. Many veterans make careers in policing. Some bring war home," March 30, 2017, https://www.themarshallproject.org/2017/03/30/when-warriors-put-on-the-badge.

59. "Governors Unite In the War against Opioids," *NYT*, February 24, 2016.

Epilogue

1. I viewed the oft-run FN advertisements during television coverage of the 2017 U.S. Open, from August 27 to September 10. Those ads were identical or very similar to ones dated April 17, 2017, that I viewed online on September 9, 2017: https://www.youtube.com/watch?v=FURYw8unEXE, https://www.ispot.tv/ad/wY6q/fn-509-the-battlefield, https://www.youtube.com/watch?v=SRhep9kaKhc. FN International and FN Herstal were part of the Herstal Group, a Belgian weapons maker controlled by the regional government of Wallonie. The group also owned American brands like Browning and Winchester Firearms. As of 2016, FN International had a headquarters in Virginia, with manufacturing facilities in South Carolina;

see http://www.fnamerica.com/about/ and http://www.grip.org/sites/grip .org/files/RAPPORTS/2000/2000-06.pdf. For ads flagged by the *NYT*, see the introduction.

2. National Rifle Association TV Commercial, "The Rule of War," n.d. [2016?], https://www.ispot.tv/ad/ADCY/national-rifle-association-rule-of-war. The ad featured Dom Raso, described by the NRA as a "Veteran US Navy Seal" who "spent 12 years hunting down radical Islamic terrorists"; see https://www.nraspeaksforme.com/our-campaign/na%C3%AFve-clingers/. Examples of and commentary on the "man card" campaign are abundant online; see also Jonathan M. Metzl, *Dying of Whiteness: How the Politics of Racial Resentment Is Killing America's Heartland* (New York, 2019), 61–63.

3. Hady Amr, "We Can and Must Apply Some of the Lessons from the Post-9/11 Period to Our Domestic Terror Problem," *Brookings* (blog), Brookings Institution website, August 6, 2019, https://www.brookings.edu/blog/order -from-chaos/2019/08/06/what-the-post-9–11-war-on-terror-can-teach-us -about-responding-to-domestic-terrorism-today/. Among criticisms of that approach, see Max Abrahms, "Don't Give White Nationalists the Post-9/11 Treatment," *Atlantic*, August 7, 2019.

4. "Donald Trump on Waterboarding: 'Torture Works,'" *WP*, February 17, 2016.

5. See, for example, Olivia Nuzzi, "Donald Trump's Pals Say Hillary Clinton Is a Lesbian Murderer, Bill Is a Cocaine Fiend," Daily Beast, May 13, 2016, http://www.thedailybeast.com/donald-trumps-pals-say-hillary-clinton-is-a- lesbian-murderer-bill-is-a-cocaine-fiend.

6. My claim that supporters of torture also endorsed "kill the bitch" rests on my reading of crowd reactions to the two appeals as shown at the time in TV media. I know of no close analysis of opinion polls comparing the two appeals. Certainly Trump and Michael Flynn (a retired army general and Trump supporter who served briefly as his natural security advisor and then pled guilty to federal crimes) often paired the two appeals, sometimes loosely and sometimes tightly.

7. Marie Gottschalk, *Caught: The Prison State and the Lockdown of American Politics* (Princeton, NJ, 2015), 184–85.

8. Gottschalk, *Caught*, 191.

9. Joseph Margulies, "The Fury of the Mob: Comparing the Calls to Prosecute Clinton and Bush," *Verdict: Legal Analysis and Commentary from Justia*, October 17, 2016, republished as "Lock Up Hillary! Lock Up George W! What's the Difference?," *Newsweek*, October 20, 2016.

10. For Sessions's frequent references to "winnable war" in 2017, see statements in "Speeches of Attorney General Jeff Sessions," U.S. Department of Justice, https://www.justice.gov/ag/speeches-attorney-general-jeff-sessions. For "multi-front war," see speech of September 19, 2017.

11. On their repeated use of "invasion," see "How Trump Campaign Used Facebook Ads to Amplify 'Invasion' Claim," *NYT*, August 6, 2019.

12. "U.S. Prepares to House Up to 20,000 Migrants on Military Bases," *NYT*, June 21, 2018.

13. That history is briefly reviewed in Jana Lipman, "Detaining Refugee Children at Military Bases May Sound Un-American, but It's Been Done Before," *The Conversation*, June 18, 2019, https://theconversation.com /detaining-refugee-children-at-military-bases-may-sound-un-american -but-its-been-done-before-115190.

14. "Trump Accuses Jewish Democrats of 'Great Disloyalty,'" *NYT*, August 20, 2019.

15. See figure 1.2, "State by State Incarceration Rates, 2012," in Gottschalk, *Caught*, 12 (in turn drawn from The Sentencing Project). See also "List of U.S. States by Incarceration and Correctional Supervision Rate," Wikipedia, https://en.wikipedia.org/wiki /List_of_U.S._states_by_incarceration_and_correctional_supervision_rate.

16. Gottschalk, *Caught*, 134. She adds, "Some predominantly white states [she singles out Idaho] operate some of the most dehumanizing and dangerous prisons in the country" (120).

17. On the appointment of Jeffrey Anderson to head BJS, see "How One Quiet DOJ Appointment Could Undermine the Push for Meaningful Police Reform," *Pacific Standard*, November 30, 2017, https://psmag.com/news /jeffrey-anderson-doj-police-reform.

18. "Distinguished Hoosier Recognized Again (August 18, 2008)," USA Patriotism!, http://www.usapatriotism.org/articles/hp/distinguished_again. htm. Since the article closed with this indication—"By Jim VanNatta Copyright 2008"—I assume the words quoted were his.

19. VanNatta paraphrased in "Newsweek Backs Off Guantanamo Article," *Boston Globe*, May 17, 2005.

20. VanNatta quoted in "Yee Ministers to Detainees, Counsels U.S. Officers on Treatment," *Seattle Times*, January 19, 2005.

21. Gottschalk, *Caught*, 42.

22. "Indiana Bill Targets Reducing County Jail Populations," *News and Tribune* (Indiana), March 2, 2015.

23. Bruce Lemmon, Commissioner, introduction to the *2015 Annual Report of the Indiana Department of Correction* (n.d.), https://www.in.gov /idoc/files/2015DOCAnRep.final.pdf.

24. Indiana Department of Correction, *Offender Population Report* (August 2019), https://www.in.gov/idoc/files/Indiana%20Department%20of%20 Correction%20August%202019%20Total%20Population%20Summary.pdf.

25. What prisoners could see is based on my personal observations. On prison staff as volunteers at the museum, see IDOC (Indiana Department of Corrections) Talk message board, thread entitled Weekly Views, July 24, 2009 ("17 Miami Correctional Facility staff and family members gathered at the Grissom Air Museum to clean the F-14 Tomcat."), http://idoctalk.proboards. com/thread/414/weekly-views-friday-july-2009. Note also "Grissom Helps Students Say 'No' to Drugs, *Air Force Print News Today*, October 25, 2013, http://www.grissom.afrc.af.mil/news/story.asp?id=123368439.

26. David Schulker, "The Recent Occupation and Industry Employment Patterns of American Veterans," *Armed Forces and Society* 43 (2017):

695–710; James A. Walker, "Employment and Earnings of Recent Veterans: Data from the CPS," *Monthly Labor Review* (July 2010): 1–9; U.S. Census Bureau, "Employment Status and Occupations of Gulf War-Era Veterans," November 2014, https://www2.census.gov/library/publications/2014/acs/acsbr13–22.pdf.

27. Ben Taub, "The Spy Who Came Home," *New Yorker*, May 7, 2018.

Index

Page numbers in italics refer to illustrations.

Grissom Air Force Base, 160, 166, 167, 169
Guantánamo Bay detention camp, 168, 191, 203, 211
Gulf War (1991), 98, 124, 125, 153, 234
gun control, 14, 132, 135, 140, 142, 174, 226
Gun-Free School Zones Act (1990), 146

habeas corpus, 95
Haiti, 153
Hamel, Veronica, 156
Hanhardt, William, 170
Hattam, Victoria, 32
health care, 67, 213
Hearst, Patty, 82–83
Heckler & Koch (arms manufacturer), 111, 113
Helms, Jesse, 153
heroin, 51
Hersh, Seymour, 191, 192
Hill Street Blues (television program), 156
Hinckley, John, Jr., 90
hip-hop, 80
Hispanics, 7, 52, 102, 115, 146
Holder, Eric, 210
Homicide (television program), 77
homosexuality, 43, 73–75, 82
Hoover, J. Edgar, 15, 33, 47–48
Hope, Bob, 51
Horton, Willie, 117
Hruska, Roman, 14
Hughes Aircraft, 30
human rights, 197
Humphrey, Hubert, 12, 13, 38
Hurricane Katrina, 230
Hussein, Saddam, 102, 124, 125, 152, 153, 177–80, 182, 186
Huston, Tom, 36
Hutchison, Kay Bailey, 137

Ice-T, 80
immigrants, 63, 71, 184, 205, 211; demonization of, 145, 215, 229, 231; deportation of, 146, 214, 215, 221, 228; detention of, 146, 148, 199, 208, 214, 216, 221; in disaster relief workforce, 230; vigilantism against, 214
Indiana, 233
inflation, 37, 65, 70
innocence projects, 150
insanity defense, 208
international law, 175, 192
Interstate Highway System, 65
Iran, 175, 176, 199
Iran-Contra scandal, 90, 98, 102, 120
Iraq, 102, 152–54, 175–77, 223, 233; private security forces in, 209; U.S. invasion of, 179–80, 186, 188, 189, 206
"I Shot the Sheriff" (Clapton), 79–80
Islamic State, 186
Israel, 188, 189, 190, 229
It Takes a Village (Clinton), 146

Jackson, Jesse, 136
James, William, 85
Japan, 189
Japanese internment, 7, 179
Jaworski, Leon, 46
Jeffords, Susan, 156
Jenkins, Philip, 72, 73, 85–86
Jenkins, Walter, 13, 75
Job Corps, 21
Johnson, Lyndon: crime policies of, 2, 4, 9, 13–16, 19, 20, 26, 34, 37, 44, 54, 60, 86; critics of, 12, 13; death of, 69; military service idealized by, 21, 22, 107; poverty attacked by, 96; rehabilitative ideal under, 38; rhetoric of, 2, 14–15, 235; Vietnam veterans and, 24–26; Vietnam War escalated by, 14, 68, 119

164, 166, 168, 205, 217; education in, 137, 211; growth of, 55, 61, 62, 67, 88, 104, 133, 135, 148, 164–66, 171, 208, 212; immigrants in, 146, 148, 199, 208, 214, 216, 221; juvenile, 148, 208, 210; as labor pool, 17–19, 23, 206–7, 215–16, 230; military, 148, 208; privatization of, 137, 210, 221; rebellions and activism in, 10, 39, 40–41, 211; as reform, 220; reform of, 209; sexual abuse in, 193, 210; solitary confinement in, 32, 39, 193, 202, 210–12, 219, 230; state *vs.* federal, 149; "supermax," 32, 41, 211, 219; in Texas, 220–21; in U.S. *vs.* Western Europe, 67–68; veterans in, 53; women in, 67, 149, 166, 211, 233. *See also* rehabilitation

privatization, 64, 137; of immigrant detention, 214, 216; of policing, 1; of prison health care, 213; of prisons, 137, 210, 221; of security, 209

Progressive (magazine), 200

Prohibition, 16

Project 100,000, 20–22, 23, 25

Project Transition, 25, 48

prostitution, 73

psychiatric research, 18

Punishing Criminals (van den Haag), 41–42

punk rock, 80

Putin, Vladimir, 229

Quayle, Dan, 80

Question of Torture, A (McCoy), 198

racial profiling, 174

Radical History Review, 198–99

Rambo films, 156

Ramparts (magazine), 44

Randolph, A. Philip, 102

Rangel, Charles, 101

rap, 80

rape, 67

Reagan, Nancy, 92, 95, 97

Reagan, Ronald, 5, 64, 122; bellicose rhetoric of, 52, 91–100, 102, 103–5, 141; crime policies of, 87–91, 96, 97; drug war waged by, 43, 44, 87, 91–92, 94–96, 120; Ford opposed by, 59; Latin American entanglements of, 101, 146; prison growth backed by, 162; U.S.-Mexico border militarized by, 145

reality television, 159–60

Rebel Without a Cause (film), 15

recidivism, 39, 112, 133, 134

Reconstruction, 17

red-light cameras, 1

Reeve, Christopher, 156

Reeves, George, 156

regulation, 67

rehabilitation, 19, 23, 46, 79; George H. W. Bush's lip service to, 121; Carter's support for, 71; decline of, 35, 38–42, 56, 58, 60, 66; Johnson's support of, 14, 38; military service linked to, 18, 49; New Deal reformism linked to, 17; Nixon's support of, 43; Obama's support for, 211; in U.S. *vs.* Western Europe, 67, 68

Reich, Robert, 167

Rejali, Darius, 199

religious right, 81–92

rendition, 191, 201

Reno, Janet, 138–39, 141

Resolution Trust Corporation, 114

Ridge, Tom, 185

"right on crime" movement, 220

riots, 12, 36

Rockefeller, Nelson, 41, 45, 60, 65

Rockford Files, The (television program), 78

Rodgers, Daniel, 96, 97

Roe v. Wade (1973), 1, 67, 91

Roof, Dylan, 206

Roosevelt, Franklin D., 3, 17, 66, 71, 119

Rosemary's Baby (film), 80